Community Health and Wellness:

a Socioecological Approach

Anne McMurray

For Kate and her generation

Community *Health* and *Wellness:*
a Socioecological Approach

Anne McMurray

Faculty of Nursing and Health Sciences
Griffith University

M Mosby

Sydney • Baltimore • Boston • Carlsbad • Chicago • London • Milan
Minneapolis • New York • Philadelphia • Portland • St Louis • Toronto

Publisher: Geoff Hasler
Acquisitions Editor: Vaughn Curtis
Project Manager: Rebecca Henson

McMurray, Anne
Community health and wellness : a socioecological approach.

Bibliography.
Includes index.
ISBN 1 875897 61 5.

1. Public health—Social aspects—Australia. 2. Health promotion—Social aspects—Australia. 3. Social medicine—Australia. I. Title.

362.120994

Edited by Kay Waters
Cover and text design by Leigh Ashforth @ watershed art & design
Illustrated by Dimitrios Prokopis
Photographs by Jo Grant
Indexed by Max McMaster
Printed by McPherson's Printing Group, Melbourne

Mosby Publishers Australia Pty Ltd
19/39 Herbert Street, Artarmon NSW 2064
AUSTRALIA

Contents

Preface

Too frequently when we speak of community health we actually mean community health services and the diseases and problems that are dealt with on a day-to-day basis. This book aims to refocus our perspective and understanding towards how health is produced within a community through a joint effort. It addresses the society–health interface not only by presenting an integrated model of influence but also by illustrating it with very practical examples.

The Ottawa Charter for Health Promotion has provided a practical pathway for implementation since its adoption in 1986. At the World Health Organization annual meeting in 1998 the World Health Assembly reinforced the need for comprehensive approaches with a special focus on 'settings' and investment in health. Indeed, the research on health determinants underlines with great clarity the importance of pathways to health that bring together the empowerment of communities, the strengthening of supportive environments and the reduction of inequities.

The approach taken in this book is interdisciplinary. It allows students to follow the present state of research and practice with great clarity. I hope it will be used widely in teaching and training—for a broad range of health professionals as well as for other professions whose work significantly impacts on community health.

Ilona Kickbusch

DIRECTOR, DIVISION OF HEALTH PROMOTION,
EDUCATION AND COMMUNICATION, WHO, GENEVA
AUGUST 1998

Acknowledgements

Several people have been invaluable in the development of this work. I would like to express my sincere gratitude to Amanda Curry for her assistance in the early stages of the writing, and to Wendy Zweck for her calm and competent management of the entire process. I would also like to thank Bill Katjar for his insightful illustrative concepts. The book would not have been possible without the help of Vaughn Curtis, Rebecca Henson and the team at Mosby, and the editorial assistance of Kay Waters. I thank them for their perseverance. Finally, I would like to express my appreciation to all those students who continue to stimulate my understanding of communities and how we, as nurses and health professionals, can assist them in meeting their needs for health and wellness in a rapidly changing society.

Community health:

the building blocks

Introduction

The four chapters in part one of this book describe the foundation from which community health is created. The first aspect of this foundation, described in chapter 1, is the ecological perspective that conceptualises health as being generated from a process of people interacting with their environment in a way that creates a feedback loop of sustainability. Healthy communities sustain, and are sustained by, healthy environments. The health of a community is also dependent on striking a balance between the capabilities, aspirations and health-related needs and goals of individuals and the whole population in the context of their environment.

The next building block is constructed from the remnants of the old public health, which revolved around achieving the greatest good for the largest number of people as determined by experts in health and health care. This system of determining public health from the top down has been replaced by a 'bottom-up, inside-out' approach, wherein people are seen to be the best judges of what they need to achieve and sustain health. Community health is created by people working collaboratively to shape and develop their community in a way that will allow them to achieve positive health outcomes. Community development is therefore integral to community health. The role of health professionals in helping to create and sustain health is one of partnership. Health professionals and other family and community advocates function as enablers and facilitators of community health, encouraging community participation in all aspects of community life. Professional expertise is a resource for community development but decision-making in health matters flows from indigenous leadership, generated from within the community in the context of ecological exchange. Strategies for health therefore emerge from many layers of interactions and interrelationships between people and the physical, social and cultural contexts of their lives.

Chapter 2 contends that effective community health promotion involves a commitment to the global strategies embodied in the Ottawa Charter for

Health Promotion: building healthy public policies, creating supportive environments, strengthening community action, developing personal skills and reorienting health services. These strategies are guided by the philosophy of primary health care, where empowered communities strive for access, equity and self-determination using all sectors of their environment to collaborate in determining health goals and appropriate processes for achieving them. Primary health care principles therefore situate all people's aspirations for health within an ethos of cultural sensitivity and social justice. These principles are incorporated into the Jakarta Declaration, which advocates situating all health promotion activities in healthy settings: healthy neighbourhoods, healthy schools, healthy workplaces, healthy villages, cities and communities.

Information is the key ingredient in strengthening the foundation of health promotion programs, and a major component of the information base is epidemiological data, which is the topic of chapter 3. Without a solid base of evidence that change is required, resources will not be forthcoming to aid the process, nor will there be any convincing arguments for people, cultures or governments to change their risky behaviours and unhealthy systems, and work towards increasing levels of personal and population health.

Chapter 4 provides a glimpse at the landscape within which community health is sustained. Its premise is that ecological interrelationships between people and the contexts of their lives gives expression to community culture. To assess a community's capacity for sustaining health requires local understandings of that culture, of community health status and community risk, of how people behave with respect to health, how they support one another, how they view health and their links to the external environment.

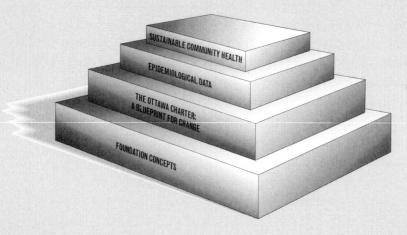

Public health, community health and community development

1

As human beings, we are all part of what is essentially a social world. As members of a community, our lives are closely interwoven with the lives of others, some living in close proximity to us, others sharing common characteristics but not inhabiting our geographical space. We also hold membership in various population groups on the basis of gender, age, physical capacity or culture. In the context of all of these group memberships, we interact with a moveable feast of richly diverse communities.

Each of these interactions, whether with our families, social groups or physical environment, is *ecological* in that there is an opportunity for exchange of ideas or energy. As a result, we and the environment are transformed, even in a small way. Ecological exchange yields both constraints and enhancements to personal and population health. Some of the more familiar constraints on health and wellbeing arise from the effects of contaminants in the physical environment, such as air and water pollution, infectious diseases, and injury. Some degree of risk is also present in the social environment, in the workplace, school and neighbourhood. Conversely, interactions with our environment in recreation, education and social interchange also present opportunities for achieving higher levels of health and wellbeing. Interactions between community members and the health care system are also imbued with challenges and opportunities for health improvements, especially when these are informative for ongoing health promotion, health monitoring, and protection from further illness. This chapter describes the essential nature of communities as a foundation for enabling community health and development. As a health professional, you will want to become conversant with the language of community health, and so that is where we will begin.

Objectives

By the end of this chapter you will be able to:

- *define health, community health, public health, community development and primary health care*

- *explain the different philosophical approaches of community health and public health*

- *discuss health from a social and ecological perspective*

- *identify the difference between health education and health promotion*

- *discuss the health promotion implications of a socioecological model of health.*

What is a community?

In the most basic terms, the word *community* simply means that which is common. We often think of a community as the physical or geographical place we share with others, but an ecological view takes this a bit further by defining a community as an interdependent group of plants and animals inhabiting a common space. People depending on one another, interacting with each another and with aspects of their environment, distinguish a living community from a collection of inanimate objects. Communities are thus dynamic entities that pulsate with the actions and interactions of people, the spaces they inhabit and the resources they use.

Some communities are also defined on the basis of personal factors such as age or gender, and some by virtue of their vulnerability to a health concern (Barnes et al. 1995). So, in addition to belonging to a certain neighbourhood or city, a person may be a member of a community of females, a community of adolescents or a community of middle-aged workers. In many cases, a person decides to become a member of a certain community by choice. For example, people may see themselves as members of the cycling community when they decide to engage in that sport. What is *communal* or *common* is the sport of cycling. Similarly, those of us who surf, swim, fish, jog or walk along the beach share the communal bonds of the beach community by choice.

What is community health?

When you think about communities in this way, the reciprocal relationship between people and their environment becomes readily apparent. Community health, then, is based on a synthesis of healthy people and healthy environments. Of course, some communities are better endowed than others with natural resources that encourage healthy lifestyles. However, communities with few resources but a strong commitment to health and wellness can also achieve a high level of community health.

A healthy community is one with a visible commitment to achieving the health and wellbeing of individuals, families and various groups of people. To begin with, there must be a common notion of health, one that is shared by community members as well as health professionals. From an ecological perspective, the goal of community health must be *sustainability*. To be sustainable, a community must be able to continue indefinitely without causing excessive disturbance or damage (Beare & Slaughter 1993). In today's society, where communities are interdependent upon one another and the global community, total sustainability represents an ideal. However, varying levels of sustainability can be achieved through *conservation* of both personal and physical resources, and by valuing *diversity*. This means that the community is bound by a common commitment to conserve not only its natural habitat, but all aspects of the physical, social and cultural environment that enable both current and future inhabitants to maintain health and wellness. Valuing diversity celebrates the different contributions that comprise the kaleidoscope of opinions, ideas and networks of the community.

What is health?

Health has been described in many ways over the years. The classic definition is that adopted by the World Health Organization (WHO) in which health is defined as 'a state of complete physical, mental and social well being and not merely the absence of disease or infirmity' (WHO 1974, p 1). This definition encompasses a holistic view of health. Holistic means focusing on the *whole*, not just the physical components. So the WHO definition is holistic in that it refers to physical, mental and social factors. However, it fails to capture the dynamic or *action-oriented* nature of being healthy and well. Health is not a static entity; it is ever changing.

Another aspect that should be included in a comprehensive definition of health is the extent to which people define themselves as healthy. Health is relative, and examples abound of individuals who have some type of functional disability, yet consider themselves healthy and well. Similarly, a community may have the disadvantage of isolation, or few natural resources conducive to health, yet the community may well be considered healthy on the basis of the attitudes and natural attributes of the people who live there.

Healthiness and wellness

Two important elements of healthiness are *balance* and *potential*. When people are healthy, their lives are in balance. There is harmony between the physical, social, emotional and spiritual. When communities are healthy there is a balance between the various barriers to health (unemployment, poverty, lack of fresh vegetables) and those things that encourage health (sporting facilities, neighbourhood clubs, medical facilities). When people are healthy, they recognise the potential for higher levels of *wellness*. For example, healthy, fit people go to the gym and eat a nutritious diet; students balance study with recreation; young families immunise their children; older people keep active and socialise with others. Similarly, healthy communities participate in greening their environment, keep an eye on crime rates and make available resources for promoting physical fitness and healthy lifestyles in their schools and workplaces.

This broad view of health and wellness is *socioecological*. The social world provides the context within which people interact with the environment. When we define health from a social perspective we acknowledge the social capital of the community. This means that health is valued, and people are valued in a climate of trust and mutual respect that extends to all facets of life (Cox 1995). The ecological part of the definition draws the diverse social and environmental aspects together into a whole, to work towards achieving equilibrium and harmony, even when aspects of the personal, social or physical environment are changing.

According to the WHO, 'health depends on our ability to understand and manage the interaction between human activities and the physical and biological environment' (WHO 1992, p. 409). Our understanding of these interactions is guided by the principles of basic ecology, which acknowledge that everything is connected with everything else in some way and, because of this, is subject to constant change (McFarlane & McFarlane 1996).

Ecological community health goes beyond the simple or shallow ecology that is focused on the three 'R' maxims of 'reduce', 'reuse' and 'recycle' to a deep ecology requiring collective questioning, at increasingly deeper levels, of our basic assumptions and meanings about the world, our culture, life and our relationship with the natural environment in everyday activities (Lacroix 1996). The deep ecological focus is thus different from a simple environmental focus in that there is a valuing of the intimate connection between the environment and population health. Health can then be seen as a living manifestation of people's compatibility with the ecosystem (McMichael 1991).

Health is thus a multidimensional concept. It is a communal artefact that evolves from sustaining the links between the activities of people and their environment (Bateson 1989). These links are in turn moderated by biology, attitudes and constantly changing circumstances. At any point in time, health is therefore a balance between striving to reach the highest potential for wellness and the compromises demanded by the physical, psychological, cultural, social and political environment.

The health of the community is, in effect, *population health*. It involves simultaneous consideration of the needs and goals of the population groups inhabiting the community, and examination of the conditions of life that either enhance or impede their health or the health of the community itself. Community health can thus be seen as a balance between the capabilities, aspirations and health-related needs and goals of individuals, various groups, and the whole population within the context of their environment.

What is public health?

Until the mid-1970s, there was no clear understanding of the distinction between the terms 'public health' and 'community health'. From the turn of the century, public health organisations were primarily concerned with eradicating infectious diseases using a regulatory approach of surveillance and control. The focus was on tracking epidemics or potential epidemics and ensuring that government regulations were in place for the ongoing monitoring of illness in the population, and to respond quickly to situations of need. For the most part, their activities were unquestioned by the general public.

From the 1930s to the 1970s, public health was defined according to a *biomedical* model where the emphasis was on understanding the causes of illness in order to apportion resources appropriately. These resources were concentrated in hospitals and acute-sector services that were in reality more concerned with public illness than public health (Davies & Kelly 1993).

Medical and other public health professionals were trained to recognise patterns of disease, environmental hazards and models of health service delivery that would result in adequate levels of health for the largest number of people. This is the goal of public health: to secure adequate health for the majority of the population.

Historically, the health-related decisions made by public health experts were guided by current medical knowledge, political factors and the availability of financial and personal resources. So, for example, in those parts of the world where health personnel and resources were plentiful, people were expected to have higher levels of health. Where vaccines were available, and where the politics of the day encouraged medical research, diseases should be curtailed. However, this has not always been the case. Despite a long history of eradicating some illnesses and improving health status in some populations, public health officials have realised for some time that there is only a tenuous association between the provision of services and achieving acceptable levels of health (Navarro 1993).

For years, people tended to overestimate the achievements of medicine in eradicating disease, yet an examination of three centuries of public health information reveals that medical advances explained only 10% of improvements in the health of the population, the remainder being attributed to public health efforts, improved nutrition and better quality of life (Allen & Hall 1988). Even today, there are developed nations rich in knowledge and technology yet poor in the public health policies that mobilise their assets on behalf of the public's health (Salmon 1995). This dilemma has been the subject of heated discussion for two decades, and was the precipitating factor that led health planners and policy advisors in many countries to convene an international meeting that would consider a new direction in health for all peoples of the world.

Primary health care

In 1978, the challenge of public health—that is, securing the highest level of health for the greatest number of people—formed the agenda for a meeting of public health delegates from 134 countries throughout the world. The meeting was held in Alma Ata (a city in the former USSR). For years, various health ministries had been grappling with the failure of public health systems to achieve health for all people, and this meeting was planned to develop new solutions and new directions in public health. The delegates' deliberations culminated in the Declaration of Alma Ata, which was essentially a commitment to embody public health goals within the philosophy of primary health care. The Declaration defined *primary health care* as follows:

> essential health care based on practical, scientifically sound and socially acceptable methods and technology made universally accessible to individuals and families in the community through their full participation and at a cost that the community and country can afford to maintain at every stage of their development in the spirit of self-reliance and self-determination. It is the first level of contact with individuals, the family and community with the national health systems bringing health care as close as possible to where people live and work, and constitutes the first element of a continuing care process (WHO UNICEF 1978, p. 6).

The Declaration represented a watershed in public health, as its focus was on empowering people to have control over decisions that affected health in their own families and communities. The primary health care approach conceptualised health as a fundamental right, an individual and collective responsibility, an equal opportunity concept and an essential element of socioeconomic development (Holzemer 1992). This represented a stark contrast to the historical 'top-down' approach to planning for public health, as people at the grass roots level of societies were now to have a greater say in planning from the 'bottom-up', or 'inside out' instead of 'outside in' (Courtney 1995). As McMichael (1993) suggests, this new approach would see experts *on tap* rather than *on top*.

Communities throughout the world embraced the concept of primary health care and the opportunity to become more involved in decisions affecting their health. The Declaration of Alma Ata thus signalled a shift in thinking from the 'old public health', wherein health professionals decided what was best for the community, to a 'new public health', where communities themselves would decide priorities and preferences for health from the grass roots, where people live, work and play. The consumer movement, which unified people with common health goals, and the information revolution, which put people in touch with one another, both played a part in encouraging heightened awareness and greater community involvement in health. From the perspective of those at the top, it was a welcome change to have governments recognise the influence of all sectors of society on the health of the population, as the Declaration clearly acknowledged the importance of technology, community planning, economic factors and settings such as the workplace in securing and maintaining community health.

Perhaps most importantly, the declaration launched what is now commonly known as the 'Health For All' (HFA) movement, a global attempt to work towards health for all people by the year 2000. Health for All, or the 'new public health' was not a call for global eradication of disease, but rather a pledge by the WHO and its member states to foster better health within the broader context of social and economic development (Maglacas 1988). It was about broadening concepts of health, refocusing from illness to health, renewing resources for health, and democratising health and health services (Hudson-Rodd 1994). And so another link was established: that between community health and community development.

Community development

Community development is a process of empowering communities to improve their health and wellbeing. This approach can be contrasted with the dichotomy of consumer–provider, where one party (in this case, health professionals) provides, and the other (the public) consumes. In the consumer–provider model there is a distinct power differential in that the provider holds the key to such resources as information, services or consumables, and the consumer must abide by the rules set down by the provider to gain the information, goods or services. The community development approach replaces this power structure with a partnership arrangement, where one person or group collaborates and negotiates with another for needed information, services or consumables.

One of the challenges of community development is to ensure that health professionals do not impose their agenda on the community. Instead, members of the community decide what they wish to change, what services they need to assist change, and what support mechanisms would maintain the change. The role of the health professional, then, is to provide enough information for the community to have the knowledge to plan for improved health outcomes. The objective of the health professional is to foster *community competence*, the ability of community members to collaborate and negotiate effectively to get what they need (Goeppinger, Lassiter & Wilcox 1982). The health professional adopts a role as *advocate* rather than decision-maker, encouraging *indigenous leadership* wherein decisions originate from local individuals (Courtney 1995).

Helping communities involves trusting in their abilities and advocating on different levels. As social advocate, the health professional adopts a respectful and culturally sensitive approach. As political advocate, it is essential to become knowledgeable about the health and welfare systems and the processes that govern both resource allocation and policy development. As professional advocate, the health professional must preserve the professional competence and solidarity that will help him or her maintain credibility in the community, and therefore act as an effective resource (McMurray 1993).

This is the essence of community health promotion: advocating for communities, collaborating with community members, sharing information and resources and helping them construct pathways to change. The process is developmental in that by working together, people's skills, knowledge and self-confidence are developed, ultimately empowering them to go on to the next undertaking. Facilitating and enabling this type of change in communities also plays a role in developing the skills of the health professional. Each community and each community development strategy is unique, so every opportunity to work with a community yields new information that the health promoter can use to consolidate and refine health promotion skills. Community development is thus a deliberate two-way process of mutual development that occurs in the process of achieving health goals.

Several principles guide community development:

- *Integration*—community development must be accomplished with integration of social, political, cultural, environmental, personal and spiritual elements. By adopting a holistic approach, issues of class, gender, race/ethnicity, age, disability or sexuality can be considered for their contribution to health.
- *Community ownership*—the community, rather than health professionals, must own the structures and processes of change. This ensures independence of strategies and action, which empowers the community for decision-making and the pace of development. It also circumvents any need for coercion or oppression from outsiders.
- *Recognition of the political nature of community change*—the links between individual and public issues are crucial and mutually dependent; for example, political processes give rise to unemployment, which in turn has an effect on health and family functioning. Community development must not be oppressive or grounded in conflict.

- *Advocacy and partnership*—the role of the health professional is to preserve the human rights of community members, ensure integrity of the processes of change, and strengthen social interactions by bringing community members together and helping them communicate with genuine dialogue, understanding and social action. Such an approach must be inclusive, so all community members are encouraged to participate. In addition, the health professional must help the community recognise and define need, by bringing together residents, service providers and researchers.

- *Vision*—community development must be undertaken with a view toward sustainability and holistic nurturing, rather than mechanistic, linear solutions to health and developmental problems. Its overall purpose is to promote health and wellbeing for all people (Ife 1995).

What is health promotion?

Within a primary health care framework, *health promotion* encompasses all activities that enable and facilitate health. These activities may be political at either the global or the local level. At the local level, this may involve lobbying the government for better roads or more parklands, or helping to institute a recycling scheme. At the global level, it may involve becoming personally aware of the problems of other countries, and making sure their health issues are publicised. For example, Chukwuma (1996) describes the global problem of toxic waste, which should become part of our global awareness. We know that relaxed attitudes and non-stringent environmental controls have allowed multinational corporations to relocate polluting industries to non-industrialised countries, where hazardous trace elements are disposed of in the soil. This is one of the major threats to health, for as McMichael & Hales (1997, p. 426) state:

> *while human societies continue to depend upon a linear waste-generating metabolism which is at odds with the circular metabolism of the rest of nature (wherein every output becomes an input), the atmosphere, land and oceans will tend to fill with waste emissions, and slowly renewable resources will be depleted.*

In many cases, local populations are more susceptible to toxic poisoning from the environment because of poor health, nutrition and hygiene, and increased population density that includes large groups of vulnerable people, such as children and pregnant women. Being poor and having few food-preservation facilities, these people tend to consume foods locally cultivated in trace-element-contaminated areas. Compounding this problem is the medical profession's inability to accurately diagnose trace-element-induced health problems. As health professionals, it is our responsibility to do what we can to ensure that we, our communities and our policy makers understand the politics of sustainable health and to see the impact of local decisions on global health.

Promoting health in any setting, whether a city, village, school or organisation, is based on the premise that health development potential can be fostered through a series of defined strategies (Kickbusch 1997). Thus the role of the health promoter is to work in partnership with community members to better understand the community's goals for health and its potential for achieving health. This also involves helping the community to identify and thus overcome any barriers or impediments to sustaining health and preventing illness. Health promotion activities may also be social—for example, working with young people to help them clarify values and goals for the future. Health promotion may be aimed at different population subgroups, such as creating day care centres for the elderly to prevent them from becoming socially isolated, or working with new parents to ensure they have the informal support system they need. The role of the health promoter thus involves being a change agent, or an advocate for health. Some health promotion activities may be educational and thus may fall under the rubric of health education.

Health education

According to Green and Kreuter (1991), *health education* refers to any planned educational intervention that is aimed at the voluntary actions people can take to look after their health or the health of others. Several elements in this definition are crucial to success. One is *planning*. Successful health education programs are carefully planned with respect to the audience, the timing, the setting, the credibility of the health educator, and the method of evaluation. Without such planning, the information may fail to educate for several reasons.

First, there may be less than optimal delivery of the educational material. Second, if the presentation(s) does not occur when the audience is receptive to the message or when the environment is conducive to learning, the information may fall on 'deaf ears'. Third, the information may be ignored if it is not seen as coming from a reliable source. Finally, if there is no evaluation of the program or presentation, the health educator will have no way of knowing whether these efforts have been effective, or whether change may have merely occurred by chance. So the next time, a whole new approach will have to be devised rather than having the benefit of feedback on what did, or did not, work previously.

Another important aspect of the definition of health education is that it must be *educational*. Many of today's health education presentations represent a combination of educational content and entertainment value. This 'mix' is sometimes called 'edutainment' and is based on the notion that people learn best when they are enjoying themselves. The edutainment approach has achieved considerable success in health education as well as in other aspects of health promotion.

The final important element within the definition of health education is that it is designed to bring about *voluntary* change. The implication of this for the health education planner is that the health education program or presentation will be designed to *influence* rather than *coerce* change. People themselves will decide whether or not to make a change. The role of the health educator is thus to present a basis for *informed choice* by providing the options, choices and access to resources that will help people choose healthy pathways to living. In order for those choices to be sustainable, people in the community must feel a sense of investment, or ownership, in the changes and their effectiveness in meeting the long-term health goals of the community.

Community health promotion: the Ottawa Charter for Health Promotion

Promoting the health of a community extends individual health education and health promotion to a broader scope of activities. In most countries of the world, this level of health promotion is guided by the Ottawa Charter for Health Promotion (WHO-Health and Welfare Canada 1986).

In 1986, eight years after the Declaration of Alma Ata, the members of 38 nations met in Ottawa, Canada, to evaluate progress in achieving health for all by the year 2000. From this meeting, the Ottawa Charter for Health Promotion was developed as a blueprint for future community health promotion initiatives. The Charter emphasised the importance of promoting health at a global level, and identified the fundamental conditions and resources for community health. These include peace, shelter, education, food, income, a stable ecosystem, sustainable resources, social justice and equity (WHO-Health and Welfare Canada 1986). The Charter (summarised in figure 1.1) identified five major strategies for health promotion that circumscribed the public health activities of disease control and resource allocation, yet adopted the primary health care approach of grass roots community development and an ecological view of health. The five strategies are as follows:

1 *Build healthy public policy*

This strategy is aimed at encouraging all those involved in health care to ensure that health becomes incorporated into all public policy decisions. This represents a change from the traditional approach, where decisions in the health sector were relatively confined to the health industry. The Charter suggested intersectoral collaboration, where there is a mutual recognition that the policies of other sectors, such as education, housing, industry, social welfare and environmental planning, also affect, and are affected by, those that guide the health of our communities.

2 *Create supportive environments*

This strategy embodies the socioecological approach to health. The Charter encouraged all people to recognise the importance of conserving and capitalising on those resources that enable people to maintain health, whether they be physical or social resources.

3 *Strengthen community action*

The Charter identified information and learning opportunities as the focus for empowering communities to make informed choices for better health. This type of community action exemplifies the community development approach.

4 *Develop personal skills*

This strategy guides communities to provide adequate and appropriate education and opportunities for skills development so that people can influence their communities to make local decisions for effective use of resources in order to attain health.

5 *Reorient health services*

Those involved in decisions affecting community health must operate from a base of evidence on what best works to foster the health of people. Included in this strategy is the need for research and the dissemination of knowledge from the multiple perspectives of those concerned with social, political, economic and physical resources as well as health.

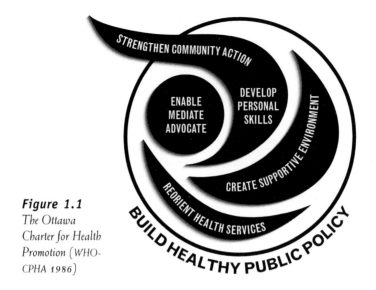

Figure 1.1
The Ottawa Charter for Health Promotion (WHO- CPHA 1986)

In 1997, the strategies of the Ottawa Charter were endorsed in the Jakarta Declaration on Health Promotion into the 21st Century (WHO 1997). The Jakarta Declaration, which emerged from the 4th International Conference on Health Promotion, is an attempt to direct efforts in health promotion toward the social, economic and environmental conditions which either constrain or facilitate health by focusing on social responsibility for health, re-framing health as an investment in the future, establishing partnerships for health, and empowering the community (WHO 1997). These principles are elaborated on in chapter 12.

Implications for community health promotion

Effective health promotion requires access to information and some unique skills. To become knowledgeable in all health matters or to keep up to date on the latest research results would take nothing short of an encyclopaedic mind. However, in this era of rapid information exchange, it is possible to access current information on a wide range of health-related topics almost instantaneously. The Internet has proven a boon to the exchange of health information, as it has for other types of information. Not too many years ago, health professionals spent considerable time building their personal networks of people researching common topics. Now, in an instant, anyone can access the latest research findings on heart disease, asthma, physical training regimes or hundreds of other topics.

For the public, there is general information on the Internet that helps keep them abreast of changes in health knowledge and, in some cases, protocols for good practice in health and medical services related to specific illnesses. This makes the job of health promotion more interesting, as people are often well-informed and may already have ideas for community health promotion. On the other hand, where the community is not well informed on a topic, the community health promoter can assist them by providing credible and current information as a basis for planning.

Besides information, the most important element in health promotion is a broad understanding of human development and behaviour, and the ability to communicate well. These three characteristics are fundamental to the role of a health advocate. To work with a community requires a sensitive approach to different people's needs at different stages of their development. For example, in dealing with asthma, similar community resources may be used to encourage both young and elderly asthmatics to cope with their conditions, but the strategic organisation of those resources, and the approach to health education for each group, will differ considerably. Similarly, promoting sexual health in small rural areas or within small enclaves of certain ethnic groups may require a vastly different approach from that used to reach the typical urban teenager. The most important issue is to start where the people are, allowing the community to become empowered by having a voice in all decisions that affect the health and well-being of its people.

Enabling and facilitating the development of community health also requires a commitment to the notion of health as a socioecological construct. As was mentioned at the beginning of this chapter, we are primarily social creatures who live in communal environments. We energise and are energised by those environments, which are constructed on foundations layered by historical, personal and situational events. Within this framework, health is not given to people, but generated by them. Our role is thus one of mediating, enabling and facilitating the processes, people and systems that can be mobilised to achieve health goals.

The promotion of health involves getting to know the will of the people and the resources unique to the community, and how these are linked with the wider context, even to the extent of the global community. The health promoter must form multiple partnerships for change, engaging with the immediate community, and understanding and respecting local, immediate dynamics and needs, but within a framework of sustainability. It is an approach that requires resourcefulness, information exchange, receptivity to new ideas and strategies, a tolerance for difference, a willingness to change and a common goal of community development. Within this framework, health can be generated and cultivated from within, rather than without, from bottom up rather than top down, as the community develops the will and capacity for relevant and appropriate change.

THINKING CRITICALLY
Community health

▶ What are the three most important resources for health that are obvious in your community?

▶ In what way is each of these resources dependent on other factors in the environment?

▶ Identify a group in your community who share a common vulnerability to a health issue or concern.

▶ List two types of community advocates in your community who have already undertaken measures to encourage community competence.

▶ Identify three major threats to health in your community and one possible solution for each.

REFERENCES

Allen, J. & Hall, B. 1988, 'Challenging the focus on technology: a critique of the medical model in a changing health care system', *Advances in Nursing Science*, vol. 10, no. 3, pp. 22–34.

Barnes, D., Eribes, C., Juarbe, T., Nelson, M., Proctor, S. et al. 1995, 'Primary health care and primary care: a confusion of philosophies', *Nursing Outlook*, vol. 43, no. 7, pp. 7–16.

Bateson, M. 1989, 'Health as artifact', *Journal of Professional Nursing*, vol. 5, no. 6, pp. 322–5.

Beare, H. & Slaughter, R. 1993, *Education for the Twenty-First Century*, Routledge, London.

Chukwuma, C. 1996, 'Perspectives for a sustainable society', *Environmental Management and Health*, vol. 7, no. 5, pp. 5–20.

Courtney, R. 1995, 'Community partnership primary care: A new paradigm for primary care', *Public Health Nursing*, vol. 12, no. 6, pp. 366–73.

Cox, E. 1995, 'Changing patterns of work and living', *Proceedings of the Third National Women's Health Conference*, pp. 274–6.

Davies, J. & Kelly, M. 1993, *Healthy Cities: Research and Practice*, Routledge, London.

Goeppinger, J., Lassiter, P. & Wilcox, B. 1982, 'Community health is community competence', *Nursing Outlook*, vol. 30, pp. 464–7.

Green, L. & Kreuter, M. 1991, *Health Promotion Planning: An Educational and Environmental Approach*, Mayfield Publishing Company, Mountain View, California.

Holzemer, W. 1992, 'Linking primary health care and self-care through case management', *International Nursing Review,* vol. 39, no. 3, pp. 83–9.

Hudson-Rodd, N. 1994, 'Public health: people participating in the creation of healthy places', *Public Health Nursing,* vol. 11, no. 2, pp. 119–26.

Ife, J. 1995, *Community Development: Creating Community Alternatives—Vision, Analysis and Practice,* Longman, Melbourne.

Kickbusch, I. 1997, 'Health-promoting environments: the next steps', *Australian and New Zealand Journal of Public Health,* vol. 21, no. 4, pp. 431–4.

Lacroix, D. 1996, 'Awakening an ecological self in nursing', in *The Ecological Self in Australian Nursing,* ed. D. Lacroix, Royal College of Nursing, Canberra, Australia, pp. 1–26

Maglacas, A. 1988, 'Health for all: nursing's role', *Nursing Outlook,* vol. 36, no. 2, pp. 66–72.

McFarlane, R. & McFarlane, J. 1996, 'Ecological connections', in *Community as Partner,* 2nd edn, eds E. Anderson & J. McFarlane, Lippincott, Philadelphia, pp. 82–121.

McMichael, A. 1991, 'Global warming, ecological disruption and human health: the penny drops', *Medical Journal of Australia,* vol. 154, pp. 449–501.

McMichael, A. 1993, 'Public health in Australia: a personal reflection', *Australian Journal of Public Health,* vol. 17, no. 4, pp. 295–6.

McMichael, A. & Hales, S. 1997, 'Global health promotion: looking back to the future', *Australian and New Zealand Journal of Public Health,* vol. 21, no. 4, pp. 425–8.

McMurray, A. 1993, *Community Health Nursing: Primary Health Care in Practice,* 2nd edn, Churchill-Livingstone, Melbourne.

Navarro, V. 1993, 'Has socialism failed? An analysis of health indicators under capitalism and socialism', *Science and Society,* vol. 57, no. 1, pp. 6–30.

Salmon, M. 1995, 'Public health policy: Creating a healthy future for the American public', *Family and Community Health,* vol. 18, no. 1, pp. 1–11.

World Health Organization 1974, *Basic Documents,* 36th edn, WHO, Geneva.

World Health Organization 1992, 'Health and the environment: a global challenge', *Bulletin of the World Health Organization,* vol. 70, no. 4, pp. 409–13.

World Health Organization 1997, *The Jakarta Declaration on Health Promotion into the 21st Century,* WHO, Geneva.

World Health Organization-Health and Welfare Canada-CPHA 1986, 'Ottawa Charter for Health Promotion', *Canadian Journal of Public Health,* vol. 77, no. 12, pp. 425–30.

World Health Organization UNICEF 1978, *Primary Health Care,* WHO, Geneva.

Primary health care: enabling health and wellness

As mentioned in chapter 1, primary health care is a framework for community health that includes advocacy at many levels. Promoting primary health care involves helping individuals and families achieve and maintain healthy lifestyles, empowering communities to organise their resources for healthful living, and lobbying politicians and policy makers at all levels to include health considerations in all policy and resource decisions.

Primary health care principles formed the basis for the Ottawa Charter for Health Promotion and, more recently, the Jakarta Declaration on Health Promotion Into the 21st Century. The principles urge a social justice approach to health promotion, which places human rights and individual and community choice at the heart of healthy communities. Because the notion of social justice and the principles of primary health care — equity, access, self-determinism, intersectoral collaboration and empowerment — are not uniformly understood, this chapter provides an explanation of terms to encourage a common framework and common understandings in advocating for community health.

Objectives

By the end of this chapter you will be able to:

- distinguish between primary health care and primary care

- define the principles of primary health care

- explain the links between social justice and primary health care

- discuss the application of primary health care principles in promoting community health

- devise a management plan to address a community health issue using primary health care principles.

Distinction between primary care and primary health care

The main advantage of using primary health care as a framework to guide health promotion activities lies in working within a clear international goal (Health For All), explicitly defined strategies (the Ottawa Charter for Health Promotion) and common, recognisable terminology. This adds consistency across different programs and between different people developing similar programs. As we launch into the new millenium, primary health care is internationally recognised as a way of structuring community health activities, but in some cases the terms *primary care* and *primary health care* are used interchangeably, and this occasionally causes confusion.

Primary care

When people require health care because of injury or illness, the *first* line of care is *primary*. But primary care is more than just the initial decision as to what must be done. It extends to the primary management of a person's condition. Primary care may involve only one intervention, or treatment over an extended period of time, but it is still primary because it is aimed at helping people with whatever problem required care in the first place. Physicians, nurses, dentists, physiotherapists and a range of other health professionals provide primary care—that is, depending on the circumstances, they may be responsible for managing a health problem.

So, for example, if an athlete suffers an injury on the sports field, the trainer will often provide *first aid* and then refer the athlete to a physician, who will assume the role of primary care provider. Similarly, a nurse in a hospital emergency department or in a community clinic may provide initial treatment for an emergency, and then either refer the person to the local GP to manage the condition, or manage it her/himself, depending on the situation. In the latter case, the nurse would be acting as a primary care provider, and this often happens in remote locations where there is no medical doctor.

Another situation where someone other than a medical doctor acts as primary care provider is in the workplace. Many manufacturing and mining companies, for example, employ health professionals to undertake the management of occupational health and safety. For some workplace-based problems the occupational health nurse is the most appropriate person to assume the role of the primary care provider.

Primary health care

Primary health care includes primary, or initial care, to address a problem, but it also encompasses the broader activities of government and other sectors of society. The goal of primary health care is to help communities and the people in them to achieve lasting improvement in the quality of their lives (Ferrinho et al. 1993). Embedded within the philosophy of primary health care are several principles that guide community health promotion activities.

Primary health care principles

The major principles of primary health care are *equity, access, empowerment, community self-determinism* and *intersectoral collaboration.* These are all interconnected, but we will examine them separately here to underline the importance of each principle to the overall philosophy of primary health care.

Equity

It was mentioned in chapter 1 that primary health care is an equal opportunity concept, and this is embodied in the principle of equity. Health for all people means equal opportunities for all people, whether they differ by geography, race, age, gender, language or functional capacity. An ecological view of community health extends beyond these familiar aspects of equity to consider sustainability as an equity issue. *Sustainable health* means that any present measures taken to improve our environment must not compromise the ability of future generations to meet their needs (Lowe 1994). So in a socioecological framework, the principle of equity has broadened beyond the needs of the present generation to consider those of future inhabitants of our communities when planning community health programs.

Clearly, then, the principle of equity requires us to include such global issues as global warming, overpopulation, the destruction of forests and the processing of industrial waste in our community health promotion strategies. But there is another consideration here in working towards a sustainable, equitable future: what may be sustainable in one community may disadvantage another. Equity, then, involves not only awareness of the needs of future generations in making resource decisions, but simultaneous assessment of their impact on other people and communities.

To engage in primary health care activities therefore requires political and social consciousness—that is, deliberate consideration of the needs and agendas of *all* people. This is where the notion of *social justice* permeates all primary health care activities. Social justice, or equity for all, must supersede individual goals, so that the least advantaged people in a community receive equal care and service to those who are advantaged by virtue of tangible (finances) and intangible (knowledge) resources. A commitment to primary health care dictates that we remain aware of the health needs of our local community, and how they relate to those of others. It is also important to understand the capacity of both local and global resources to meet health needs across the spectrum of advantage and disadvantage. By approaching health planning in terms of the 'big picture', we can 'think global and act local'.

One of the most common inequities that has a negative impact on health is socioeconomic status. The wealthy usually have access to better food and a better lifestyle balance than the poor, and in many countries the disparity in health status between most and least affluent appears to be growing (Chu 1994; Whitehead 1995). In many cases, the best laid plans for equitable distribution are subordinated to economic arrangements. In the developing nations this is primarily due to a lack of resources, whereas in developed countries it is often a function of over-bureaucratised health care structures and public policies that are focused more on the needs of vested interests than on social justice (DeBois Inglis & Kjervik 1993).

A broad review of international studies on health and illness reveals that inequities in social and economic conditions continue to be linked to poorer health outcomes (Whitehead 1995). This is exacerbated among the indigenous people of the world. In some age groups, the rate of illness among the Aboriginal poor and unemployed is as much as 50–60% above the rest of the population (AIHW 1996). Within the Australian Aboriginal and Torres Straight Islander (ATSIC) community, the infant mortality rate remains 3 to 5 times higher than for non-indigenous people (AIHW 1996). Only marginally better rates exist for indigenous people in other countries as well, particularly South Africa, the US, Canada and New Zealand (Bullen & Beaglehole 1997; Brady 1995; Matseoane 1997). In some cases the disparity between indigenous and non-indigenous people is due to a lack of access to information and other resources, and in some cases it is linked to social and family conditions.

Family support is an important element in helping people maintain health and, with increasing rates of separation and divorce, many one-parent families experience lower health status. In ATSIC communities, nearly a quarter of the population lives in a family headed by a single parent, compared with 9% in the rest of the Australian population, so a combination of factors contributes to social disadvantage (Hartley 1995). Clearly, equity issues, and the links between the social and racial agendas, must be addressed before any gains can be made in achieving sustainable health for the population.

Access

Under the primary health care philosophy, access to health care requires that health care be available where people live and work (WHO UNICEF 1978). One of the greatest barriers to access is geographic location. People who live in rural and remote areas have fewer resources than those in urban environments. In some countries, labour regulations and fears over job security prevent access to health services. For example, as male unemployment rates have risen, female production workers spend long hours on the job, leaving them little or no time to attend to their own or their families' health needs.

This is particularly the case in some cultures where it is inappropriate for the male to assume household duties. As a consequence, women spend long hours preparing meals and cleaning their homes prior to and after their paid work. In most cases, occupational health services are non-existent in their place of employment and they have no community access to preventive programs such as cervical screening. As could be expected in this situation, rates of post-partum infections and other female problems have grown proportionally with increasing levels of female employment (Momsen & Kinnaird 1993).

> CASE STUDY

Sri Lankan tea plantation workers

It is interesting to reflect on the assumption held by many people in developed countries that access to employment equates with access to health, and this is sometimes the case. In developing countries, however, the opposite is often true. Sri Lankan Tamil tea plantations provide one example of where workplace health services have attempted to respond to conditions of ill health precipitated in the workplace.

The women workers typically begin their day at 4.00 a.m., when they rise to fetch water, prepare meals and get the children ready for creche or school prior to reporting themselves for paid work at 7.00 a.m. They may take a break to feed their children during the day but generally work until 5.30 p.m., when they return home to begin the evening chores of cleaning, laundry and preparing the evening and the following day's midday meal. This routine goes on six days a week and involves climbing steep slopes in the plantations, being exposed to chilly winds, rain and hot sun, and carrying up to 25 kg in a basket strapped to their backs.

At home, the women cook over firewood stoves, so smoke inhalation and respiratory complaints are common. With food preparation being the exclusive domain of women, these conditions are much more prevalent in women than men. Exacerbating the situation is the fact that tight wage and work schedules allow little time for food purchase, but many foods are also inaccessible. In addition, much of the drinking water is polluted, and personal hygiene facilities are poor.

Their culture dictates that women's wages be collected by husbands, fathers or another adult male family member, and sometimes the money is spent on gambling and alcohol rather than on food or goods that would improve the quality of the family's life. This intersection of culturally embedded family life and occupational health is now being addressed in Sri Lanka through a comprehensive health plan sponsored by the Asian Development Bank and by improvements in health infrastructure made by large plantation owners. With sponsorship from UNICEF, women now have access to health education, supplementary child feeding, and pre- and post-natal care. Despite the fact that these are curative rather than preventative measures, the result has been greater access to health for those employed in this sector (Momsen & Kinnaird 1993).

Another barrier to access is related to technology. One of the aims of primary health care is to develop healthy public policies that promote the use of appropriate technologies. The issue of technology has been debated in many forums, and tends to polarise opinions, particularly in the ethical arena (Lee & Paxman 1997). We have the technology to keep very small birthweight infants alive, yet should we do so at the expense of others? Similarly, is it appropriate use of technology to sustain the life of the very oldest old? Is it appropriate to provide access to high-technology medicine for very old or very young people if they have merely become part of clinical trials to test the devices? Is it appropriate to deny access to the type of health care provided in big cities to those who live at a distance? Should fertility treatment, for example, be allocated on the basis of gender or age equity, or on the basis of human desire for a child regardless of the public health problem of overpopulation?

There are no clear answers to these questions of appropriateness, as they tend to become clouded with moral judgements. Perhaps a fundamental question that needs to be addressed is related to the role of moral and ethical issues in public health decisions, and this is being widely debated throughout the world from the perspective of both access and equity (Downie & Calman 1994).

Yet another barrier to access is lack of education or information. The question in this case is, should the informed person who demands certain services from the health care system have an advantage over those ignorant of what is available? The Internet poses a new twist to this dilemma. Those who can afford Internet access surely have an advantage over those who are deprived by either finances or distance.

These dilemmas are not new, as technological developments have had an impact on health for many years. For example, when the refrigerator was first invented, it represented the single most important device preventing illness by guarding against contamination of foods. It was, however, accessible only to those who could afford it, and no public health authority ever considered providing refrigerators for all people. Today, partly because of global communication and increased consumer sophistication, new technologies have become part of the public interest, and people everywhere tend to enter debates over the ethics of resource allocation and their right to technological innovations (Ham 1997).

Empowerment

One of the most remarkable features of primary health care is the shift in power relations that has ensued from reorienting health care away from health professionals' agendas to that of people themselves. Wallerstein (1992) describes empowerment as a process of social action that promotes individual and community control, political efficacy, improved quality of community life and social justice. People become empowered when they believe in their ability to create change. Instead of being directed towards choices made by outsiders, empowered community change comes from within the community.

The role of the health professional in the change process is markedly different from the past, when at times people were coerced into changing their health behaviours on the basis that it was good for them. The fundamental flaw in this approach is the assumption that what was good for people could be described within standardised, generic prescriptions decided by experts who, despite being well versed in the latest medical literature, were field illiterate. Without knowledge of the 'field' or 'grass roots', it is impossible to incorporate cultural differences that provide wider and more relevant choices for people in achieving health and wellness.

To participate in securing health for people in an empowered community thus requires *cultural sensitivity*, one of the cornerstones of social justice. Cultural sensitivity means not simply tolerating differences between groups of people, but understanding the dynamics of another culture in a way that captures both the words and the music—that is, being able to assess elements within the behaviour patterns or social roles of a culture that make it special and that are, or can be, conducive to health.

Some examples of cultural differences in health behaviours stand out clearly—for example, the way some ethnic groups use hot and cold foods to overcome various illnesses. Others are subtle, such as the way in which religious or spiritual beliefs contribute to health (Brady 1995). For years, researchers have examined the relationship between religion and health, and their findings in many countries, with numerous religions, in different eras, all point to a significant, positive effect of being religious on health.

However, despite a variety of explanations, no single factor has emerged as the definitive link between religion and health (Levin 1994). This lack of clarity further reinforces the notion that various conceptions of health and healthful living can only be understood from within and alongside a community, which is where all health promotion interventions must begin.

Self-determinism

If we as health professionals are to encourage communities to become self-determined, it is important to understand human behaviour and some of the things that prevent or discourage people from taking responsibility for their own health goals. It helps to recognise that some people tend to seek out information about their health, while others prefer to leave health matters and various strategies for managing their health to professionals. Still others believe in fate—that relative states of health are predetermined and so there is little use in trying to change.

These individual preferences for decision-making must be respected; but when information and options are provided sensitively and in a way that will be readily understood, most people will choose to take responsibility for their health. At the community level, this can be tricky, as different people's group allegiances may compete with various community health goals as defined by others.

For example, a community may contain a mix of people who have different notions about nutrition. One group may want to establish a school canteen with fresh foods; another may want a cheaper, fast food option. To encourage healthy eating patterns in the children who attend the school, competing agendas will need to be discussed, options considered, and information provided that will help the community make a self-determined decision.

In this and similar cases, the health professional can play an important advocacy role in getting people together to explore their options, but at the same time must adopt a role as a mediator and facilitator, ensuring that everyone has a say and that any required information is brought to the community to inform decisions as they are generated. This has proved effective in school-based healthy eating programs, where the objective is to get young people to make healthy choices because they are informed, not coerced (Dixey 1996).

Community self-determinism cannot be achieved unless there is equity in the relationship between the health professional and the community; that is, the health professional is clearly recognised as a partner, rather than the leader, in decision-making. In the end, the community must define not only its priorities but also what is accessible, affordable and essential to achieve health goals (Barnes et al. 1995).

Community participation and self-determinism rely on several considerations. People need to decide that they do indeed belong to the community. They need to recognise community concerns and issues, whether these relate to geography, interests or common vulnerabilities to ill health (Meleis 1992). They also usually need assistance in mapping out the way in which their concerns are communicated to others, including those with access to resources, and to know who they can rely on for help with particular needs. Equally important, they need to be assured that different levels of participation are valued, so that different people may make a choice for participation that does not make unreasonable demands on their other responsibilities (Barnes et al. 1995).

Cultural sensitivity also plays a large role in helping people determine directions and strategies for change. For example, in some African countries it is a cultural expectation for breastfeeding mothers to abstain from sexual relations. It is also customary, and a highly valued family tradition, that breastfeeding will continue for at least two years. To preserve the sanctity of the mother–child relationship there is also tolerance for the perceived need of males to satisfy their sexual needs outside the family during this time and this is where the issue of culture becomes problematic. As we have now become aware, the rate of HIV infection in Africa (and in other countries) is escalating and the transmission of the virus is clearly sexual.

To further complicate the problem, the cultural group in this example has entrenched beliefs that prevent males from either using protection during sexual intercourse or confining sexual relations to the home. The dilemma is at once cultural, social and public health related: how does the community strike a balance between cultural sensitivity, self-determinism and saving lives? The answer lies in assisting the community to address issues of: access (to information, in this case); equity, involving the rights of all members of the community, including the unborn; and empowerment to make and enact self-determined changes without overriding cultural norms. One of the ways in which this may be approached is by casting beyond the immediate problem to the wider environment and enlisting the help of others in non-health sectors of society.

▶ CASE STUDY

The Haida Gwaii Diabetes Project

The Haida Gwaii are members of two First Nations villages in the Queen Charlotte Islands, British Columbia, Canada. 'First Nations' is the term given to indigenous, or Aboriginal, people, which signifies that they were the first, or original, inhabitants of Canada. Health researchers have known for many years that diabetes is a prevalent problem among Aboriginal people worldwide, and that to be effective, prevention programs must be developed by members of the community in ways that are both culturally considerate and empowering. In response to this need, a group of researchers from the University of British Columbia devised a strategy for encouraging self-determinism among members of the villages to develop their own diabetes teaching and prevention program.

The researchers joined with local family physicians and Haida community health workers (CHR) to plan a research project on diabetes prevention that would be acceptable to the community. The community health workers acted as intermediaries between the researchers and the community, explaining the people's concerns about research that had been conducted in the past. Researchers had been seen to have 'parachuted in', taking samples for research, and then disappeared. The people felt strongly about the taking of blood, hair or other body substances, as these were seen by the Haida people as subject to misuse and a violation of their cultural mores.

The CHRs also explained the rich traditions of the culture, including their approaches to healing and health maintenance, and a commitment to sustaining health for the next generation. The CHRs then identified certain key leaders of the villages, provided assurances that no body substances would be taken, and ascertained their willingness to engage in discussion with the research team. After consulting with these key informants and attending traditional Haida feasts, the research team members were able to organise focus group discussions attended by many villagers to discuss the meaning of diabetes, how they felt about living with the illness, their ideas about causation and prevention, and their traditional approaches to healing.

During these interactions the researchers were able to answer questions and, more importantly, to convey the message that their role was one of partnership with the community, that they were there to help the community solve its own problems. The community then developed a framework for health promotion based on both traditional and acquired knowledge. Rather than simply 'parachuting out', the non-resident team members have now formed a liaison with the community to act as external partners in any future endeavours (Herbert 1996).

Intersectoral collaboration

Intersectoral collaboration requires co-operation between different community sectors, including (but not limited to) those managing health, education, social services, housing, transportation and local government. Intersectoral collaboration involves a kind of fluid and flexible network of coalitions, where different alliances between sectors may respond to certain needs and have a finite existence. Others may be longer-term, and still others may be part of a long-range plan that requires sequential activities.

For example, if the Haida Gwaii community mentioned above decided to institute a campaign to examine family health issues while preserving the community's sense of cultural identity, an intersectoral group may begin planning for the changes by involving the spiritual elders first. After a series of conversations with these community leaders, a plan may be devised to educate adults and young people. Collaborative meetings would then include people responsible for workplace and school health, local and national political leaders and community health professionals, with roles and responsibilities apportioned according to the expertise of the various participants.

In other cases, the community may wish to begin with screening, to provide evidence that change is needed. Health department personnel could provide policy and planning documents to guide the process, the local council could provide access to screening facilities if none existed, state transportation authorities may get involved in helping either the health professionals or the people get to where the screening was occurring, and local employers may choose to promote the idea in the workplace. In this case, several sectors would be involved at the same time.

This type of collaboration is effective in most cases where a health issue may be jeopardising community health. For example, in an urban community where heart disease is prevalent, intersectoral collaboration could be used to devise a heart health program for males at risk of heart disease, and it might work something like this: for several months, the health department and various industries would work together to screen working males at risk. Then a government and employee group may liaise to explore the issue of program planning for exercise and nutrition. Private enterprise may then enter into discussions between local government, fitness personnel and medical specialists to guide the program's implementation, and the education department may be invited to work with the public media to promote the program.

Intersectoral collaboration also involves the provision of health information and programs to other sectors to help them see the value of adding health to their operations. Health professionals contribute to the education industry by integrating health issues into the curriculum. Health and safety personnel contribute to the environment and transportation industry by providing information on pollution hazards and road safety, and members of the recreation and fitness industries propound the merits of corporate health programs for private or public industry.

Intersectoral collaboration lies at the heart of community participation. It is a two-way process of planning for health goals with the participation of all aspects of the community and, in turn, adding value to the community by increasing health. It may include an 'all-in' approach, an 'all-at-once' approach, or a series of small stages where smaller subgroups of people collaborate to achieve small gains that will contribute to larger solutions.

At the global level, intersectoral collaboration involves various sectors collaborating to achieve a healthy society and, ultimately, health for all people. This is an intensely political activity: state and national governments must be ready to allocate economic resources to health budgets and to respond to their local electorates, while advancing the cause of global population health. The essential elements for successful intersectoral collaboration at this level include national primary health care policies that support decentralised control, local goal-setting, service planning and provision, mutual accountability, responsibility, co-operation and respect (Barnes et al. 1995). These issues are discussed in depth in chapter 16.

As always, social justice concerns must supersede individual gain so that the least advantaged receive equitable and accessible health resources. At the global level this may require redeploying a portion of economic resources to aid developing countries even while there are unmet needs in domestic health. This is a contentious issue at a time of shrinking resources, but it is the ultimate expression of social justice and, in some cases, a political necessity, as nations rely on each other's support in a range of areas.

Intersectoral collaboration in action: the Healthy Cities Project

Perhaps the most famous and enduring example of intersectoral collaboration is the Healthy Cities Project, which was one of the first specific initiatives of the Health for All campaign. In 1974, the Canadian Health Minister, Marc Lalonde, released a document on health called the Lalonde Report, which for the first time identified the government's responsibility to create favourable environments within which people could achieve health gains (Hancock 1992).

The report was based on the rationale that without an environment conducive to health it was futile to try to preach the gospel of healthy lifestyles to individuals. Others agreed, and recognised that in many cases health promotion campaigns would be blaming the victim if they were not targeted at *both* the people *and* the environmental circumstances within which they were expected to make healthy choices. So public health initiatives began to adopt a wider focus, and finally, in 1986, representatives from seventeen European cities met in Lisbon and declared the city as the prime target for environmental change. This was based on the fact that more than half the world's population lives in cities, where health problems are most concentrated and resources most plentiful (Flynn 1992).

The cities that have chosen to participate have developed health goals in ways that are appropriate for their particular conditions, but all are based on the premise that a healthy city is one where:
- health is a social, rather than medical, matter
- health should be the responsibility of all city services
- health should be monitored by physical, social, aesthetic and environmental indicators

■ health must be the product of intersectoral collaborative efforts
■ cities should be not merely survival units, but a cradle of good health (Baum & Brown 1989).

Health professionals have been instrumental in helping city residents launch their projects on the basis of a strategic vision for health (Hancock 1992) and to provide assistance with evaluating progress (Hancock 1992; Chapman & Davey 1997). This type of support makes visible the role of the health professional as a partner and advocate, in helping communities change. In transmitting to the community information about the health care system and the processes that govern resource allocation, the health professional enacts a role as political advocate and this requires a comprehensive breadth of system-wide knowledge.

Healthy cities projects have expanded and become widely diverse, drawing support from health professionals, representatives of recreation, police, social services, voluntary organisations and people of all ages to effect changes that, in turn, have informed health policy. The movement now incorporates thousands of cities worldwide, all with a common aim of using intersectoral collaboration and community participation to reduce inequalities, strengthen health gain and reduce morbidity (illness) and mortality (death) (Davies & Kelly 1993). In 1993, the WHO commenced Phase Two of the European Healthy Cities Project, defining this as the 'action phase'. Cities that have joined the project are required to demonstrate action on reducing inequalities in health status, improvement in access to the prerequisites to health, lifestyle change, creation of better environments and health care reform (WHO 1993).

Healthy Cities is a prime example of how intersectoral partnerships can effectively implement the principles of primary health care, using the strategies of the Ottawa Charter for Health Promotion: building healthy public policy, creating supportive environments, strengthening community action, developing personal skills and reorienting health services (WHO-HWC-CPHA 1986). At the regional level, such powerful lobbies as The Council of Europe's 'Sustainable Communities' program and the OECD's 'Ecological Cities' project have aligned themselves with the Healthy Cities Projects (Hancock & Davies 1997). Such broad endorsement from the highest levels of society has encouraged collaborative alliances between local government and health councils to develop and manage health plans that underline the importance of the environmental movement to the quality of people's lives and thus to community health.

THINKING CRITICALLY
Primary health care

▶ List four ways in which indigenous people are more vulnerable to ill health than are others.

▶ Describe three ways in which the AIDS epidemic has precipitated debate on the difference between moral and public health issues.

▶ Discuss the term 'empowerment'. Is it possible to empower communities? What is the relationship between self-empowerment and community empowerment?

▶ Identify two major issues that need to be addressed when planning for a Healthy City.

▶ Explain three ways in which your own health has been compromised by access and/or equity issues.

REFERENCES

Australian Institute of Health and Welfare 1996, *Australia's Health, 1996*, AGPS, Canberra.

Barnes, D., Eribes, C., Juarbe, T., Nelson, M., Proctor, S. et al. 1995, Primary health care and primary care: a confusion of philosophies, *Nursing Outlook*, vol. 43, no. 7, pp. 7–16.

Baum, F. & Brown, V. 1989, 'Healthy Cities (Australia) Project: issues of evaluation for the new public health', *Community Health Studies*, vol. 13, no. 2, pp. 140–9.

Brady, M. 1995, 'Culture in treatment, culture as treatment. A critical appraisal of developments in addictions programs for indigenous North Americans and Australians', *Social Science and Medicine*, vol. 41, no. 11, pp. 1487–98.

Bullen C. & Beaglehole R. 1997, 'Ethnic differences in coronary heart disease cases and fatality in Auckland', *Australian and New Zealand Journal of Public Health*, vol. 21, no. 7, pp. 688–93.

Chapman, P. & Davey, P. 1997, 'Working "with" communities, not "on" them: A changing focus for local government health planning in Queensland', *Australian Journal of Primary Health—Interchange*, vol. 3, no. 1, pp. 82–91.

Chu, C. 1994, 'Integrating health and environment: the key to an ecological public health', in *Ecological Public Health: From Vision to Practice*, eds C. Chu & R. Simpson, Institute of Applied Environmental Research, Brisbane, pp. 1–10.

Davies, J. & Kelly, M. 1993, *Healthy Cities: Research and Practice*, Routledge, London.

DeBois Inglis, A. & Kjervik, D. 1993, 'Empowerment of advanced practice nurses: Regulation reform needed to increase access to care', *Journal of Law, Medicine and Ethics*, vol. 21, pp. 193–205.

Dixey, R. 1996, 'Healthy eating in schools and "eating disorders"—are "healthy eating" messages part of the problem or part of the solution?', *Nutrition and Health*, vol. 11, pp. 49–58.

Downie, R. & Calman, K. 1994, *Healthy Respect: Ethics in Health Care*, Oxford University Press, New York.

Ferrinho, P., Robb, D., Cornielje, H. & Rex, G. 1993, 'Primary health care in support of community development', *World Health Forum*, vol. 14, pp. 158–62.

Flynn, B. 1992, 'Healthy Cities: a model of community change', *Family and Community Health*, vol. 15, no. 1, pp. 13–23.

Ham, C. 1997, 'Lessons and conclusions', in *Health Care Reform: Learning from International Experience*, ed. C. Ham, Open University Press, Buckingham, pp. 119–40.

Hancock, T. 1992, 'The Healthy City: Utopias and Realities', in *Healthy Cities*, ed. J. Ashton, Milton Keynes, Philadelphia, pp. 22–9.

Hancock, T. & Davies, K. 1997, *An Overview of the Health Implications of Global Environmental Change: A Canadian Perspective*, Canadian Global Change Program, Ottawa, Royal Society of Canada, Ottawa.

Hartley, R. 1995, *Families and Cultural Diversity in Australia*, Allen & Unwin, AIFS, St Leonards, NSW.

Herbert, C. 1996, 'Community-based research as a tool for empowerment: the Haida Gwaii diabetes project example', *Canadian Journal of Public Health*, vol. 87, no. 2, pp. 109–12.

Lee, P. & Paxman, D. 1997, 'Reinventing public health', *Annual Review of Public Health*, vol. 18, pp. 1–35.

Levin, J. 1994, 'Religion and health: Is there an association, is it valid, and is it causal?', *Social Science and Medicine*, vol. 38, no. 11, pp. 1472–82.

Lowe, I. 1994, 'Priorities for a sustainable future', in *Ecological Public Health: From Vision to Practice*, eds C. Chu & R. Simpson, Institute of Applied Environmental Research, Brisbane, pp. vii–viii.

Matseoane, S. 1997, 'South African health care system at the crossroads', *Journal of the National Medical Association*, vol. 89, no. 5, pp. 350–6.

Meleis, A. 1992, 'Community participation and involvement: theoretical and empirical issues', *Health Services Management Research*, vol. 5, no. 1, pp. 5–6.

Momsen, J. & Kinnaird, V. (eds) 1993, *Different Places, Different Voices: Gender and Development in Africa, Asia and Latin America*, Routledge, London.

Wallerstein, N. 1992, 'Powerlessness, empowerment and health: Implications for health promotion programs', *Health Promotion*, vol. 6, no. 3, pp. 197–205.

Whitehead, M. 1995, 'Tackling inequalities: A review of policy initiatives', in *Tackling Inequalities in Health*, eds M. Benzeval, K. Judge & M. Whitehead, King's Fund, London, pp. 22–52.

World Health Organization-Health and Welfare Canada-CPHA 1986, Ottawa Charter for Health Promotion, *Canadian Journal of Public Health*, vol. 77, no. 12, pp. 425–30.

World Health Organization-Regional Office for Europe 1993, *Setting Standards for WHO Project Cities: The Requirements and the Designation Process for WHO Project Cities*, WHO, Copenhagen.

World Health Organization UNICEF 1978, *Primary Health Care*, WHO, Geneva.

3

Epidemiology: community health and community risk

P lanning for health in a community must rest on a solid base of inform- ation that allows the health planning team to think globally and act locally. This information includes an understanding of local, state, national and global goals for health, and knowledge of community resources and barriers to health, some of which may be related to the motivation and preferences of community residents. Equally important is information on the current health status of the people who live in the community, so that comparisons can be made with wider trends and patterns of health and illness. This type of data gathering and analysis is *epidemiological research* and is aimed at revealing community strengths and risk factors that are fundamental to promoting community health.

Although many types of research data provide useful information for health planning, epidemiological data have traditionally provided the scien- tific basis for clinical decision-making, which was essentially left to medical researchers. With the advent of the 'new public health', research on, and with, communities is participatory, and combines a number of methodolog- ical approaches that are discussed in chapter 17. This chapter is confined to an explanation of the scientific foundations of epidemiological research, to encourage all health-related decision-making to begin from a basis of comprehensive and comparative knowledge of community health problems.

Objectives

By the end of this chapter you will be able to:

• *justify the need for epidemiological assessment of a community*

• *explain the concept of populations at risk*

• *describe the web of causation model for epidemiological investigation*

• *discuss the significance of the Global Burden of Disease Study*

• *explain the relationship between epidemiological information and the principles of primary health care.*

What is epidemiological research?

Epidemiology is the study of the frequency, distribution and determinants of health and illness, the patterns of disease occurrence in human populations and the factors that influence these patterns (McMurray 1993). The word *epidemiology* means the study of epidemics. An *epidemic* is where a health or illness condition occurs in a population in excess of what would normally be expected. At the expected level, it would be described as *endemic*. Studying epidemiological factors in a population or a segment of a population is a form of *applied research*, because the information is applied to solving a practical problem. The ultimate goal of epidemiological research is to devise strategies for control or eradication of the epidemic.

Epidemiological studies also provide information that can be used as a basis for preventative strategies by linking health promotion efforts to the amount and type of *risk* that exists in a population. In order to anticipate the risk of illnesses or epidemics developing in a community or among a particular population, it is important to understand historical factors and patterns of health and illness among other communities and other populations and the relationship between *risk factors*, *exposure*, and development of illnesses or epidemics.

A *risk factor* is an attribute or exposure that is associated with an increased probabilty of a particular outcome, such as the occurrence of a disease (AIHW 1996). This does not mean that if the risk factor is present it will cause a disease, but it is a starting point for understanding the potential for illness or a condition that will jeopardise optimal health in the population. Research into community risk factors allows health planners to construct a profile of community risk so that preventative measures can be undertaken to reduce the likelihood of an epidemic occurring among the population.

Risk factor indicators measure population and fertility trends, economic and other determinants of health status, and behavioural patterns that suggest risk factors for various diseases (AIHW 1995). Of course, risk factors are only one health indicator, because the health of a population is also influenced by health resources and service use, but examining patterns of risk provides a starting point for developing prevention and control programs to improve community health. Community risk factors may include the number of people who are overweight or 'at risk' for heart disease, the rate of unemployment, or the age-related rates of people engaging in physical activity or eating a nutritious diet.

Determinants of health

The key determinants of health in a population include such things as people's biological endowment, their individual responses, their social and physical environment, the economic conditions of their lives, and the accessibility and quality of health services (Health Canada 1996). Some of these are individual determinants such as biological or behavioural factors, while others are population-level determinants, which indirectly influence individual health. These latter factors include poverty, isolation, unemployment, housing and other environmental influences (Whitehead 1995).

Although health services are essential in determining health status, the non-medical care factors—behaviour, the environment, human biology and socioeconomic status—remain the most important factors affecting the health of the population (Lee & Paxman 1997). However, any attempt to address health needs must be based on understanding the complex interaction between each type of factor and between individual variations of factors that may affect health. This is the objective of epidemiological study.

The interactions between various factors are illustrated in the example shown in figure 3.1. This case, like many examples of ill health or health risk, suggests a set of links between the things that influence health. For example, gender may have an effect on employability, which may influence a person's (or family's) level of poverty, which may affect access to health resources, which may change the level of child health, which may affect family dynamics. Each of these factors may have a compound effect on health status, and it is difficult to determine the extent to which each of these may be affecting the health of the family, or of the population of a certain community. So this is where specific information is required.

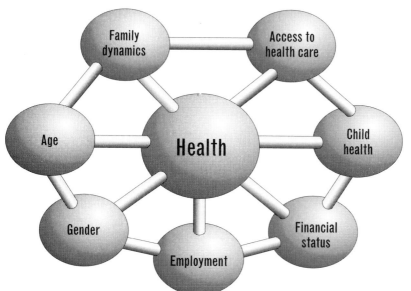

Figure 3.1
Interactions between factors affecting health

Categorising epidemiological information

In order to better understand the interplay between factors associated with a health-related condition or an epidemic of illness, data from population-based studies must be incorporated into our knowledge of health and health care in a community. These data are both descriptive and substantive. *Descriptive* information includes observations of existing conditions that are documented through surveillance and screening programs. The *substantive* contribution to the data includes the natural history, patterns of occurrence and risk factors associated with a disease or condition (Valanis 1988). In both cases, the methods and terminology of epidemiological research must be used in a standardised way so that the information is consistent with other studies and can be used as a part of larger population studies. In order to achieve this consistency, the terminology is explained here:

- *Morbidity* refers to the number of people in a certain population affected by an illness or condition. Morbidity is described in terms of incidence and prevalence.

- *Incidence* is the number of new cases of the condition occurring in a specific population during a specified period of time.
- *Prevalence* is the number of both old and new cases occurring in a population during a specified period of time.
- *Mortality* refers to the number of deaths from the illness or disease.
- *Rates* are a mathematical computation of the frequency of occurrence of a condition in a population. The rate is expressed as an equation estimating the likelihood that the condition would occur in a member of the population. The most popular rates are incidence and prevalence rates. Incidence rates measure the number of new cases of the condition within a given time period, while prevalence rates calculate the total of new and old cases. These are expressed as an equation, with the incidence and prevalence rates expressed as the numerator and the population at risk shown as the denominator (see figure 3.2).
- The *population at risk* is the total number of those in the population who are susceptible to the condition. This may include the number of non-immunised children at risk for measles, or the rate of those who work in occupational environments with high noise exposure. This fraction is multiplied by a base number which is usually expressed as 1000 or 100 000 depending on the size of the population.

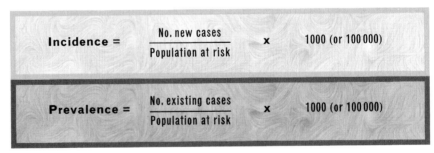

$$\text{Incidence} = \frac{\text{No. new cases}}{\text{Population at risk}} \times 1000 \text{ (or } 100\,000\text{)}$$

$$\text{Prevalence} = \frac{\text{No. existing cases}}{\text{Population at risk}} \times 1000 \text{ (or } 100\,000\text{)}$$

Figure 3.2 *Population rates as used in epidemiological studies (McMurray 1993)*

Using epidemiological information

Rates can be expressed as *crude rates*, which are computed for the population as a whole. They may also be *specific* to certain subgroups, or *adjusted* on the basis of demographic characteristics, such as age, race or sex (Selby 1996). For example, a community may choose to publish the crude rate of cancer among its population, but this would not provide information specific enough to encourage women to have pap smears, or for families to immunise their children, or for males to be screened for prostate cancer. On the other hand, age-adjusted rates of cancer of the cervix, and age- and sex-adjusted rates of prostate cancer could be used to heighten awareness of the need for screening among the population at risk. Similarly, linking prevalence rates or local incidence rates of measles among children may be useful in encouraging parents to have their children immunised against this disease.

Other analytic tools can be used to provide more specific measures for health planning. For example, the *relative risk* computes the extent to which a factor can be predictive of risk in a population. This is expressed as a ratio of the difference between the incidence rate in those who are exposed to the hazard, and those who are not. If the difference between the two is significantly higher in the population exposed to the hazard, it is identified as a risk factor. In cases where no incidence rates are available, but a disease or condition occurs, an *odds ratio* can be calculated retrospectively. This is done by comparing the mathematical odds of the condition occurring when the risk factor is present with when it is absent (Selby 1996).

Despite having sensitive tools available to calculate risk, it is important to distinguish between *cause* and *association*. Health and illness are products of a complex web of factors: hereditary predisposition, biology, history, environment, stressors and life events. For a variable to be defined as a causative agent, several conditions must be met. First, the cause and effect association must be coherent or logical in light of historical knowledge of the health condition. In addition, the association between the factor and the illness or health condition that eventuates must be consistent over time and must occur in the same direction (Selby 1996).

For example, if many studies reveal that a large number of people become ill after ingesting food from a certain source, the source can be considered a causative agent of the illness. Another condition requires the association to be significantly strong, and the factor must consistently produce the condition. Finally, the factor must always occur prior to the illness.

In most cases, a condition is the result of interconnections and interplay between many elements, some of which have a *synergistic*, or combined, effect that can alter either the *latency* period (the lag between exposure and development of the condition) or *potency*, once the condition begins to develop. Attributing cause must therefore be done with caution and substantiated with careful research design and analysis. Similarly, the measurement of risk must be tempered with information related to patterns of health, illness and behaviour in a constantly changing social environment.

Risk revisited

Individual perceptions of risk are linked to people's definitions of health and their health-related beliefs, and this has been the subject of numerous research studies. Recently, the notion of people being 'at risk' has been replaced in the health literature by a more specific identification of *risky behaviours* that have been deduced from morbidity and mortality data (McKie et al. 1993).

Risky behaviours include such things as unhealthy food consumption, disease, sedentary lifestyle, smoking, excessive use of alcohol and other substances, unsafe sexual habits, participating in dangerous sporting activities and being exposed to such stressors as violent and abusive behaviours (McKie et al. 1993). Naturally, longer exposure to any of these risky behaviours, or the compound effects of multiple factors, would be expected to result in greater overall risk of ill health or injury. However, identification of risky behaviours fails to capture the social and cultural relatedness of risk. For example, the elite athlete would not consider her/himself to be engaging in risky behaviours while running a rigorous marathon; nor would the person whose culture dictates a relaxed, sedentary lifestyle consider her/himself at risk for failing to take up running for exercise.

As stated in chapter 1, health is a communal artefact. By placing too much emphasis on individual behaviour and individual predispositions, we tend to blame the victim when things go wrong. If, on the other hand, the cultural embeddedness and social orientation of health is acknowledged, the focus of our health promotion strategies can be more justly placed on creating environmental conditions within which members of a community will seek higher levels of health and wellness. In the process, individuals will benefit from communal participation, which can serve as a self-reinforcing feedback loop to encourage further participation.

Epidemiological models

In order to closely examine the interplay of factors that affect health and illness, epidemiological studies are guided by a conceptual model or framework. The most popular model for epidemiological investigation is the epidemiological triad model. The triad configures health and illness as a composite of three equivalent factors—the agent, host and environment—each of which may interact to cause a certain condition, or a cluster of symptoms in the population (Valanis 1988). For example, where there is an outbreak of salmonella poisoning in a certain group of people, the agent is the salmonella organism, the host is the group of people who ingest the organism, and the environment includes all the conditions that encourage people to consume the substance containing the organism or that encourage the organism to thrive. These environmental conditions may include the existing health status of the host, community resources to diagnose and treat the medical condition that ensues from ingesting the agent, and educational resources that will help people learn to take preventative precautions so that the epidemic can be stemmed and will not recur. Figure 3.3 illustrates the model.

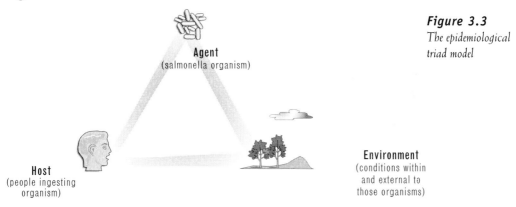

Agent
(salmonella organism)

Host
(people ingesting organism)

Environment
(conditions within and external to those organisms)

Figure 3.3
The epidemiological triad model

Agent

The agent in an epidemiological triad may vary according to *type*. It may be physical, chemical, biological or even the absence of a substance (for example, as happens in a metabolic deficiency such as Type 1 diabetes). It may also be a combination of these. For example, a physical agent such as an extremely hot climate may combine with the type of chemical agents that are found in air pollution to create a potent substance that could poison a group of people, especially if they are susceptible hosts.

Transmission also varies, and is an important consideration when analysing the interaction between factors. The agent may be transmitted directly (for example, in semen or blood products as occurs in the case of the HIV virus) or indirectly, through *vehicles, vectors* or *air*. Milk, for example, may transmit diptheria in babies, and food is a vehicle for salmonella. Lice, in some cases, can transmit typhus, and airborne agents may travel in dust or water droplets (Valanis 1988). Agents may gain *entry* to the host through a variety of methods, including inhalation (as occurs with the flu), ingestion (salmonella) or through the transfer of body fluids (HIV).

Host

Characteristics of the host also vary. *Susceptibility* of the host is influenced by many factors. Some of these are: *demographic* factors such as age, gender or marital status; *personal* factors including immunity or nutritional status; or social factors such as having a family or neighbourhood support system. Of course, the most important host factor is *exposure* to the agent, but exposure alone is not enough to guarantee that the condition or epidemic will occur, as there is never a foolproof way of predicting how an array of factors will interact.

Environment

Environmental factors may include: geography and climate (physical factors); the presence of biological and chemical factors; or socioenvironmental factors such as whether the environment is rural or urban, crowded or isolated, supportive or non-supportive. The impact of the environment cannot be overstated, particularly in considering the synergistic effects of many environmental factors. Where it is warm, people can often be encouraged to go outside and exercise. Where there is social support, families can often overcome a lack of resources. Conversely, where there are extraordinary air pollution levels, the strongest individuals may still succumb to respiratory problems. Illnesses and epidemics thus grow out of unpredictable interactions, some within the host, agent and environment, and some between the three categories of factors.

One environmental factor that is often overlooked in epidemiological studies is the policy environment. Since the inception of the consumer movement, lobby groups have emerged on a number of occasions to bring pressure on government departments to respond quickly to epidemics or potential epidemics. In many cases, these grass roots movements have been directly responsible for improvements in health through public awareness campaigns and informal investigations of factors related to health.

One of the most widely publicised recently has been the groundswell of protest against breast implants that have caused ill health in many women worldwide. The consumer lobby has effectively brought about closer monitoring of the manufacture and implanting of these devices, with the result that a potential epidemic has been aborted. Another current initiative of the consumer movement concerns an epidemic of hepatitis A, which has affected children in several countries.

> CASE STUDY

Hepatitis A

Hepatitis A is a highly contagious virus that enters the body through the faecal–oral route and attacks the liver. There are an estimated 1.4 million cases reported annually throughout the world. Infection occurs through close person-to-person contact or by ingesting contaminated food or water. In some cases, it is transmitted through sharing blood products. The virus has been known to cause a range of symptoms such as fatigue, nausea, vomitting, fever/chills, jaundice, pain in the liver area and abdomen, dark urine and light-coloured stools. Most patients begin recovery within three weeks, although some may experience symptoms for up to six months.

From an epidemiological perspective, some of the most important factors related to the disease are age and incubation period. The highest incidence is in children, and infants less than a year old rarely show clinical signs of the illness, so those handling soiled diapers (parents, child care workers) can become infected without knowing they were exposed. With an incubation period of 20–50 days, if those people are also responsible for handling food, they can spread the disease before they are aware they have it.

In some parts of the world, hepatitis A is endemic, so those travelling to infected areas may become infected and not know it until some time later. The prevalence may also be increased in occupations where people must engage in risky behaviours, such as laboratory workers or handlers of primates that may harbour the virus. Recreational risky behaviours such as needle-sharing or anal intercourse may also increase the likelihood of infection.

Recently, an epidemic of hepatitis A in the US linked to contaminated strawberries provided the impetus for a consumer-driven policy change. Young children in several states became ill after eating dessert cups containing the strawberries; those affected included 1400 people attending a sporting event. As public health officials tried to trace the source of the virus, a media debate arose over whether the berries were contaminated during cultivation or during processing and packing.

The debate quickly focused on government surveillance, and facts on food-related illnesses revealed a plethora of different cases throughout the previous year. It was learned, and publicised by the consumer group, that between 9 and 33 million Americans become sick every year from some form of food poisoning. Several agencies were responsible for food monitoring, and these were accused of piecemeal policies that allowed the food safety program to be little more than a recall agency for contaminated food. The lobby became vocal and widespread throughout the country, with the end result that within months of the epidemic, President Clinton went to Congress with a request for a substantial increase in the budget for food monitoring.

The groups continue to push for a single food-safety agency, with optimism for the future. In a similar case, several recent epidemics of hepatitis B in Australia and New Zealand have been linked to contaminated oysters. These incidents, and sporadic outbreaks of salmonella, have prompted public health researchers to join consumer groups in pressing for a systematic and consistent approach to surveillance for pathogens in the food chain that would extend from raw ingredients through manufacture, distribution and consumption (Veitch & Hogg 1997).

These examples illustrate the complex nature of responding to epidemiological problems. The initial step must always be to unravel the cluster of factors and their interrelationships. In the case of hepatitis A it is important to: look at the behaviours of the children and their history, in order to ascertain exposure; question their caregivers (whether home or child care); and look at the physical environment. In addition, it is important to examine the social factors, which may include education and cultural understandings that may affect early diagnosis and subsequent treatment. Figure 3.4 illustrates the triad model as it relates to hepatitis A. (Information courtesy of CNN Interactive.)

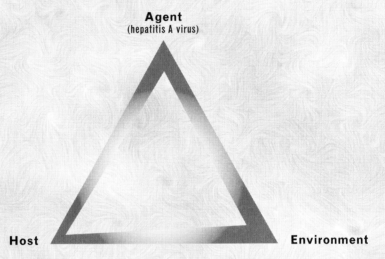

Agent
(hepatitis A virus)

Host

- adults and children exchanging infected implements
- children, workers in child care
- those with little knowledge of sanitation
- migration from areas of high incidence
- fishers, families eating infected fish
- military, other travellers
- health care, laboratory workers, handlers of infected primates
- haemophilliacs requiring transfusion in countries without blood screening
- male homosexuals
- those sharing I.V. injections

Environment

- playgrounds, social environments where food, faecal material is exchanged
- lack of sewage, potable water
- lack of educational materials
- cultural insensitivity
- infected fishing waters
- inadequate food processing, surveillance

Figure 3.4 *The epidemiological triad model illustrating risk factors for hepatitis A*

Another way to configure epidemiological studies is within the web of causation model. This approach provides a visual illustration of the complex interplay between individual, cultural, political and communal factors as well as those arising from biology and the environment, as shown in figure 3.5.

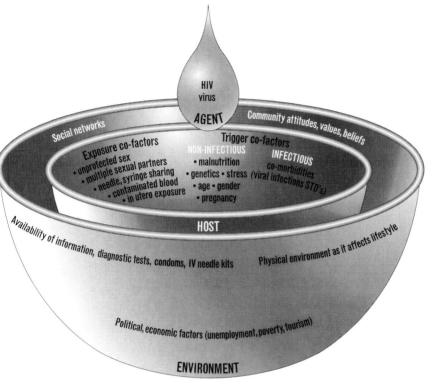

Figure 3.5
The web of causation model illustrating risk factors for HIV infection (adapted from McMurray 1993)

Agent Orange

One interesting epidemic that arose from a combination of political, social, cultural, environmental and biological factors is the case of Agent Orange related illness. The case of Vietnam veterans' exposure to dioxin through Agent Orange has been called the most complex epidemiological problem ever imagined (Lewis 1996). The challenge for those attempting to resolve both medical and legal issues related to the incident has been to determine the extent of harm done to millions of Vietnam veterans by exposure to Agent Orange, in order to allocate equitable compensation to the soldiers.

Agent Orange was a herbicide used as a defoliant in the Vietnam War from 1962 to 1971, and during these years the US dumped more than 19 million gallons of the chemical (a 50:50 mixture by weight of two phenoxy acids 2,4-D and 2,4,5-T) onto the jungles of Vietnam. As the soldiers returned to the US and Australia, clusters of symptoms became apparent. Some suffered skin rashes, others were afflicted with more serious disorders such as malignant tumours. As time went by, a number of symptoms appeared in the children born to these men and their partners. At the same time, the information revolution was allowing communication between people separated by great distances and the beginnings of both formal and informal epidemiological research, tracking common symptoms among those who had served in Vietnam.

The cluster of symptoms found in Australian veterans and their families was similar to those occurring in the US veterans. Their respective associations, Veterans' Affairs in the US, and the Returned Servicemen's League in Australia, were becoming the repositories of numerous stories of illness. As the evidence grew, the veterans began piecing together a case for compensation. The media became involved and the case expanded rapidly, culminating in a 1984 class action being brought against seven companies that had manufactured the chemical. The companies paid $280 million to settle the suit.

In 1991, a group of researchers at the Harvard School of Public Health convened a panel of thirteen scientists to weigh the evidence on the human carcinogenicity of the chemical 2,4-D, reviewing toxicological and epidemiological literature. They concluded that, although a cause–effect relationship could not be established, the epidemiological evidence pointed to an association between the chemical and non-Hodgkin's lymphoma (Ibrahim et al. 1991).

In the US, the Agent Orange Act of 1991 (Public Law 102-4) established a presumption of service connection secondary to herbicide exposure for non-Hodgkin's lymphoma, soft tissue sarcomas, and chloracne or other acneform disease consistent with chloracne. In 1992, the Department of Veterans' Affairs and the National Academy of Science (NAS) signed an agreement to review and analyse the pertinent literature. After reviewing approximately 6420 abstracts of scientific and medical articles and studying 230 epidemiological studies, consulting outside experts and conducting public hearings, they prepared a report separating diseases into four categories based on a sliding scale of the certainty of their association with herbicide exposure.

The committee found 'limited/suggestive evidence' of a link between exposure to the herbicide and spina bifida, respiratory cancers, acute disorders of the nervous system, prostate cancer, a form of bone marrow cancer called multiple myeloma and the metabolic disorder porphyria. It found 'sufficient evidence' of an association between the herbicide and cancer of the connective tissue, diseases of the lymph nodes and lymph tissues, and the skin disease chloracne. Insufficient evidence was found for links between Agent Orange and bone cancers, leukaemia, other birth defects, and circulatory and respiratory disorders. There was also some evidence that the use of the herbicide is associated with cancers of the brain, bladder and gastrointestinal system (Veterans' Affairs 1996).

An Australian group of researchers then conducted an analysis of the NAS report. Like their American counterparts, they found insurmountable difficulties in verifying the associations. These were related to the absence of an index of personal exposure to herbicides and the difficulty of quantifying risk. However, the Australian researchers accepted the NAS report's inclusion of non-Hodgkin's lymphoma, chloracne, soft tissue sarcoma, porphyria cutanea tarda and Hodgkin's disease, and added multiple myeloma, leukaemia and respiratory cancers. Although there was not sufficient evidence of association, they also suggested that prostate cancer be added to the list of possibilities and that continuing studies investigate this latter association once the veterans reach the age of highest prevalence of this condition (Maclennan & Smith 1996).

Slowly, and with great difficulty, the veterans themselves and those they co-opted have tried to construct a web of causation to show the relationship between Agent Orange and their illnesses. Their investigations revealed that the chemical product has actually been around and used by the military since the 1940s, yet serious testing did not begin until the 1960s, *so dose–response data*—that is, the amount of exposure sufficient to cause a reaction—has never been estimated. (The web of causation model illustrating risk factors for Agent Orange related diseases is shown in figure 3.6.)

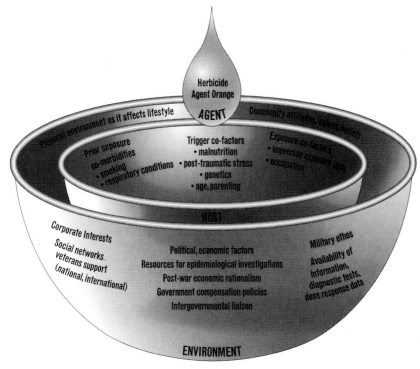

Figure 3.6

The web of causation model illustrating risk factors for Agent Orange related diseases

Another problem was in the manner of exposure. It was unclear whether 'exposure' should include only those directly exposed through participating in dumping the chemical from planes, being physically sprayed while on the ground, handling the drums of chemical, or simply ingesting particles through air or water. Another problem is linked to *co-morbidities*, and this is common in many attempts to isolate causative agents. A person's history of risky behaviours such as smoking, occupational exposure (such as a farmer would have) or prior respiratory illness represents a potential confounding effect when trying to associate exposure and outcome. The *latency* of the illness provides yet another potential confounding element, as some illnesses such as cancer take many years to develop and their symptoms may be vague and slow to manifest themselves.

In the case of the war veterans, there may also have been other illnesses masking the symptoms. Many returned home suffering post-traumatic stress related symptoms, and it could be expected that the health status of some would have also been compromised by having a significant change in diet and lifestyle. A large number of the young soldiers were anxious to establish a family—settling into parenthood was another drastic lifestyle change after their tour of duty. As their children were born, symptoms such as skin rashes began to appear in their offspring.

Another element in the web concerns the political and economic environment. Following the Vietnam War, most countries were on the precipice of an era of economic rationalism. Finances for the type of epidemiological research that was required were limited, and the military was being streamlined, as were all government departments. The information networks that made visible the necessary pieces of the puzzle were generated by the veterans themselves and their support organisations, and the likelihood of the chemical companies sponsoring their investigations was remote.

In 1996, the Agent Orange Benefits Act of 1996 was declared in the US; since October 1997 this has provided health care, monthly allowance and vocational rehabilitation to children of Vietnam veterans with spina bifida. This has been a significant landmark in the case, as it represents the first time that genetic health effects have been linked conclusively to herbicide exposure (Spina Bifida Association of America 1996).

It is interesting that despite some very difficult obstacles the links have been confirmed, and a clearer picture may benefit others in the future. With the Vietnam soldiers it was impossible to study the specific facts of a dose–response relationship. Future studies of people such as farmers and those involved in chemical manufacturing with occupational exposure to herbicides may reveal this level of detail and the relative and compound risks. The case also has implications for other environmental toxins. Following the enormous personal and financial cost incurred by Agent Orange we can only hope that in the future, society (and most certainly the military) will err on the side of caution with respect to environmental chemicals.

The Agent Orange epidemiological study was spawned through grass-roots activism. However, other studies have made a significant contribution to our knowledge of community health through systematic, long-term investigation of the multiplicity of factors that contribute to a particular condition. In perhaps the most comprehensive epidemiological study ever undertaken, a group of researchers has conducted an investigation into the factors contributing to the most prevalent conditions of our time.

The Global Burden of Disease Study

In order to inform national and international health policies for prevention and control of disease and injury, a group of researchers mounted a search of epidemiological data sources worldwide. Their goal was to determine the patterns of death, in 1990, for 14 age–sex groups in eight regions of the world, for 107 causes of death (Murray & Lopez 1997a). Their Global Burden of Disease (GBD) Study found the following:

■ The leading causes of death in 1990 were ischaemic heart disease, cerebrovascular accidents (stroke), lower respiratory infections, diarrhoeal diseases, perinatal disorders, chronic obstructive pulmonary disease, tuberculosis, measles, road traffic accidents and lung cancer.

■ Five of the ten leading killers are communicable, perinatal and nutritional disorders largely affecting children.

■ Of all deaths in children under 15 years of age, 98% occur in the developing world. Most of these deaths are related to childhood malnutrition, poor water and sanitation, and personal and domestic hygiene (Murray & Lopez 1997a, b).

■ The prevalence of most disability is highest in sub-Saharan Africa and lowest in established market economies (Murray & Lopez 1997c).

■ Developed regions account for 11.6% of the worldwide burden from all causes of death and disability, and account for 90.2% of health expenditure worldwide (Murray & Lopez 1997b).

■ Health trends in the next 25 years will be determined mainly by the ageing of the world's population, the decline in age-specific mortality rates from communicable, maternal, perinatal and nutritional disorders, the spread of HIV and the increase in tobacco-related mortality and disability (Murray & Lopez 1997d).

The GBD Study is interesting in its statistical power. Data were gathered from many regions of the world, and aggregated to produce a 'big picture' report card on community health. The findings are relevant to policy planners; however, at the local level, there will need to be close examination of the trends according to social, cultural, age and gender categories. It will be interesting, in the future, to see how this epidemiological information is operationalised to effect improvements to community health.

THINKING CRITICALLY

Epidemiology

▶ What information would you need to conduct an epidemiological assessment of a mining community?

▶ Generate a web of causation for occupational injuries in a migrant population.

▶ Discuss risk and risky behaviours related to alcohol consumption.

▶ Explain the relationship between epidemiological information and ensuring primary health care in a community.

▶ Discuss the significance of the Global Burden of Disease Study to health planning in your community.

REFERENCES

Australian Institute of Health and Welfare 1995, *Australian Health Trends, 1995*, AGPS, Canberra.

Australian Institute of Health and Welfare 1996, *Australia's Health, 1996*, AGPS, Canberra.

Health Canada 1996, *Towards a Common Understanding: Clarifying the Core Concepts of Population Health for Health Canada, A Discussion Paper*, Conceptual Framework Subgroup on Population Health, Health Canada, Ottawa.

Ibrahim, M., Bond, G., Burke, T., Cole, P., Dost, F. et al. 1991, *Weight of the evidence on the human carcinogenicity of 2,4-D*, Center for Risk Analysis, Harvard School of Public Health, Boston.

Lee, P. & Paxman, D. 1997, Reinventing public health, *Annual Review of Public Health*, vol. 18, pp. 1–35.

Lewis, B. 1996, *Some facts about Agent Orange/Dioxin*, New Jersey Agent Orange Commission, New Jersey.

Maclennan, R. & Smith, P. 1996, *Veterans and Agent Orange. Health Effects of Herbicides Used in Vietnam,* Veterans' Independent Consultation Group, Inc, Brisbane.

McKie, L., Al-Bashir, M., Anagnostopoulou, T.,Csepe, P., El-Asfahani, A et al. 1993, Defining and assessing risky behaviours, *Journal of Advanced Nursing,* vol. 18, pp. 1911–16.

McMurray, A. 1993, *Community Health Nursing: Primary Health Care in Practice,* 2nd edn, Churchill-Livingstone, Melbourne.

Murray, C. & Lopez, A. 1997a, 'Mortality by cause for eight regions of the world: Global Burden of Disease Study', *The Lancet,* vol. 349, May 3, pp. 1269–76.

Murray, C. & Lopez, A. 1997b, 'Global mortality, disability, and the contribution of risk factors: Global Burden of Disease Study', *The Lancet,* vol. 349, May 17, pp. 1436–42.

Murray, C. & Lopez, A. 1997c, 'Regional patterns of disability-free life expectancy and disability-adjusted life expectancy: Global Burden of Disease Study', *The Lancet,* vol. 349, May 10, pp. 1347–52.

Murray, C. & Lopez, A. 1997d, 'Alternative projections of mortality and disability by cause 1990-2020: Global Burden of Disease Study', *The Lancet,* vol. 349, May 24, 1498–1504.

Selby, M. 1996, 'Epidemiology, demography and research', in *Community as Client: Application of the Nursing Process,* 2nd edn, eds E. Anderson & J. McFarlane, Lippincott, Philadelphia.

Spina Bifida Association of America 1996, *The Agent Orange Benefits Act of 1996,* SBAA, Washington.

US Government, Veterans' Affairs 1996, *Agent Orange and Herbicide Exposure,* USGPS, Washington.

Valanis, B. 1988, 'The epidemiological model in community health nursing', in *Community Health Nursing: Process and Practice for Promoting Health,* 2nd edn, eds M. Stanhope & J. Lancaster, Mosby, St Louis, pp. 149–71.

Veitch, M. & Hogg, G. 1997, 'Must it have been something I ate?', *Australian and New Zealand Journal of Public Health,* vol. 21, no. 1, pp. 4–7.

Whitehead, M. 1995, Tackling inequalities: A review of policy initiatives, in *Tackling Inequalities in Health,* eds M. Benzeval, K. Judge & M. Whitehead, King's Fund, London, pp. 22–52.

4

Health and sustainability: community as client

Sustainable health is health that endures over time. It encompasses not only the current state of health in a population or a community, but all of those factors that will provide conditions favourable to creating and maintaining the health of future generations. It is a difficult goal to achieve in today's society, where people's health is inextricably bound to an increasingly compromised physical environment and less than optimal social conditions. However, sustainable health is crucial to the healthy survival of the species.

The key to sustaining health lies in a commitment to an ecological notion of health. This chapter takes a look at the community as an ecosystem with resources, opportunities and threats to health and healthy lifestyles. In viewing the community this way, we as health professionals can direct our efforts toward helping people recognise and maximise resource capabilities to sustain the health of their particular community and that of the global population.

Objectives

By the end of this chapter you will be able to:

* *explain community health within an ecological perspective*

* *assess the constraints and facilitating factors that influence a community's health potential*

* *discuss the role of a community advocate in encouraging sustainable community health*

* *explain the link between health indicators and patterns of health services utilisation*

* *identify strategies for healthy community development.*

Health in relation to place

If we accept the notion that community health is community development, communities must be seen as dynamic, functional entities where thoughtful planning creates conditions within which people can strive for health and their preferred quality of life. Working effectively with communities to achieve health goals requires a focus not only on the people who live there, but on the community as a whole. In effect, the *client* or recipient of community health promotion efforts is not only the collective of people, but the physical space and social habitat with which they interact. This requires an understanding of the relationship between people and place.

People develop a sense of equilibrium within a defined context—whatever is defined as their *place*. This is a relationship characterised by *mutuality*, where what happens in one aspect affects the other. So people and their communal, physical environment operate in a kind of symbiotic relationship. A person's sense of place is an expression of communal culture and, as such, helps set the agenda for activities related to health and illness, and the way services are used to sustain each (Hudson-Rodd 1994). In turn, culture shapes the way people define health and the ways in which they interact within their place. For this reason, health promotion programs are best developed with the *setting* in mind. As suggested in chapter 2, these can be directed at healthy cities, healthy villages, healthy workplaces and healthy schools; each of these emphasises aspects of the place as well as the people involved.

Health in relation to place is both a product and a resource. It is a product of all aspects of the environment, including the health care system, and an essential resource for living a full and rich life. As a member of a certain community, most people recognise the elements that will contribute to their personal health or the health of their family, but few spend much time focusing on the strengths and weakenesses of the communal environment. So in many cases the first task of the community health professional is to heighten awareness among people of the links between community resources, community risk factors and health. This requires a kind of ecological enculturation, wherein people incorporate an *ecological perspective* into their family and community culture.

Ecological enculturation

There are several ways in which ecological enculturation can be encouraged within a community. One approach is to collaborate with local education, health, recreation, sporting and business groups to ensure that the younger generation develops an affinity with the environment and that all citizens are aware of the strengths and resources particular to their community. Another is to use the local media to raise public awareness of the importance of the environment in creating and sustaining health. The media is especially useful for communicating to the local community what is happening in the wider arena.

For example, newspapers, magazines and television broadcasts provide access to deliberations taking place at the major environmental meetings, whether these are international summits sponsored by the United Nations or the World Bank, or scientific meetings addressing the implementation of strategies for preserving the environment. These meetings signal to young people especially that people everywhere are taking the environment seriously. They also reflect an important sign of the times we live in—the increasing trend towards globalisation.

Globalisation refers to the interdependence of nations around the world. No one country can produce all the goods and services it needs to sustain its people and thus no one nation can afford to be insular in any policies affecting its people. We need one another; we must trade and barter with one another and, to do this, we must understand the nature of each other's resources, how they are allocated, and how they will be replenished.

The environment is the most important resource in the world, and therefore all people interested in preserving the future must become aware of how environmental issues in one place affect all others.

Some of the most important environmental discussions of our time have taken place in the past several years. The 1990s saw the first large summit on the environment, the Rio Summit of 1992. This meeting of nations was to have been a watershed for the environment. People around the world believed that such a visible discussion of environmental preservation would signal a commitment to action; yet, in 1997, a new summit had to be convened to further warn all nations of the world about the lack of progress in devising a plan for sustainability. A global environmental policy has yet to be agreed upon, but nations are finally collaborating on standards for such things as acceptable waste disposal and automobile emissions. At the societal level, this will be an invaluable step, given the expectation that each country will become mobilised by the precedents set by others and the need for co-operation for a healthier future.

The mass media is having some effect at the local level, primarily in the industrialised nations, particularly in encouraging healthier lifestyles and greater awareness of the environmental effects of various patterns of consumption and waste disposal. The Internet has now become an invaluable medium for these types of messages. However, the Internet will have to be as closely monitored as the more traditional media to ensure that the gains made by increasing awareness of health and environmental issues are not negated by the commercialised promotion of poor health practices (Chukwuma 1996).

On the positive side, there are now numerous websites on the Internet devoted to articulating principles of sustainable health and development. A well-prepared article linking health and environmental issues can often provide the impetus for public debate, especially when the author is a credible source and where people are empowered to respond through such mechanisms as letters or chatlines. One such article from the 'betterworld' website advises that:

> Becoming sustainable individually and collectively requires all of us to commit our lives to building communities of fully empowered, compassionate, nonviolent, honest, loving human beings who live joyfully and beautifully within the limits of their physical environment (Leland 1995, p. 2).

This is the broader picture of sustainable health.

Sustainability

Lowe (1994) reports that a community is sustainable when it has at its disposal an amount of land that supplies all the resources it consumes and absorbs all the waste it produces. Likewise, sustainability in community health can be taken to mean that the community has a type of health—illness *carrying capacity*—that is, all the health resources it needs and the capacity to respond to all the illness it produces. Many researchers believe the world is exceeding its carrying capacity, primarily due to overpopulation, and at present we add 100 million people per year to the world's population. In a mere 54 years the world will have twice as many people as today (Nelder 1997). If even 5% of today's population (such as the US) consumes significantly more than its sustainable share of the global environment, the earth's ecosystems will be doomed to fail in a relatively short period. What a provocative question it would be to ask if China, which has a similarly large population, grew to enjoy the same standard of living, and thus the same rate of consumption, as the US (Leland 1995). Clearly, sustaining the environment in one country is fundamental to the health of *all* people.

Another threat to sustainability in health is the degradation of our natural resources. It is ironic that people are living longer these days because of economic and technological developments, yet it is these very developments that have exploited, and thus degraded, the environment so necessary to their survival (Evans, Barer & Marmor 1994). This has led one critic to lament that the term 'sustainable development' is a misnomer, as one counters the other (Ife 1995). The need for fresh water in many countries is both crucial and critical. Water scarcity leads to food scarcity, and some predict even more wars and conflicts than we are experiencing at present, as competition for land, water, food, trees and minerals continues to destroy large chunks of our civilisation and create numerous 'eco-refugees' (Hancock & Davies 1997; Nelder 1997).

In the most overpopulated countries, overreliance on pesticides and herbicides, wasteful or improper irrigation, unsustainable growing practices and overproduction have diminished topsoil and the productive capacity of the land. Global warming has the capacity to produce massive floods, the withdrawal of forests, and the death of species or entire ecosystems, leading to massive extinctions regardless of conservation efforts. We may lose 20% of all the species on the planet within the next 20 to 40 years, most in the tropical rainforests, yet we continue to burn fossil fuels and spill carbon dioxide into the air at unprecedented levels (Nelder 1997). The potential health effects of these practices are of enormous significance, and some will only be revealed in generations to come.

Global environmental changes have now been linked unequivocally to physical ailments. At present there appears to be an epidemic of acute respiratory disease responsible for up to 4 million deaths per year in children under age five. Air pollution, both indoor and outdoor, appears to play a central role in this epidemic (Christiani 1993). Researchers in the US are finding that there is a direct link between hospital admissions for respiratory and cardiac diseases and increases in air pollution, particularly acid aerosols and ozone (CEOH, AATS 1996).

Early environmental studies identified a number of workplace hazards linked to various forms of chemical pollution, including silicosis in miners, scrotal cancers in chimney sweeps, and pulmonary disease in those who worked with asbestos. Some environmental agents may be acting as 'endocrine disruptors', interacting with human endocrine systems, leading to possible mental and reproductive abnormalities (Lee & Paxman 1997). Environmental changes have also caused numerous sociocultural changes, with land and water shortages causing forced migration, urbanisation and poverty and their related effects on health.

The answer lies not only in promoting widespread awareness of the issues at the level of consumption, but also in healthy public policies that weave sustainable health considerations into all decisions related to economic development (WHO 1992a). This includes regulatory policies that govern automobiles, food safety, chemicals such as lead, and threats of injury such as firearms, developed in consultation between government and public health personnel.

Distribution of health services

Sustainable health is also jeopardised by unequal distribution of health services throughout the world and, in some cases, within certain communities. LaFond (1995) examined the experiences of five developing countries (Nepal, Pakistan, Vietnam, Ghana and Uganda) to investigate internal and external influences on sustainable health. She concluded that most health care interventions are short-lived, and health gains transient, because national governments cannot afford to maintain the recurrent cost of certain interventions.

Aid provided from developed countries is often insufficient, particularly when it is tied to specific programs, such as immunisation. Although immunisation is an important part of community health, when donations are earmarked for such a specific target, other aspects of health may become neglected. As a consequence, some types of assistance fragment health systems into disconnected activities with limited health benefits, and thus fail to lead to sustainable outcomes. This is contrary to the philosophy of primary health care, where long-term community self-determination, and thus sustainability, is the goal.

The solution is clear, but costly. Foreign aid must include training opportunities in order to build long-term local capabilities for delivering health care so that community self-determinism can be achieved. Unless programs of assistance are substantial enough to create wide-ranging programs for sustainable health, they may actually impede, rather than advance, the achievement of health goals, thus defeating attempts to provide access and equity in health care (LaFond 1995).

Some would say that in the industrialised countries we have achieved sustainability in health because we have services at our disposal. However, this is an oversimplification, because of disparities in both illness and usage and because of issues that mediate patterns of utilisation. As you saw in chapter 3, epidemiological information permits community health risk appraisal. At any given time, in any given country, statistical predictions can be made that indicate the number of people expected to develop a range of cancers and respiratory and cardiac illnesses, and the number likely to meet their demise through road trauma.

What our risk appraisals cannot do, however, is predict how people will respond to these threats: how many will undertake screening for cancer, slow their driving speed or have regular medical checkups. The 'worried well', who seek medical care more often than others, are another unknown quantity (Lynch et al. 1996). Irrespective of health status or health services, some people are simply more preoccupied with health, while others tend to see health matters as a low priority.

So the unpredictable nature of people's behaviour represents another factor that influences sustainability in health. In addition, new technological innovations are being developed so rapidly that it is almost impossible to predict what proportion of resources they will require from year to year. The capacity for sustainability is thus difficult to measure with any precision, at either the global, national or local level. However, we must continue to document the resource base, and thus our carrying capacity, and so we proceed with 'best guess' approaches based on national health indicators and patterns of past usage.

Indicators of health

Health economists attempt to predict health consumption, and thus the need for resources to monitor health status, identify and investigate health problems and hazards, inform people about health issues, mobilise community resources, develop supportive policies to assist communities, regulate hazardous substances, provide services for the ill, prepare sufficient health care personnel, evaluate the provision of services, and research innovative solutions to public health problems (Lee & Paxman 1997). These services must be developed according to community indicators of need (shown in figure 4.1), which include the following:

1 *Health status*

The health status of a community refers to epidemiological indicators such as mortality and survival rates for those with an illness such as cancer or coronary heart disease. A population's health status is also indicated by the number of people with a disability, by the number of perinatal and infant deaths that occur, and the general level of health of its children, including the rates of child injury. Injury rates among adults are also included in the health status indicators, and these include motor vehicle injuries and those resulting from family violence. Other health status indicators among the adult population are the rates of chronic and communicable diseases, mental illnesses and, for both children and adults, dental (oral) health status (AIHW 1995).

2 *Health determinants and risk factors*

Determinants of health in a population are also compiled through epidemiological study. They include population trends (birth, immigration, ageing), fertility rates, the general economic status of the community, anthropometric (structural) measures such as the proportion of the population who are overweight, measures of physiological functioning, nutritional status and usual dietary intake, the number of people who participate in physical activities, and the rates of drug use and abuse (AIHW 1995).

3 *Health resources*

Resources for health include the proportion spent on health by the government, the adequacy of the health labour force, including those prepared for public health activities, and the amount and distribution of services for both treatment and prevention (AIHW 1995).

4 Health service use

Usage information includes the number of people with illnesses who regularly use medical and dental services, hospitals and community health clinics, and those designated for aged care. Preventive and screening services include participation in screening programs such as mammography clinics and pap smears (AIHW 1995).

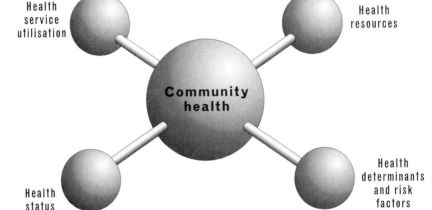

Figure 4.1
The interrelationship of factors influencing the health of individuals, families and communities

Separating out the factors that influence health and health service use allows a base of information from which to forecast whether resources will match need in a certain population over a particular time frame. However, this information is not entirely predictive of what happens at the community level without more precise, local data. This involves an assessment of how the community is constituted and what attitudes, opinions, values and ideas people have with respect to health in their community.

It is then important to ascertain whether people's opinions about their health are followed by certain healthful behaviours. Sometimes this can be done by examining patterns that show a breakdown of which people have used which services in the past. For example, data can be collected on the number and type of families who had their children immunised, which family types tend to use their local GP for medical care, which ones use the hospital emergency room, which groups attend screening programs, what proportion of older people have family caregivers, and which types or age groups of individuals tend to maintain high levels of fitness.

CASE STUDY

Health and health service utilisation in Belmont, WA

The author and colleagues devised a study in one Australian community to examine patterns of utilisation of health services. The objective of the study was to provide a profile of the community in terms of people's preferences and patterns of usage. First, we selected an inner-city community we thought might be typical of other Australian urban communities. We drove around and took an inventory of the types of houses there, the number of recreational facilities, schools, industries, transportation and health care facilities. Next, we secured demographic information about the community so that we had a clearer idea of such indicators as the proportion of single dwellers, two-parent and one-parent families, extended families, migrants, age groups and socioeconomic status.

We then compared these indicators with the national average and concluded that the community could be considered a 'typical' Australian, urban community. Our next step was to plan a series of family interviews, to try to gain a community, rather than health service, perspective on what services people use, and whether they found these accessible and satisfactory. We trained a group of senior nursing students to ensure standardised interviewing procedures, and then mapped out the community to allocate each student a certain number of streets to survey.

The study yielded some very interesting information. For example, we learned that our sterotype of older people was incorrect. Many who had a long-standing, life-limiting illness were managing very well at home, and considered themselves quite healthy. They were, in effect, enjoying a relatively good health status in that they had access to sufficient supportive resources. We also learned that in one-parent homes, the mothers tended to take their young children to the emergency department of the hospital for treatment, rather than to the GP, primarily to save time in their busy lives. And we learned that gender roles are changing. We asked people to identify the family health guardian—the person to whom other family members turned for advice or assistance. This question was asked on the basis that we were uncertain about whether changing family structures would create different family health roles.

Our results indicated that for approximately 20% of the families interviewed, the role of the health guardian was assumed by either the male or both partners. For the elderly, family caregivers were similarly divided according to gender. This has implications for the development of resource materials, which are typically stereotyped on the assumption that caregivers are always female.

The study findings were subsequently sent to the relevant health department so that health planners could consider the findings as a basis for evaluating service provision. This type of profiling allows health planners to think global but act local, to recognise the preferences and choices that will determine how community members will access health services and work towards sustaining health at the local level. We now consider the study a prototype for future study in other communities as a basis for comparison (McMurray et al. 1998).

Community assessment

In any community it is important to have statistical information on epidemiological status and health indicators; it is also important to learn how the characteristics of the people who inhabit the community might influence their health-related decisions. One such characteristic concerns whether the community generally feels ownership, whether community residents feel responsible for, and will be accountable for, health and to one another (Abel et al. 1995).

Communities are inherently social organisations and, as such, community residents are an important resource (Boothroyd et al. 1994). People contribute to the community through such things as their informal caring activities and their sense of community identity and belonging. Community networks allow community members to meet basic social needs by providing a sense of connection, opportunities to participate in decision-making, a sense of safety and security, a buffer against stress, and leisure activities; all of these have the capacity to contribute to the quality of community life (Boothroyd et al. 1994). So it is important to understand community dynamics —who the key players are and how people interact with one another.

It is also important to know the geography of a community. Some communities are bound by their seclusion, while others have physical features such as mountains, rivers or railway tracks that provide barriers to communication. It is particularly important to understand people's relationship with the land, and whether the majority of community members are long-term residents. The assumption may be made that if people feel a sense of long-term connection with the community, they may be more amenable to persuasion aimed at preserving the local physical environment.

In many cases, people themselves have a clear idea of the sustainability of their local environment and how it can circumscribe their lifestyle opportunities. This is exemplified in the struggle of indigenous people to retain their land, and the plight of rural communities to remain in their homes even when they cease to provide economic viability. When health professionals gain an in-depth understanding of people's affinity with the land and their cultural history in time and space, they have greater insight into how to frame their health promotion strategies. It is also necessary to know what age groups and family types characterise the majority of people.

In the past, numerous inventories or checklists have been generated to guide community health assessment. However, these tend to approach assessment from predetermined assumptions, and run the risk of leaving unexpected issues undocumented. The following categories are therefore presented as an informal guide to community assessment, in the expectation that the process will be open to suggestion by community members, in the spirit of full participation.

Some of the questions to ask community members include the following:

- Are there large proportions of elderly or young families that will require particular health services in either the present or the future?
- What is the cultural mix?
- How does the community see itself?
- What do people think of living in this community?
- Do they believe it is conducive to health?
- What is the level of awareness of health and ecological issues?
- What are the environmental strengths?
- What do they think the community needs most?
- Is there access to transportation for those who need health services?
- What should be sustained?
- What structural features exist and what social and structural changes do they think are required for sustainability?
- What notable differences in opinion exist?

Once this information is known, the next level of assessment should move on to their relationships with the external environment. These questions are as follows:

- Who are the gatekeepers, or key funders of health?
- Are there adequate numbers and types of health professionals?
- What are their priorities for the short, medium and long term?
- In what way are these tied to political goals? What *are* the political goals?

All health programs, especially screening programs, require financial resources. Where a community has a visible problem that is high on the list of government health priorities, it is easier to argue for the necessary funds for an intervention program. However, many issues remain problematic to the community, yet are invisible to, or dismissed by, government funding agencies because of the need, in a climate of economic restraint, to justify return on investment.

Tuberculosis is a case in point. A generation ago, tuberculosis occurred in many countries in epidemic proportions; however, the rate of infection of the disease subsided after worldwide chest X-ray screening brought those afflicted with tuberculosis into treatment. As the number of those with the illness declined, screening was thought to be cost ineffective, on the basis that funds could be better spent in other areas of health need; and of course the AIDS epidemic has attracted a large portion of current resources.

However, there has been a resurgence of cases of tuberculosis and it is now the largest cause of death from a single infectious agent in the world, particularly in developing countries (WHO 1992b). The WHO is developing a focused global program to heighten awareness of the program, to mobilise support on a major scale, and to provide direct guidance and support to national programs.

Community assessment as a political activity

Because of the competition for resources, community assessment must be conducted within the political and economic context of the community and the wider health budgeting arena. This is reflected in the language of health promotion. It has become the norm in many parts of the world to describe health as an investment, especially in this era of economic rationalism, where every government expenditure must be rationalised (Kickbusch 1997). Few health promotion investments are easily quantifiable, and in many cases it is extremely difficult to demonstrate return on investment in terms of either human or other resources.

Part of the difficulty in demonstrating return on investments in health is related to the lag between health interventions and outcomes. For example, programs to counter domestic violence, which has profound effects on the health of many families, have a long period between innovation and outcomes. Family violence is rife in numerous communities throughout the world, yet many people complain of inadequate resources to respond to the problem with viable solutions. In some cases, this is because of the problem being politicised to the extent that funding is often dependent on policy makers' ability to see a return on their investment within the term of their political appointment.

It usually takes years to see improvements in health, and it is often impossible to identify which health gains are due to particular interventions. It is interesting that the greatest return on investment in health comes from such simple forms of daily exercise as walking, but the gains in terms of cardiovascular health and prevention of bone disease take many years to demonstrate.

One of the problems encountered by health professionals wishing to establish intervention programs is the lack of specific information from which to argue the need. Where there is competition for funds between programs, an immunisation program, for instance, is readily measurable within a fairly reasonable time frame. A domestic violence prevention program aimed at teaching young people about relationships is not.

One way of dealing with this type of situation is to think of a creative way of documenting assessment data. For example, the need for a health education program that would prevent domestic violence could be argued on the basis of the prevalence of violence-related injuries, particularly when injury prevention is high on the list of government priorities for community health.

The final step in community assessment is therefore linked to identifying the key players within the community who will provide ongoing support for any necessary changes to community health. Those questions can be framed as follows:

■ Who are the key players who will be willing to engage in serious resource dialogue to sustain both community health and economic viability?
■ What networks and coalitions can be built?
■ Who in the community are the opinion leaders?
■ Who are those who play important roles in resource allocation?
■ How does the community show its capacity for caring?
■ What precedents have been set?

This line of questioning means addressing the issue of equity, but it also aims at making subtle aspects of the community *transparent*, so that the processes, as well as the structures of change, can be made visible. Then programs may be developed which tap in to the strengths of the community and acknowledge the constraints in the environment, whether these be personal, physical, social or financial constraints.

Without this community ownership and commitment, the likelihood of sustainability in programs designed to respond to local needs will be difficult to achieve. In the long term, only community involvement can sustain the supportive social networks, good jobs and safe neighbourhoods that are fundamental to good health (Frank 1995). To ascertain the community's capacity for change, community assessment must revolve around the themes described in figure 4.2.

People
- people–place relationships
- networks for communication
- support systems, family caregivers
- community leadership

Place
- geographic area
- natural and developed resources
- other structural features
- access to transportation

Health patterns
- epidemiological data
- demographic characteristics
- local patterns of service utilisation

Gatekeepers
- local, state, national priorities for health
- financial resources
- competing political goals
- health professionals

Figure 4.2 *Community assessment inventory*

Community assessment is a bit like a SWOT analysis. The object of the exercise is to reveal the *Strengths, Weaknesses, Opportunities* and *Threats* to community health. Once that has been achieved, the information can be shared among members of the community to look for acceptable solutions to existing problems, and strategies for maintaining these over time. The health professional then acts as a community advocate—a resource person who *mediates* between people and those responsible for freeing up the resources they need, *enables* community groups to achieve their goals by helping to build coalitions for change, and *monitors* their progress by collecting information to inform them of the benchmarks they achieve along the way and to help them revise their goals for the future.

The key to accurate assessment is community participation. Planning for equitable, accessible and culturally sensitive health services and resources can only be achieved by incorporating local knowledge and insight into the risk factors and determinants of health that are peculiar to that community.

THINKING CRITICALLY

Sustainable health

▶ List three ways in which rural and urban communities tend to differ in the extent to which they are ecologically enculturated.

▶ List five factors that hinder the global community in achieving sustainable health.

▶ Identify three community networks in your own community that help people sustain high levels of health.

▶ Identify two major strengths and two major barriers to health in your community.

▶ Discuss the pros and cons of political influences on community health.

REFERENCES

Abel, P., Boland, M., Durand, B., Geolot, D., Goodson, J. et al. 1995, 'Workforce and community health care needs: A model to link service, education, and the community', *Family Community Health*, vol. 18, no. 1, pp. 75–9.

Australian Institute of Health and Welfare 1995, *Australian Health Trends*, 1995, AGPS, Canberra.

Boothroyd, P., Green, L., Hertzman, C., Lynam, J., McIntosh, J. et al. 1994, 'Tools for sustainability: iteration and implementation', in *Ecological Public Health: From Vision to Practice*, eds C. Chu & R. Simpson, Institute of Applied Environmental Research, Brisbane, pp. 111–21.

Christiani, D. 1993, 'Urban and transboundary air pollution: human health consequences', in *Critical Condition*, ed. E. Chivian, MIT Press, Cambridge MA.

Chukwuma, C. 1996, 'Perspectives for a sustainable society', *Environmental Management and Health*, vol. 7, no. 5, pp. 5–20.

Committee of Environmental and Occupational Health, Assembly of the American Thoracic Society 1996, 'Health effects of outdoor air pollution', *American Journal of Respiratory and Critical Care Medicine*, vol. 153, no. 3 p. 50.

Evans, R., Barer, M & Marmor, T. 1994, *Why are Some People Healthy and Others Not?*, A. deGruyter, New York.

Frank, J. 1995, 'Why "Population Health"?', *Canadian Journal of Public Health*, vol. 86, no. 3, pp. 162–4.

Hancock, T. & Davies, K. 1997, *An Overview of the Health Implications of Global Environmental Change: A Canadian Perspective*, Canadian Global Change Program, Royal Society of Canada, Ottawa.

Hudson-Rodd, N. 1994, 'Public health: people participating in the creation of healthy places', *Public Health Nursing*, vol. 11, no. 2, pp. 119–26.

Ife, J. 1995, *Community Development: Creating Community Alternatives—Vision, Analysis and Practice*, Longman, Melbourne.

Kickbusch, I. 1997, 'Health-promoting environments: The next step', *Australian and New Zealand Journal of Public Health*, vol. 21, no. 4, pp. 431–4.

LaFond, A. 1995, *Sustaining Primary Health Care*, Earthscan, London.

Lee, P. & Paxman, D. 1997, 'Reinventing public health', *Annual Review of Public Health*, vol. 18, pp. 1–35.

Leland, B. 1995, 'The heart of sustainability', editorial, *BWZ*, 1–4.

Lowe, I. 1994, 'Priorities for a sustainable future', in *Ecological Public Health: From Vision to Practice*, eds C. Chu & R. Simpson, Institute of Applied Environmental Health Research, Brisbane, pp. vii–viii.

Lynch, W., Edington, D. & Johnson, A. 1996, 'Predicting the demand for health-care', *Healthcare Forum Journal*, vol. 39, no. 1, pp. 20–5.

McMurray, A., Hudson-Rodd, N., Al Khudairi, S. & Roydhouse, R. 1998, 'Health and health service utilisation in Belmont: A community case study', *Australian and New Zealand Journal of Public Health*, vol. 22, no. 1, pp. 107–14.

Nelder, C. 1997, 'Envisioning a sustainable future', *BWZ*, pp. 1–15.

World Health Organization 1992a, *Our Planet, Our Health: Report of the WHO Commission on Health and Environment*, WHO, Geneva.

World Health Organization 1992b, *Tuberculosis control and research strategies for the 1990s: memorandum from a WHO meeting*, WHO, Geneva.

Sustainable health
for the individual and family

CONTENTS

Introduction

Part two introduces the notion of health and wellness along a continuum of developmental stages, guided by the model of health and wellness introduced in part one. Chapter 5 examines children as a population group. Healthy childbirth and healthy children are the most important predictors of sustainable health, in the community and in civilisation as a whole. In creating and sustaining the health of children, we invest in the health of all people. Chapter 5 is based on the contention that each community has a unique capacity for nurturing young people regardless of constraints that may be related to environmental, economic, social, political and cultural factors. The role of the health advocate is to help community members analyse that capacity, and to investigate the health determinants and risk factors that must be addressed in order to sustain health and wellness.

The health status of adolescents in any community provides a barometer of a community's progress in generating health and wellness. At this most crucial stage, a large segment of the population is launched from childhood to adulthood, from dependence to independence. How adolescents negotiate this transition is the most important indicator of how health and wellness will be valued in their adult lives. The effects of peer pressure and social structures are among the most important determinants of healthy lifestyle choices. The adolescent's choices, and the extent to which these are supported by others, often establish a pattern for life, for health or illness. Chapter 6 explores some of these choices and the risk factors that most profoundly affect the health of adolescents and thus the health of future adults.

Healthy adulthood depends on individual choices tempered by hereditary, social and environmental conditions. In the adult population the outcomes of health service provision are also visible, as by the time most people reach adulthood they have encountered the health care system at least once. These encounters may be aimed at redressing a clinical problem, at providing an opportunity for future illness prevention, or both. The way adults use the health care system is therefore important to the pattern of living that will sustain or impede the quality of their lives as they age. In chapter 7 the major risk factors and lifestyle determinants of healthy adulthood and the role of the health care system are discussed in a way that acknowledges the dual influence of the environment and personal choices on health.

Chapter 8 examines the features of healthy ageing. Risk factors for premature illness are described, and are contrasted with exemplars of healthy ageing among older groups of people. The health professional's role in assisting the elderly to expect, and then to achieve, health and wellness is paramount at this time of life, as older people rely more heavily than others on advice and guidance from those they encounter in a range of health services. A model for healthy ageing is presented to serve as an example for self-determination in achieving a long and healthy life.

Chapter 9 provides an insight into the contemporary family, discussing the importance of the family as an infrastructure for sustainable health. The influence of the family on all stages of development, from childhood to old age, are addressed. The role of the family in health has traditionally been described in terms of structural, rather than process, issues, but in a rapidly changing society it is essential to address the interaction between the two. As the new century approaches, family structures present a kaleidoscope of configurations. Along with these new structures are evolving processes for securing and maintaining the health of family members and dealing with outside influences. Culturally determined roles are also being reformed and reframed, as communications technology brings families from one community into contact with many others, creating a realm of new expectations. The impact of technology and changing family structures and processes is discussed in this chapter with respect to the role of the health advocate, based on the perspective that understanding is the key to helping others achieve health and wellness.

In chapter 10, gender issues are discussed under the rubric of healthy men and healthy women. Too often, gender issues have tended to polarise health promotion activities toward either females or males, sometimes at the expense of the other. In discussing these issues within the same chapter, distinctions and areas of congruence are illuminated, with emphasis on the ways in which both women and men can capitalise on their unique strengths and overcome their peculiar weaknesses to better capitalise on resources in their personal, social, cultural and physical environment.

Chapter 11 addresses a range of issues relevant to the health of Aboriginal people. Aboriginal people are the most vulnerable among us, as they experience considerably lower health status than their non-Aboriginal counterparts. Chapter 11 is built on the premise that cultural knowledge and understanding is fundamental to encouraging health among Aboriginal people. Equity and cultural sensitivity dictate that community health and development goals must first address measures to ensure that the health needs of Aboriginal people are met. The notion of cultural safety is discussed as instrumental to working with Aboriginal people, and this includes understanding their spiritual nature, and their connection with elements of their external environment, including the land. Reconciliation between Aboriginal and non-Aboriginal people is thus crucial, and a comparative view of reconciliation efforts in South Africa, Canada, the US, Australia and New Zealand is presented. The chapter concludes with health promotion strategies designed to facilitate and enable Aboriginal health in ways that integrate spiritual, cultural, biomedical and psychosocial needs.

5 Healthy children

One of the most important indicators of health in any community is the extent to which it is able to nurture the health of its young. Healthy children tend to become healthy adults, so community initiatives aimed at securing child health are an important investment for community health in general. In some communities the capacity for nurturing young people is hindered by economic, social, political and cultural factors, while in others children thrive and become fit for life. What distinguishes the latter, healthy type of community from all others is rational planning. To chart a course for healthy children requires consideration of all the components of health included in the model presented in the previous chapter. This includes health status, health determinants and risk factors, health service utilisation and health resources. This chapter addresses the creation and maintenance of equitable, accessible and culturally sensitive child health and wellness within such a framework.

Objectives

By the end of this chapter you will be able to:

- *identify the five most important influences on child health in contemporary society*

- *describe two risk factors that seriously compromise the health of children*

- *discuss family development issues influencing child health and wellbeing*

- *identify three community goals for sustaining child health*

- *explain how a primary health care framework can be used in planning for child health.*

The healthy child

What is a healthy child? If we revisit our definition of health from chapter 1, health, and thus the health of children, is characterised by balance and potential. Healthy children are those whose physical health and fitness is balanced with their social, emotional and spiritual lives, and who are developing towards their highest potential for health and wellbeing, given the constraints of their particular circumstances. In some cases, these constraints are related to genetic endowment, or a lack of access to resources, either for health services or for normal developmental activities. Some children may have access to resources but may live in a family environment that is less than conducive for healthy development. And for some, behavioural factors, either theirs or their parents', create situations of risk that jeopardise health status. Risks to child health thus include risks at birth, environmental risks, behavioural risks and those related to the adequacy of health resources (Fink 1989). These factors are summarised in figure 5.1.

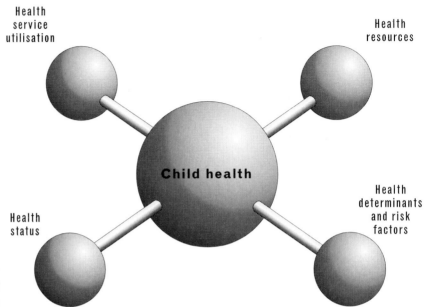

Health
service
utilisation

Health
resources

Child health

Health
status

Health
determinants
and risk
factors

Figure 5.1
*The interrelationship
of factors influencing
the health of children*

Health determinants and risk factors

A kaleidoscope of factors contribute to the health of children. Some of these are biological and include genetic inheritance, while others are related to family influences and the child's physical and social environment. The most important influence on the health and wellbeing of children exerts its effect before the child is born, during pregnancy.

Healthy pregnancy

A healthy pregnancy is the first step towards having healthy children. For the expectant mother this includes eating a balanced diet that ensures adequate nutritional intake for her and the child, participating in regular exercise, maintaining harmony between physical, social and emotional health, and securing medical monitoring to ensure appropriate foetal development. Healthy pregnancy includes being physically fit for childbirth. During a normal pregnancy, regular exercise (three times per week) is beneficial for both mother and child, particularly if this reflects the woman's typical pattern of activity. Fortunately, in this era, more women than ever before are physically active, and many continue their exercise during pregnancy (Zhang & Savitz 1996). Of course, experienced athletes often engage in higher levels of activity than non-athletes, but the rule for both types of women is to not exercise to the stage of exhaustion, so that the by-products of exercise and body temperature do not increase to the extent of harming the foetus. Walking is an ideal weight-bearing exercise for pregnant women, and such non-weight-bearing exercises as cycling on a stationary bike, or swimming, allow a good workout while minimising the risk of injury.

The importance of diet in pregnancy cannot be overstated. The effects of antenatal diet are experienced not only in childhood, but also in later life, when osteoporosis, renal disease, cardiovascular disease and a host of other conditions reflect the early nutritional status of the developing foetus (Barker et al. 1990; Mason et al. 1996). The mother's weight gain during pregnancy is an important indicator of the infant's birthweight, which, in turn, is another determinant of the child's future health status. So from the earliest indication of pregnancy, the mother needs to carefully plan her diet to ensure adequate and appropriate nutrients for her and the baby, and to balance diet with exercise and other lifestyle factors. This will also be influenced by the cultural and environmental context of the woman's life, as some food preferences and dietary patterns are set in cultural customs. In addition to culture, financial resources also determine whether a woman's diet will be adequate (Bronner 1996).

The woman's psychological and social wellbeing are also important, and affect all other lifestyle choices. We have known for years that mothers who are comfortable with the idea of being pregnant, who have a good relationship with their partner, and who have friends, a social network and a supportive, extended family tend to adapt better to pregnancy (Nuckolls, Cassel & Kaplan 1972).

Antenatal care is also an important determinant of a successful pregnancy. Even where the mother expects no problems with the pregnancy, the need for regular checkups is essential to ensure that the child is developing as it should, and that the mother is maintaining her own health. The value of continual monitoring throughout pregnancy cannot be overestimated, as the research indicates that infants born to mothers having no antenatal care run a ten times greater risk of dying at birth than those whose mothers do seek care during pregnancy (Green & Ottoson 1994). It has also been suggested by some nutrition experts that pre-conception advice should be offered to girls at school, and continue throughout the child-bearing years (Dickerson 1995).

Infant mortality and risk

Each country uses the infant mortality rate as an indicator or benchmark of the health of its population. Infant mortality is the greatest threat to potential parents. In most of the industrialised countries, the rate of infant mortality or *perinatal death rate* has declined markedly over the last two decades. To a large extent this is due to advances in biomedical technology that allow us to keep very low birthweight babies alive. But despite technology, approximately 75% of all deaths that occur during the first month of life are attributable to low birthweight (Martin 1992).

Parents today are more aware than their predecessors of risk factors that are universally known to increase the risk of having a low birthweight baby. The role of diet in successful pregnancy has been acknowledged for years, and most people understand the link between iron deficiency and low birthweight babies. However, research continues to unravel the links between dietary intakes of vitamins and minerals during pregnancy and a variety of birth outcomes. For example, recent longitudinal studies have revealed that supplements of folic acid during pregnancy are effective in preventing recurrence of conditions as disabling as anencephalus and spina bifida (MRCVSRG 1991). With the current resurgence of this type of research, and general interest in diet and nutrition, one could expect that mothers of the future will be better prepared than their predecessors to ensure healthy pregnancies (Bower et al. 1997).

Other factors putting the child at risk of low birthweight include smoking or alcohol abuse during pregnancy, and the mother's age, with mothers giving birth either below 15 years or above 35 years of age running a greater risk than others (Green & Ottoson 1994). In some cases, however, multiple factors compound each other, leading to an even greater risk. For example, we know that the effect of nicotine from cigarette smoking is detrimental to the foetus. Yet a higher proportion of women of lower socioeconomic status smoke than do those of higher socioeconomic status (Jacobson & Wilkinson 1994). But these factors may not be due only to behavioural responses. One group of researchers found that black women smokers in the US have a higher level of a major metabolite of nicotine than white women who smoke a comparable number of cigarettes (English, Eskenazi & Christianson 1994). So for those women, the risk of having a low birthweight baby increases because of their biological makeup, their smoking behaviour and their socioeconomic status, which is typically lower than that of the white population.

Socioeconomic status is a complicated risk factor with respect to infant birthweight. Most people would be shocked to learn that the infant mortality rate among Americans ranks among the highest of the industrialised nations. Infants born in Canada, Sweden, Japan and eighteen other countries have a better chance of surviving during their first year than infants born in the US (Martin 1992). This situation is undoubtedly linked to the disparity in socioeconomic status within the US. The gap between rich and poor results in a situation where some mothers have access to appropriate dietary and lifestyle supports during pregnancy, while others cannot afford the proper foods and often are unaware of the need for a nutritious diet. In addition, this reflects a situation of extreme poverty, where women often live in poor housing conditions, with little access to transportation, child care and health services. Poverty, in turn, is more prevalent among women of colour, placing them more at risk for unhealthy pregnancy than their white counterparts (Knutson, Leavitt & Sarton 1995).

In many developing countries, women have little or no education and often have no access to the type of information they need for both a healthy pregnancy and subsequent family planning. The World Bank, which sponsors substantial research in this area, reports that educated women have smaller families and better spacing between children, and their children tend to be healthier and better educated (World Bank 1991). Yet, educating parents on pregnancy care is only part of the solution, as often infant malnutrition is linked to environmental and cultural problems (Bronner 1996). For example, land degradation in some countries has resulted in a limited food supply (Hertz, Hebert & Landon 1994). In some places, the allocation of food, like other resources, is culturally determined, and males are often given higher priority than females. Education programs for sustainable community health must therefore look beyond the immediate need of the pregnant woman and the family, and address social policy issues related to the entire population, including cultural issues, equity of access and, ultimately, social justice.

Genetics

Healthy pregnancy is an important element in population health because it represents the beginning of the biological pathway to a community's health (Frank 1995). However, many children come into the world without the genetic endowment that would enable them to grow and develop into healthy and fit adults. As a result, some children spend at least a portion of their childhood with some degree of disablement and some are destined to live their lives with chronic, life-limiting disease or with intermittent episodes of acute illness. On the other hand, many children who are born with disabilities develop into healthy adults and learn to manage their condition, particularly if they live in a supportive family environment. Sometimes a child with a disability draws family members closer together, but in other families the strain intensifies the child's experience of disability, and seriously compromises family stability.

There are those who believe the old adage that 'forewarned is fore-armed' and that if expectant parents understand their chances of having a child with a disability they will be better able to cope with the situation, or to make choices for alternative action. For this reason, genetic testing is now the norm among mothers considered at risk of having a child with a genetic illness. The type of testing varies depending on parental risk factors and local health care resources. In places where there are sufficient health care resources, all pregnant women undergo amniocentesis. This involves withdrawing a sample of amniotic fluid from the mother's uterus and testing it for biochemical and chromosomal defects. In some cases, alpha-fetoprotein tests are conducted which can identify such abnormalities as neural tube defects, twin pregnancy, central wall defects or Down syndrome (Green & Ottoson 1994).

Since 1990, the Human Genome Project (HGP) has made consider-able advances in diagnosing genetic conditions (Williams & Lessick 1996). The Project is aimed at mapping the estimated 100,000 genes lying on twenty-three pairs of chromosomes in the human body and determining the sequence of the three billion base pairs of nucleotides that make up DNA. This information will then be compiled on data bases and be made available to scientists and the public upon its completion around the year 2005. However, as with many biomedical advances, the HGP cannot be seen as a 'magic bullet' that will solve many public health problems, and scientists are proceeding with caution to examine the impact of the knowledge they are uncovering. One of the most important roles of the HGP is thus to consider the ethical, legal and social implications of this information so that it is managed in a socially responsible way for the benefit of future generations (Williams & Lessick 1996; Lee & Paxman 1997).

It has been known for some years now that older mothers (beyond age thirty-five) may be at greater risk for having a child with a genetic defect.

Genetic testing of older mothers has become common medical practice in many places, especially with the current trend for parents to delay child-bearing until their thirties or beyond. The tests are usually followed by an explanation to the parents of the degree of statistical risk of them having a child with a genetic problem, and for some parents this poses a heart-wrenching dilemma. Since genetic testing began, even prior to the HGP, health professionals have had to give careful consideration to their role as advocates for parents in these situations. Although the benefits of genetic testing include better reproductive planning, relief from uncertainty and sometimes the potential for gene therapy, some families prefer to forego the opportunity for testing (Williams & Lessick 1996).

In some cases, such as in testing for the carrier gene for cystic fibrosis, parents have declined the offer of being tested because they feel there is some psychological benefit in being unaware of their carrier status (Fanos & Johnson 1994). As a family and child advocate, the role of the health professional is to maintain a non-judgemental attitude, regardless of the family's decision(s), and to provide support and information at each step of the decision-making process. This involves being knowledgeable enough about all sides of the issues to provide appropriate guidance without coercion, and helping preserve the family's autonomy in decision-making, whether the decisions involve testing, participating in genetic research, or managing the pregnancy. Most importantly, the role of the health professional is to foster family empowerment and thus work toward the primary health care goal of self-determinism.

Diet and nutrition

From birth onwards, maintaining adequate nutrition is the most essential ingredient for healthy childhood. For at least the first six months of life, breast milk is the most ideally balanced diet for newborn infants, and provides immunity from many diseases for the infant. However, in many places, because of the pressure on women to return to work quickly, the number of children who have been breastfed is declining. Campaigns to encourage women to breastfeed have been under way in most countries, but nowhere is the need so acute as in the developing countries, where not only are infants often deprived of the superior nutritious value of breast milk, but they may also suffer from gastrointestinal illnesses acquired from contami-nated bottle formulas and, in many cases, a lack of medication to treat these conditions (WHO 1996).

Because good nutrition is the basic ingredient for helping children grow strong and fit, most communities allocate considerable resources to encouraging healthy diets in day care centres and school health programs. Promoting good nutrition is now a crucial part of school health because of the large numbers of families in which both parents must remain in full-time employment. In many places, the scope of school health services has expanded over the last decade from a focus on treating children for accidents and injury to creating a healthy environment for growth and development. Intersectoral collaboration is used to capitalise on the ideas of education and health departments and thus to devise thoughtfully planned programs aimed at good nutrition, physical education, guidance and counselling. The co-operative nature of these programs is the key to their success, and many encourage family involvement (Igoe & Speer 1992), so it is not uncommon to see parent volunteers managing healthy canteens that once sold junk food, and acting as teacher aides and role models for healthy living.

The trend toward community participation in school health programs exemplifies the primary health care approach, where health professionals, teachers and parents work collaboratively as partners in ensuring the health of children. Increasingly, we can expect to see more emphasis placed on school as the setting for healthy lifestyle development, as economic problems send more and more parents into the workplace. Along with this will be the need for government policies to co-ordinate school health promotion efforts, which to date have been fragmented in their development and therefore somewhat inconsistent from one place to another (Baker 1994).

Health, fitness and lifestyle

Along with a nutritious diet, children need to maintain a level of physical activity sufficient to promote cardiovascular fitness and the muscular capacity to complement bone growth through periods of rapid development. Despite peaks and troughs of interest in physical fitness over the past three decades, as the new century nears, we see declining fitness levels in the children of many countries. To some extent, this can be attributed to ease of transportation, the growth of technology which has seen more children in sedentary play, and a lack of role modelling by parents, who are themselves tied to sedentary lifestyles (Heath et al. 1994).

In the US, declining activity in adolescence and adulthood has led to obesity of epidemic proportions costing the health care system millions of dollars annually in health care (Grubbs 1993; Heath et al. 1994). However, the research shows little evidence that American children are becoming less fit over time, or that they are less fit than European children, which refutes the popular impression that they spend countless hours watching television (Simons-Morton et al. 1997). In Australia there is also cause for optimism. As in the US, some children participate in very little physical activity, but as a population group there has been a distinct trend towards increasing levels of activity since the 1980s (AIHW 1996) and this may be reason to believe that the next generations will continue to value being fit and healthy.

Obesity among children is among the most prevalent risk factors for disease (Blank Sherman et al. 1992). In Australia, between 15 and 30% of children are overweight, with trends heading towards the American statistic of one in three children being overweight (Grundy 1995). Australia is a country that prides itself on an emphasis on sports, yet the relationship between sport and fitness is poorly understood. Despite the fact that two out of three pre-adolescents and adolescents participate in out-of-school hours sporting activities, young people between the ages of six and sixteen do not maintain even a minimal standard of cardiovascular fitness (Naughton & Carlson 1995). Some researchers feel that the problem should be confronted in the classroom as well as on the sporting fields, to reinforce the importance of sport as a lifelong physical activity rather than simply as entertainment or recreation (Naughton & Carlson 1995).

One approach to teaching children about physical fitness is to refocus physical education from an emphasis on *how* the game is played to *why* it is necessary for health and wellbeing. This type of approach can also be used to educate young children about such risky behaviours as smoking and drug abuse. Quite often, programs addressing substance abuse are not introduced until high school, yet epidemiological studies reveal that some children begin smoking and/or drinking alcohol as early as grade four, indicating, as some public health professionals believe, that we must begin to consider cigarette smoking as a paediatric disease (Bush & Iannotti 1993; Lee & Paxman 1997). As with physical fitness, children need explanations of the dangers of tobacco smoking, but they also need a plausible reason for alternative behaviour. Programs that emphasise the incompatibility of smoking and drug use with being fit and healthy (and thus capable of playing sport) tend to be better received than giving children heavy-handed directives that emphasise only that risky behaviours are bad for them.

Childhood asthma

The importance of exercise and diet is especially important for children with asthma, one of the most neglected problems in community health (Bauman 1996). The child with asthma has frequent airway obstructions that are caused by inflammation and excess mucous in the airway, and constriction of the bronchial passageway. Often the asthma attack is triggered by a respiratory illness, allergens or pollutants in the air (including tobacco smoke), or emotional factors, exercise or changes in humidity and temperature (Beeber 1996). Parental smoking is considered an important factor in precipitating childhood asthma, or at least wheezing attacks, which is considered a surrogate measure of asthma. Researchers have identified the influence of parental smoking patterns but the exact influence of exposure to this kind of passive smoking is unknown in the subsequent development of asthma (Cunningham et al. 1996).

Worldwide rates of asthma are increasing dramatically, but for reasons unknown, Australia and New Zealand experience higher prevalence, morbidity and mortality than any other developed countries. Researchers have studied a range of causal factors such as antenatal and parental smoking post-natally, heredity, respiratory infectious agents and air quality, but the only factors that seem peculiar to the Australasian region seem to be pollens, moulds and house dust mites (Bauman 1996). Interestingly, Australian Aboriginal children have a lower prevalence of asthma than their white counterparts, yet the reason remains unknown, although environmental factors are suspected (Veale et al. 1996).

It would appear that a number of factors in combination have led to the increase in prevalence of childhood asthma. One of these is related to ozone. Ozone is a known air pollutant but its exact role in either causing or triggering asthma is unknown. When air pollutants are slow to disperse because of atmospheric stagnation and high levels of ultraviolet radiation, ozone levels increase in the ambient air. However, in large cities with high pollution levels caused by industrial and automobile exhaust, oxidation of the ozone occurs, leaving the ambient air with a relatively greater concentration of nitrogen dioxide than ozone (Devereux et al. 1996). This suggests that the web of causation includes not only the specific factors precipitating asthma or an asthma attack, but the combination of environmental conditions favourable to the disease. Prevention and control of asthma presents a classic case for collaboration between health and environmental scientists and the need for wide dissemination of knowledge between and among different populations.

Emotional and social risk factors

Asthma is only one of many illnesses with a suspected emotional and social component. Increasingly, the patterns of morbidity in children show the effects of stressors in the social and cultural environment of contemporary family life (Vimpani & Parry 1989). A holistic view of health dictates that our efforts to promote child health in the community must focus on children living in harmony with their physical, social and cultural environment. So the first place to address child health issues is within the family, where individual health and wellbeing is constituted.

The family and parenting

The needs of infants and young children have not changed over the years. They still need physical care, love, nurturing, protection and a sense of belonging. But the context in which their needs are met has changed with every generation. It is easy to explain children's difficulties in terms of parent absence, especially as many couples work outside the family home and sometimes are also transient, following jobs that may take them far from extended family support networks. However, other historical events have also conspired to change the way people parent these days.

At the turn of this century, most issues concerning parenthood were under the direction of medical doctors. In the 1920s it became common practice to consult nurses or paediatricians for all matters relating to child care. By the late thirties, kindergarten and child guidance professionals were recognised as the new experts on child rearing. In the sixties and seventies, expert knowledge emerged through women's organisations such as those that addressed natural childbirth and/or breastfeeding. Today, parenting knowledge comes from a mixture of professionals—psychologists, social workers and 'lay' experts (Rieger 1991)—all of whom seem to have written a book on the subject. This insidious professionalism of what was once exclusively the domain of the family has placed considerable pressure on today's first-time parents to consult a guru at every turn; as a consequence, some have all but relinquished the right to make up their own minds about child care. Many young parents feel guilty at being forced to spend so little time with their children, and because of conflicting research reports about the effects of institutional child care for very young children, often feel anxious and depressed about their role as parents, usually with no older generation available to soothe their fears.

Today's urban lifestyles often leave young families feeling alone and lacking in meaningful relationships with others as they emerge daily from the workplace exhausted and in need of reassurance. In the past, families either inherited or selected their support networks, and had time to discuss issues related to child-rearing. Now people live in isolation, crowded or otherwise, and come to rely on health professionals as their source of guidance and support. And because they often lose the perspective of what is normal *for their child*, they accept the blame for any little deviation from what are often unrealistic expectations.

Exceptions to this scenario occur in many cultural groups that still provide a strong support base for babies and their parents. But increasingly, young mothers from these extended family networks are returning to the workforce and suffering the additional strain of falling into cracks between the old culture and the new. So even in those groups with strong traditions of child care there is a need to have members of the older generation understand what may be new parenting styles. A further frustration lies in the fact that today's new parents are caught between two competing social attitudes: one that venerates parenthood and thus scorns the quick return to work of the mother, and the other that considers paid work as the only legitimate occupation. This latter notion is reinforced by government policies, which usually offer disproportionate subsidisation of child care for working parents (Cox 1993).

The role of the health professional in helping parents nurture their young revolves around the primary health care principle of empowerment. As family and child health advocates we must act as a filter to ensure that our guidance gets through to them in their busy lives but does not sabotage family health competence (Dunst & Trivette 1996). Parents must be included as participants in decisions related to their children, and our role is to support their decisions and assist them to reveal and explore the full range of options and choices pertinent to decisions (Rushton, McEnhill & Armstrong 1996). At the policy level we need to uncover the hidden facets of family issues that would inform public policy debate, including care giving within the family, sharing of care between the public and private sphere, and reassessment of models and resources for care (Cox 1993). Keeping family issues on the public agenda provides a greater chance of creating healthy public policies and thus a family-friendly, and child-friendly, society.

Child poverty

One of the most important social issues of our time is the profound effect of poverty on child health. Poverty is associated with increased neonatal and childhood mortality rates, greater risk of injuries resulting from accidents, child abuse or neglect, higher risk for asthma and lower developmental scores on a range of tests at multiple ages (Aber et al. 1997). Child poverty is a problem for many countries, even developed countries where the gap between rich and poor continues to broaden (Chu 1994). One study, conducted by the Children's Defense Fund in the US, found that while the gross national product of that country grew by more than one-fourth from 1979 to 1989, child poverty increased by 21% (Johnson et al. 1991).

A more recent study in the US examined the effects of family structure, race and poverty over a fourteen-year period and found that poverty was the most important predictor of ill health in childhood (Montgomery, Kiely & Pappas 1996). They discovered that more than two out of three black children in single-mother households were living in poverty, although the association was not related as much to race as to single parenting, especially where there was no child support. In the UK, Australia, New Zealand and many other countries, poverty also exerts a profound effect on the health of children (Fancourt 1997; Whitehead 1995). A comparative analysis of eight industrialised countries confirmed that the situation is worse in the US because of the large proportion of single-mother headed families with the lowest socioecomic status (Montgomery, Kiely & Pappas 1996).

Childhood stress

Children today are exposed to a great many stressors. From a review of the past twenty years of literature on stress and illness in children, Grey (1993) reports that those children with more stressful experiences are significantly more likely to experience illness or hospitalisation, or use health services more frequently than others. Some children are simply more vulnerable than others, and this may be a result of several factors, biological and temperamental as well as experiential (Connell 1989). Although the literature is somewhat ambiguous about the cause and effects of stress, studies of the relationship between stressful events and physical and psychological illness in children have yielded similar results to those of adults. These indicate that for all groups of children, stress tends to be followed by some sort of illness (Grey 1993).

Nowhere are the effects of stress more evident than in the child victims of war. In many parts of the world, hundreds of thousands of young children are left to forage for food and water, deprived of access to immunisation, and exposed to infectious diseases. Their physical states are doubly compromised by torture, trauma, rape and other abuses, and the emotional stress of separation from family members and dislocation from their homes (Cliff & Noormahomed 1993). Their lives represent one of the most pressing global child health problems and one that must demand attention from all health policy makers, particularly when budgetary decisions are being made to support international community development programs and thus health for all.

Child sexual abuse

One of the problems in addressing child sexual abuse at the community level is the lack of data defining the extent of the problem, and the knowledge that many incidents of abuse go unreported. Researchers in a number of countries estimate that approximately 20% of female children experience some form of inappropriate sexual contact (Anderson, Martin & Mullen 1993; Britton & Hansen 1997; Fleming 1997). These figures may also be underestimated because of the secrecy and shame surrounding sexual abuse, the criminal sanctions against it, and the dependent age and status of the child (Fleming 1997).

Risk factors for child sexual abuse are numerous, and most point to a cluster of factors that include being physically abused, having a mother who is mentally ill, and social isolation (Fleming, Mullen & Bammer 1997). Sexually abused children usually come from families where there is a high frequency of other social and interpersonal problems. These contribute to both the risks and the long-term deleterious effects of the abuse, including the risk of sexually transmitted diseases and psychiatric illness (Britton & Hansen 1997; Romans 1997).

As a community, we cannot respond effectively to child abuse without considering the overall needs of the child in the context of his or her life (Cloke 1997). Research studies worldwide have produced overwhelming evidence for social and interpersonal problems as the sequelae of abuse in childhood; and some problems are exacerbated by the outcomes of disclosing the abuse (Nagel, Putnam & Noll 1997). All forms of abuse seem to have effects that last into adulthood; and, where the abuse is sexual in nature, there is usually a direct effect on sexual adjustment and the capacity for intimacy in adult life (Romans 1997). In some cases this can lead to intergenerational perpetuation of the cycle of abuse (Shah 1997).

Responding to the abused child requires cultural sensitivity as well as the normal consideration of the needs of young, and therefore vulnerable, children (Powell 1997). Assessing children for child abuse needs to be done sensitively, whether in the school or a health care service. This is one area where intersectoral collaboration between education, police, social welfare, health professionals and neighbourhood groups has produced comprehensive guidelines for surveillance, monitoring and response (Mulroy 1997). Assessing children also involves understanding the family's perspective, as different cultures have varying ideas of what may be considered maltreatment of a child, and what should be done about it (Powell 1997). Families must be supported, yet the vulnerable protected. In all societies, the problem must be addressed with a focus on preventive strategies that are visible and comprehensive. These include early detection and response, childhood education, ongoing support for families, better informed treatment options and community education.

Accidents and injuries

Childhood is the time when considerable emphasis must be given to teaching about safety and safe behaviour. At the same time, the environment within which young children grow must be designed to minimise the opportunity for accidents. On any given day, one Australian child dies accidentally, and 160 more are admitted to hospital suffering from a preventable injury (Moller & Kreisfeld 1997). In Canada, the rate is 125 accidents requiring medical attention to every death, and in England and Wales, childhood accidents cause the death of 700 children each year, with 10,000 being permanently disabled, and 100,000 requiring hospitalisation from injuries (Canadian Red Cross Society 1995; Obeid 1997).

In the US, the figures are magnified to reflect the greater population density. As many as 11 deaths and 1000 disabling injuries occur *every hour*, so that 12 to 14 million children annually receive medical treatment for accidental injury (Sleet 1990; Hammett & Kirby 1997). Injuries also continue to be the leading cause of death among children (Peterson & Stern 1997). These rates reflect enormous personal cost to families, and to the children themselves, but they also represent a huge burden on the health care system.

For very young children the most common accidents are choking, fires and automobile accidents where the child is a passenger (Canadian Red

Cross Society 1995). The most important preventive measure that can be taken by community health professionals is to teach parents about the need for close supervision of young children and explain how to take precautions within the home—for example, checking heaters, cooking equipment and electrical distribution, and ensuring the child has no exposure to matches or lighters used for cigarette smoking. The community also has a responsibility for industrial safeguards, such as ensuring adequate labelling of manufactured goods such as flammable clothing, nursery furniture and electrical appliances. This is one area where collaboration with consumer organisations is extremely helpful.

Childhood drownings are the most common cause of death for toddlers in many countries, and one of the most prevalent forms of childhood injury (AIHW 1996). Some of these accidents occur because of the erratic behaviour of the 1–3 year age group. Their capabilities change at least daily, and parents often are stretched to the limit in keeping up with them. However, other factors such as socioeconomic status may put some families more at risk than others of having a drowning or a serious submersion injury. Although some researchers believe that lower-income families have a more relaxed attitude toward supervising children, often it is that they lack the knowledge and the means to make their children's environment safe (Peterson & Stern 1997).

For poorer families, sub-standard housing often creates a plethora of risk factors: balconies and windows without child safety catches, spaces in the home needing repair, unsafe electrical appliances, and crowded streets near high traffic areas with few alternative parks and play areas. One of the greatest hazards is that of accidental poisoning. Children most at risk are those under three years of age, who have little concept of danger and whose curiosity drives them to taste just about anything. The most harmful substances children ingest include petroleum distillates such as fuels, solvents, cleaners and polishes, but many other household products can cause serious poisoning, even things like eucalyptus oil or alcoholic beverages (Wiseman 1995).

Another domestic hazard relates to the risk of accidental injury from furniture. Young children slip through the crevices in beds, especially bunk beds, and they fall from chairs and sofas. The Child Accident Prevention Foundation of Australia reports that 19% of injuries in the first year of life are associated with baby equipment (CAPFA 1997). There is a particularly high risk in single-mother headed families, where the mother may be less well equipped to provide continuous and vigilant protection from harm because of employment obligations and, in some cases, the lack of emotional and material resources to ensure child safety (Obeid 1997; Peterson & Stern 1997).

Climate and geography are also factors in childhood injuries. Warm climates see young children outdoors, either in swimming pools or on the streets, and riding bicycles, for longer periods of the year than in colder climates (Acton, Nixon & Clark 1997). Bicycle injuries are one of the major sources of head injury in children. Head injuries are devastating, not only because of their profoundly disabling and long-lasting effects on the child, but also because they represent such an enormous cost to society, estimated at eight billion dollars per year in the US alone (Childsecure 1997). Many bicycle accidents involve collisions with automobiles. Automobile accidents remain the leading cause of accidental death in all age groups of children, and laws have now been introduced in all states of Australia, the US and all provinces of Canada for the mandatory wearing of seat-belts and the use of car seats for all young children.

Accident reduction strategies must include a concerted community effort. Bicycle helmet and car seat legislation must be combined with community awareness campaigns, strict labelling codes for manufacturers, bicycle safety instruction in schools, and environmental modifications such as safer road design and maintenance. Under the age of five, children's judgement cannot be relied upon, and so parental supervision is the most important element in maintaining child safety. After age five, children must still have constant reinforcement and the best way for this to occur is through appropriate modelling by parents, teachers and other authority figures (Peterson & Stern 1997).

Safety instruction and guidance must be ongoing because as a child grows, so does the number of dangers they are exposed to. Such instruction must consider the different stages of child development so that educational messages can be appropriately directed to the way in which different age groups conceptualise the information. This is extremely important, as misunderstandings may increase a child's anxiety, in some cases causing *increased* rather than decreased carelessness (Moss-Morris & Paterson 1995; Peterson & Stern 1997). Stories are usually most appropriate for teaching children about safety, because the information can be embedded within recognisable events and thus will usually be better remembered.

Most accidents occur when parents or children are tired or ill, or under stress, when routines are disrupted or when someone other than the usual carer is supervising the child (Canadian Red Cross Society 1995). Bicycle and other automobile accidents tend to occur when the child is travelling to and from school, and one Australian study found that these occurred mid-block, on local urban roads, during the after-school hours (Stevenson et al. 1992). This indicates the need for both parents and teachers to be aware of the importance of child safety. One Canadian study, for example, found that helmet use was more frequent for children travelling to and from school than for those simply riding around the local neighbourhood, and this may indicate that safety behaviours are only employed when some form of monitoring is taking place. This is similar to the seat-belt situation. Many people travelling short distances fail to use seat-belts, on the basis that they are not going far from home and that there is no one observing the behaviour (Farley, Haddad & Brown 1996). So greater attention may need to be paid to those things that influence children adopting safe practices, including whether they hesitate to use helmets because of the decreased risk, or the lack of peer pressure, or lack of reinforcement by teachers or parents.

It is important to provide parents with accurate information on the risks involved in childhood activities, as many fail to understand the severity of outcomes of neighbourhood accidents. In addition, it is often up to the health professional to provide parents with information on safety standards related to home appliances, bicycle helmets and car seats, and on the importance of modelling safe behaviours. The research that links safety precautions to risk reduction outcomes has been somewhat ambiguous to date, but there is now an accumulating body of evidence for the effectiveness of such things as seat-belts, car seats and bicycle helmets, and this information needs to be transmitted to parents in a way that will encourage and support their efforts (Thompson, Rivara & Thompson 1989).

In addition to helping parents, as community advocate it is important to understand the factors within the environment that predispose its young residents to a greater incidence of accidents. For example, areas of old, overcrowded housing have been shown to be associated with higher accident rates, particularly for young males (Wade, Chapman & Foot 1981). Suburban streets are also hazardous for young children, and many injuries occur in residential driveways as a result of vehicles backing up (Winn, Agran & Castillo 1991). Rural areas have their own peculiar risks, related not only to the environment but to the attitudes of rural children, who tend to use such precautions as seat-belts and bicycle helmets less frequently than urban students (Schootman et al. 1993).

In addition to parent information, child accident prevention informa-tion must be directed to the children themselves, and in most schools this is a major feature of the primary and pre-primary school curriculum. Neylon (1993) suggests that the major advantages to teaching children positive health and safety practices early in their school experience is that exposure to the messages is guaranteed, given that all children attend school. In addi-tion, young children starting school show a particular interest in their health, growth and development, and often have the capacity to influence their parents once they take the information home (Gans et al. 1994).

It is important to remember that no health and safety promotion program will be successful unless it is based on the principles of primary health care. *All* families, rich or poor, rural or urban, must have access to the information. Educational information must be culturally sensitive and directed at all cultural groups residing in the community. Presentations must be designed to provide information for informed decision-making, in order to promote self-determinism rather than coercion, and must be accompanied by environmental modifications that include intersectoral input. Compre-hensive strategies to address child safety issues must include involvement from health, education, transport, the business community, the community council, consumer organisations and any relevant political forces within a community to ensure safety and protection for all young people.

Child health resources

The most important community resources for child health are directed at prevention of illness or injury. Ideally, the involves an intersectoral approach, where parents, educators, public health planner, local commun-ity councils and all members of the public combine their efforts to ensure the health and safety of young people The most significant prevention issue involves protecting children from infectious diseases through immunisation.

Immunisation

Immunisation is one of the most vital health resources for ensuring the health of a community's children. Ten major diseases can now be controlled by vaccination, including diptheria, tetanus, pertussis (whooping cough), polio, measles, tuberculosis, yellow fever, mumps, rubella and *Haemophilus influenzae* type b (Hib) infection (Burgess 1997). One of the most impor-tant decisions parents must make is whether to have their children immunised, yet many fail to do so because of either a lack of understanding or misinformation about the risks involved. Immunisation involves giving the child a vaccine designed to stimulate production of specific *antibodies* that protect the child from developing a particular infectious disease. When the majority of children in a population are vaccinated against the disease, there is seen to be a high level of *herd immunity*; that is, the chances of the infectious agent being spread amongst others is markedly reduced (Burgess 1997). The public health goal—to maintain good health for the greatest number of people—requires that as many children as possible in the population be immunised.

At present, 80% of the world's children are immunised against diptheria, tetanus, pertussis, polio, measles and tuberculosis, and the goal of the WHO is to increase the levels of immunisation, so that by the turn of the century there will be total eradication of at least poliomyelitis and measles (Cochi, Hull & Ward 1995; Henderson 1995). Although immunisation is one of the most effective public health measures in the world, between two and three million preventable deaths still occur from six diseases: measles, whooping cough, tetanus, polio, tuberculosis and diptheria (Green & Ottoson 1994; Hanna et al. 1994; Thompson 1997). Measles alone accounts for one million deaths a year. Total eradication of poliomyelitis and measles, as the WHO intends, will not only benefit the community in terms of child health, but will save at least 1.5 billion dollars annually in the cost of routine vaccination (Burgess 1997).

Immunisation schedules vary slightly throughout the world, but the WHO mandates that all children should be immunised against diptheria, pertussis, tetanus, polio, measles and, in many countries, tuberculosis. In the US the level of immunised children tends to range between 70 and 80% of the population, with certain subgroups having levels lower than 50% (Green & Ottoson 1994). In Australia and Canada, immunisation levels are maintained at approximately 90%, possibly because of the fact that it is provided through the Medicare scheme of universal health insurance. However, in Australia and in some parts of New Zealand the rate has begun to decline, in part because of a parent-led campaign criticising pertussis immunisation on the basis that it presents a risk of causing brain damage in the child (Hanna et al. 1994).

Some believe that the concerns of many Australian parents were galvanised by an emotionally charged nationally televised program in 1997 depicting public health officials as covering up the true facts on immunisation. Similar public anti-immunisation movements have occurred elsewhere in the past and all are cause for alarm (Thompson 1997). Thompson (1997) recounts that similar situations have occurred before, in other places. In the 1970s in the UK, and the 1980s in the US, there were some suggestions from parents of children with neurological disabilities that their children's problems may have been caused by pertussis vaccination. A documentary in the UK showed a court case in which it was claimed that thirty-six of these children had been brain-damaged over the previous twelve years, and because the children had in fact been vaccinated, they were awarded damages.

Following this case, the Vaccine Injury Act was introduced in the UK in 1979 and the rate of vaccinations began to plummet. Almost immediately, a severe epidemic of whooping cough occurred, with five thousand children hospitalised. Two thousand children came down with pneumonia, 83 developed encephalopathy and 28 died. A similar event occurred in the US where, by 1984, 255 lawsuits had been filed against the drug companies manufacturing the vaccine. As a result, the cost of the vaccine rose from 15 cents per dose to $8.50 per dose, representing a substantial economic burden on families with no national health care scheme. All but one of the companies manufacturing the vaccine withdrew from production, further inflating the cost. Meanwhile, extensive research studies were conducted to examine the association between pertussis vaccination and neurologic illness. Although some association was demonstrated, it was calculated to be negligible in the population as a whole. For those children who did succumb to acute neurological disease, it was suggested that there may have been pre-existing underlying brain or metabolic abnormalities, but the results of the research have not proven this conclusively.

These events represent the hazardous side of consumer activism. As you saw in chapter 3 with the case of Agent Orange related disease, agitation by public lobbies has in the past created pressures for health care reform, with positive outcomes. However, the recent fear over side effects from immunisation has acted as a deterrent to many parents, with the result that Australia currently has its lowest rate of childhood immunisation in many years. Other problems include variability in adhering to immunisation schedules within different families, and the inconsistencies of parents immunising children even within one family. In one study conducted in Kuala Lumpur, it was found that, despite government subsidisation for immunisation, many people had immunised their children for one disease but neglected to obtain the full coverage (Gan 1993). A survey in one State of Australia revealed that although most children start the immunisation schedule, many either do not complete the schedule or complete it too late (Hanna et al. 1994).

In the US, where it is a prerequisite of entry to school that children be immunised, research studies have shown that where the parents do not obtain the first scheduled immunisation, they tend to not start immunisation at all (Hanna et al. 1994). In some cases, family mobility prevents the children from finishing a course of immunisation once they have begun. In other cases, parents have been unable to keep track of whether each child has had the full schedule. One answer, according to Canadian authorities, is to consider re-initiating immunisation for all children beginning school (or pre-school) where there is no available record that the child has had the full schedule of immunisations. Evidently, better surveillance is required and, perhaps more importantly, public campaigning in all countries to provide parents with accurate and rational information on the necessity for children to be immunised. As Thompson (1997) clearly explains, the health of the entire community is at stake:

> *If none of the children in a child care centre of 150 children were immunised, and a whooping cough outbreak occurred, about 135 children would come down with the disease. On average, one child would get encephalitis as a result of the disease. If every child in the centre was immunised correctly with four doses of DTP, possibly one child at the centre every 170 years could get encephalitis as a result of the immunisation (p. 8).*

Goals for child health

The major health issues for children's health in today's society include the following:
- safety/injury prevention
- immunisation
- healthy lifestyle/fitness/activity
- diet/nutrition
- mental/emotional health.

In order to achieve child health in any community, *all* of these risk factors must be acknowledged and incorporated into the goals and targets of the community. An intersectoral approach is essential and this is congruent with the strategies of the Ottawa Charter for Health Promotion

(WHO-Health and Welfare Canada, 1986). The five strategies for child health are as described below.

Building healthy public policy

Healthy public policy for children involves ensuring that policies governing illness and injury surveillance, health and fitness promotion, family support systems and sustainable environments are all developed coherently, so that all influences on health are acknowledged by society. This includes developing and monitoring manufacturing safety standards, housing standards and legislation (such as that governing seat-belts and bicycle helmets) that guides safe behaviour. Laws mandating the licensing of child care workers also fall into this category. In some cases, and in some communities, new priorities for health targets will need to be set. For example, where opportunities for immunisation are inequitable, or where access to of physical fitness or mental health initiatives for children are not available, the community may have to press for policy changes.

Policies must respond to children's holistic needs for balance and potential. This means that physical education programs must be considered integral to education programs and not just an 'add-on' to learning. Sporting activities and recreational facilities must be secured to offer opportunities for building strong bodies and spirited minds, and these must be considered as important to community development as economic ventures. Resources must also be allocated for parent education and parent support, particularly for working parents and separated parents, who need to be equally aware of and involved in sustaining the health of their children. Policy development for healthy children thus exemplifies the need for intersectoral collaboration at all levels. This includes communication and co-operative decision-making by agencies responsible for decisions related to family law, local education, health, sport and recreation departments, local councils, state and provincial governments, consumer groups and the environment.

Perhaps the most important policy decision governments must make is to acknowledge the importance of antenatal care in sustaining the health of the entire population. The profound impact of nutrition on health has become unquestionable throughout the past several decades. Research studies have addressed the relationship between nutrient and vitamin requirements *in utero* and subsequent states of health and illness in later life. Antenatal care that ensures adequate dietary intake and careful monitoring of growth patterns has the capacity to increase lifespan, enhance quality of life and reduce the cost of illness care for the population, making it the most important policy focus in public health.

Creating supportive environments

This strategy includes planning for child-friendly physical environments, developing school-based safety education programs and providing resources for positive parenting. Any attempt to reduce childhood accident rates must include community-wide initiatives such as introducing bicycle paths, protected play areas and safe playground equipment. The importance of the setting for health and safety must be recognised. Children spend a large proportion of their time in school settings, and there must be adequate resourcing within health budgets to ensure that schools are safe, and healthy settings within which young children can not only learn, but thrive.

Supportive environments for child health also include those conducive to healthy pregnancy. Services that provide health surveillance and monitoring for pregnant women must be widely available, and this includes workplace-based resources. With the demise of child health nurses in many neighbourhoods, new parents must have access to alternative sources of information and support. Parenting resource centres should be a priority in both urban and rural communities, and they must provide information that is culturally appropriate and family friendly.

Strengthening community action

In order to empower communities, parents, grandparents, teachers and others need to be made aware of their community's strengths and resources as well as the areas of particular risk to young children. Health advocacy involves validating their ideas and informed choices by assisting them to implement health and safety initiatives at the local level. Grandparent-to-child programs have been established in some areas with overwhelming success. The underlying premise of these programs is surrogate caring. Many older people live at a distance from their grandchildren; likewise, other children have a need for grandparenting but, for whatever reason, have no grandparent available to them. The result of bringing the two together is increased caring and a sense of intergenerational connectedness. Another advantage is that for sole supporting working parents, an extra support person who is also older and mature can be invaluable in helping to care for children.

Parent-to-parent programs are another way of strengthening community action. These programs, which allow opportunities for sharing, often provide an outlet for new parents to express concerns and to share resources and strategies for parenting. In addition, they provide an opportunity to socialise with others in similar situations, and thus guard against the ill effects of the isolation that new parenting often brings. The health professional's role in such groups is a facilitative one, bringing people together to strengthen their combined resources and helping them compile a data base of resources for any additional services required.

Developing personal skills

It is up to health, education and community welfare groups to ensure that the community has appropriate educational opportunities for skills development for health carers, teachers, parents and the children themselves. This is fundamental to effective teamwork that focuses on the child, rather than the vested interests of the various people involved with helping children maintain health. Eliminating teacher in-service sessions is often excused on the basis of competing priorities; but teachers need to be constantly updated on the changing needs of children and the latest findings relevant to their health. Similarly, child care workers need to have access to the most up-to-date information and the evolving research information that guides their practices. Developing and updating personal skills needs to be viewed in terms of the inextricable link between physical and emotional health in pregnant women, their children, and the population in general. Care must therefore be taken in setting goals so that child health goals are seen in the context of developing healthy parents and healthy parenting.

Reorienting health services

In the past, public health services included a relatively equitable distribution of child health nurses throughout the community to support and assist parents in maintaining the health of their children. In Australia, the role and function of the child health nurse is changing and, increasingly, child health surveillance and family support is becoming integrated into the generalist community health nursing role. The end result of this rationalisation of services is inequity in service provision, with some families enjoying neighbourhood centres for monitoring and guidance while others, particularly those in rural areas or in the outer suburbs of large cities, have to rely on central hospital-based services and their local GP. For the health professional, in many cases no central resource centre exists, and information and/or support related to changing practices or culturally appropriate services is difficult to access.

In the UK, where community health services are provided on a geographic basis, the situation is less acute. Health visitors and district nurses are responsible for a geographically determined segment of the population and they assume responsibility for most of the family's health needs in collaboration with a designated community GP. This ensures childhood screening, surveillance, family counselling and referrals to other services for all family members. A similar service is provided by public health nurses in Canada. In the US, where the system is dominated by a 'user pays' scheme, the cost of health care precludes this type of service for everyone.

The issue for all involved in child health is to recognise that the organisation of services is changing rapidly in response to shrinking health care budgets. In the interests of access and equity, all health professionals must work more closely together to ensure that families do not fall through the cracks in service provision. This involves greater teamwork than ever before, and careful evaluation of services and health outcomes. Regardless of the type of service, all health encounters should be carefully documented, a task that is made less onerous by the introduction of computers. It is also important to conduct systematic research into health issues and outcomes in a variety of contexts and with a focus on the environment. Many epidemiological investigations begin from a worker in the field noticing a cluster of certain types of illnesses, or observing the outcomes of a change in the health environment. This type of informal research is integral to the role of all health professionals and is absolutely essential to heighten awareness of the interplay between the environment, individual and group behaviour, and biological factors. Research findings must be used to inform and thus empower the community to become involved in decision-making related to health services. This creates health advocacy strategies that are congruent with primary health care principles of access, equity, cultural sensitivity and self-determinism.

THINKING CRITICALLY

Child health in the community

▶ Identify five important influences on child health in today's society.

▶ Identify four agencies responsible for some aspect of child safety in your community.

▶ Compare and contrast the health and safety risks of school children in the following:

• a rural community where the majority of children live on farms

• an inner-city neighbourhood with a majority of families of low socioeconomic status

• a middle-class oceanside community

• a suburban community 15 km from a large metropolitan area.

▶ Describe two goals and two targets for improving the health and safety of children in your community.

▶ Describe three activities in a local school or recreational setting that illustrate primary health care in practice for young children. For each, explain the importance of the setting in promoting child health.

REFERENCES

Aber, J., Bennett, N., Conley, D. & Li, J. 1997, 'The effects of poverty on child health and development', *Annual Review of Public Health*, vol. 18, pp. 463–83.

Acton, C., Nixon, J. & Clark, R. 1997, 'Bicycle riding and maxillofacial trauma in young children', *Medical Journal of Australia*, vol. 165, no. 5, pp 249-51.

Anderson, J., Martin, J., Mullen, P., Romans, S. & Hertison, P. 1993, 'The prevalence of childhood sexual abuse. Experiences in a community sample of women', *Journal of the American Academy of Child and Adolescent Psychiatry*, vol. 32, pp. 911–19.

Australian Institute of Health and Welfare 1996, *Australia's Health*, 1996, AGPS, Canberra.

Baker, C. 1994, 'School health policy issues', *Nursing and Health Care*, vol. 15, no. 4, pp. 179–84.

Barker, D., Osmond, C. & Simmonds 1990, 'Foetal and placental size and risk of hypertension in adult life', *British Medical Journal*, vol. 301, pp. 259–62.

Bauman, A. 1996, 'Asthma in Australia: dawning of a public health approach', *Australian and New Zealand Journal of Public Health*, vol. 20, no. 1, pp. 7–8.

Beeber, S. 1996, 'Smoking and childhood asthma', *Journal of Pediatric Health Care*, vol. 10 no. 2, pp. 58–62.

Blank Sherman, J., Alexander, M., Gomez, D., Kim, M. & Marole, P. 1992, 'Intervention program for obese school children', *Journal of Community Health Nursing*, vol. 9, no. 3, pp. 183–90.

Bower, C., Blum, L., O'Daly, K., Higgins, C., Loutsky, F. et al. 1997, 'Promotion of folate for the prevention of neural tube defects: knowledge and use of periconceptional folic acid supplements in Western Australia, 1992 to 1995', *Australian and New Zealand Journal of Public Health*, vol. 21, no. 7, pp. 716–21.

Britton, H. & Hansen, K. 1997, 'Sexual abuse', *Clinical Obstetrics and Gynecology*, vol. 40, no. 1, pp. 226–40.

Bronner, Y. 1996, 'Nutritional status outcomes for children: ethnic, cultural and environmental contexts', *Journal of the American Dietetic Association*, vol. 96, pp. 891–903.

Burgess, M. 1997, 'Immunisation in the year 2020 and beyond', *Australian and New Zealand Journal of Public Health*, vol. 21, no. 2, pp. 115–16.

Bush, P. & Iannotti, R. 1993, 'Alcohol, cigarette, and marijuana use among fourth-grade urban school children in 1988/89 and 1990/91', *American Journal of Public Health*, vol. 83, no. 1, pp. 111–15.

Canadian Red Cross Society 1995, *Childsafe Manual*, The Red Cross Society, Ottawa.

Child Accident Prevention Foundation of Australia 1997, *Kidsafe House*, CAPFA, Queensland Health, Brisbane.

Childsecure 1997, *Big Safety for Little Kids*, Childsecure, Bethesda.

Chu, C. 1994, 'An integrated approach to workplace health promotion', in *Ecological Public Health: From Vision to Practice*, eds C. Chu & R. Simpson, Institute of Applied Environmental Research, Brisbane, pp. 182–94.

Cliff, J. & Noormahomed, A. 1993, 'The impact of war on children's health in Mozambique', *Social Science and Medicine*, vol. 36, no. 7, pp. 843–8.

Cloke, C. 1997, 'Save the children', *Nursing Times*, vol. 93, no. 14, pp. 35–7.

Cochi, F., Hull, H. & Ward, N. 1995, 'To conquer poliomyelitis forever', *The Lancet*, vol. 345, pp. 1589–90.

Connell, H. 1989, 'Stress in childhood', in *Community Child Health: An Australian Perspective*, eds G. Vimpani & T. Parry, Churchill-Livingstone, Melbourne, pp. 423–38.

Cox, E. 1993, 'The place of family in social policy', *Family Matters*, vol. 34, pp. 28–30.

Cunningham, J., O'Connor, G., Dockery, D. & Speizer, F. 1996, 'Environmental tobacco smoke, wheezing, and asthma in children in 24 communities', *American Journal of Critical Care Medicine*, vol. 153, pp. 218–24.

Devereux, G., Ayatollahi, T., Ward., R., Bromly, C., Bourke, S., Stenton, S. et al. 1996, 'Asthma, airways responsiveness and air pollution in two contrasting districts of northern England', *Thorax*, vol. 51, no. 2, pp. 169–74.

Dickerson, J. 1995, 'Good preconception care starts in school', *Modern Midwife*, Nov., pp. 15–18.

Dunst, C. & Trivette, C. 1996, 'Empowerment, effective help-giving practices and family-centered care', *Pediatric Nursing*, vol. 22, no. 4, pp. 334–43.

English, P., Eskenazi, B. & Christianson, R. 1994, 'Black-white differences in serum continine levels among pregnant women and subsequent effects on infant birth weight', *American Journal of Public Health*, vol. 84, pp. 1439–43.

Fancourt, R. 1997, 'Child health in times of social and economic change', *New Zealand Medical Journal*, vol. 110, pp. 95–7.

Fanos, J. & Johnson, J. 1994, 'CF carrier status: the importance of not knowing', *American Journal of Human Genetics*, vol. 55, no. 3 (suppl.), p. A292.

Farley, C., Haddad, S. & Brown, B. 1996, 'The effects of a four-year program promoting bicycle helmet use among children in Quebec', *American Journal of Public Health*, vol. 86, no. 1, pp. 46–51.

Fink, R. 1989, 'Issues and problems in measuring children's health status in community health research', *Social Science and Medicine*, vol. 29, no. 6, pp. 715–19.

Fleming, J. 1997, 'Prevalence of childhood sexual abuse in a community sample of Australian women,' *Medical Journal of Australia*, vol. 166, pp. 65–8.

Fleming, J., Mullen, P. & Bammer, G. 1997, 'A study of potential risk factors for sexual abuse in childhood', *Social Science and Medicine*, vol. 21, no. 1, pp. 49–58.

Frank, J. 1995, 'Why "population health"?', commentary, *Canadian Journal of Public Health*, vol. 86, no. 3, pp. 162–4.

Gan, C. 1993, 'Utilization of maternal and child health facilities by the urban poor of Kuala Lumpur', *Southeast Asian Journal of Tropical Medicine and Public Health*, vol. 24, no. 2, pp. 302–6.

Gans, K., Bain, S., Plotkin, B., Lasater, T. & Carleton, R. 1994, 'Implementation and institutionalization of heart health programming in schools: The Pawtucket heart health program experience', *Journal of Health Education*, vol. 25, no. 2, pp. 89–96.

Green, L. & Ottoson, J. 1994, *Community Health*, 7th edn, Mosby, St Louis.

Grey, M. 1993, 'Stressors and children's health', *Journal of Pediatric Nursing*, vol. 8, no. 2, pp. 85–91.

Grubbs, L. 1993, 'The critical role of exercise in weight control', *Nurse Practitioner*, vol. 18, no. 4, pp. 21–6.

Grundy, M. 1995, 'Children plumping up', *Aussie Sport Action*, vol. 6, no. 4, pp. 10–11.

Hammett, W. & Kirby, S. 1997, *Protecting Young Children in the Home*, North Carolina Extension Service, North Carolina State University, Charlotte.

Hanna, J., Wakefield, J., Doolan, C. & Messner, J. 1994, 'Childhood immunisation: factors associated with failure to complete the recommended schedule by two years of age', *Australian Journal of Public Health*, vol. 181, pp. 15–21.

Heath, G., Pratt, M., Warren. C. & Kann, L. 1994, 'Physical activity patterns in American high school students: results from the 1990 Youth Risk Behaviour Survey', *Archives of Pediatrics and Adolescent Medicine*, vol. 148, no. 11, pp. 1131–6.

Henderson, D. 1995, 'Vaccination policies and practices', *Australian Journal of Public Health*, vol. 19, pp. 634–8.

Hertz, E., Hebert, J. & Landon, J. 1994, 'Social and environmental factors and life expectancy, infant mortality, and maternal mortality rates: results of a cross-national comparison', *Social Science and Medicine*, July, vol. 39, no. 1, pp 105–14.

Igoe, J. & Speer, S. 1992, 'The community health nurse in the schools', in *Community Health Nursing: Process and Practice for Promoting Health*, 3rd edn, eds A. Stanhope & J. Lancaster, Mosby, St Louis, pp. 707–30.

Jacobson, L. & Wilkinson, C. 1994, 'Review of teenage health: time for a new direction', *British Journal of General Practice*, vol. 44, pp. 420–4.

Johnson, C., Miranda, L., Sherman, A. & Weill, J. 1991, *Child Poverty in America*, Children's Defense Fund, Washington.

Knutson, L., Leavitt, R. & Sarton, K. 1995, 'Race, ethnicity and other factors influencing children's health and disability: Implications for pediatric physical therapists', *Pediatric Physical Therapy*, vol. 7, pp. 175–83.

Lee, P. & Paxman, D. 1997, 'Reinventing public health', *Annual Review of Public Health*, vol. 18, pp. 1–35.

Martin, D. 1992, 'Children in peril: a mandate for change in health care policies for low-income children', *Family Community Health*, vol. 15, no. 1, pp. 75–90.

Mason, J., Musgrove, P., Watson, F. & Habicht, J. 1996, 'Undernutrition', in *Quantifying Global Burden Health Risks: The Burden of Disease Attributable to Selected Risk Factors*, eds C. Murray & A. Lopez, Harvard University Press, Cambridge.

McEvoy, A. & Erikson, E. 1990, *Youth and Exploitation*, Learning Publications, Inc., Montreal.

Medical Research Council Vitamin Study Research Group 1991, 'Prevention of neural tube defects: results of the Medical Research Council Vitamin Study', *The Lancet*, vol. 338, pp. 131–7.

Moller, J. & Kreisfeld, R. 1997, *Progress and Current Issues in Child Injury Prevention*, National Injury Surveillance Unit, Australian Institute of Health and Welfare, Canberra.

Montgomery, L., Kiely, J. & Pappas, G. 1996, 'The effects of poverty, race, and family structure on US children's health: data from the NHIS, 1978 through 1980 and 1989 through 1991', *American Journal of Public Health*, vol. 86, no. 10, pp. 1401–5.

Moss-Morris, R. & Paterson, J. 1995, 'Understanding children's concepts of health and illness: implications for developmental therapists', *Physical and Occupational Therapy in Pediatrics*, vol. 14, no. 3/4, pp. 95–108.

Mulroy, E. 1997, 'Building a neighbourhood network: interorganizational collaboration to prevent child abuse and neglect', *Social Work*, vol. 42, no. 3, pp. 255–64.

Nagel, D., Putnam, F. & Noll, J. 1997, 'Disclosure patterns of sexual abuse and psychological functioning at a one-year follow-up', *Social Science and Medicine*, vol. 21, no. 2, pp. 137–47.

Naughton, G. & Carlson, J. 1995, 'Physiological aspects of youth sport: developmental or detrimental?' *Sport Health*, vol. 13, no. 20, pp. 5–7.

Neylon, J. 1993, 'Health promotion for school children', *Nursing Standard*, vol. 7, no. 30, pp. 37–40.

Nuckolls, K., Cassel, J. & Kaplan, B. 1972, 'Psychosocial assets, life crisis and the prognosis of pregnancy', *American Journal of Epidemiology*, vol. 95, no. 5, pp. 431–41.

Obeid, A. 1997, 'Preventing childhood accidents: the poverty factor', *Health Visitor*, vol. 70, no. 1, pp. 30–1.

Peterson, L. & Stern, B. 1997, 'Family processes and child risk for injury', *Behaviour Research and Therapy*, vol. 35, no. 3, pp. 179–90.

Powell, C. 1997, 'Protecting children in the accident and emergency department', *Accident and Emergency Nursing*, vol. 5, pp. 76–80.

Rieger, K. 1991, 'Motherhood ideology' in *Issues Facing Australian Families*, eds R. Batten, W. Weeks & J. Wilson, Longman Cheshire, Melbourne, pp. 46–53.

Romans, S. 1997, 'Childhood sexual abuse: concerns and consequences', *Medical Journal of Australia*, vol. 166, pp. 59–60.

Rushton, C., McEnhill, M. & Armstrong, L. 1996, 'Establishing therapeutic boundaries as patient advocates', *Pediatric Nursing*, vol. 22, no. 3, pp. 186–9.

Schootman, M., Fuortes, L., Zwerling, C., Albanese, M & Watson, C. 1993, 'Safety behaviour among Iowa junior high and high school students', *American Journal of Public Health*, vol. 83, no. 11, pp. 1628–30.

Shah, R. 1997, 'It is easier to build strong children than to mend broken men', *Iowa Medicine*, Mar., pp. 110–11.

Simons-Morton, B., McKenzie, T., Stone, E., Mitchell, P., Osganian, V. et al. 1997, 'Physical activity in a multiethnic population of third graders in four states', *American Journal of Public Health*, vol. 87, no. 1, pp. 45–50.

Sleet, D. 1990, 'Perspectives on childhood injury and injury prevention in the United States, WA', *Child Injury Prevention*, May, pp. 32–4.

Stevenson, M., Lo, S., Laing, B. & Jamrozik, K. 1992, 'Childhood pedestrian injuries in the Perth metropolitan area', *Medical Journal of Australia*, vol. 156, pp. 234–8.

Thompson, R., Rivara, F. & Thompson, D. 1989, 'A case-control study of the effectiveness of bicycle safety helmets', *New England Journal of Medicine*, vol. 320, no. 21, pp. 1361–7.

Thompson, S. 1997, 'Vaccination: protection at what price?' *Australian and New Zealand Journal of Public Health*, vol. 21, no. 1 (suppl.), pp. 1–8.

Veale, A., Peat, J., Tovey, E., Salome, C., Thompson, J. et al. 1996, 'Asthma and atopy in four rural Australian aboriginal communities', *Medical Journal of Australia*, vol. 165, no. 4, pp. 192–6.

Vimpani, G. & Parry, T. (eds) 1989, *Community Child Health in Australia*, Churchill-Livingstone, Melbourne.

Wade, F., Chapman, A. & Foot, H. 1981, 'The physical environment and child pedestrian accidents in the United Kingdom', *Man-Environment Systems*, vol. 11, pp. 25–30.

Whitehead, M. 1995, 'Tackling inequalities: a review of policy initiatives', in *Tackling Inequalities in Health*, eds M. Benezeval, K. Judge & M. Whitehead, King's Fund, London, pp. 22–52.

Williams, J. & Lessick, M. 1996, 'Genome research: Implications for children', *Pediatric Nursing*, vol. 22, no. 1, pp. 40–7.

Winn, D., Agran, P. & Castillo, D. 1991, 'Pedestrian injuries to children younger than five years of age', *Pediatrics*, vol. 88, no. 40, pp. 776–82.

Wiseman, H. 1995, 'Accidental childhood poisoning', *Health Visitor*, vol. 68, no. 4, pp. 163–4.

World Bank 1991, *Tobacco Use: A Public Disaster*, The World Bank, New York.

World Health Organization 1996, *The World Health Report 1996: Fighting Disease, Fostering Development*, WHO, Geneva.

World Health Organization-Health and Welfare Canada-CPHA, 1986, 'Ottawa Charter for Health Promotion,' *Canadian Journal of Public Health*, vol. 77, no. 12, pp. 425–30.

Zhang, J., & Savitz, D. 1996, 'Exercise during pregnancy among US women' *Annals of Epidemiology*, vol. 6, no. 1, pp. 53–9.

6 Healthy adolescents

Adolescence is one of the most critical stages of a person's development, for it is in this crucial transition from childhood to adulthood that many risky behaviours are experimented with and sometimes adopted as lifestyle patterns. What distinguishes the adolescent progressing through the tortuous path to healthy adulthood from others who fall victim to high-risk behaviours such as smoking, overeating, abusing alcohol or other harmful substances, unsafe sexual activities and self-inflicted injury remains a mystery to health professionals. This chapter explores some of the research that has attempted to illuminate the various factors related to adolescent health status: risk factors that precipitate unhealthy adolescence, and some of the health resources that would facilitate healthy adolescence.

Objectives

By the end of this chapter you will be able to:

- *identify the two most important influences on healthy adolescence*

- *describe at least four factors that put adolescents at risk for ill health*

- *discuss family issues influencing adolescent health and wellbeing*

- *identify three goals for sustaining adolescent health in a community*

- *explain how a primary health care framework can be used in planning for improvements to adolescent health.*

The healthy adolescent

When most people think of healthy adolescents they usually imagine physically fit young people engaged in social activities —at least that is what the media attempts to portray in magazines, movies and commercials. This is a picture of balance and potential, of happy, physically well people striving to reach their life goals. But in reality, many young people's lives contradict this image. Frustrated by societal expectations, information overload, forecasts of gloomy employment prospects and retracting family support, some teenagers suffer from anxiety, depression and poor physical health. Maintaining a 'mix' of emotional, social and physical wellbeing is therefore one of the greatest challenges of the adolescent period, and often it is the vigilant eye of the school nurse, teacher or sports coach that identifies signs of distress or ill health. Understanding the dynamics of healthy adolescence is therefore fundamental to health advocacy, and once again our model of factors influencing health (figure 6.1) provides a guide to examining this important stage of life.

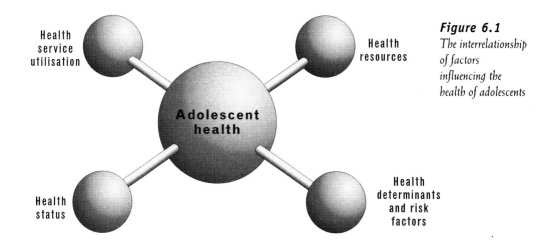

Figure 6.1
The interrelationship of factors influencing the health of adolescents

Health determinants and risk factors

In adolescence, all energies are focused on preparing for adulthood, and sculpting an adult identity seems to take precedence over other issues (Erikson 1963). Young people 'try on' a range of identities to develop a sense of themselves in relation to the world and others. Many find this difficult, particularly balancing these changes with maintaining supportive relationships with family and friends. Researchers report that many young people suffer from increased alienation and emotional distress during this period of rapid change, because of the erosion of families, schools and other institutions that in the past provided a scaffold for development (Bronfenbrenner 1986). Some of this erosion can be linked to a climate of economic restraint, and the pressures on institutions to do more with less. Also, to some extent the problems of young people are related to their expectations today, which by far surpass those of previous generations. But personal expectations are embedded in societal expectations, which engulf and often overwhelm young people just when they are supposed to be gaining the freedom to be individuals. A common conviction among those attempting to help guide adolescents to become healthy adults is that the problems of youth are complex and continue to be a major public health problem.

Mental health issues

Researchers have examined the associations between emotional distress in adolescence and the health problems of young people (Barron & Yoest 1994). Many health planners assert that mental health problems such as depression, youth suicide, health damaging behaviours and the alienation of young people are among the most pressing problems for the new millenium (Jacobson & Wilkinson 1994; Lamarine 1995; Sawyer & Kosky 1996).

A large proportion of young people's emotional distress stems from relationship problems which, during adolescence, seem to invade all facets of their lives. This is magnified considerably for the 5–10% of adolescents who who are gay, lesbian or bisexual (Nelson 1997). A heterosexist society often leads to feelings of stigma and social isolation, which create an additional strain on the gay person's transition through adolescence. Many young gay people become victims of family or societal violence, and fall prey to unhealthy lifestyles. As a result, they are over-represented in the statistics for depression, anxiety disorders, substance abuse, homelessness, sexually transmitted diseases and youth suicide (Nelson 1997).

Adolescents in general are at risk of responding to stress in ways that are less than helpful, particularly with the pressures of studing and/or balancing work and family relationships. One of the greatest difficulties in helping them is their hesitancy to use traditional health services. Another problem has been called the 'inverse care law', which contends that those most at risk are least likely to seek or want advice (Jacobson & Wilkinson 1994).

Homelessness

When difficulties with family members cannot be resolved, many run away from home, as do as many as one million adolescents in the US each year (McEvoy & Erikson 1990). Some return several times; others fail to find a niche within which to grow and find a direction, and instead revert to a life on the streets. This group is now recognised as a major health problem in many communities, particularly large inner city areas, where they are easy prey for exploitation within the world of drugs and prostitution. Often their health issues are masked by the stigma of homelessness, which sees them subjected to moral rather than public health attention, much like the victims of HIV infection in the early days of that epidemic.

The homeless are at risk for a host of different illnesses, addictions and mental instability (Breakey 1997). The question is whether there have been any real public health gains for young people in the past few decades. At the turn of last century, the problems of youth were related to infectious diseases, being unemployed and living in large, inner city areas with poor hygiene, and insufficient clothing, heating and nutritious food (Vimpani & Parry 1989). Today, many homeless youth live in exactly these conditions. The problem requires a concerted, intersectoral response that recognises that adequate housing, income support, education and employment are funda-mental to healthy lives (Breakey 1997). For many homeless youth, lack of these essentials leads to a range of physical and emotional problems.

Suicide

Regardless of whether the family home is abandoned, some adolescents find it impossible to gain a sense of the present or the future, and instead decide to end their lives. Youth suicide rates have reached alarming proportions in many countries (Runyan & Gerken 1989; AIHW 1995). Despite some documented evidence for a link between social disadvantage and suicide, suicide rates in third-world countries are markedly lower than in industri-alised nations. In the US, the spread of cases is interesting. Suicide among white males is the third-largest cause of death for American adolescents, at an annual rate of 11 per 100,000 population, yet the rate for Afro-Americans is roughly half that for the more privileged white Americans (Cantor, Slater & Najman 1995; Green & Ottoson 1994).

In the UK, the incidence of successful suicides is somewhat lower, at 6 per 100,000 among males and 1 to 2 per 100,000 among females between the ages of sixteen and nineteen (NHS Health Advisory Service

1995). In Australia, the suicide rate among this age group is the highest of all the industrialised countries, with 15 per 100,000 for males and one per 100,000 for females (ABS 1996). There are now more deaths in Australia from suicide than from motor vehicle crashes, which have always accounted for a large proportion of injury to young people (AIHW 1995). In some cases the rates of suicide are underestimated. Suicide by motor vehicle crash is generally difficult to detect, as is suicide by overdose in a drug abuser. The rates are also affected by the method used. Males tend to use firearms, with dire consequences, whereas females tend to attempt poisoning, not always successfully. For both sexes, poisoning by motor vehicle exhaust has become a more common means of suicide; drowning, jumping from high places, and cutting and stabbing are used less frequently (AIHW 1995).

The research is guarded over what types of problems and circumstances will tip a vulnerable person over the edge. Some studies have found a correlation between suicide rates in the population and unemployment (Morrell et al. 1993). But this is a complex relationship influenced by many individual, social and cultural factors (Cantor & Slater 1997). West and Sweeting's (1996) research in the UK suggests that unemployment is damaging to mental health, even though some people may be unemployed because of illness. They conclude that fear or anticipation of unemployment may also affect mental health and may contribute to the overall grim picture that puts adolescents at risk for suicide.

Brent's (1995) review of the literature reveals that the most important set of risk factors for completed and attempted suicide in adolescents are those of mental disorders and substance abuse. He reports that over 90% of all youthful suicide victims have suffered from at least one psychiatric disorder, and names this as *the* most important risk factor. However, stressful life events, particularly if there have been multiple stressors, lack of family cohesion, interpersonal conflict, interpersonal loss, personal and parental legal/disciplinary problems, physical/sexual abuse, a recent move and exposure to suicide, all may lead a young person to this extreme act (Brent 1995). Another group of researchers suggests that the two main issues that lead an adolescent to suicidal thoughts, and thus to attempt suicide, are family and school problems. They claim that it is not necessarily a person's academic performance that causes the distress, but rather the disparity between academic performance and the expectations of either the teenager or his or her family (Dukes & Lorch 1989).

Concern over youth suicide is one of the things that has precipitated increased interest in the health issues of young people. Until the 1990s, when these rates skyrocketed, the needs of adolescents were either hidden or ignored by many health authorities. West and Sweeting (1996) attribute this to the traditional gap between paediatrics and adult medicine, the relatively low use of medical services among young people, and the use of broad bands for official statistics, especially mortality rates, which often obscure the adolescent period. A further reason relates to societal impressions of the teenage years as a time of fitness and wellness. This notion is currently being dispelled by surveys of young people themselves and, unfortunately, actions which decry a healthy state of transition (Jacobson & Wilkinson 1994).

Studies in recent years have found that young people, especially young women, report high levels of symptoms such as respiratory complaints, headaches, stomach disorders, skin problems and concerns about weight, as well as mental health problems such as nervousness, anxiety, sleep problems and depression (West & Sweeting 1996). These authors suggest that the findings of this body of research may represent only the tip of the iceberg. In a major review of psychosocial disorders among young people, Rutter and Smith (1995) argue that, in contrast to physical health, mental health has deteriorated since the Second World War. Young women seem to suffer more mental health problems than males, but this may be attributed to the fact that females have a greater willingness to admit to psychological distress, and thus seek help for it (D'Espaignet & Rickwood 1995).

Both male and female adolescents today find themselves in a social malaise, where their environment is pervaded by economic recession, unemployment, low-paid jobs and the sense of having no future (West & Sweeting 1996). Paradoxically, this sense of futility occurs within a context of information overload, so the young person is on the one hand bombarded by stimuli engendering action, and on the other by messages that say 'don't bother'. Many react to these mixed messages by becoming anxious and depressed. Some go on to manifest suicidal behaviours, crime, alcohol and drug abuse, depression and eating disorders.

Eating disorders

The two most common eating disorders affecting adolescents are anorexia nervosa and bulimia, both of which are thought to be a product of social preoccupation with physical attractiveness in general, and thinness in particular (Dixey 1996). Anorexics avoid food to the point of emaciation, while bulimics tend to binge on large volumes of food and then purge their bodies by laxatives, self-induced vomiting, excessive exercise, or a combination of these methods (Estok & Rudy 1996). The malnourishment caused by both these conditions puts young people at risk for dehydration, infections, cardiac problems, menstrual problems and, for those with bulimia, oesophageal irritation and dental erosion (Estok & Rudy 1996). An increase in the prevalence of eating disorders is becoming evident in all but the developing countries (Wakeling 1996). However, the incidence has recently shown an increase in second-generation migrants from developing nations and many non-Caucasian populations (Nadaoka et al. 1996; Wakeling 1996). Thus eating disorders have become a worldwide public health problem.

As with many of the problems of youth, researchers hold mixed views about what prompts a young person to become anorexic or bulimic. The spectrum of symptoms is generally considered to result from a combination of emotional, physical, sociological and family factors, and it has recently been hypothesised that there may even be a genetic predisposition for some (Zerbe 1996). Population studies have concluded that the increased prevalence is connected with social changes in everyday life, such as the greater availability of food, and changes in the role of women in society. This is illustrated by women in the urban workforce becoming increasingly preoccupied with their appearance, compared with previous times when most remained in the home (Nadaoka et al. 1996).

Studies in the UK reveal that half of all British women are overweight, so the fact that 60% are dieting is a good thing (Dixey 1995). The other side of this equation is, however, the link between dieting and eating disorders. Dieting is thought to potentiate disordered eating through cycles of dieting and regaining weight (Dixey 1995). However, dieting remains popular, especially among women in the middle classes. This is thought to be related to class identity, where these women engage in conspicuous 'healthist' behaviours (such as dieting) for purposes of 'differentiation and mutual affirmation' (Crawford, in Dixey 1995, p. 52).

Research in the US reveals increased rates of eating disorders among young men, especially male homosexuals and those engaged in sports that emphasise thinness and appearance, such as dance, gymnastics, running or rowing. In some cases, addiction to activity also becomes part of the eating disorder syndrome (Zerbe 1996). Most studies, from various parts of the world, conclude that there is a strong relationship between eating disorders and depression and low self-esteem, especially when this is manifest in obsessive-compulsive traits, and so the only thing that seems certain is that the eating disorder seems to occur as the culmination of some type of emotional turmoil (Gotestam, Eriksen & Hagen 1995; Willcox & Sattler 1996; Zerbe 1996).

Many blame the media for women's preoccupation with thinness on the basis that the mass media is the main dictator of society's female norms (Tiggermann 1995). Some responsibility must also be apportioned to the beauty and fashion industry, and community groups have been lobbying in several countries to promote images of normal-sized women rather than the waif-like models currently projected in magazines and other media. The dangerous message in most of the fashion magazines is one of overvaluing appearance as a measure of personal worth (Zerbe 1996). This kind of thinking needs to be overturned from a very young age, particularly when younger children are constantly bombarded with pictures of ultra-thin models on television. Unfortunately, the insidious influence of these images is not usually felt until there are severe symptoms and an entrenched, disordered body image that may take years to reverse. Health professionals must become aware of the influence of these images on the health and wellbeing of young people and join consumer groups in lobbying for change. Their guidance must be based on recognised patterns of behaviour and an understanding of the outcomes of eating disorders, and this information must be provided to parents, sports coaches, teachers and all those involved with fostering healthy teenage development and progression into healthy adulthood.

Lifestyle choices

Although family and social factors often influence the extent to which adolescents can achieve high levels of health and wellness, lifestyle choices play a large part in determining how they will negotiate the transition into healthy adulthood. Gillis (1994) reports that the contribution of lifestyle choices to subsequent morbidity and mortality is greater in adolescents than in any other age groups. The most important of these choices are related to alcohol and drug consumption, smoking, safe sexual practices, diet and activity patterns. In many cases, the pattern for one of these behaviours is similar to that of the others. This is exemplified in some research carried out in the US, which identified a relationship between physical activity and several other health behaviours. The results of the study, which was conducted on a large, nationally representative sample, showed that little or no involvement in physical activity was associated with cigarette smoking, marijuana use, poor dietary habits, television viewing, failure to wear a seat-belt, and perception of low acdemic performance (Pate et al. 1996).

Researchers are thus beginning to refocus their investigations from studies of the risks related to one isolated behaviour to those which examine *patterns* of behaviour. Even the term *risk* has a different connotation today than in the past. Early associations of risk tended to calculate mathematical odds of something occurring, in much the same way as an habitual gambler would calculate the probability of winning. Today, the term 'risk' is associated with negative outcomes and is often used to link irresponsible behaviour to those outcomes (McKie et al. 1993). The danger inherent in this type of forecasting is that it allows health professionals to caution, or in some cases even badger, a person about his or her behaviour. This is in effect 'victim-blaming' and is incongruent with a primary health care approach in which the environment or social context is considered as important as individual behaviour. Within a primary health care perspective, healthful choices can only be made where there are healthy opportunities, complete with access and equity in the distribution of supportive mechanisms.

Recreational drug use

The importance of studying patterns of adolescent behaviour is best illustrated in the case of drug and alcohol consumption. Behaviours begun in adolescence may provide a 'gateway' for continuation or progression to greater levels of substance abuse in adulthood. Early detection of risky consumption patterns is therefore useful for anticipating what might happen in the future (Chou & Pickering 1992; Kandel, Yamaguchi & Chen 1992). In addition, despite wide and unresolved debate on the issue, experimentation with 'soft' substances such as alcohol and marijuana may lead to abuse of more lethal substances, or at least to a wider range of substances (Kandel 1975). A further point concerns the cumulative effect of toxic substances from adolescence to adulthood, which is poorly understood. In the absence of any clear dose–response data, *any* level of consumption of toxins such as nicotine and alcohol must be considered as a compromise to adult health status.

Factors associated with substance abuse in adolescents have been studied in many different settings. The research reveals a higher rate of substance abuse among school dropouts than among those who remain in school. Once again, this signals an important interaction between factors, in this case socioeconomic status and social opportunity. This interaction is evident in the fact that the dropout rate is highest in many groups who are socially disadvantaged (Swaim et al. 1997). Other interactions have been noted in relation to family violence. Young people who develop alcohol and drug problems often have been victimised by family violence and child mal-treatment (Miller, Maguin & Downs 1997). It may be inappropriate, however, to make any kind of generalisations about substance abusers, given that the culture within which they consume their preferred substances changes dramatically with time.

We cannot describe substance abuse as a single phenomenon, because of the wide variability in types and levels of abuse and abusers. Cocaine provides a case in point. In the 1980s many older adolescents and young adults who could afford cocaine began the habit of inhaling the substance through their nostrils. It was seen to be a drug they could manage while out for the evening, and it began to be associated with dancing and other party situations. In the 1990s public health officials have had to contend with a new type of cocaine addict—the injecting cocaine user, who tends to use the drug in private situations, as heroin has always been used. Informal reports reveal that the cocaine injector tends to become a bit 'crazy' when high, losing all sense of judgement, and it suspected that it is now cocaine, rather than heroin, users who are sharing needles, engaging in unprotected sex and thus spreading the HIV virus (Swaim et al. 1997).

Drugs in sport

One aspect of drug use that has thus far been poorly researched is the use of drugs in sport. Following such high-profile cases of abuse as Ben Johnson's positive drug test at the 1988 Olympics, and, more recently, the accusations of drug use among the Chinese swimming team at the 1996 Olympics, the public has become much more aware of the perva-siveness of drugs in sports. One little-known fact is that some psychoactive drugs designed to enhance performance actually *decrease* performance because of adverse cardiovascular effects and impaired judgement (Schwenk 1997). A major problem is that of anabolic steroids. Steroid use is becoming more prevalent among teenagers involved in sports despite tighter legislation, school-based education and drug testing in competitive events (Tanner, Miller & Alongi 1995). In two separate research studies conducted in the US, it was found that 14 to 15 years tends to be the age when teenagers begin to use steroids. Both studies revealed that just over 1% of females and 4 to 6% of males take steroids to increase strength and/or improve muscle mass (DuRant et al. 1993; Tanner et al. 1995).

Young people other than elite athletes take steroids because they believe it makes them look attractive, which is a major influence on most adolescents. The hazards of steroid use need to be recognised not only for the physiological effect of the drugs, but because adolescent users of anabolic steroids are also likely to use other drugs: marijuana, cocaine, cigarettes, smokeless tobacco, alcohol and mood-altering substances. Studies of these types of patterns of drug use also identify the added danger of sharing needles and the risk of HIV and other infections (D'Elio et al. 1993; DuRant et al. 1993). Any attempt at health education targeting adolescents must therefore take a comprehensive approach to encouraging healthy lifestyle change rather than singling out any one behaviour.

Tobacco smoking

Cigarette smoking is the largest preventable cause of death in the industrialised world (Breslow 1982). In Australia, an average of fifty deaths per day are directly related to smoking, and adolescents are the group most at risk for taking up smoking (Girgis et al. 1995). Recent studies on alcohol and drug use have found a pattern of association between smoking and drinking among Australian students in years seven, nine and eleven (Hibbert et al. 1995). These researchers found that frequent use of tobacco and alcohol was also associated with more frequent marijuana use, particularly for frequent drinkers. Interestingly, their study also revealed that coffee use is already common in the early teens, and this is a pattern of drug taking that extends into the rest of people's lives, once they develop a caffeine habit. This research looked at patterns of smoking and alcohol use, and found that the consumption of both nicotine and alcohol becomes more common in the mid-teens, with marijuana use most common in older teens. This pattern is consistent with the notion of a sequential progression in the initiation of drug use across the teen years; that is, using one drug often leads to using another.

Gender differences have also been evident in the research. A study by Hibbert and colleagues (1995) found that, like other American and British studies of gender differences in smoking rates, females smoke at a higher rate than males and are more likely to smoke on a regular basis than young men. The authors cite several studies linking smoking to cervical cancer, early menopause, complications of oral contraceptive use, unfavourable outcomes of pregnancy and vulnerability to lung cancer, concluding that smoking among female adolescents remains a serious public health problem. Another trend examined in the study indicated that older female adolescents are now smoking marijuana and drinking alcohol at similar rates to males, and this is cause for alarm as both genders consume alcohol at potentially health-threatening levels (Hibbert et al. 1995).

Smoking is a particular problem for countries like China, which contains one-fifth of the world's population and more than 30% of the world's smokers (Zhu et al. 1996). China now leads the world in tobacco production and the price is obvious, as more Chinese now die of lung cancer than any other cause. Based on the knowledge that the earlier a person begins to smoke, the more likely it is that they will become a regular smoker, a group of researchers recently conducted a large national study among Chinese elementary school children. Their findings revealed that most young people aged between ten and twelve begin to smoke as a result of peer pressure. As in other countries, there is a direct link between young people's smoking and low socioeconomic status, having parents, siblings or teachers who smoke, and not believing that smoking is harmful to health (Zhu et al. 1996). Health promotion efforts in that country thus need to focus on young people's beliefs and the effect of role modelling on their behaviour, in order to prevent the current alarming rates of smoking-related mortality from escalating further. This will require a collaborative approach from all levels of society.

Sexual health

Another area of high risk for adolescents is sexual behaviour. The two most important reasons for concern about sexual health practices are teenage pregnancy and sexually transmitted diseases. Both these outcomes of unprotected sex have a profound effect on adolescents, yet many young people still report that their education in sex, sexuality and sexually transmitted disease is either non-existent, inappropriate or acquired through their own sexual experience (Few, Hicken & Butterworth 1996). Researchers at the Alan Guttmacher Institute in the US report that 30 to 50% of teenagers have their first sex education course after grade ten, which for many is too late, as they have already been sexually active (Rodriquez & Moore 1996). Another view, however, is that regardless of the type or amount of education provided, adolescents may be at risk because messages or information are ignored or dismissed as not relevant to them. This may be linked to their stage of cognitive development in that without prior experience of a negative outcome they may be hesitant to take appropriate risk reduction steps.

This proposition was examined in the research conducted by Hewell and Andrews (1996), who studied contraceptive use among female adolescents who had experienced either an abortion or a negative pregnancy test. They found that 99% of the post-abortion group and 50% of those having a negative pregnancy test began to use reliable contraception immediately following; however, by the time of their follow-up clinic visit, those figures had dropped to 28% and 6% respectively. This led them to conclude, as had previous researchers, that risk-taking behaviours in adolescents are the result of short-term thinking and the propensity to not plan ahead or anticipate the consequences realistically (Fortenberry 1997; Hewell & Andrews 1996). For some reason, adolescents entertain the idea that they are magically protected from dangers that only happen to other people, a phenomenon some have called 'magical thinking' (Zigler & Stevenson-Finn 1987).

Teenage pregnancy

The teenage mother's developmental stage has profound effects on the outcomes of pregnancy. It is interesting that, despite the worldwide trend to greater use of contraception, there remains a rise in the proportion of teenage pregnancies (Jacobson & Wilkinson 1994). The UK has one of the highest rates of teenage pregnancy in Western Europe. Half the pregnancies under age sixteen, and one-third of those among 16 to 19 year olds end in termination (Fullerton 1997). To some extent, the problem is linked to such influences as having a mother or sister with a previous history of pregnancy, ready access to health services, and poor employment prospects (Fullerton 1997; Seamark & Pereira Gray 1997).

Pregnancy generates developmental change at any age, but in the adolescent it can create a developmental crisis as the young girl struggles to deal with two stages at once: adolescence and young adulthood (Rodriquez & Moore 1996). Deciding what to do about the pregnancy compounds the stress of these transitions, and this is often the case for approximately 40% of the world's population who have the option of legal abortion (Yang 1995). Where childbirth is the outcome, the strains of parenting can provide an enormous burden. This is the case for the majority of those who experience teenage pregnancy, as many of these girls come from socio-economic conditions of relative deprivation (Irvine et al. 1997; Jacobson & Wilkinson 1994).

Choosing between persevering with the pregnancy and having an abortion is one of the most difficult issues that confront young adolescent women, as this can pervade a young woman's life forever. In some cases, the abortion issue is expedited by social structures, such as those in Singapore, where abortion is legal. It is also mandatory for any teenager under age sixteen to be counselled at the Institute of Health (Yang 1995). In many other countries, especially the US, the anti-abortion or 'pro-life' movement is publicly visible, and at times wields a powerful influence on the pregnant adolescent's decision. Small wonder then that teenage mothers tend to experience conflicts. These often lead to emotional outbursts, dramatic mood changes and acute depression which, if the choice is made to continue with the pregnancy, can lead to child abuse (Zigler & Stevenson-Finn 1987). Other risks to the child occur because of the teenage mother's early stage of development. Because of their physiological immaturity, they tend to have a higher risk of complicated pregnancies, including hypertensive disorders and low birthweight babies (Cunningham & Boult 1996; Yang 1995). In many cases, teenage mothers also smoke and ingest alcohol and other substances, compounding the risk to the child.

From a social perspective, teenage pregnancy has a devastating effect on many teenage girls. Even in some African communities, where teenage pregnancy is somewhat more culturally tolerated than in other areas, the result is as devastating as elsewhere, in terms of interrupting the young girl's education and thus cutting off at least some opportunities for employment and thus resources for parenting (Buga, Amoko & Ncayiyana 1996). At the societal level, supporting teenage mothers and their child(ren) is costly, and consumes funds that could otherwise be deployed elsewhere in the health and social system. This is a particular problem in the US, where the rates of teenage pregnancy are the highest of most developed nations (Hewell & Andrews 1996; Yang 1995). Rodriquez and Moore (1996) report that half of American teenage mothers go on welfare within a year, and 77% within five years. They calculate that the annual cost of providing first-year welfare services to a single mother and child is $9200, whereas the cost of family planning for a sexually active teenager is $64. These figures speak for themselves.

Sexually transmitted diseases

The threat of sexually transmitted diseases has always existed, but the AIDS epidemic has caused renewed alarm. The HIV epidemic now has an incidence rate of 16,000 new cases per day, totalling more than thirty million worldwide. Ninety per cent of these cases are in developing countries (Ferrari 1997). The extent of the epidemic in the population is unparalleled in recent history. The link between HIV infection and other sexually transmitted diseases (STD) is also of grave concern. In the US, approximately three million teenagers acquire an STD each year, which is thought to increase the risk of subsequent HIV infection (Coyle et al. 1996; Wasserheit 1992).

Approximately 20% of all current cases of HIV have been diagnosed in people in their twenties, and there is a possibility that they may have contracted the virus as adolescents. Another cause for alarm is the fact that still so little is known about HIV. Not so long ago it was thought to be confined to the homosexual community, but this is no longer the case, with heterosexual relations and sharing of needles accounting for a large proportion of infections (Li et al. 1996). One fact that has been demonstrated conclusively is that using a condom prevents transmission, yet recent research reveals that, despite one in four 16 to 19 year olds being sexually active, many teenagers are still not using condoms with any pattern of consistency (Coyle et al. 1996; Hiltabiddle 1996; Yang 1995).

With the increased publicity about HIV and AIDS, condom use, at least among university students, has recently been reported at as high as 60% in Australia, Scotland and France (Rodden et al. 1996). However, there has been great variability in the research, with rates of condom use fluctuating according to such factors as age, education and ethnicity (Rodden et al. 1996). So the fact remains that, despite a worldwide increase in condom use throughout the 1980s, many young people continue to be at risk from a range of STDs, AIDS and pregnancy.

Countering risk: healthy adolescence

In the US, McKie and colleagues (1993) attempted to construct an equation that would predict the probability of ill health from a pattern of risky behaviours; but individual subjective factors were found to mediate between expectations and reality. In other words, the way a person perceives her or his ability to function is variable, and thus far, health promotion experts have not been able to settle on a consistent approach to changing people's attitudes. The optimal approach to helping people change is to adopt a community epidemiological approach, where a web of causation can be constructed to illuminate factors such as age, gender, social, cultural and environmental context and examine the interactions between them. This type of approach has been used to embed other health promotion interventions within the context of school, home, neighbourhood and community (Sawyer & Kosky 1996).

Tresidder and colleagues (1997) studied the risky behaviours of a group of sixteen-year-olds who had left school compared with school attenders and found higher rates of alcohol, cigarette and marijuana consumption, sexual abuse and drink driving. They felt that these teenagers were missing the 'connectedness' to school that serves to protect adolescents against a range of 'acting out' behaviours, including drug use, higher risk of injury and risk of pregnancy (Resnick, Harris & Blum 1993). One analysis of studies in ten countries found a strong association between regular smoking, for example, and alienation from school (Nutbeam & Aaro 1991). Young adolescents leaving school are a group at particular risk of ill health because they do not have the peer support or health surveillance offered in most school health services. Health education for this group must therefore be targeted at the neighbourhood and community.

One group of researchers studied the effects of a smoking prevention campaign for teenagers over a four-year period in one state of the US. After extensive evaluation they concluded that the most effective health education for this group is a combination of media exposure and school-based education because these two settings have the most powerful influences on young people (Flynn et al. 1994). This approach is supported by sex education experiences in the UK, which emphasise the importance of teaching sessions that are informative, allow for values clarification, develop social skills and encourage active participation in learning (Few, Hicken & Butterworth 1996). Australian researchers have also found the multifaceted approach to be more effective (Sawyer & Kosky 1996).

One group in the US developed a program to teach adolescents about pregnancy and STDs which included five primary components: school organisation, curriculum and staff development, peer resources and school environment, parent education and school–community linkages. Their program, *Safer Choices*, emphasised the school climate and organisational culture to encourage the view that safer sexual choices were part of the social norms of the school and the group. Out-of-school support activities were also included, with newsletters and other school–community initiatives. One of the features of the program was that it fostered group empowerment through peer support groups as well as emphasising individual responsibility (Coyle et al. 1996).

Goals for adolescent health

The major health issues affecting adolescents include the following:
- mental/emotional health
- healthy lifestyle
- minimisation of risky behaviours.

The place to begin improving adolescent health is at the societal level, encouraging all members of the community and society at large to recognise the major factors that place adolescents at risk for unhealthy choices. Once again, the strategies of the Ottawa Charter provide a framework for addressing the issues separately and collectively.

Building healthy public policy

Policies to encourage healthy adolescence include those that address the need for teachers and other educators to be supported in their attempts to counsel young people. This is important because health promotion must be offered in the setting that is most conducive to change. For adolescents, this is primarily the school. Too often, teachers work in isolation, providing guidance and support to teenagers as an 'add-on' to their already overburdened work roles, with little recognition for their efforts. This must be addressed by all sectors of the community interested in cultivating a generation of young people.

Another area where public policy can help encourage healthy lifestyles among young people is in legislating for changes conducive to healthy choices. This includes such things as providing needle exchanges and condoms, reducing hotel hours, increasing the minimum age for the purchase of cigarettes, and close monitoring of retail outlets selling harmful substances. Some studies have demonstrated that government preventative policies have had a positive effect on risks to public health. For example, the efforts of the anti-smoking lobby have been attributed with reducing smoking in the US by 80% (Whitehead 1995). Similarly, needle exchange programs in the US have reduced HIV infection among intravenous drug users, with no evidence of increased drug use as a result (Glantz 1996). However, mandated changes must be undertaken with sensitivity to people's civil liberties, particularly in the context of widespread debate concerning public control over individual private behaviours.

Some people resent being forced to wear bicycle safety helmets or being cut off from drinking at the bar when they have obviously had enough alcohol. Others believe that condoms and needle exchanges encourage sexual promiscuity and drug taking. Glantz (1996) equates this to a situation where disapproval of motorcycles is expressed in forbidding the use of motorcycles without safety helmets. Another argument against government control is that health and education departments may be making judgements concerning the wellbeing of their charges that are designed more for protection from litigation than the welfare of the young person. These community concerns need to be aired and discussed at all levels of the community. The most important issue for health professionals is to ensure that people have access to accurate information when making decisions about health and lifestyles, so that the views of the vocal minority do not override opportunities for all community members to make informed choices.

Healthy policies must also be based on the priorities of the time. For example, policies have been slow to respond to the problems of homelessness, suicide and teenage pregnancy. However, some initiatives are exemplary. In Finland, for example, researchers have found that building healthy public policy and reorienting health services have had a marked effect on teenage pregnancies and abortions in that country (Kosunen & Rimpela 1996). In 1970 the Finnish government introduced the Primary Health Care Act, which guaranteed equal access to family planning services, including contraception in all municipalities. School sex education was also incorporated into all curricula and reaches virtually every adolescent. Since that time, the national rates of teenage pregnancy and abortion have dropped by approximately one half, with some regional variations that may reflect a problem with urban teenagers not having easy access to the service. A similar effect has been found in the Netherlands, where the rates of abortion (the indicator of unplanned pregnancy) have plummeted to the lowest in the Western world (Kosunen & Rimpela 1996).

Creating supportive environments

An environment conducive to healthy adolescence is one in which adolescents feel safe to explore and to stretch their imaginations for the future. School is a major influence on whether teenagers feel free to question and learn. The formal education system must provide opportunities for safe and guided discussion on a range of topics, including relationships and sexuality. This has been confirmed in studies of violence prevention programs at school, where confidentiality and adequate space and location were seen as the keys to sucessful intervention (Fiester et al. 1996). To support young people, mechanisms must be put in place whereby teachers and parents can exchange ideas, clarify values and provide advice to adolescents that is consistent with family and societal expectations, yet allows freedom and creativity. Coyle and colleagues' (1996) model (Safer Choices) underlines the need for a comprehensive approach that is policy driven and yet empowering for adolescents and their parents. The findings of Tresidder and colleagues (1997) on the importance of the school environment indicate a need to incorporate out-of-school support systems for young people who may fall through the cracks in health promotion campaigns because they are out in the workforce or unemployed. This is particularly important for homeless adolescents, who are at risk for numerous subsequent problems.

Strengthening community action

Community action to improve the health of adolescents must also involve fostering personal skills among parents, teachers, the business community and all others who provide support to young people. One study conducted in Canada found that parents' health-promoting lifestyles were significantly correlated with those of their adolescent daughters, providing support for the importance of parental modelling (Gillis 1994). This and other studies point to a need for parent support centres that shift the focus from paternalistic advice-giving to family-friendly suggestions for higher levels of health and wellness. In Africa, where many single mothers find their daughters caught in the cycle of teenage pregnancy, it has also been considered more useful to guide both women together (Cunningham & Boult 1996).

The accessibility of services is as important as their substance. With both parents often working and with no available extended family support, there is a need for health information services in local neighbourhoods. At present, services to adolescents are provided through formal agencies such as school health services and family planning associations. Parents have little access to the information being given to their children unless the child chooses to initiate discussion with them. In many cases, there is not only a generation gap problem, but cultural conflicts as well, as migrant children quickly assimilate the values of their new culture without the involvement of their parents. Primary health care practice requires that access, equity, self-determination and cultural sensitivity be extended not only to the adolescent group, but also to their parents and other relevant community members. Provision of accessible, coherent and culturally congruent family support centres would help achieve health goals for both groups and locate the source of information to where it can be most effective—at the heart of the community.

Developing personal skills

This strategy is perhaps the most important from the perspective of the adolescent. The teenage years are the pivot point for the development of personal skills for adult survival. The most important element in developing personal skills is to educate adolescents on matters related to their health and to support them in changing. Many researchers have found that individual teaching can be most effective when it integrates functional knowledge (what must be done to improve health or prevent illness), motivational knowledge (how beliefs affect behaviour), outcome expectancy (belief in the effectiveness of preventative action) and self-efficacy (confidence that one can use skills effectively) (Becker 1974; Coyle et al. 1996; Hiltabiddle 1996). Perhaps most importantly, health teaching efforts need to be cognisant of the adolescent's egocentrism. As was mentioned previously, most adolescents believe themselves to be utterly unique and often invulnerable. This may explain why, despite evidence of the dangers of certain behaviours, many still do not adopt healthy lifestyles (Hewell & Andrews 1996; Hiltabiddle 1996; Jacobson & Wilkinson 1994).

In addition to individual health education, one of the most effective means of changing behaviour is by peer modelling, whereby healthy, fit role models within their social sphere are used to convey health promotion messages. The two most important skills for healthy behaviour are social decision-making and problem-solving skills (Elias & Kress 1994). These can best be learned in the context of examples, either in the classroom or within sports coaching or other venues in which teenagers interact. In being provided with opportunities for problem solving and negotiating a range of views, young people learn to integrate social–cognitive, affective, behavioural and social relationship areas with critical thinking for both academic achievement and future healthful behaviours (Elias & Kress 1994). Such education sessions must also be culturally and linguistically appropriate (Barg & Lowe 1996).

The dialogue for exchange must be not only appropriate for different ethnic groups but also must respond to the unique culture of adolescence. Incorporating their music, art and other artefacts of adolescent life into the sessions allows young people to readily identify with the context as well as the content. This is essentially an environmental approach in that it refocuses the emphasis of health teaching within a contextual frame of reference.

Reorienting health services

One of the most important reactions of adolescents is alienation from societal institutions, including those that provide health care. School health centres are usually designed to be attractive to teenagers, and provide an invaluable teaching service. Drop-in centres and neighbourhood health clinics must also be designed for easy and confidential access, and these can be designed in collaboration with teenagers themselves (Goudie 1996). Hot lines for confidential guidance provide an invaluable service for those who hesitate to seek face-to-face information. In addition, there needs to be easy access to crisis care for those in need. Staff of emergency departments and psychiatric institutions may therefore need ongoing awareness training for dealing with the special needs of adolescents.

Places where young people congregate should also be the repository of information on health issues, especially to meet the needs of those who have left school or who have otherwise 'fallen out of the nest' (Tresidder 1996, p. 229). In order to reach these adolescents, health education messages must be made available in shopping malls, computer game parlours, sports organisations and youth clubs. Radio and television stations that attract a large teenage audience provide an opportunity to reinforce the messages of authority figures with those from such teenage allies as radio disc jockeys.

One of the most consistent findings from studies of teenage preventive behaviours is their lack of knowledge on health issues. The latest findings of research studies must be made available to adolescents, their teachers, parents, school health nurses and all others who may find themselves in a position to offer guidance and support. Of equal importance is the need to have a truly collaborative approach to helping adolescents. Commitment to a *client*, rather than *provider*, approach is necessary to ensure that the lines of communication remain open to all members of the health care team attempting to encourage positive health practices.

One of the most innovative approaches to promoting adolescent health is the harm reduction approach, in which drug education, for example, focuses on preventing the potential harms related to drug use rather than trying to prevent the drug use itself (Duncan et al. 1994). This major paradigm shift in drug education is based on the assumption that everyone in society uses some form of drugs, licit or illicit. The focus is on ensuring safety and survival—instead of being castigated, drug users are taught safe methods of injecting, sniffing or using implements related to their behaviour. This approach also includes such structural supports as designated drivers, free taxis, coffee stops along highways, and changing social norms related to responsible drinking and responsible drink serving, needle exchange programs and free condoms.

The harm reduction approach is becoming widely accepted by many different countries, in recognition that people have always, and will continue to, engage in high-risk behaviours. The shift in thinking is that if health professionals can at least encourage those people and the general public to think about preventing the most serious outcomes, it may help to educate 'users'. It may also increase the availability of treatment services and change public perceptions in a way that will encourage treatment and instigate legal reform (Duncan et al. 1994).

THINKING CRITICALLY
Adolescent health

▶ Identify four high-risk behaviours of adolescents and three risk reduction strategies for each.

▶ Discuss the contention that the context is the most important element in any health promotion program.

▶ Identify three measures that can be taken to ensure cultural sensitivity in teaching adolescents about healthy sexuality.

▶ Describe four health promotion resources available to adolescents in your community.

▶ Describe three strategies for an adolescent smoking prevention program corresponding to individual factors that should be considered in any health promotion program.

REFERENCES

Australian Bureau of Statistics 1996, *Estimated resident population by sex and age*, cat. no. 3201.0, AGPS, Canberra.

Australian Institute of Health and Welfare 1995, *Health in Australia: What You Should Know*, AGPS, Canberra.

Barg, F. & Lowe, J. 1996, 'A culturally appropriate cancer education program for African-American adolescents in an urban middle school', *Journal of School Health*, vol. 66, no. 2, pp. 50–4.

Barron, C. & Yoest, P. 1994, 'Emotional distress and coping with a stressful relationship in adolescent boys', *Journal of Pediatric Nursing*, vol. 9, no. 1, pp. 13–20.

Becker, M. 1974, *The Health Belief Model and Personal Health Behavior*, Charles B. Slack, New Jersey.

Breakey, W. 1997, 'It's time for the public health community to declare war on homelessness', editorial, *American Journal of Public Health*, vol. 87, no. 2, pp. 153–5.

Brent, D. 1995, 'Risk factors for adolescent suicide and suicidal behavior: Mental and substance abuse disorders, family environmental factors, and life stress', *Suicide and Life Threatening Behavior*, vol. 25 (supp.), pp. 52–62.

Breslow, L. 1982, 'Control of cigarette smoking from a public policy perspective', *Annual Review of Public Health*, vol. 3, pp. 129–51.

Bronfenbrenner, U. 1986, 'Alienation and the four worlds of childhood', *Phi Delta Kappan*, vol. 67, pp. 430–6.

Buga, G., Amoko, D. & Ncayiyana, D. 1996, 'Adolescent sexual behaviour, knowledge and attitudes to sexuality among school girls in Transkei, South Africa', *East African Medical Journal*, vol. 73, no. 2, pp. 95–100.

Cantor, C. & Slater, P. 1997, 'A regional profile of suicide in Queensland', *Australian and New Zealand Journal of Public Health*, vol. 21, no. 2, pp. 181–6.

Cantor, C., Slater, P. & Najman, J. 1995, 'Socioeconomic indices and suicide rate in Queensland', *Australian Journal of Public Health*, vol. 19, no. 3, pp. 417–20.

Chou, S. & Pickering, R. 1992, 'Early onset of drinking as a risk factor for future alcohol-related problems', *British Journal of Addiction*, vol. 87, pp. 1199–1204.

Coyle, K., Kirby, D., Parcel, G., Basen-Engquist, K., Banspach, S. et al. 1996, 'Safer choices: A multicomponent school-based HIV/STD and pregnancy prevention program for adolescents', *Journal of School Health*, vol. 66, no. 3, pp. 89–94.

Cunningham, P. & Boult, B. 1996, 'Black teenage pregnancy in South Africa: some considerations', *Adolescence*, vol. 31, no. 123, pp. 691–700.

D'Elio, M., Mundt, D., Bush, P. & Iannotti, R. 1993, 'Healthful behaviors: Do they protect African-American, urban preadolescents from abusable substance use?', *American Journal of Health Promotion*, vol. 7, no. 5, pp. 354–63.

D'Espaignet, E. & Rickwood, D. 1995, 'Trends in psychological distress among young Australian women aged 16–24: effects of age, occupation and final year examination', *Proceedings of the Third National Women's Health Conference*, Australian National University, Canberra, pp. 310–14.

Dixey, R. 1996, 'Healthy eating in schools and "eating disorders"—are "healthy eating" messages part of the problem or part of the solution?', *Nutrition and Health*, vol. 11, pp. 49–58.

Dukes, R. & Lorch, B. 1989, 'The effects of school, family, self-concept, and deviant behaviour on adolescent suicide ideation', *Journal of Adolescence*, vol. 12, pp. 239–51.

Duncan, D., Nicholson, T., Clifford, P., Hawkins, W. & Petosa, R. 1994, 'Harm reduction: An emerging new paradigm for drug education', *Journal of Drug Education*, vol. 24, no. 4, pp. 281–90.

Dunst, C. & Trivette, C. 1996, 'Empowerment, effective helpgiving practices and family-centered care', *Pediatric Nursing*, vol. 22, no. 4, pp. 334–43.

DuRant, R., Rickert, V., Ashworth, C., Newman, C. & Slavens, G. 1993, 'Use of multiple drugs among adolescents who use anabolic steroids', *New England Journal of Medicine*, vol. 328, no. 13, pp. 922–6.

Elias, M. & Kress, J. 1994, 'Social decision-making and life skills development: A critical thinking approach to health promotion in the middle school', *Journal of School Health*, vol. 64, no. 2, pp. 62–6.

Erikson, E. 1963, *Childhood and Society*, 2nd edn, Norton, New York.

Escobedo, L. & Peddicord, J. 1996, 'Smoking prevalence in US birth cohorts: the influence of gender and education', *American Journal of Public Health*, vol. 86, no. 2, pp. 231–6.

Estok P. & Rudy, E. 1996, 'The relationship between eating disorders and running in women', *Research in Nursing and Health*, vol. 19, pp. 377–87.

Fanos, J. & Johnson, J. 1994, 'CF carrier status: the importance of not knowing', *American Journal of Human Genetics*, vol. 55, no. 3 (suppl.), p. A292.

Farley, C., Haddad, S. & Brown, B. 1996, 'The effects of a four-year program promoting bicycle helmet use among children in Quebec', *American Journal of Public Health*, vol. 86, no. 1, pp. 46–51.

Ferrari, J. 1997, 'Global HIV-AIDS scourge underestimated', *The Weekend Australian*, Nov. 29–30, p. 49.

Few, C., Hicken, I. & Butterworth, T. 1996, 'Alliances in school sex education: teachers' and school nurses' views', *Health Visitor*, vol. 69, no. 6, pp. 220–3.

Fiester, L., Nathanson, S., Visser, L. & Martin, J. 1996, 'Lessons learned from three violence prevention projects', *Journal of School Health*, vol. 66, no. 9, pp. 344–6.

Flynn, B., Worden, J., Secker-Waler, R., Pirie, P., Badger, G., et al. 1994, 'Mass media and school interventions for cigarette smoking prevention: Effects two years after completion', *American Journal of Public Health*, vol. 84, no. 7, pp. 1148–50.

Fortenberry, J. 1997, 'Health care seeking behaviors related to sexually transmitted diseases among adolescents', *American Journal of Public Health*, vol. 87, no. 3, pp. 417–20.

Fullerton, D. 1997, 'A review of approaches to teenage pregnancy', *Nursing Times*, vol. 93, no. 13, pp. 48–9.

Gillis, A. 1994, 'Determinants of health-promoting lifestyles in adolescent females', *Canadian Journal of Nursing Research*, vol. 26, no. 2, pp. 13–28.

Girgis, A., Doran, C., Sanson-Fisher, R. & Walsh, R. 1995, 'Smoking by adolescents: large revenue but little for prevention', *Australian Journal of Public Health*, vol. 19, no. 1, pp. 29–33.

Glantz, L. 1996, 'Annotation: Needle exchange programs and the law—time for a change', *American Journal of Public Health*, vol. 86, no. 8, pp. 1077-8.

Gotestam, K., Eriksen, L. & Hagen, H. 1995, 'An epidemiological study of eating disorders in Norwegian psychiatric institutions', *International Journal of Eating Disorders*, vol. 18, no. 3, pp. 263–8.

Goudie, H. 1996, 'Making health services more accessible to younger people', *Nursing Times*, vol. 19, no. 92, pp. 45–6.

Green, L. & Ottoson, J. 1994, *Community Health*, 7th edn, Mosby, St Louis.

Hewell, S. & Andrews, J. 1996, 'Contraceptive use among female adolescents', *Clinical Nursing Research*, vol. 5, no. 3, pp. 356–63.

Hibbert, M., Rosier, M., Carlin, J., Caust, J. & Bowes, G. 1995, 'Patterns of common drug use in teenagers', *Australian Journal of Public Health*, vol. 19, no. 4, pp. 391-9.

Hiltabiddle, S. 1996, 'Adolescent condom use, the health belief model, and the prevention of sexually transmitted disease', *Journal of Obstetrics and Gynecologic Nursing*, vol. 25, no. 1, pp. 61–7.

Irvine, H., Bradley, T., Cupples, M., & Boohan, M. 1997, 'The implications of teenage pregnancy and motherhood for primary health care: unresolved issues', *British Journal of General Practice*, vol 47, pp. 323–6.

Jacobson, L. & Wilkinson, C. 1994, 'Review of teenage health: time for a new direction', *British Journal of General Practice*, vol. 44, pp. 420-4.

Jacobson, L., Wilkinson, C. & Pill, R. 1995, 'Teenage pregnancy in the United Kingdom in the 1990s: the implications for primary care', *Family Practice*, vol. 12, no. 2, pp. 232–6.

Kandel, D. 1975, 'Stages of adolescent involvement in drug use', *Science*, vol. 190, pp. 912–14.

Kandel, D., Yamaguchi, K. & Chen, L. 1992, 'Stage of progression in drug involvement from adolescence to adulthood: further evidence for the gateway theory', *Journal of Studies in Alcohol*, vol. 53, pp. 447–57.

Kosunen, E. & Rimpela, M. 1996, 'Towards regional equality in family planning: teenage pregnancies and abortions in Finland from 1976 to 1993', *Acta Obstet Gynecol Scand*, vol. 75, pp. 540–7.

Lamarine, R. 1995, 'Child and adolescent depression', *Journal of School Health*, vol. 65, no. 9, pp. 390–3.

Li, Y., Gold, J., McDonald, A. & Kaldor, J. 1996, 'Demographic pattern of AIDS in Australia, 1991 to 1993', *Australian and New Zealand Journal of Public Health*, vol. 20, no. 4, pp. 421–5.

McEvoy, A. & Erikson, E. 1990, *Youth and Exploitation*, Learning Publications, Inc., Montreal.

McKie, L., Al-Bashir, M., Anagnostopoulou, T., Csepe, P., El-Asfahani, A. et al. 1993, 'Defining and assessing risky behaviours', *Journal of Advanced Nursing*, vol. 18, pp. 1911–16.

Miller, B., Maguin, E. & Downs, W. 1997, 'Alcohol, drugs, and violence in children's lives', *Recent Developments in Alcoholism*, vol. 13, pp. 357–85.

Morrell, S., Taylor, R., Quine, S. & Kerr, C. 1993, 'Suicide and unemployment in Australia 1907-1990', *Social Science and Medicine*, vol. 36, pp. 749–56.

Nadaoka, T., Oiji, A., Takahashi, S., Morioka, Y., Kashiwakura, M. et al. 1996, 'An epidemiological study of eating disorders in a northern area of Japan', *Acta Psychiatrica Scandinavica*. vol. 93, pp. 305–10.

Nelson, J. 1997, 'Gay, lesbian, and bisexual adolescents: providing esteem-enhancing care to a battered population', *The Nurse Practitioner*, vol. 22, no. 20, pp. 94–109.

NHS Health Advisory Service 1995, *Child and Adolescent Mental Health Services: Together We Stand*, HMSO, London.

Nutbeam, D. & Aaro, L. 1991, 'Smoking and pupil attitudes towards school: the implications for health education with young people', *Health Education Research*, vol. 6, no. 4, pp. 415–21.

Pate, R., Heath, G., Dowda, M. & Trost, S. 1996, 'Associations between physical activity and other health behaviors in a representative sample of US adolescents', *American Journal of Public Health*, vol. 86, no. 11, pp. 1577–81.

Resnick, M., Harris, L. & Blum, R. 1993, 'The impact of caring and connectedness on adolescent health and well-being', *Journal of Paediatric Child Health*, vol. 29 (suppl.), pp. 3–9.

Rodden, P., Crawford, J., Kippax, S. & French, J. 1996, 'Sexual practice and understandings of safe sex: assessing change among 18 to 19 year old Australian tertiary students 1988 to 1994', *Australian and New Zealand Journal of Public Health*, vol. 20, no. 6, pp. 643–9.

Rodriquez, C. & Moore, N. 1996, 'Perceptions of pregnant/parenting teens: reframing issues for an integrated approach to pregnancy problems', *Adolescence*, vol. 30, no. 119, pp. 685–706.

Runyan, C. & Gerken, F. 1989, 'Epidemiology and prevention of adolescent injury', *Journal of the American Medical Association*, vol. 262, pp. 2273–9.

Rutter, M. & Smith, D. (eds) 1995, *Psychosocial Disorders in Young People: Time Trends and Their Causes*, John Wiley, Chichester.

Sawyer, M. & Kosky, R. 1996, 'Mental health promotion for young people: A proposal for a tripartite approach', *Journal of Paediatric Child Health*, vol. 32, pp. 368–70.

Schwenk, T. 1997, 'Psychoactive drugs and athletic performance', *The Physician and Sportsmedicine*, vol. 25, no. 1, pp. 32–46.

Seamark, C. & Pereira Gray, D. 1997, 'Like mother, like daughter: a general practice study of maternal influences on teenage pregnancy', *British Journal of General Practice*, vol. 47, pp. 175–6.

Swaim, R., Beauvais, F., Chavez, E. & Oetting, E. 1997, 'The effect of school dropout rates on estimates of adolescent substance use among three racial/ethnic groups', *American Journal of Public Health*, vol. 87, no 1, pp. 51–5.

Tanner, S., Miller, D. & Alongi, C. 1995, 'Anabolic steroid use by adolescents: prevalence, motives and knowledge of risks', *Clinical Journal of Sports Medicine*, vol. 5, no. 2, pp. 108–15.

Tiggermann, M. 1995, 'The role of the media in adolescent women's drive for thinness', *Proceedings of the Third National Women's Health Conference*, Australian National University, Canberra, pp. 164–7.

Tresidder, J. 1996, 'Perspectives on adolescent health in the 1990s', *Australian and New Zealand Journal of Public Health*, vol. 20, no. 3, pp. 229–30.

Tresidder, J., Macaskill, P., Bennett, D. & Nutbeam, D. 1997, 'Health risks and behaviour of out-of-school 16 year olds in New South Wales', *Australian and New Zealand Journal of Public Health*, vol. 21, no. 2, pp. 168–74.

Vimpani, G. & Parry, T. (eds) 1989, *Community Child Health in Australia*, Churchill-Livingstone, Melbourne.

Wakeling, A. 1996, 'Epidemiology of anorexia nervosa', *Psychiatry Research*, vol. 62, pp. 3–9.

Wasserheit, J. 1992, 'Epidemiological synergy: Interrelationship between human immuno-deficiency virus infection and other sexually transmitted diseases', *Sexually Transmitted Diseases*, vol. 19, pp. 61–77.

West, P. & Sweeting, H. 1996, 'Nae job, nae future: young people and health in a context of unemployment', *Health and Social Care in the Community*, vol. 4, no. 1, pp. 50–62.

Whitehead, M. 1995, 'Tackling inequalities: a review of policy initiatives' in *Tackling Inequalities in Health*, eds M. Benezeval, K. Judge & M. Whitehead, King's Fund, London, pp. 22–52.

Willcox, M. & Sattler, D. 1996, 'The relationship between eating disorders and depression', *Journal of Social Psychology*, vol. 136, no. 2, pp. 269–71.

Yang, M. 1995, 'Adolescent sexuality and its problems', *Annals of the Academy of Medicine*, vol. 24, no. 5, pp. 736–40.

Zerbe, K. 1996, 'Anorexia nervosa and bulimia nervosa', *Postgraduate Medicine*, vol. 99, no. 1, pp. 161–9.

Zhu, B., Liu, M., Shelton, D., Liu, S. & Giovino, G. 1996, 'Cigarette smoking and risk factors among elementary school students in Beijing', *American Journal of Public Health*, vol. 86, no. 3, pp. 368–75.

Zigler, E. & Stevenson-Finn, M. 1987, *Children: Development and Social Issues*, Heath, Lexington, MA.

7

Healthy adults

By the time most people reach adulthood they have usually experienced at least one illness or injury serious enough to seek medical help. For most adults these are acute episodes, resolved without major intervention or residual effects. For others, however, chronic, disabling conditions either cause premature mortality or compromise quality of life. The difference between these two groups is related to many factors, including the same types of things that influence child and adolescent health. However, from a population perspective, adults show distinctive variations in health status related to age, gender, place of residence and family structure. So, in addition to those factors identified in our model of health (shown in figure 7.1), this chapter will also focus on these demographic differences.

Objectives

By the end of this chapter you will be able to:

- *identify the most prevalent causes of morbidity and mortality among the adult population*

- *identify the risk factors and determinants of health and illness in adults*

- *describe lifestyle factors that affect the health of adults*

- *discuss the role of health care services in maintaining the health of adults*

- *explain how the health of adults can be improved using the strategies of the Ottawa Charter for Health Promotion.*

The healthy adult

Adulthood is the time of a person's life when the intersecting influences of biology, the environment and lifestyle are most apparent. By the time people have become adults, their innate predispositions have combined with the circumstances of their lives to set a pattern for the future. For most, the prospect for a long life free of disability is good, but for approximately 18% of the population, especially older males, the quality of their lives will be compromised by sight, hearing, speech, mobility, emotional or mental conditions, or the need for medications (AIHW 1996a). Such disabilities are, however, only one part of the equation for a healthful life (see figure 7.1).

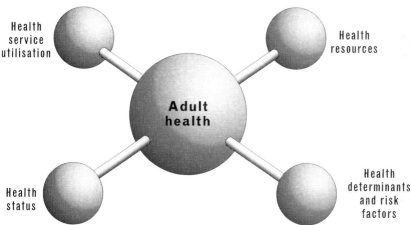

Health service utilisation

Health resources

Adult health

Health status

Health determinants and risk factors

Figure 7.1

The interrelationship of factors influencing the health of adults

Health determinants and risk factors

For more than a century, health researchers have been trying to explain relative states of health and illness in various population groups. A decade ago, the Centers for Disease Control and Prevention in the US analysed the relative weight of factors leading to morbidity and mortality in adults and concluded that the tendency to die prematurely was due to four main factors: human biology (20%), environmental factors (20%), inadequate health care (10%) and unhealthy behaviour and lifestyles (50%) (AIHW 1996a; Lee & Paxman 1997). One study conducted in 1993 found that the role of lifestyle factors in mortality has changed little since 1977. Half of all deaths can still be attributed to tobacco, diet and activity patterns, alcohol, microbial and other toxic agents, firearms and motor vehicle injuries, sexual behaviour and illicit drug use (McGinnis & Foege 1993). The Global

Burden of Disease Study shows some variation in the cause of death world-wide, but confirms the risks of an unhealthy lifestyle, especially in the industrialised nations (Murray & Lopez 1997).

The implication of this information is that poor health is not necessarily our destiny. Population-based approaches to improving health need to consider the cultural, social, educational and economic environment, which has a profound effect on lifestyle choices. Lifestyle choices, in turn, cannot be made without consideration of occupation, marital status, major life events and social networks. So as health advocates we need to encourage personal healthy behaviours but also address structural issues such as poverty, housing, educational and social support services, and employment opportunities (AIHW 1996a; Lee & Paxman 1997). Creating opportunities for, and supporting, healthy choices are thus the most important objectives of public health and health promotion programs.

Individual and family lifestyle choices are also moderated by the availability of accessible, affordable and culturally appropriate services to treat and prevent illness and to sustain wellness. One of the greatest challenges, however, lies in determining the effectiveness of various services or programs. As mentioned previously, health is generated by a multitude of factors and it is particularly difficult for health planners to measure health outcomes as a direct response to certain interventions. For example, the outcomes of government-sponsored anti-smoking or anti-pollution campaigns may not be fully realised for years. In the time lag between exposure to a program and health outcomes, many things change, including people's behaviour. Although there is a lack of precision in attributing health gains to particular services or activities, it remains important to undertake program planning and development from a data base of local knowledge and information that allows comparison with other places and other groups. We continue to measure morbidity and mortality rates, the extent to which people are exposed to health information, the ways in which they gain knowledge and skills to sustain their personal health, and their self-reported quality of life and satisfaction with services.

Mortality and morbidity

In the 1990s the major causes of death in industrialised nations are diseases of the cardiovascular system, cancer and injuries, all of which are thought to be modifiable by lifestyle practices (AIHW 1996a; Lee & Paxman 1997). Mortality (death) and morbidity (illness) rates are calculations of the number of deaths or incidences of illness according to the corresponding population. A more meaningful statistic, however, is the *age-standardised* death or mortality rate, which allows comparison of populations with different age distributions, usually presented separately for males and females (AIHW 1996a; WHO 1995). This allows consideration of such issues as the influence of ageing on the incidence and prevalence of chronic illness and disability, and the fact that some conditions are peculiar to certain age groups. Age distinctions are also useful in linking events in early life, such as early childhood nutrition, which shows variable outcomes in adult life.

In most countries the age-standardised mortality rates have declined dramatically, primarily due to health technologies and better medical information. Information on mortality is usually presented as *life*, rather than death, expectancy (Murray & Lopez 1997). For example, Japan has the highest life expectancy for both males and females, while those from Eastern European countries have the lowest. Life expectancy in Australia is now 75 years for males and 80 years for females, an improvement of 16 years for males and 17 years for females from 50 years ago, when infectious diseases caused many early deaths (AIHW 1996a).

Healthy lifestyles

The leading causes of today's morbidity and mortality rates are tightly woven parts of the fabric of modern living: rich foods, alcohol, drugs, sedentary work and leisure, stress, guns, automobiles and other machinery (Green & Ottoson 1994). Government controls on toxic waste production and disposal, gun control laws, and tobacco and alcohol can only go part of the way in discouraging harmful behaviours. Health promotion campaigns have had to tread a delicate balance between urging people to take responsibility for their lives in such a way as to blame the victim, and adopting a too heavy-handed approach to public control over what some believe should be private matters.

Promoting healthy lifestyles must begin from where people see themselves and their health status. Being healthy is a personal code, embedded in the cultural system to which people belong (Kleinman 1988). Lifestyle practices are influenced by the way people see themselves positioned within culture, and within the larger scheme of the social world, and this influences their receptivity to health messages. Promoting healthy lifestyles must therefore be considered within a population approach so that the effect of socioeconomic environments and relationships on biological pathways to health can be acknowledged and supported by resources for community development and enrichment (Frank 1995; Nutbeam 1995).

Physical activity

One of the most important targets for health promotion is physical activity. In today's post-industrial society more people than ever lead a sedentary lifestyle. Technology has made daily physical activity unnecessary and one-third of the adult population in Western countries choose to also be inactive in their leisure time (Guerzoni 1996). This is of great concern when the costs of exercise are compared with the costs of treating illness. Regular exercise such as daily walking is free, and health gains are enormous in terms of keeping fit, burning off extra calories and coping with stress. Regular physical activity also appears to reduce depression and anxiety, improve mood and enhance people's ability to perform daily tasks throughout their life span (Lee & Paxman 1997).

Embarking on a program of physical activity may also act as a catalyst for other positive lifestyle practices. When a person adopts physical leisure activities they tend also to quit smoking, lose weight and have less stress (Johnson, Boyle & Heller 1995). Researchers have shown that combining moderate vigorous sporting activity and quitting cigarette smoking are independently associated with lower rates of death from all causes and from coronary heart disease (CHD) in middle-aged and older men (Paffenbarger et al. 1993).

Coronary heart disease

Coronary heart disease provides a good example of the need for physical exercise. Despite the fact that mortality rates from CHD have declined dramatically in the past twenty years, the disease remains the major cause of death in industrialised countries (Crowley, Dunt & Day 1995; Murray & Lopez 1997). The greatest improvements in mortality from CHD have occurred in the US, Australia and Japan (Green & Ottoson 1994). Numerous research studies have identified the three major modifiable risk factors for CHD as smoking, hypertension and hypercholesterolaemia (Crowley, Dunt & Day 1995; Shea & Basch 1990). Health promotion programs have succeeded in lowering the rates of smoking and hypertension, but cholesterol levels have remained constant.

Weight control remains a problem. In males, the body mass index (weight/height^2) has gradually increased over the past two decades, and this is indicative of a gradual increase among the rest of the population of the Western world (Galuska et al. 1996; Knuiman et al. 1995). Preventive measures for coronary heart disease will therefore need to focus on exercise and reducing dietary intake (Crowley, Dunt & Day 1995; Young et al. 1996).

Weight control programs, especially for women of low socioeconomic status, have had only modest successes (Jeffery & French 1996). From a purely economic perspective, exercise, especially walking, is the most cost-effective form of illness prevention available. The cost of treatment of CHD is estimated at approximately $1.13 billion a year in Australia and $43 billion annually in the US (Crowley, Dunt & Day 1995; Green & Ottoson 1994). Although certain biological factors increase a person's risk of CHD (older age, male gender, prior family history and having a high-stress personality type), non-modifiable factors are compounded by lifestyle choices. The implication is for healthy lifestyle practices to begin early in life.

Smoking

The Director-General of the WHO reports that in the past four decades, since the hazards of tobacco use have been known, tobacco smoking has killed more than 60 million people in the industrialised countries alone (WHO 1996). Unless this trend is reversed, 10 million people will die each year of smoking-related causes, with 70% of these deaths in developing countries. In addition to the mortality rates, millions of people worldwide will suffer needlessly from a tobacco-related disease each year. These diseases will cost governments thousands of millions of dollars, with thousands of millions more lost because productive lives are cut short by tobacco use (WHO 1997). Smoking is thus the greatest public health problem of our time.

Tobacco is a risk factor for some 25 diseases and accounts for approximately 15% of deaths from all causes, including cardiovascular disease (CHD and stroke), cancers and obstructive pulmonary disease, in all age groups. This figure is closer to 50% in those with a lifetime smoking history (AIHW 1996b; WHO 1997). The debate over whether or not passive smoking is hazardous to health has now been resolved. We have a large, cumulative body of evidence indicating that for non-smokers, environmental tobacco smoke can result in aggravated asthmatic conditions, impaired circulation, respiratory conditions and, in infants, a greater risk of dying from Sudden Infant Death Syndrome (SIDS) (Haglund 1997).

In the industrialised nations, the annual cost of smoking-related deaths is exorbitant. In Australia, for example, where approximately 28% of people smoke, the cost of health care for smokers has been estimated at some $672 million. The cost is ten times that amount ($68 billion) in the US, where one-quarter of the population smokes (Escobedo & Peddicord 1996). The rate of smoking is proportionally higher for Aboriginal people (Andrews, Oates & Naden 1997). Recent American research also confirms the strong tendency for people with lower educational levels to smoke, particularly young males, who now have a smoking prevalence rate of 65%, or three times the national average (Escobedo & Peddicord 1996).

In Europe, Asia and many developing countries, smoking presents an even greater public health problem than in other countries. The prevalence of smoking in India, for example, has been estimated at as much as 45 to 48% among males. Indian women, who chew betel quid rather than smoking tobacco, are now dying of oral cancer at a rate greater than from breast cancer (Haglund 1997; Narayan et al. 1996). In China, where more than one-third of males smoke, it is predicted that by the year 2020 there will be 2 to 3 million deaths annually from tobacco-related disease (Haglund 1997; Zhu et al. 1996).

Smoking and diet

We have only recently begun to understand the mechanisms of smoking-related illness, although we have known for years that the carcinogens in cigarette smoke attack tissues in the larynx, oral cavity, oesophagus, lungs and urinary bladder. This creates damage by generating free radicals, which place increased demand on the antioxidant systems that protect cells from damage (Margetts & Jackson 1993). Further exacerbating the problem is the fact that most smokers have a lower intake of foods that provide protective antioxidant nutrients, such as vitamin C (English, Najman & Bennett 1997). There is now conclusive evidence of the links between smoking, inadequate diet and a hazardous intake of alcohol (Breslau et al. 1996; English, Najman & Bennett 1997). Once again, this points to the need for lifestyle modification programs to address risk factors and a lifestyle that may reinforce unhealthy patterns of living. The WHO decrees that this cannot be accomplished without broad popular support at the local level, where national and international initiatives for tobacco control must begin. These include providing protection from environmental tobacco smoke, anti-smoking health education programs, and support for smoking cessation (Haglund 1997; WHO 1997).

Environmental risk factors

Another combination of risk factors that jeopardises the health of adult populations is related to the effects of environmental influences, and the interaction of these with personal and sociocultural factors. Calvert and Ewan (1995) report that explicit assessment of this type of risk has been one of the most difficult tasks in public health. They attribute this to the uncertainty and controversy that always accompany the process of adjusting to major changes in the environment, and making 'best guesses' about human health. Some studies have been quite innovative in trying to identify the health implications of environmental development. One group of researchers devised a study to examine the pollutant levels of a proposed freeway as precipitating ill health and injury, while others examined the impact of living near a flight path (Dunt, Abramson & Andreassen 1995; Morrell & Taylor 1997). Research of this nature is in its infancy; it will take many years of systematic investigation to reveal the full extent of environmental problems associated with this type of development.

Research into workplace pollutants and subsequent health and safety education has heightened awareness of the need for reduction in workplace air pollution, and this comes at a time when more people are also quitting smoking (Brown et al. 1997). However, there is still much to be learned about the health effects of environmental pollutants. Studies on air pollution in all corners of the globe have now provided an inventory of chemicals defiling our air, primarily from automobile exhaust emissions and industrial waste.

Until very recently, environmental scientists were the only ones concerned about such pollutants as carbon monoxide, sulphur dioxide, hydrocarbons, lead, nitrogen oxides, dust, ash, and ozone. As the new century approaches and there is greater public awareness of such environmental factors as global warming and changes in the ozone layer, atmospheric idiosyncracies, transportation and consumption patterns, and systems of waste management, we can expect wider public participation in exploring their health implications (Calvert & Ewan 1995). Over the past two decades, significant gains have also been made in environmental legislation in a number of countries including the US, Australia and New Zealand. Importantly, the legislation has been developed through intersectoral planning and community participation (Calvert & Ewan 1995).

Cancers

One of the most prevalent diseases of adulthood is cancer, the second most frequent cause of death after CHD and stroke (AIHW 1996a). Although some cancers share common risk factors, most have a unique set of risk factors and vary according to age, gender and race. The most obvious of these are breast cancer, which occurs primarily in women, and prostate cancer, which occurs only in men. Most mortality rates from cancer have remained constant in the last half of this century, primarily because of early detection, although early detection has also resulted in an increase in the *incidence* of cancers such as breast and prostate (AIHW 1996a).

The rates of lung cancer mortality have also increased, despite lower smoking rates in the past two decades, but this reflects the smoking patterns of twenty years ago, given the onset of disease, or time lag between exposure to the risk and outcome. The risk of cancer is highest in adult life, and among older males. Younger adult females have proportionately higher rates because of cancers of the cervix, uterus, ovary and breast (AIHW 1996a).

Survival rates from cancer have improved over the past two decades. The survival rate is an indication of the biology of the disease and host factors, the availability of health services and medical intervention. Because these factors are not always comparable, especially where health services differ, international comparisons are imprecise. However, the trend indicates an improvement in relative survival at five years for Australian women from 70% in the 1970s to approximately 77% in the late 1980–90s. This compares with 64 to 70% in the UK, 69 to 80% in Scandinavia, 73 to 75% in Canada and 62 to 81% in the US (Taylor & Coates 1997).

Accidents and injuries

Another major risk for adults is that of accident and injury. The mortality rate from injuries is not significant compared with other causes of death. However, injuries result in major impediments to both quality of life and productivity (AIHW 1996a; Hingson et al. 1996). Alcohol is a major factor in nearly 50% of motor vehicle injuries. These are currently declining slightly due to improved public education programs, better law enforcement, stricter penalties, better roads and improvement in vehicle safety design. However, as the population grows, so too will automobile travel. It will take a concerted effort by government, industry, community organisations, health education personnel and people themselves to prevent the problem from becoming worse in the future.

Other injuries among adults include occupational injuries or falls at home (from bicycles, horses, ladders or scaffolding and so on), accidents related to using power tools, farm machinery, and poisonings (AIHW 1996a).

However, the most contentious form of injury is that caused by violence, particularly violent crime, which is becoming an all-too-pervasive characteristic of society. A large proportion of violent episodes occur within situations of family conflict, and these will be discussed in chapter 9. Most of the other types of violence in society are sensationalised by the press, but for every story that makes the headlines there are many more buried in both the suburbs of large cities and in the corners of rural communities.

Violence is perpetrated not only by criminals and those in altered states of consciousness brought about by substance use. Many countries, most notably the US, are currently experiencing a firearm and handgun-related epidemic of violence (Gardiner, Norton & Alpers 1996). Because burglaries and other crimes against property are on the increase everywhere, many people have either armed themselves or are less hesitant than in the past to use force in protecting their property. Some attribute the propensity to strike back to television violence, but this is as yet unresolved. One side of the debate argues that there is no direct link between what is modelled on television and what occurs in real life; but the opposing view is that young people are brought up to believe that violent retribution is a normal response in situations where a person is attacked or where efforts toward achieving some sort of goal are thwarted.

The issue of firearms use is one that should be of grave concern to public health professionals. In Australia and New Zealand, pro-gun lobby groups promote the notion that most incidents of firearm misuse are committed by either unlicensed owners with illegal weapons or the mentally ill. However, a study of all non-fatal firearm injuries in a three-year period in New Zealand revealed that a large number were perpetrated by licensed gun owners, including half of those involved in domestic disputes (Gardiner, Norton & Alpers 1996).

The role of government in regulating weapons continues to be a contentious issue. The worst episode of mass violence ever experienced in Australia occurred in 1996 in Tasmania, where 35 people were killed and 18 others were seriously injured by a deranged, lone gunman. The episode sparked an international debate on gun laws, and provided the stimulus for the world's most comprehensive set of gun control regulations. Interestingly, health organisations, with few exceptions, were slow in registering their views, perhaps indicating that there is still a need to normalise the social conditions within which we live as part of our health agenda (Peters 1996). In any event, it is imperative that further research be conducted on violence in the community, as much to dispel misconceptions about the conditions within which these events occur as to draw people's attention to the way violent lifestyles compromise the health of our communities.

Respiratory illness

Respiratory conditions are another frequently occurring cause of death in adults. These include chronic obstructive lung disease, asthma, emphysema and bronchitis (AIHW 1996a; Lee & Paxman 1997). Environmental factors, especially air pollution, are thought to play a role in each of these, although the precise nature of that role remains unknown. Most respiratory ailments occur as a result of some potent combination of hereditary, environmental and lifestyle factors. In many cases, occupational exposure either triggers or exacerbates a respiratory condition, especially where workplace dust is poorly controlled. The research is guarded on the role of occupational exposure and asthmatic episodes, and some uncertainties remain about the relative contribution of occupational exposure as a risk factor for asthma. However, studies have identified significant relationships between employment as a sawmill worker, laboratory technician, spray painter, baker, plastics and rubber worker, welder or cleaner and the risk of developing the disease (Beach et al. 1996; Kogevinas et al. 1996; Siracusa et al. 1995).

HIV and AIDS

The most prevalent cause of mortality among adults today is AIDS. In fact, 10% of all AIDS cases reported to the Centers for Disease Control and Prevention in the US have involved individuals 50 years of age and older, 10% of these being among persons over age 60. AIDS has been reported more in these older groups than in those 24 years old or younger, and the number is rising faster among the older population than in younger age groups (Whipple & Walsh Scura 1996). In some adult populations, particularly white, middle-class groups, the risk of HIV infection seems remote. In part this attitude is a product of public misinformation that has led people to believe that HIV is a disease of homosexual males and intravenous (IV) drug users.

A large proportion (71%) of all HIV infections worldwide are a result of heterosexual transmission. In the industrialised world, homosexual transmission is responsible for a much larger proportion (93% and 88% respectively) but the number of people infected through heterosexual intercourse is increasing (Choi & Catania 1996; Kault 1996; Li et al. 1996;

WHO 1996; Zierler & Krieger 1997). In countries like China, the majority of cases (73%) occur as a result of IV drug use (Yu et al. 1996). Although proportionately fewer adults contract AIDS than other illnesses (CHD, cancer or injuries), it is a major public health problem because of its lethal nature, and because it is preventable through healthy sexual practices.

Because of the myth of 'homosexual only' transmission, people have been particularly slow to understand the escalating risk of women contracting the disease. The risk is especially acute in women of colour, but again this is a reflection of socioeconomic status. Studies of women in the US, Zaire, Zimbabwe and South Africa illustrate the links between women being economically destitute and having to engage in sex for material sustenance (Zierler & Krieger 1997). In many parts of the industrialised world, women exchange sex for drugs, thus doubling the risk of contracting the disease. In the African countries this is sometimes at the request of their families for purchasing land or building materials or to repay debts. At the same time, men's labour migrations at times of shrinking jobs become a source of infection as they seek sexual contact along their routes (Zierler & Kreiger 1997).

Men's sexual behaviour in the industrialised nations has also put women at risk. One US study of women living in inner-city, low-income housing developments found that approximately one-third were put at risk by the behaviour of their sexual partners, whether through sexual activity or their use of injected drugs (Sikkema et al. 1996). In this study, women were found to have high levels of HIV risk knowledge, but they did not fully understand how to use a condom, and held misconceptions about the physical appearance of most people with HIV infection. Many had also contracted other sexually transmitted diseases, which is a known co-factor for HIV infection (St. Louis, Wasserheit & Gayle 1997). The authors concluded that health education programs must be designed to incorporate 'prevention messages and skills focused on partner relationships and the issues of power imbalance in traditional sexual relationships, social and economic dependence on a male partner, and the priorities of daily life for impoverished women' (Sikkema et al. 1996, p. 1127).

Countering risk: healthy adulthood

Community-wide programs to support lifestyle change are enjoying considerable success in helping the adult population with risk reduction. Several health promotion programs designed for prevention of illness and injury have used multiple strategies to help their respective communities achieve health enhancement objectives. These include the North Karelia (Finland) Project, the Stanford Five City Project and the Minnesota Heart Health Program in the US, the North Coast Healthy Lifestyle Program and the Shepparton Healthy Heart Project in Australia. Each has been aimed at multiple risk factor reduction strategies (smoking, diet, nutrition, physical activity, blood pressure). These have included community participation, media promotion, school-based health education, worksite health promotion, screening and referral of high-risk individuals, and education programs for health professionals (Crowley et al. 1995).

One issue of pressing concern to most public health planners is the rate of road trauma. The rate of fatal motor vehicle and motorcycle accidents among young men has sparked a concerted effort by many governments to set designated goals for reduction of road traumas. These address the need for greater community ownership and participation in road safety (ACT Government, Road Safety Strategy, 1994). In the US, vehicle-related deaths have declined in the past 25 years by 10,000 per year, despite the fact that the number of vehicles has doubled, miles driven have increased and cars have become smaller. The improvements have been attributed to the establishment of minimum safety standards, seat-belt laws and reduced alcohol allowances for drivers (Robertson 1996). One group of researchers attributes the success of implementing these measures to an intersectoral, community approach that organises multiple city departments and private citizens to focus on saving lives, rather than simply confining their efforts to a single measure such as drink-driving law enforcement. They calculated that this type of comprehensive approach could yield a 10 to 15-fold saving relative to program expenditures (Hingson et al. 1996).

Another important area in which risk factors need immediate attention is in preventing further escalation of the AIDS epidemic. The research suggests that there has been a worldwide shift from homosexual transmission to transmission by injecting drug users and heterosexual or bisexual unprotected intercourse. However, these patterns are not consistent for all populations. In some large cities, commercial sex workers have demonstrated responsible precautions; in other places, particularly in Asian countries, they have been less regulated than in other countries. Transmission by injecting drug users has led to an epidemic of hepatitis C, which is looming large on the horizon as a major public health problem (Kault 1996).

Both epidemics have remained a serious threat to indigenous people, particularly those in rural areas, who have not as yet had adequate or culturally appropriate health education programs designed for their particular needs. These people have also been poorly traced, so that patterns of infection are not clear (Kault 1996). Health education programs must target indigenous people and others who seem to be falling into the cracks in traditional awareness campaigns. The messages must incorporate what is now known about individual sexual behaviour among different groups of people and further investigate individual and group differences.

We also need to closely examine the link between education and preventive behaviour. Studies have found a link between higher educational attainment and protective behaviour, and this needs to be explored further (Choi & Catania 1996). This information is essential to ensure that resources spent on educating people are targeting the appropriate areas of need.

Goals for adult health

Goals for adult health should be to reduce the incidence of:

- cardiovascular disease and stroke
- cancer
- lung and respiratory diseases
- accidents and injuries
- infectious diseases.

These goals can be achieved primarily through programs that educate people about the risk factors predisposing to illness, those that facilitate healthy lifestyles in individuals and families, and through mechanisms that create healthy environments within which optimal lifestyles can be achieved. The Ottawa Charter guides the development of each of these strategies.

Building healthy public policy

The gun laws that have been introduced into Australian society are expected to have a marked effect on the rates of violent crime, although the response to the laws, introduced in 1997, will not be known for some years. One government initiative that has proven effective is the Australian National Road Safety Action Plan. The plan provides an excellent example of intersectoral collaboration for healthy public policy developed as a response to the high rate of road trauma, especially among younger men. The plan provides a blueprint for a co-ordinated approach to reducing the rates of trauma. It includes safety and law enforcement legislation, education programs and encouragement of safe practice, transport and land use planning, safety standards and engineering, and evaluation of progress.

These measures have been developed to incorporate physical, economic and social aspects of the driving environment, and will target all concerned with road safety, including automobile manufacturers, drivers, educators and the police (AIHW 1996c). In the UK, where a similar program has been introduced, the rate of casualties has dropped by 35% in a three-year period despite a growth in road traffic of 49% over the same period. Interestingly, drivers in that country are now almost three times as likely to be breath tested, but are less likely to fail the test than ten years ago. This is reflected also in the mortality rates. The number of deaths from drink-driving in that country has almost halved (UK Department of Transport 1996).

Health promotion policies governing smoking have experienced a very tortuous path. One of the difficulties with introducing anti-smoking policies has been an immensely powerful tobacco industry, which until 1997 denied that cigarettes caused any illness, and successfully defended all lawsuits against them. This occurred despite confirmation in 1950 by the Royal College of Physicians in London, the US Surgeon General, and the World Health Organization that smoking causes lung cancer (Wynder & Muscat 1995). However, the industry, which maintains lobbyists in all States of the US, succeeded in covering up its culpability in smoking-related mortality, perhaps because of government complacency encouraged by substantial revenues from tobacco tax. In 1997, a relatively small tobacco company, the Liggett group, created a worldwide controversy by openly admitting that research findings linking smoking and lung cancer had been suppressed for four decades by the tobacco industry.

What followed was an historic agreement between the US government and the nation's largest companies to pay upwards of $500 billion to settle a number of damages claims by the victims and their families. The settlement was made on the proviso that once settled, the companies would receive immunity from further class-action lawsuits. Because of this judgement, in 1997 the government instituted control over nicotine, under the Food and Drug Administration Act. The tobacco companies will end cigarette sales from vending machines and self-service displays, pay the medical bills of those with lawsuits pending, and fund an anti-smoking blitz intended to reduce youth smoking by 60% in the next decade. If this is successful, millions of young lives could be saved.

Several governments have, in the past, attempted to control the tobacco industry by forcing them to reduce the amount of carcinogens in the cigarettes they produced. By 1993, health hazard labelling had been introduced by most of the large tobacco companies, and the amount of tar and nicotine in cigarettes drastically reduced (by almost one-third). The latter development, however, has had a rebound effect on the health of some smokers. An unanticipated effect of the reduction in tar and nicotine is that smokers of low-yield cigarettes compensate for the low delivery of nicotine by inhaling the smoke more deeply and by smoking more intensely, causing a greater concentration of carcinogenic agents in their lungs. To make matters worse, this new, intense type of smoking is particularly noticeable among those employed in smoke-free environments. These are the smokers who slip outdoors as frequently as their job allows and puff deeply on their cigarettes to get the maximum effect in a short period of time, so they can hasten back to work.

Paradoxically, policies designed to improve workplace health and to prevent unhealthy levels of smoking toxicity are having the opposite effect. The message here is that once a health public policy has been developed, it must be constantly evaluated, so that both the intended and unintended outcomes can be part of the strategic planning processes for the future. A Canadian example also illustrates the need for ongoing evaluation. In 1994, a tobacco tax cut was introduced, much to the chagrin of the Canadian anti-smoking lobby. Research conducted by Statistics Canada revealed that almost immediately, the rate of decline in smoking was slowed (Hamilton et al. 1997). This case demonstrates the need for vigilance in public policy development, and the need for all health promotion programs to be based on the growing body of information from all parts of the world.

Creating supportive environments

As mentioned previously, nutrition and dietary habits play a large role in preventing illness. The good news in nutrition and diet is that people of all socioeconomic strata are beginning to change their eating patterns, perhaps in response to the combination of health education campaigns and supportive environments (Dobson et al. 1997). Supportive environments have also been effective in encouraging adults to take up a physical activity, as witnessed by the growth in the fitness industry.

Many community-wide programs have also been established to provide peer support to those suffering from illness or injury. In the past, many people died from the major illnesses of adulthood, such as CHD, cancer and respiratory disease. Today, with technological advances prolonging their lives, they live with the disease for longer periods than in the past. In addition, shrinking health budgets have shortened their hospital stay, resulting in a greater proportion of their rehabilitation time being spent in the home and community. This has necessitated a greater reliance on family and other informal carers providing support and advice throughout the illness trajectory.

Although this places a burden of care on family members, numerous community self-help and support groups have emerged from within communities. These people have mobilised their own resources to provide the informal support required by those suffering from cancer and other diseases (Ramsey 1992). Usually staffed by those who have survived some type of cancer, these groups provide assistance and guidance for those who need advice on a range of issues that assists their adjustment following the acute episodes of their illness, with positive results (Ramsey 1992).

Strengthening community action

The health problems of adulthood cannot be overcome without a supportive community infrastructure. Crime and violence in the community, the AIDS epidemic, carcinogens in the atmosphere, the plight of impoverished families, all must be seen as integral to the health of all community members. The role of the health professional is to ensure community-wide dissemination of current information on each of these topics, so that the community can make informed decisions about such things as crime and injury surveillance, providing support systems for the victims of illness, lobbying for environmental controls or assisting others less able to deal with their lives.

Examples of effective community action can be seen in a range of community programs to protect neighbourhoods from crime and injury. The Neighbourhood Watch program is perhaps the best known. Its strengths are that it is recognisable and widespread, and all members of the community where it has been introduced are able to recognise a safe location should the need arise. Similarly, community action spawned the Mothers Against Drink Driving (MADD) movement, which has successfully attracted thousands of members who have been able to lobby government bodies for a range of improvements to road safety and harsher penalties for those who drink and drive. However, some inequities exist between rural and urban communities (Hancock et al. 1996). Clearly, some people are disadvantaged by geography and other aspects of their lives. The goal must be to ensure that all people receive support and the opportunity to participate in planning for the development of their community.

Developing personal skills

One of the classic examples of developing personal skills has been the world-wide movement to teach women breast self-examination (BSE). Although mammography is now available to a large proportion of women in the industrialised nations, BSE is the cheapest and easiest way of screening those at risk of breast cancer, providing the technique is practised correctly. Health professionals can help address this problem by teaching community members to help one another learn appropriate techniques. Similarly, self-help groups that assist new mothers or the elderly are empowering and thus important to community self-determinism.

▶ CASE STUDY
The Mpowerment project

One project in the US that best illustrates peer support at the community level is a community project designed to help young gay men protect themselves against HIV infection. The Mpowerment project was based on the alarming fact that young gay men continue to engage in unprotected anal intercourse, and are still becoming infected with the HIV virus. A group of health professionals thus planned a community-level approach on the basis that they needed to reach large numbers of men, and that these men may not be susceptible to individual-level interventions, given the influences of their social environment. The other reason for selecting the approach was that it is known that most gay men do not seek out formal AIDS prevention services. The intervention was therefore planned around three principles: the men's social concerns, the anticipated power of peer influence, and the need to mobilise and empower the gay community.

The program was developed from the theoretical perspective of the diffusion of innovations, which posits that people are most likely to adopt new behaviours or innovations if others who are similar to them and who they respect, accept them. Small group peer-led meetings, social events and outreach activities were organised, wherein the group members, rather than the health professionals, encouraged participation in role plays and discussions about safe sexual practices. Evaluation of the program revealed that not only had the men increased their rate of protected sexual activity, but they had extended the message to others, diffusing the information throughout the gay community (Kegeles, Hays & Coates 1996).

Reorienting health services

The case study above illustrates not only the value of developing personal skills in the community, but also the need to shift the way health services are designed and delivered. In this case, the health education program was collaboratively designed by the gay men themselves and the group of health professionals studying its outcome. It represented a prime example of community-empowered health promotion. At the planning stages, health service professionals must investigate a range of these types of approaches.

Their planning must incorporate a contemporary vision of what is included in public health, including environmental issues as well as AIDS, other infectious diseases, cancers and smoking-related illnesses. Today we have realised some gains in publicising the importance of the social environment as well, but much remains to be done. We must continue to put forward the case of violence as a public health issue. Health services must be reoriented toward integrating information from a wide range of sources: consumer and scientific, formal and informal.

Health planning needs to explore the optimal mix of epidemiological and surveillance information, cost effectiveness and delivery mechanisms that will achieve the breadth and scope required. We also need to ensure the appropriate mix of individuals and groups to work toward health goals (St. Louis, Wasserheit & Gayle 1997). Preventive services must be tailored to the needs of the population subgroup, whether rural, urban, indigenous or non-indigenous. Most importantly, health services, whether for care or prevention, must be co-ordinated, so that health departments do not become compartmentalised and thus lose sight of the context within which health can be created and sustained. Only by working in partnership with community-based organisations, employers, churches, service clubs and neighbourhoods, and by reorienting health services to the setting in which they will be most acceptable to people, will we achieve the level of health that the population of the twenty-first century deserves.

THINKING CRITICALLY

Adult health

▶ Identify the three lifestyle issues most important to the health of adults.

▶ Describe how you would plan a health promotion campaign to encourage greater physical activity among a group of 40 to 45 year old women.

▶ Identify five important issues that must be addressed in a program to encourage sexual health among gay and/or bisexual males.

▶ Design a set of strategies for reducing the rate of criminal violence in your community.

▶ Explain how health services in your community can be reoriented to reflect the principles of primary health care.

REFERENCES

Andrews, B., Oates, F. & Naden, P. 1997, 'Smoking among Aboriginal health workers: findings of a 1995 survey in Western New South Wales', *Australian and New Zealand Journal of Public Health*, vol. 21, no. 7, pp. 789–91.

Australian Institute of Health and Welfare 1996a, *Australia's Health*, 1996, AGPS, Canberra.

Australian Institute of Health and Welfare 1996b, *Tobacco use and its health impact in Australia*, AGPS, Canberra.

Beach, J., Dennis, J., Avery, A., Bromly, C., Ward, R. et al. 1996, 'An epidemiologic investigation of asthma in welders', *American Journal of Respiratory Critical Care Medicine*, vol. 154, pp. 1394–400.

Breslau, N., Peterson, E., Schultz, L., Andreski, P. & Chilcoat, H. 1996, 'Are smokers with alcohol disorders less likely to quit?', *American Journal of Public Health*, vol. 86, no. 7, pp. 985–0.

Brown, A., Christie, D., Taylor, R, Seccombe, M. & Coates, M. 1997, 'The occurrence of cancer in a cohort of New South Wales coal miners', *Australian and New Zealand Journal of Public Health*, vol. 21, no. 1, pp. 29–32.

Calvert, D. & Ewan, C. 1995, 'Risks to health, risk management and environmental health impact assessment', editorial, *Australian Journal of Public Health*, vol. 19, no. 4, pp. 325–6.

Choi, K. & Catania, J. 1996, 'Changes in multiple sexual partnerships, HIV testing, and condom use among US heterosexuals 18 to 49 years of age, 1990 and 1992', *American Journal of Public Health*, vol. 86, no. 4, pp. 554–6.

Crowley, S., Dunt, D. & Day, N. 1995, 'Cost-effectiveness of alternative interventions for the prevention and treatment of coronary heart disease', *Australian Journal of Public Health*, vol. 19, no. 4, pp. 336–46.

Dobson, A., Porteous, J., McElduff, P. & Alexander, H. 1997, 'Whose diet has changed?', *Australian and New Zealand Journal of Public Health*, vol. 21, no. 2, pp. 147–54.

Dunt, R., Abramson, M. & Andreassen, D. 1995, 'Assessment of the future impact on health of a proposed freeway development', *Australian Journal of Public Health*, vol. 19, no. 4, pp. 347–56.

English, R., Najman, J. & Bennett, S. 1997, 'Dietary intake of Australian smokers and non-smokers', *Australian and New Zealand Journal of Public Health*, vol. 21, no. 2, pp. 141-6.

Escobedo, L. & Peddicord, J. 1996, 'Smoking prevalence in US birth cohorts: the influence of gender and education', *American Journal of Public Health*, vol. 86, no. 2, pp. 231–6.

Frank, J. 1995, 'Why "population health"?', commentary, *Canadian Journal of Public Health*, vol. 86, no. 3, pp. 162–4.

Galuska, D., Serdula, M., Pamuk, E., Siegel, P & Byers, T. 1996, 'Trends among overweight US adults from 1987 to 1993: a multistate telephone survey', *American Journal of Public Health*, vol. 86, no. 12, pp. 1729–35.

Gardiner, J., Norton, R. & Alpers, P. 1996, 'Non-fatal firearm misuse: license status of perpetrators and legality of the firearms', *Australian and New Zealand Journal of Public Health*, vol. 20, no. 5, pp. 479–82.

Green, L. & Ottoson, J. 1994, *Community Health*, 7th edn, Mosby, St Louis.

Guerzoni, E. 1996, 'Getting physical', *Sport Health*, vol. 14, no. 4, pp. 10–11.

Haglund, M. 1997, *The Next Wave of the Tobacco Epidemic: Women*, National Institute of Public Health, Stockholm.

Hamilton, V., Levinton, C., St. Pierre, Y. & Grimard, F. 1997, 'The effect of tobacco tax cuts on cigarette smoking in Canada', *Canadian Medical Association Journal*, vol. 156, pp. 187–91.

Hancock, L., Sanson-Fischer, R., Redman, S., Reid, A. & Tripodi, D. 1996, 'Knowledge of cancer risk reduction practices in rural towns in New South Wales', *Australian and New Zealand Journal of Public Health*, vol. 20, no. 5, pp. 529–37.

Hingson, R., McGovern, T., Howland, J., Heeren, T., Winter, M. et al. 1996, 'Reducing alcohol-impaired driving in Massachusetts: the saving lives program', *American Journal of Public Health*, vol. 86, no. 6, pp. 791–7.

Jeffery, R. & French, S. 1996, 'Socioeconomic status and weight control practices among 20 to 45 year old women', *American Journal of Public Health*, vol. 86, no. 7, pp. 1005–10.

Johnson, N., Boyle, C. & Heller, R. 1995, 'Leisure-time physical activity and other health behaviours: are they related?', *Australian Journal of Public Health*, vol. 19, no. 10, pp. 69–75.

Kault, D. 1996, 'Assessing the National HIV/AIDS strategy evaluation', *Australian and New Zealand Journal of Public Health*, vol. 20, no. 4, pp. 347–51.

Kegeles, S., Hays, R. & Coates, T. 1996, 'The Mpowerment project: a community-level HIV prevention intervention for young gay men', *American Journal of Public Health*, vol. 86, no. 8, pp. 1129–36.

Kleinman, A. 1988, *The Illness Narratives*, Basic Books, New York.

Knuiman, M., Jamrozik, K., Welborn, T., Bulsara, M., Divitni, M. et al. 1995, 'Age and secular trends in risk factors for cardiovascular disease in Busselton', *Australian Journal of Public Health*, vol. 19, no. 4, pp. 375–82.

Kogevinas, M., Antó J., Soriano, J., Tobias, A., Burney, P. & the Spanish Group of the European Asthma Study 1996, 'The risk of asthma attributable to occupational exposures. A population-based study in Spain', *American Journal of Respiratory and Critical Care Medicine*, vol. 154, pp. 137–43.

Lee, P. & Paxman, D. 1997, 'Reinventing public health', *Annual Review of Public Health*, vol. 18, pp. 1–35.

Li, Y., Gold, J., McDonald, A. & Kaldor, J. 1996, 'Demographic pattern of AIDS in Australia, 1991 to 1993', *Australian and New Zealand Journal of Public Health*, vol. 20, no. 4, pp. 421–5.

Margetts, B. & Jackson, A. 1993, 'Interactions between people's diet and their smoking habits: the dietary and nutritional survey of British adults', *British Medical Journal*, vol. 307, pp. 1381–4.

McGinnis, J. & Foege, W. 1993, 'Actual causes of death in the United States', *Journal of the American Medical Association*, vol. 269, pp. 2207–12.

Morrell, S. & Taylor, R. 1997, 'A review of health effects of aircraft noise', *Australian and New Zealand Journal of Public Health*, vol. 21 (suppl.), no. 2, pp. 221–36.

Murray, C. & Lopez, A. 1997, 'Global mortality, disability and the contribution of risk factors: Global Burden of Disease Study', *The Lancet*, vol. 349, May 17, pp. 1347–52.

Narayan, K., Chadha, S., Hanson, R., Tandon, R., Shekhawat, S. et al. 1996, 'Prevalence and patterns of smoking in urban India', *British Medical Journal*, vol. 312(7046), pp. 1576–9.

Nutbeam, D. 1995, 'Health outcomes, health promotion and improved public health in Australia', *Australian Journal of Public Health*, vol. 19, no. 4, pp. 326–8.

Paffenbarger, R., Hyde, R., Wing, A. & Lee, I. 1993, 'The association of changes in physical activity level and other lifestyle characteristics with mortality among men', *New England Journal of Medicine*, vol. 328, pp. 538–45.

Peters, R. 1996, 'Australia's new gun laws: preventing the backslide', *Australian and New Zealand Journal of Public Health*, vol. 20, no. 4, pp. 339–40.

Ramsey, P. 1992, 'Characteristics, processes, and effectiveness of community support groups: a review of the literature', *Family Community Health*, vol. 15, no. 3, pp. 38–45.

Robertson, L. 1996, 'Reducing death on the road: the effects of minimum safety standards, publicized crash tests, seat belts, and alcohol', *American Journal of Public Health*, vol. 86, no. 1, pp. 31–4.

Shea, S. & Basch, C. 1990, 'A review of five major community-based cardio-vascular disease prevention programs. Part 1: Rationale, design, and theoretical framework', *American Journal of Health Promotion*, vol. 4, no. 3, pp. 203–13.

Sikkema, K., Heckman, T., Kelly, J., Anderson, E., Winett, R. et al. 1996, 'HIV risk behaviors among women living in low-income, inner-city housing developments', *American Journal of Public Health*, vol. 86, no. 8, pp. 1123–28.

Siracusa, A., Kennedy, S., DyBuncio, A., Lin, F., Marabini, A., et al. 1995, 'Prevalence and predictors of asthma in working groups in British Columbia', *American Journal of Industrial Medicine*, vol. 28, pp. 411–23.

St. Louis, M., Wasserheit, J. & Gayle, H. 1997, 'Janus considers the HIV pandemic—harnessing recent advances to enhance AIDS prevention' editorial, *American Journal of Public Health*, vol. 87, no. 1, pp. 10–11.

Taylor, R. & Coates, M. 1997, 'Breast cancer five-year survival in New South Wales women, 1972 to 1991', *Australian and New Zealand Journal of Public Health*, vol. 21, no. 2, pp. 199–205.

United Kingdom, Department of Transport 1996, *Road Accidents in Great Britain 1995—The Casualty Report*, HMSO, London.

Whipple, B. & Walsh Scura, K. 1996, 'The overlooked epidemic: HIV in older adults', *American Journal of Nursing*, vol. 6, no. 2, pp. 6020–2.

World Health Organization 1995, *World Health Statistics Annual, 1994*, WHO, Geneva.

World Health Organization 1996, *The World Health Report 1996: Fighting Disease, Fostering Development*, WHO, Geneva.

World Health Organization 1997, *Message from the Director-General of the WHO for World No-Tobacco Day 1997*, WHO, Geneva.

Wynder, E. & Muscat, J. 1995, 'The changing epidemiology of smoking and lung cancer histology', *Environmental Health Perspectives*, vol. 103, no. 8 (suppl.), pp.143–8.

Young, D., Haskell, W., Taylor, C. & Fortmann, S. 1996, 'Effect of community health educa-tion on physical activity knowledge, activity and behavior', *American Journal of Epidemiology*, vol. 144, no. 3, pp. 264–74.

Yu, E., Xie, Q., Zhang, K., Lu, P. & Chan, L. 1996, 'HIV infection and AIDS in China, 1985 through 1994', *American Journal of Public Health*, vol. 86, no. 8, pp. 1116–22.

Zhu, B., Liu, M., Shelton, D., Liu, S. & Giovino, G. 1996, 'Cigarette smoking and risk factors among elementary school students in Beijing', *American Journal of Public Health*, vol. 86, no. 3, pp. 368–75.

Zierler, S. & Krieger, N. 1997, 'Reframing women's risk: social inequalities and HIV infection', *Annual Review of Public Health*, vol. 18, pp. 401–36.

8 Healthy ageing

The terms 'ageing' and 'elderly' were once used as an indication that a person had begun the downhill journey to the end of life. Yet today, as the world has experienced a proliferation in medical and health-related knowledge together with life-sustaining technology, ageing has taken on a new connotation—that of unexplored possibilities. Many people over age sixty-five lead healthy and productive lives, some thriving in ways they could not during their middle years when their life circumstances prevented them from achieving a balance between work, recreation and family responsibilities.

Where once sixty-five was thought to be the beginning of the *older* stage of life, and thus a state of *decline* in health and wellness, today we do not consider a person older until they have reached at least a decade beyond that. Even then, the emphasis in health care has shifted from the 'damage control' approach of previous times to advocating for health enhancement in the latter stage of life. This attitude is based on recent research that has shown an over-estimation of the so-called inevitable effects of ageing, and an under-estimation of the modifying effects of diet, physical exercise, personal habits, coping styles, environment and psychosocial factors (Seedsman 1995). This chapter looks at the changing attitudes towards older people and their health status, and explores some of the issues related to ageing that affect our attempts to advocate for health and wellness in the over-65 population.

Objectives

By the end of this chapter you will be able to:

- *describe the most important influences on health and wellness among the population over age sixty-five*

- *describe three risk factors that affect the health of older people*

- *discuss the concept of ageism and its implications for health care*

- *explain the patterns of health service utilisation among older adults*

- *identify health promotion strategies for the ageing population using the Ottawa Charter for Health Promotion.*

Healthy older people

People over age sixty-five constitute the fastest-growing population group in the world. The demographic trends reported by the WHO indicate that the global population will increase from 5.8 billion in 1996 to an estimated 7.9 billion by 2020, by which time the number of persons aged sixty years and above will almost double and reach 1.2 billion. More than three-quarters of these older people will be in developing countries (WHO 1997). At present, China, India, the former Soviet Union, the US and Japan are the countries with the largest proportion of elderly (Green & Ottoson 1994). Because older people use health care services to a proportionately greater extent than any other population group, it is a matter of considerable urgency that we seek ways of preventing illness and promoting healthy lifestyles among our older community members.

Health determinants and risk factors

The many factors that affect healthy ageing include biological and psychosocial conditions, the environment and access to health services. These can be analysed within the framework of our model (shown in figure 8.1).

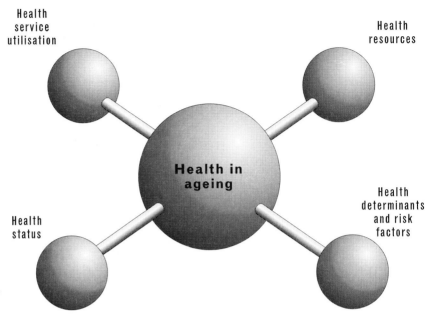

Figure 8.1
The interrelationship of factors influencing the health of older people

Healthy ageing

Goals for health and wellness are essentially the same for older age groups as for younger people. Healthy ageing means having minimal disability and dysfunction, a manageable amount of stress, the support of family and friends, a feeling of being valued, and adequate resources to cope with the requirements of daily living. Although many people develop functional disabilities with increasing age, most have also developed ways of coping with illness or incapacity from the wisdom that comes from life experiences and personal resourcefulness. A lifetime of activity, both mental and physical, a balanced diet, a sense of humour, gainful employment and an environment conducive to healthy lifestyles seems to insulate people against the worst effects of cardiovascular diseases, cancers, mental illnesses and other life-limiting disabilities or dysfunction. One prescription for healthy ageing is to:

> ...exercise...eat like a bushman...get as much sleep and rest as the body requires...maintain a sense of humour and deflect anger... set goals and accept challenges...don't depend on anyone else for your well being...be necessary and responsible; give to others, become involved...don't slow down; stick with the mainstream...maintain energy and a sense of purpose (Bortz, cited by Spradley & Allender 1996, p. 479).

Ageism

Despite the fact that ageing is a normal part of life, many older persons are subjected to *ageism*, a type of discrimination against older people on the basis of a number of misconceptions about their characteristics, attitudes and abilities. Among the most common of these are believing that older people are inherently weak, have diminished physical and mental capabilities, and are non-productive, resistant to change and dependent on others (Spradley & Allender 1996). Like younger people, the ageing population have physical, spiritual, psychological, social and cultural needs, but sometimes these are stereotyped as deficiencies. For example, an older person's irritability may be dismissed as part of ageing, when in fact it may be due to personality characteristics or a response to recent life events. Similarly, we all forget things, but an older person's casual memory slip may be labelled as dementia or Alzheimer's, when it may actually be due to motivation, the saliency of remembering, or personal interest (Wilkinson 1996).

To counter stereotyping, the onus is on health professionals and other informal carers to understand the important influence of a person's life biography and life events on health. Erickson's model of life cycle stages contends that we all have 'crises' to resolve at various stages of development. The major life crisis of old age is integrity versus despair, the resolution of which is expected to produce wisdom. But this may be an overgeneralisation of what actually occurs, because of variability among individual's responses to the circumstances of their lives (Wilkinson 1996). Some older individuals experience entirely different life crises, and their responses may be anything but despair. Attitudes vary widely—some people do not consider themselves old at eighty, while others believe they have aged at fifty.

It can be difficult to separate normal from pathological ageing because of variability in ethnicity, race and sociocultural affiliation. We know that heredity and lifestyle factors are important influences on a person's development throughout their lifespan, including the older years. A person's 'biological clock' for longevity is set at birth, although it is influenced during life by lifestyle factors (smoking, diet, exercise), social factors and medical events. The way in which older people respond to their social, cultural and physical environment is highly individualistic and represents a composite of responses to stress, life events, behaviours and social support (Nilsson 1996).

One way to address misconceptions about ageing is to continue researching people's experiences of ageing and the influence of a range of factors on the health of older groups of older people. There is a need for in-depth research studies to help dispel the sweeping generalisations that have focused on *in*competence, rather than *competence,* in the elderly. One approach is to include older people at each stage of the process. As participants, they can help guide questions toward issues relevant to them. This approach helps counter ageist stereotypes, as my colleagues and I found in our study of community perceptions of health and wellbeing. Our findings revealed that the same issues that concerned the young were most important to older families—namely, nutrition, exercise and ensuring a sustainable environment for subsequent generations (McMurray et al. 1998).

Research that garners older people's perceptions and that focuses on culturally embedded health needs helps to inform health promotion programs and strategies that can be tailored to individual and group needs. This type of approach provides a better basis for health planning than relying on the assumptions of health professionals (Askham 1996).

Risk factors for illness

Some 80% of older people have a chronic medical condition (AIHW 1996; Spradley & Allender 1996). These include the common illnesses of adults mentioned in chapter 7, such as cardiovascular and respiratory disease, cancers, diabetes, arthritis, vision and hearing loss, and hypertension. But many physiological changes that occur with ageing are simply a reduction in function.

Mental illness

For approximately 15% of the over-65 age group, mental illnesses are a problem, though many respond to treatment. But as in younger groups, the capacity of older people to cope with various mental conditions varies with ethnicity, socioeconomic status, marital status, urban–rural residence and family support (Green & Ottoson 1994). Dementia will be one of the biggest challenges of the future, as the demographics of an increasingly older population signal a sharp increase in its prevalence (Lorenson 1992). One of the most severe forms of dementia is Alzheimer's disease.

Alzheimer's disease is one of the most devastating conditions of ageing, because it is absolute and insidious. People suffering from Alzheimer's disease cannot rely on the past as a blueprint for the present or future, because they have forgotten everything learned earlier in life. As the disease develops, the person loses the capacity for judgement and reasoning, and in some cases is unaware that he/she is not functioning normally. In most cases, other family members have been unaware of their elderly family member's memory lapses, and so when the disease is diagnosed it is usually quite advanced.

One of the most difficult challenges of Alzheimer's is the stress placed on family caregivers, who often have to cope daily with intense agitation and anxiety. Also, Alzheimer's is caused by a combination of factors, some non-modifiable (age, genetics). This makes prevention difficult. Health promotion efforts must be directed at supporting family caregivers and ensuring the safety and security of the person suffering from the disease.

Medication use

For older people who develop chronic illnesses, often the most difficult aspect of their condition is coping with medications. Studies of medication use estimate that 80–90% of those over age 65 use medications regularly (Dicker 1997). Taking medications, especially where multiple drugs are required for one or a combination of conditions, is a particular source of distress among older people. For those with few problems, a medication regime may be relatively straightforward. But older people who develop multiple problems or an exacerbation of an existing condition may be referred to a number of health services, often for specialised diagnosis. In many cases, one drug is added to another, with one prescriber being unaware of the medications already being taken. This is as much a function of poor case management as the older person's inability to understand and explain his or her routine medication use. The result is *polypharmacy*, or multiple drug taking, which can have disastrous results.

▶ CASE STUDY

Polypharmacy

Mrs Griffin was sixty-seven when she was diagnosed with diabetes mellitus. She had had several episodes of near-fainting, and each time she would take a double dose of the arthritis medication she had been taking for twenty years and lie down until she felt better. Because she was also thirsty, she would have a drink; if late afternoon this would be a little nip of sherry or a 'shandy' (beer and ginger ale). She continued to take her thyroid medication, a 'silver compound' from the herbalist, sleeping pills at night, and some other tablets that her deceased husband used to take to 'make his blood richer'. The day she was diagnosed with diabetes, she had had a more serious spell than previously, and fell unconscious. Her daughter took her to the emergency department of the local hospital, where she was assessed by an internist, prescribed an insulin regime and referred to the diabetes educator for guidance. Her GP was notified, but she did not visit him after her discharge from hospital, because all he ever did was take her blood pressure, tell her to go on a diet, and send her the bill. Each time she went home to the bush, she saw the country doctor, who always reassured her that she would 'live forever'. Besides, the diabetes educator would make sure she was okay.

About six months after her diagnosis, she felt she had accomplished a manageable balance of diet, exercise and insulin tablets, so she went on a tropical vacation. While there, she was severely traumatised by a toxic insect bite. Within hours she had been admitted to hospital, where she suffered a mild stroke. She became severely depressed and never quite recovered her normal state after the stroke. She was put on anti-depressants for her mood states and an anti-hypertensive medication for her blood pressure, and returned home within a month. Three months later, she had a massive coronary and died on the way to hospital. She had just had her seventieth birthday. When the family sorted through her medications and contacted the GP, he was shocked to learn of the arsenal of medicines she had been taking, especially when he learned that she had been taking them in combination with alcohol and caffeine substances.

No one had thought to check that she had discarded the old pills for the new ones or that she was aware of the interaction between her prescriptions, over-the-counter medications and alcohol. No one medical practitioner had co-ordinated her medication regime or examined the potential for synergistic reactions. For the past two years, her preoccupation had been with diabetes. No one could provide any meaningful explanation for why her body had just 'packed up'.

The case above is not extraordinary. Many older people consume multiple medications without understanding their function, the sequence in which they should be taken, the compound effects, or the toxicity and side effects of each. So recognition of the problem has been the first important step toward more careful monitoring of polypharmacy among the older age groups in the community. The next step is wider public dissemination of medication information so that families and community members can be made aware of the dangers of self-medication and take steps to more closely monitor the effects of drugs taken in combination with each other.

Gender issues and ageing

Some patterns of health and illness are related to gender. At all stages of the life cycle men and women have different rates and types of illness, but this is most marked in later life. Women live longer, but are more likely than men to experience chronic ill health. They also report more recent and minor illnesses and have a higher prevalence of severe handicap. The prevalence of disability is higher for older men than women, and they are more likely to report cancers, diseases of the nervous system and sense organs, respiratory and digestive diseases than women, who are more likely to report circulatory system and genito-urinary disease, although the number of older women with coronary artery disease is increasing. Men over sixty-five are more likely to be overweight, to smoke and to be risk drinkers than women (AIHW 1996; Moser 1997).

Contrary to popular opinion, most of the conditions of ageing do not result in clinical sequelae. For example, many men with prostate cancer die *with*, rather than *from*, the disease, and for a variety of reasons have not experienced symptoms. Similarly, menopause is one of the most misunderstood life transitions for older women. It is often accompanied by vasomotor symptoms such as hot flushes and sweats but, contrary to common understanding, it does not necesarily result in decreased health status, increased use of health services or increased levels of depression (McKinlay 1992).

One health risk that occurs at menopause is osteoporosis, in which loss of bone mass weakens the bone, making it easier to fracture. Osteoporosis is more prevalent in females but also occurs in males. Heredity plays a part in disease development, but most factors contributing to the condition are modifiable with healthy lifestyle practices such as maintaining a diet high in calcium, and regular, weight-bearing exercise. Smoking, alcohol, a prolonged high-protein diet, excessive caffeine intake, sedentary lifestyle, and medications such as cortisone, anticonvulsants and thyroid medication also contribute to osteoporosis (Green & Ottoson 1994).

Osteoporosis is also influenced by hormonal factors, specifically the amount of oestrogen. At menopause the decline in oestrogen accelerates loss of bone mass; but this may also occur in younger women. Women who have 'turned off' menstruation through anorexia, long-distance running or other excessive exercise for more than six months, or those whose body fat mass drops below 15% of their normal weight, may lose bone mass (Beard & Curtis 1997). The best way to prevent loss of bone mass, and conditions such as osteoporosis, is to adopt a healthy diet rich in calcium from an early age. One of the best ways to combat oestrogen loss is to exercise regularly, seven days a week if possible, regardless of age. The exercise regime should be tailored to the individual's needs, and should balance aerobic exercise, such as brisk walking, cycling or riding a stationary bike, with resistance training and stretching (Shangold 1996).

Physical activity

Physical exercise has only recently begun to be an important part of the lifestyle of older people. Many of today's over-65's have grown up believing that work (including housework) provided sufficient physical exercise. However, with the widespread trend toward healthy lifestyles in other age groups, this attitude is gradually changing. Today, in many countries and communities, health and fitness programs are aimed specifically at the older age groups, whereas in the past, health care resources, including health promotion funds, tended to be diverted towards younger people.

This new emphasis on healthy lifestyles for older people has resulted from a combination of factors. One of these is increased life expectancy, related to the explosion of both medical and scientific knowledge; another is technology, which has provided medical practitioners with the means to treat illness efficiently and effectively, and has enhanced people's capacity to be self-determined in maintaining health and positive lifestyle practices. The Internet, for example, distributes health-related information that allows the public to gain insights into health, risk factors and a range of illnesses. For many retired people, accessing this information has become a hobby, and has prompted a shift in medical attitudes toward health consumers. Because of the proliferation of public information, many older people have been able to self-manage to a greater extent, or to negotiate care strategies with their medical providers using information they have downloaded from the 'net'.

Community attitudes toward health and healthy lifestyles have also changed, with the result that more older people feel comfortable participating in outdoor activities, joining their younger counterparts in sporting and recreational pursuits that would have been unattractive to their forebears. Consumer trends have also responded to the needs of older people. Today there is widespread recognition that many over-65's have disposable income for travel, leisure activities, sportswear, reading materials, software and a range of consumer goods tailored to their special needs. To some extent, these changing community attitudes represent a response to the proliferation of research knowledge in the area of exercise science and ageing.

Professional knowledge about physical training for older people is currently experiencing a period of unprecedented growth. It was formerly believed that loss of strength was inevitable with ageing, but recent research shows that resistance training improves strength and functional ability, thereby decreasing the risk of falls. Falls are the most common source of injury in older people, and although they may be caused by a range of factors, including poor vision, foot disorders, depression, acute illness, dementia and environmental hazards, many simply occur because of a lack of muscle strength (Pollock 1992). Exercise specialists concur that strength training can help build back the muscle mass, especially in men, that has been diminished by loss of the anabolic hormones (testosterone and growth hormone) through ageing. Unless joint pain or musculoskeletal conditions contravene, resistance training may be beneficial for both males and females in older age, providing their program is undertaken with a preliminary medical assessment, and conducted under the supervision of specialist exercise trainers (Munnings 1993; Pollock 1992).

Fitness and personal attitudes

Positive attitudes toward physical activity have many advantages. Researchers have identified the benefits of regular physical exercise in the elderly as increased cardiovascular function, lower morbidity and mortality from cardiovascular disease, less body fat, better lipid profile, slowed progression of osteoporosis, better balance and co-ordination, better functional capacity, better nutrition and sleep, and in many cases reduction of anxiety, depression and other psychological disorders (Finucane et al. 1997). A recent Australian study revealed that group exercise in older community-dwelling women resulted in significant improvement in reaction times, strength, memory span and measures of wellbeing. The researchers concluded that group exercise may help reduce age-related declines in certain physiological and cognitive functions. Also, group exercise is usually accessible, inexpensive and enjoyable (Williams & Lord 1997).

As with all age groups, individual differences determine the extent to which older people will choose one or another type of activity. One type of exercise rapidly becoming popular among older and middle-aged people is the Chinese martial art, Tai Chi. Besides improving balance by teaching people to rotate the body slowly and walk with a narrower stance, Tai Chi helps people recognise the limits of their stability. It provides a slow, rhythmic sense of movement that has been shown in the few research studies conducted to date to avert falls in older people (Wolf 1997).

Exercise such as Tai Chi exemplifies the importance of balancing, or harmonising, physical and mental activity. This is crucial to the notion of a healthy lifestyle, which some mistakenly equate with physical fitness only. Seedsman (1995, p. 40) defines a healthy lifestyle as a unique pattern of living adopted by an individual in his/her 'interaction with self, the social and material world and the values, orientations and strategies that are utilised for coping with change'. A healthy lifestyle reflects an individual's overall fitness orientation and accomplishments. Being fit encompasses not just cardiovascular and respiratory fitness, muscle strength, endurance, flexibility and body composition, but also relaxation, enhanced emotional wellbeing and a positive self-image. A fitness *attitude* is thus as essential as a well-exercised body. It is sustained during ageing by investing in life and the idea that life, to its final stages, is an adventure (Seedsman 1995).

Sexuality and ageing

Sexual activity is a natural part of life, and sexual patterns established as a young person remain throughout life (Steinke 1997). Sexual relationships provide love, intimacy, closeness and physical pleasure, which enhance life (Marinaro 1997). Age may reduce the frequency of sexual activity, but this may be due to a range of factors, including boredom (Richardson 1988). For many older people, maintaining sexuality and sexual activity can help to counter other compromises to the quality of life. This may be especially so for the older woman, whose identity as a younger person may have revolved around mothering and being a wife. In later years, she may feel it is still as important to feel needed and wanted as during child-bearing years, when her sexual identity would have been more socially visible (Nay 1992). Similarly, a man may feel that his sexual identity is dismissed by society with the end of his paid employment, particularly if his sense of manliness' was derived from being the family provider.

To date, research into sexuality and ageing has marginalised the issue of sex roles in ageing and instead tended to focus on measuring sexual activity. To help older people see themselves and their health needs in a holistic way, it is important to examine the psychosocial aspects of life quality (Steinke 1997). Measuring activity patterns may reduce our information to statistical associations rather than informing us about older peoples' experiences, expressions of sexuality, or unmet needs. But the research has revealed that those who care for older people can be influenced by well-designed educational programs that make visible all aspects of emotional health, including sexuality (Steinke 1997). At the population level, this suggests that community attitudes may be influenced by carefully conceived messages that highlight the importance of sexuality at all (including the latter) stages of human development. In line with the principles of primary health care, this approach celebrates emotional health as a fundamental human right (Parke 1991).

Widowhood and loneliness

A person's coping strategies are developed over years of dealing with life's stressors, but some situations have a profound effect on emotional status, particularly if they are unexpected. One such situation is widowhood (Gallagher, Thompson & Peterson 1982). The experience of widowhood varies on an individual basis, and results in differential effects on the well-being and morale of older people (Bennett 1997). Older people have usually had some exposure to death, through losing either friends or other family members, but the loss of a spouse is often the most difficult to deal with. Because of differential mortality with ageing, elderly women are widowed at a rate higher than their male counterparts.

Today, women who are widowed have usually held traditional family roles, and so may be deprived of their self-identity and social context once their partner is gone. In many cases their physical and mental health deteriorates, as they have no one to shop for, cook for or share meals with. Older widows may also be unprepared for making financial decisions, obtaining necessary services and socialising as a single person rather than as part of a couple. The health of older men also tends to decline with widowhood. Some men find it almost impossible to perform routine household tasks and develop social networks formerly organised by their wives. In these cases, widowhood is more isolating for them than for their female counterparts (Gallagher, Thompson & Peterson 1982).

The loneliness that ensues from losing a partner can precipitate illness or aggravate pre-existing disorders in both sexes (Rosenbloom & Whittington 1993). Often the interaction of ageing and loneliness has a multiplier effect, wherein the older person develops an increasingly poor self-image and an inability to cope with further losses, or to concentrate on the present. Activity patterns shift, and many experience almost constant restlessness and dissatisfaction with life (Donaldson & Watson 1996). The process of grieving may lead to depression; in some cases people's interest in health, lifestyle and fitness declines. The most noticeable symptom of this is usually neglect of their nutritional intake, resulting in 'failure to thrive', a condition characterised by malnutrition, weight loss and depression (Newbern & Krowchuk 1994; Rosenbloom & Whittington 1993).

Meeting social needs

Adaptation to loss is a complex process requiring four major tasks: accepting the finality of the loss, experiencing the pain of grief, adjusting to the environment from which the deceased is missing, and withdrawing emotional attachment to their partner. This is a very difficult process, almost impossible without social support (Morgan 1994). It is important for the health professional seeking to provide support to the bereaved person to remember that each person grieves in their own way, and to spend some time trying to understand the meanings that this particular loss holds for that person (Gilbert 1996). Some researchers have found that the process of adapting is highly dependent on friendship networks. A confidante can have a buffering effect on the stress of bereavement. This may be very difficult for some, especially males, many of whom find themselves in later life impoverished by a lack of friends or a social network (Gallagher, Thompson & Peterson 1982).

Social isolation is one of the most pervasive conditions of ageing. For those with good physical and mental health, social networks may simply shift over time; but for those incapacitated by chronic illness or disability, being cut off from former affiliations can be devastating. Religion is an important affiliation for many older people who rely on their church and church-related organisations for continuing social connectedness.

Religion and health

A review of studies on the relationship between religion and health in many cultures, including US White and Black Protestants, European Catholics, Parsis from India, Zulus from South Africa, Japanese Buddhists and Israeli Jews, reveals that religion can have a significant, positive effect on health. These effects are evident in studies of self-limiting acute conditions, fatal, chronic diseases and illnesses with lengthy, brief or absent latency periods between exposure, diagnosis and mortality. The author of this extensive review has concluded that there are many factors related to religion that promote health, including the fact that the holding of particular religious beliefs tends to promote healthier lifestyles.

Belonging to a religion can also exert psychosocial effects. Religious affiliation and a sense of belonging engendered by the church can buffer the adverse effect of stress and anger, in an interaction between psychosocial and biological effects, possibly through psychoneuroimmunologic responses (Levin 1994). But some aspects of the relationship between religion and health are ambiguous. For some, religion seems to enhance peacefulness, self-confidence and sense of purpose; others are beset by guilt, self-doubt, shame and low self-esteem. These responses may be a result of the interaction between personal belief systems and those that flow from the religious affiliation (Levin 1994).

Socioeconomic status

Many older people live below the poverty line and this has profound health effects. In the US, approximately 13% of over-65's live at this level of poverty (Spradley & Allender 1996). Older persons living in socioeconomic disadvantage tend to have higher rates of mortality from all causes, specifically pneumonia, influenza, diabetes, lung cancer, respiratory illness and stroke (AIHW 1996). Older women are often financially disadvantaged, especially if they have not planned for surviving their spouse, and their economic worries can be unremitting and irreversible, especially if resources are not forthcoming from family members. The best prevention is retirement planning; but for many older people this retrospective insight is less than helpful.

Retirement

Many people fail to begin planning for their retirement until it is imminent, and find themselves having to sustain a living for up to one-third of their lives, whereas in the past, the time between retirement and the end of life was considerably shorter. Throughout those twenty years, the cost of living escalates, and often older retirees find they have inadequate financial resources. This can lead to a desperate need for revised financial planning in their seventies and eighties, which can leave some people vulnerable to exploitation by a range of financial advisors. One outcome may be that they are persuaded to re-mortgage their homes in schemes that would see their children financially liable following their death. Of course, this is not always the case, but it signals a need for financial counselling at many stages of life so that people can feel empowered to make their own decisions. Again, this illustrates the interaction between socioeconomic variables and the capacity for sustainable health during retirement and the older stages of life. Seedsman (1995) suggests that retirement should be a time of optimism. At this time in a person's life, the pervasive element should be resocialisation, where a life-enhancing lifestyle is substituted for old, debilitating habits. The features of this are as follows:

- constructive social relationships
- a meaningful level of social integration
- positive self-regulation to stressful aspects of the environment
- effective functioning in accordance with genetic, physiological, psychological and physical capacities
- regular involvement in a series of intrinsically motivated behaviours that are pleasurable and satisfying, including, where possible, a balanced physical activity program for a minimum of three days per week (Seedsman 1995, p. 41).

Relocation

Another factor that jeopardises the health and wellbeing of older people is relocation. Many older people have experienced multiple relocations, from their own home to the residence of a family member, and sometimes back and forth between the homes of family members. They may also experience relocations between residential facilities, health care institutions and their usual residence. Each of these moves adds stress to their lives, especially if they have been forced by illness or family circumstances to leave a home in which they had spent a substantial portion of their lives. For some, the stress is exacerbated by the unpredictability of the move, because of either its location or its duration. Relocation stress is influenced by several factors: the person's characteristics prior to the move, their attitudes toward moving, their preparation for the move, their physical and cognitive status, and the extent to which they feel they have control over the move. Males, especially older males, usually suffer adverse consequences to moving, as do those in poor mental or physical health (Green & Ottoson 1994).

At some point, most people experience a loss of *place* in both the material and the emotional sense. For the older person this is usually quite painful, as the connection between people and place becomes more entrenched with time. Some people go through a period of grieving for their home in a way that surprises others, including family members, with its intensity. Besides losing the material comforts of their house, they have also lost the symbolic meaning of their sanctuary. Their home may contain the history of establishing and sustaining the family, the sense of satisfaction that comes from providing a protective environment for loved ones, the possessions and personal touches that make the family's mark on the home, and the peculiar way in which the home has acted as an enclosure for their most significant moments and memories. In some cases, the transition to a more protective environment is required, and in time the person adjusts. However, it is important for health advocates to be sensitive to a person's environmental needs, especially at those times when the priority for care may be emphasising physical needs.

Utilisation of health services

It is widely accepted that people aged beyond sixty-five use health services more frequently than other age groups (AIHW 1995). However, closer examination of patterns of utilisation among older people reveals that they are not a homogeneous population, and that health service utilisation varies according to a range of factors. These include whether they are from rural or urban communities, their cultural norms, the extent to which they prefer to care for their own health needs, and their satisfaction with available services and service providers.

Researchers have suggested that satisfaction with services actually contributes to health status, in that those who are satisfied tend to be compliant with the recommendations of health care professionals (Hjortdalh & Laerum 1992; Showers et al. 1995). This makes it important to understand people's perspectives toward health care rather than adopt a 'one-size-fits-all' approach to service provision. In considering older people as one homogeneous group we run the risk of propagating obtrusive, over-medicalised policy, and inattention to the reasons why older people cope with problems and changes in the way that they do (McKinlay 1992). One study of seniors' needs in Canada revealed that what older people value most from health care providers is positive, appropriate communication, non-stereotyped attitudes toward them, accessible, appropriate services, and continuity of care, a finding also supported by our study (Brown, McWilliam & Mai 1997; McMurray et al. 1998).

In the industrialised countries, 70 to 80% of persons aged sixty-five years and over have good health and manage their daily activities without assistance. About 6 to 7% are in residential care; 12 to 15% of persons living in their own homes, either alone or with family members, need some form of health or social service assistance (Lorensen 1992). In Australia as well as the US, more than 90% of those over age sixty live in private homes within the community; half of these require care. This leaves millions of older people worldwide cared for by family members, most of whom are female; the majority of these informal carers do not receive extra assistance from others (Godfrey 1996; McMurray 1995; Spradley & Allender 1996). The role of the health advocate must therefore include advocating for family members, and this has implications for both health policy and practice.

Goals for healthy ageing

Healthy and successful ageing must provide:

■ a balance between independent living and social support
■ physical and emotional health
■ adequate financial and health care resources to sustain the latter stages of life
■ a place in which to feel safe and comfortable.

Once again, the strategies of the Ottawa Charter for Health Promotion provide a guide to implementing these health goals.

Building healthy public policy

The year 1999 will be the International Year of Older Persons. This is an important indicator of a global commitment to meeting the needs of our ageing population. The WHO has recently emphasised the needs of older people, underlining the importance of physical exercise for people of all age groups, including the oldest citizens. Although there is recognition of the pre-eminence of personal choices in undertaking varying levels of activity, they have suggested that public policies must support these choices with the infrastructure for healthy ageing (WHO/FIMS 1995). This type of statement by the WHO acknowledges the role of governments and policy makers at all levels in addressing the health and fitness needs of older people.

In addition to general health and exercise programs, policies must also address the nutritional needs of older people. Because a community's food supply is determined primarily by the immediate environment, local government policies must reflect the importance of ensuring equitable distribution of what may be inadequate resources. Food safety and storage is also an issue for the elderly. As mentioned in chapter 5, food safety has become a priority of the international health community, and the impetus for this has come from the needs of children. However, nutrition is an aspect of healthy lifestyles that cuts across all developmental stages, and nutrition policy must also address older people's access to fresh vegetables, fruit and protein-containing substances.

One of the most important policy decisions affecting the health of the ageing population relates to housing and other types of accommodation for the elderly. Many older people move from home to hospital, to hostel or palliative care environment and back to home. For some, these multiple transitions have distressing effects, particularly if financial support for accommodation is inadequate. Governments in many countries have experimented with a variety of funding arrangements for aged care, and none have fully met the needs of all people. In Australia, the current debate over entry fees for nursing homes has provoked an outcry on the basis that the proposed scheme is a violation of the primary health care principles of equity and access. These issues must be resolved at all levels of health services administration and include sensitivity to older people's need for self-determination, particularly in being able to select an environment that is conducive to healthy ageing and compatible with cultural needs and preferences.

Creating supportive environments

By the year 2020 most people will live in urbanised environments, including 60% of the population of developing countries (WHO 1997). In some cases this is appropriate for older people who wish to be surrounded by family and friends. Urban settings also tend to provide a greater number of resources to older people, such as day-care centres and neighbourhood self-help groups. However, the shrinking of the rural sector is an issue that has caused many older rural people considerable stress. Away from their familiar space and sense of independence, many will experience the crowding of the cities for the first time during their retirement. Rural people are known for self-reliance and independence, yet they often have little access to the means to live an empowered life, especially when they suffer from dementia or other mental illnesses. Researchers have also revealed that face-to-face contact with people in rural areas has diminished, compromising their social support network. Like urban dwellers, poverty among older people leads to decreased social activity and voluntary participation, and this extends also to family caregivers, who may have few resources and thus little respite from their role (Godfrey 1996).

Strengthening community action

Poverty among the ageing population must be addressed at the community as well as the policy level. Self-help groups and mutual assistance schemes must in some cases be initiated by health and social welfare personnel, as these are the people most likely to become aware of community strengths as well as needs. Community action can also be supported by encouraging volunteer activities within the ageing population, including widow-to-widow support groups and those that focus on a certain illness (Ramsey 1992).

Programs such as the University of the Third Age are often well received by older people, who find keeping up-to-date stimulating and informative. A Canadian study from the Centre on Ageing at the University of Victoria reports that many older people express a willingness to give time to one or more voluntary organisations, and these people should be encouraged. The researchers concluded that there is enormous value added to the role of the health advocate by including lay volunteers. If people participate in self-help, mutual aid and other voluntary groups, the research and practice interests of both lay and professional groups could expand the constituency advocating for more public involvement in the planning and delivery of health and social services (Prince & Chappell 1994; Ramsey 1992).

Another important element of social support for many older people is their religion and their ability to regularly attend church services. Relocation to a different environment may cause them enormous stress if they are also unable to return to the familiarity of friends and religious support. Our role as health advocates should include assessing their needs for communication and worship with church members. This may involve arranging transportation, social networks of lay people with similar religious affiliations, or visits by members of the church, especially for those who are incapacitated and cannot meet what they may see as the obligations of their faith.

Developing personal skills

One of the most difficult challenges in health promotion for the older population is to change entrenched attitudes. Many older people, when confronted with a serious illness, will change their lifestyle habits. It is, however, more difficult to change personal habits among those older people who have not yet experienced serious consequences of their behaviours. This has been the case in smoking cessation programs (Wakefield et al. 1996). The implications for developing personal skills are clear: people need to be provided with both personal information (such as the results of lung function tests) and the structural support for change.

Recognition of the hazards of unhealthy lifestyle practices is only part of the equation in encouraging older people to change. Behavioural change is at best difficult to achieve. Older people often need to balance control of a chronic illness such as diabetes or heart disease with trying to live a normal and fulfilling life. Some older people try to give up smoking or to lose weight numerous times before they are successful, and go through several stages ranging from discouragement to commitment, just as occurs in younger people. However, they often have fewer activities to distract them when they are trying to make major lifestyle changes, and also have a longer history of the behaviour(s) than young people. We need to support unsuccessful, as well as successful, attempts and try to understand the difficulties inherent in trying to unlearn, then relearn, ways of behaving. Most importantly, it is crucial that older people are treated as unique human beings. For some, massage, therapeutic touch and alternative therapies provide a remedy with which to counter unhealthy lifestyles. Others respond to a more cognitive, rational approach and can be convinced to reframe the negative lifestyle practice as a threat to their longevity or to the quality of their life. The most successful persuasive techniques capitalise on both the unique and shared characteristics of people attempting to change, placing at least equal emphasis on community infrastructure that would support the change.

Reorienting health services

Health promotion programs for older people need to be tailored to their particular community and to the self-identified sociocultural preferences of those who are being cared for. Given the great diversity between different age groups beyond sixty-five, between cultures and between those with different levels of health and wellness, it is important to assess their individual needs before assigning them to one or another type of care. In Japan, for example, as in many Eastern cultures, it is an accepted fact of life that elders will be cared for by the family regardless of whether or not the older people are ill or well. In other countries, care of the frail aged takes place in nursing homes, with only minimal input from family members.

The effectiveness of healthy lifestyle promotion programs is also dependent upon the physical environment within which they are received. Those programs devised for nursing home residents are often aimed at the older old, and would be inappropriate for those who live in retirement villages or mobile home parks. Similarly, those who live alone or with families in private homes may have different needs from those of communal-living seniors. A mentored approach usually works best in a group setting, where healthy older people can encourage one another toward positive health practices. One model being adopted in Denmark involves older people being provided with the option of living in integrated housing with a communal concept of living. Residents are provided with common facilities but must also commit themselves to the common community goal and be willing to help others when needed, as well as contribute to the financial running of the buildings (Lorensen 1992). Negotiating tasks and needs provides people with a sense of making their own choices and thus controlling their own destiny.

In this era of economic restraint, the emphasis is on community and home care, so even in those places where acute care has traditionally been allocated to institutions, the trend is changing. As a result there is increased burden on family caregivers, who often require substantial educational support for their role. This includes information on rehabilitation strategies as well as the intervention technologies planned for their family member. They also have a significant need for respite care to prevent situations where they are overcome by the stress of care giving. Home care represents a shift toward considering health a family matter, rather than an issue confined to the individual.

Caring for our ageing population requires careful deliberation of the 'mix' that constitutes optimal conditions for health enhancement. This includes access and equity in service provision, empowerment for the older person and his/her family, a physical and social environment within which health can be achieved until the end of life within a milieu of encouragement and caring.

THINKING CRITICALLY
Healthy ageing

▶ Identify four significant influences on healthy ageing.

▶ Describe three factors in the environment of older people that put them at risk for ill health.

▶ Discuss the relationship between healthy communities and healthy ageing.

▶ Describe three major patterns of health care utilisation by older people that affect the community health care system.

▶ Devise a set of strategies to promote healthy ageing in your community using the Ottawa Charter for Health Promotion as a guide.

REFERENCES

Askham, J. 1996, 'Ageing in black and ethnic minorities: a challenge to service provision', *British Journal of Hospital Medicine*, vol. 56, no. 11, pp. 602–4.

Australian Institute of Health and Welfare 1995, *Health in Australia: What You Should Know*, AGPS, Canberra.

Australian Institute of Health and Welfare 1996, *Australia's Health, 1996*, AGPS, Canberra.

Beard, M. & Curtis, L. 1997, *Menopause and the Years Ahead*, Fisher Books, Tucson, Arizona.

Bennett, K. 1997, 'A longitudinal study of wellbeing in widowed women', *International Journal of Geriatric Psychiatry*, vol. 12, pp. 61–6.

Brown, J., McWilliam, C. & Mai, V. 1997, 'Barriers and facilitators to seniors' independence', *Canadian Family Physician*, vol. 43, pp. 469–75.

Dicker, B. 1997, 'Promoting quality use of medicine: the med-smart project', *Geriaction*, vol. 15, no. 1, pp. 4–11.

Donaldson, J. & Watson, R. 1996, 'Loneliness in elderly people: an important area for nursing research', *Journal of Advanced Nursing*, vol. 24, pp. 952–9.

Finucane, P., Giles, L., Withers, R., Silagy, C., Sedgwick, A. et al. 1997, 'Exercise profile and subsequent mortality in an elderly Australian population', *Australian and New Zealand Journal of Public Health*, vol. 21, no. 2, pp. 155–8.

Gallagher, D., Thompson, L. & Peterson, J. 1982, 'Psychosocial factors affecting adaptation to bereavement in the elderly', *International Journal of Aging and Human Development*, vol. 11, no. 2, pp. 79–96.

Gilbert, K. 1996, '"We've had the same loss, why don't we have the same grief?" Loss and differential grief in families', *Death Studies*, vol. 20, pp. 269–83.

Godfrey, S. 1996, 'Identified gaps in the services to rural carers of frail/demented people', *Geriaction*, vol. 14, no. 1, pp. 26–31.

Green, L. & Ottoson, J. 1994, *Community Health*, 7th edn, Mosby, St Louis.

Hjortdalh, P. & Laerum, E. 1992, 'Continuity of care in general practice: effect on patient satisfaction', *British Medical Journal*, vol. 304, pp. 1287–90.

Levin, J. 1994, 'Religion and health: is there an association, is it valid, and is it causal?', *Social Science and Medicine*, vol. 38, no. 11, pp. 1475–82.

Lorensen, M. 1992, 'Health and social support of elderly families in developed countries', *Journal of Gerontological Nursing*, June, 25–32.

Marinaro, D. 1997, 'Your turn', *Journal of Gerontological Nursing*, Oct. pp. 52– 5.

McKinlay, J. 1992, 'Advantages and limitations of the survey approach: understanding older people', in *Researching Health Care: Design, Dilemmas, Disciplines*, eds J. Daly, I. McDonald & E. Willis, Routledge, London, pp. 114–37.

McMurray, A. 1995, 'Towards 2000 and beyond: who cares? The Australian experience', *Geriaction*, vol. 13, no. 8, pp. 20–3.

McMurray, A., Hudson-Rodd, N., Al-Khudairi, S. & Roydhouse, R. 1998, 'Family health and health services utilisation in Belmont, WA. A community case study', *Australian and New Zealand Journal of Public Health*, vol. 22, no. 1, pp. 107–14.

Morgan, J. 1994, 'Bereavement in older adults', *Journal of Mental Health Counselling*, vol. 16, pp. 318–26.

Moser, D. 1997, 'Correcting misconceptions about women and heart disease', *American Journal of Nursing*, vol. 97, no. 4, pp. 26–9.

Munnings, F. 1993, 'Strength training: not only for the young', *The Physician and Sportsmedicine*, vol. 21, no. 4, pp. 132–40.

Nay, R. 1992, 'Sexuality and aged women in nursing homes', *Geriatric Nursing*, Nov./Dec., pp. 312–14.

Newbern, V. & Krowchuk, H. 1994, 'Failure to thrive in elderly people: a conceptual analysis', *Journal of Advanced Nursing*, vol. 19, pp. 840–9.

Nilsson, P. 1996, 'Premature ageing: the link between psychosocial risk factors and disease', *Medical Hypotheses*, vol. 47, pp. 39–42.

Parke, F. 1991, 'Sexuality in later life', *Nursing Times*, vol. 87, no. 50, pp. 40–2.

Pollock, C. 1992, 'Breaking the risk of falls: an exercise benefit for older patients', *The Physician and Sportsmedicine*, vol. 20, no. 11, pp. 149–56.

Prince, M. & Chappell, N. 1994, *Voluntary Action by Seniors in Canada. Final Report*, Centre on Aging, University of Victoria.

Ramsey, P. 1992, 'Characteristics, processes, and effectiveness of community support groups: a review of the literature', *Family Community Health*, vol. 15, no. 3, pp. 38–45.

Richardson, J. 1988, 'Sexuality and our older patients: a brief look at myth and reality', *Australian Family Physician*, vol. 17, no. 8, pp. 647–8.

Rosenbloom, C. & Whittington, F. 1993, 'The effects of bereavement on eating behaviors and nutrient intakes in elderly widowed persons', *Journal of Gerontology*, vol. 48, no. 4, pp. 5223–9.

Seedsman, T. 1995, 'Ageing and the fitness factor: a need for clarification of the issues', *Australian Journal of Leisure and Recreation*, vol. 5, no. 1, pp. 39–43.

Shangold, M. 1996, 'An active menopause', *The Physician and Sportsmedicine*, vol. 24, no. 7, pp. 30–9.

Showers, N., Perlman Simon, E., Blumenfield, S. & Holden, G. 1995, 'Predictors of patient and proxy satisfaction with discharge plans', *Social Work in Health Care*, vol. 22, no. 1, pp. 19–35.

Spradley, B. & Allender, J. 1996, *Community Health Nursing: Concepts and Practice*, 4th edn, Lippincott, Philadelphia.

Steinke, E. 1997, 'Sexuality in ageing: implications for nursing facility staff', *Journal of Continuing Education in Nursing*, vol. 28, no. 20, pp. 59–63.

Wakefield, M., Kent, P., Roberts, L. & Owen, N. 1996, 'Smoking behaviours and beliefs of older Australians', *Australian and New Zealand Journal of Public Health*, vol. 20, no. 6, pp. 603–6.

Wilkinson, J. 1996, 'Psychology 5: implications of the ageing process for nursing practice', *British Journal of Nursing*, vol. 5, no. 18, pp. 1109–13.

Williams, P. & Lord, S. 1997, 'Effects of group exercise on cognitive functioning and mood in older women', *Australian and New Zealand Journal of Public Health*, vol. 21, no. 1, pp. 45–52.

World Health Organization 1997, 'Seeing ahead—projections into the next century', press release, WHO, Geneva.

World Health Organization/FIMS Committee on Physical Activity for Health 1995, 'Exercise for health', *Bulletin of the World Health Organization*, vol. 73, pp. 135–6.

Wolf, S., Coafler, C. & Xu, T. 1997, 'Exploring the basis for Tai Chi Chuan as a therapeutic exercise approach', *Archives of Physical Medical Rehabilitation*, vol. 78, no. 8, pp. 886–96.

9
Healthy families

Few people would challenge the notion that the family is the singularly most important influence on the health of a society. Although genetics and health services play a part in health and illness, it is the basic patterning of behaviours, attitudes, beliefs and values within the family that primarily determines whether and to what extent people make choices for healthy lifestyles. The role of the family in community health is therefore to provide the impetus and the tools for sustaining lifelong healthy practices. Families also enact a role as gatekeeper between people and their environment, particularly their social environment. In this respect, families are fundamental to community development.

This century has seen enormous changes to families in both structure and process. Some of these changes have had a detrimental effect on community health, while others have had a health-enhancing effect. This chapter examines the essential roles of the family, traditionally and in the context of changes that have led to improvements and compromises in community health.

Objectives

By the end of this chapter you will be able to:

• *describe the roles and functions of families in society*

• *identify four significant ways in which families influence health and wellness*

• *explain the three most common factors that place families at risk for ill health*

• *identify community goals for sustaining family health*

• *develop a planning framework for helping families achieve sustainable health.*

Defining the family

When we think of family, some of us think of the protective envelope that provides a refuge from the stresses and strains of the outside world. Others have the opposite reaction. To them the family is a combat zone, a kind of repository for the collective problems of both the inside and the outside world. Most of us, though, hold a view of family that lies somewhere between these two extremes. The family is the filter, or mediating structure, that functions as a gatekeeper between us as individuals, and the society in which we live. It is a conduit through which society transmits to individuals its social and cultural norms, roles and responsibilities. The family also acts as a communicative structure from within, in that it provides a structure for bonding individual attitudes, opinions and needs. These, in turn, can be used to inform societal policies and processes that vitalise communities.

The concept of family has come to mean many things to people, and to date there is no one accepted definition or standard form. The clergy often describe the family as exemplifying the morality of a society (Goode 1996). Sociologists tend to see families as primary agencies for socialisation, social control and transmission of cultural values, while psychologists see families as primary units for child-rearing and the development of personality (Goode 1996). Economists tend to view the family as a unit of consumption. Before the age of industrialisation, families represented the basic unit of both production and consumption, so they were actually crucial to the development of society (Goode 1996; Hartley 1995). Today it is widely accepted that the family training ground is the precursor to developing expectations for relationships with other people (Peplau 1994). The social and psychological support provided by families is therefore essential to the development of both healthy individuals and a healthy society (Franks, Campbell & Shields 1992; Sweeting & West 1995).

Structural–functional definitions

The family can be defined according to its structures and relationships. Families can be seen as systems of people related by blood ties, marriage, legal adoption or residence, or by bonds of reciprocal affection and mutual responsibility (Wright & Leahy 1987). Structural–functional theorists describe the family as a social system whose major goal is to maximise the congruency between the family and society. Friedman (1986) identifies four related structural dimensions that interact to weave this family goal within the family's functioning: role structure, value systems, communication processes and power relations.

1 *Role structure*

Family roles and positions within the group are characterised by more or less homogeneous and predictable behaviours which, of course, change with different circumstances and with changing societal expectations. In the typical intact or nuclear family, husband and wife undertake various formal roles related to the marriage, such as parenting, recreation, housekeeping, kinship, sexual and therapeutic roles (Friedman 1986). In some cases, one or more of these are shared between the adult members but, for the most part, family roles are gendered and organised around generations, which may at times preclude them from being interchangeable (Ganong 1995). The extent to which these roles are flexible and responsive to the situation is, however, dependent on cultural expectations or individual preferences as well as various arrangements made between the partners. So, for example, a young couple may decide at marriage that they will share household work or child care responsibilities. Similarly, children's roles may be predetermined by the family's cultural or individual expectations, but may shift and change according to circumstances, including the children's ages and stages.

2 *Family values*

The rules or norms within which a family behaves is largely dependent on the family's shared values. Family values consist of ideas, attitudes and beliefs that are usually culturally determined but also rely on the family's history and traditions. Family values include such things as the importance placed on material wealth, work, education, achievement in intellectual and recreational pursuits, equality, child-rearing practices, tolerance of others and social consciousness. A major function of families is to ensure that all members recognise these values, even if some are challenged. In many cases, a generational modification of values evolves from interactions both within and outside the family. These modifications may be transient or lead to new value systems with each subsequent generation (Friedman 1986). This is most often evident in migrant families who, in the process of acculturating to their new environment, adopt successively more of the new country's values with each generation. Similarly, adolescents typically go through a period of challenging family values. Some of the new values they adopt are simply a function of their struggle for independence and are short-lived; however, most young people tend to establish their own family system with at least some transformation or modification of the value system of their family of origin.

3 *Family communication*

In the process of communicating with one another, families learn to recognise both the shared and individual characteristics of each member. One of the most important functions of family communication is to help each member with the process of *individuation*; that is, to develop a sense of self (Friedman 1986). Healthy communication patterns also help each family member learn about others and learn to make personal choices, and this helps each person to develop self-esteem. The features of positive communication within the family are based on mutual respect for each other. They include creating opportunities to express one's feelings, thoughts and concerns; active encouragement of spontaneity and authenticity; honest, constructive resolution of conflicts; and clear, consistent, unambiguous styles of communicating that convey affection, support and acceptance (Friedman 1986).

4 *Family power structure*

This aspect of family function is closely related to communication patterns. In families without mutual respect, there is often a chaotic style of communication, where one family member dominates, controlling the actions of others. Healthy power structures are those with a more egalitarian structure, where there are flexible structures for sharing power among family members. In this style of relating, family members complement, rather than subordinate, each other. Individual members understand their respective roles in the family hierarchy and the extent to which they have authority over family decisions. The key to ensuring egalitarian power relations is thus clear, predictable understanding of family role expectations and a commitment to sharing authority.

In fulfilling these roles, family members contribute to the healthy functioning of the community. The healthy structures and patterns of inter-relationships established within the family are carried into the outside world and provide a basis for community cohesion. In addition to these structural dimensions and patterns, family health is generated by fulfilment of the following core functions:

- **Affection**—a caring, affectionate family environment provides the conditions within which family members can learn to trust one another and others outside the family.
- **Security and acceptance**—having basic physical and emotional needs nurtured within the family instils a sense of safety and security that will promote the ability to be accepting of other community members.
- **Identity and a sense of worth**—reflecting on family interactions allows family members to develop a sense of who they are and how their unique characteristics are linked to those of others.
- **Affiliation and companionship**—throughout the lifespan the family creates a sense of belonging among members, which establishes a template for bonding together and with others.
- **Socialisation**—the family transmits a cultural and social identity that will embody the family's history and values and thus contribute to the community's collective identity, particularly in multicultural communities.
- **Controls**—within the family all members come to recognise the rules and boundaries that provide realistic standards for public behaviour (Duvall & Miller 1985).

Developmental definitions

A slightly different way of looking at the family is through its developmental stages. Developmental theorists suggest that families go through various stages, each to some extent quantitatively and qualitatively different from adjacent stages. At each stage, the family is expected to achieve certain developmental tasks in order to meet the family's biological requirements, cultural imperatives and shared aspirations and values. Family researchers have identified specific stages and their correspondent tasks, but few families today fit precisely in to one specific stage. For example, the traditional stages are as follows:

■ the beginning stage of marriage, where the task is to relate harmoniously to the kin network and plan the family

■ the parenthood stage, where the young family is established as a stable unit

■ the stage of raising pre-school children, where the need for protection and space, integration and socialisation predominates

■ the children-at-school stage, where school achievement is promoted while the adults attempt to maintain a satisfying marital relationship

■ families with teenagers, where the family attempts to integrate and communicate its values, lifestyles, and moral and ethical standards

■ launching-centre families, where the children begin to leave home and the role of parents shifts to encouraging independence and, as the older children marry, welcoming new adult family members into the fold

■ the post-parenting stage, where the parents attempt to maintain a sense of physical and psychological wellbeing through a healthy environment, sustaining satisfying relationships with children and ageing parents, and re-strengthening the marital relationship

■ retired families, where the partners attempt to maintain comfortable living arrangements, maintain intergenerational family ties and, sometimes, learn to cope with the loss of a partner (Duvall 1977).

It would be obvious to anyone reading this list that few families today conform to the expectations of the past, where intact families were the norm, and family life assumed a more or less predictable pathway. Today, with escalating rates of separation and divorce, many families live in transient family groupings where the family straddles one or several stages at once. Some families also experience the blending of two families into a new configuration and, in some cases, this occurs more than once. As a result, there are stages of establishing a separated family, stages of dealing with various custodial arrangements, entering new relationships, reconstituting the family unit and planning for step-parenting.

In addition to divorce, many families have experienced older children leaving home and returning several times, depending on financial circumstances. Developmental theories are also challenged by the conventions of culture, which often determine whether the family includes members of three and four generations. So although it is useful to consider various developmentally related family tasks, a categorisation truer to today's families may be simply single or married adults living with or without children; married adults living with young, teenage or adult children; older people living alone, with partners or with children; and intergenerational families comprising any of the above.

Family systems

Another approach to studying families is within the rubric of family systems theory. Systems theory describes the family as a conglomerate of parts (such as subsystems of children) that interact with the whole and, in turn, with aspects of the environment. However, once again, in this era of rapidly changing societal expectations many families have fewer subsystems than in the past. Viewing the family as a set of systems and subsystems fails to capture the power relations that exist in families, whether these arise out of gender relationships or parent–child relationships (Wellard 1997). So today we have no consensual notion of what constitutes family. Instead, the boundaries for describing families are varied and flexible, and we are left with a more or less accepted view that the family is whoever the family says it is.

Contemporary families

Although there is probably no such thing as a typical family in today's society, the social changes of this century have brought about a profound effect on most families throughout the world. Delayed marriage, divorce, patterns of cohabitation, later age at marriage for both men and women, and the return of women to the paid workforce, have brought dramatic changes to family composition and child care arrangements. The stereotypical family of old, which consisted of two parents and their children, has ceased to be the norm. In fact, just 40% of Australian families and 50% of American families now consist of a couple with dependent children in a registered marriage (ABS 1993a; US Bureau of Census 1990). Thirty per cent of Australian families are couples without children, and approximately 15% do not live with family members at all.

The rate of 'intact' families is also declining in other countries, as is the rate of adults who live alone, either because they have never married or because of widowhood (ABS 1993a; de Vaus & Wolcott 1997; Matseoane 1997; US Bureau of Census 1990). Of those people who do not live alone, three-quarters live in households containing only two people; however, the proportion of smaller households is less for indigenous people, who tend to have a strong sense of their multi-generational lineage (Brady 1995), and this is one example of where cultural traditions override social trends. Family composition may be determined by whether the cultural norm is to reside with members of the male's family (patrilineal societies such as Australian Aborigines) or that of female relatives (matrilineal societies such as the Akan people in Ghana) (Goode 1996).

It is commonly thought that because of higher divorce rates in this era we have had an extraordinary increase in the proportion of one-parent families. Although these are increasing from what they were two decades ago, the proportion of one-parent families is similar to 100 years ago when many women died in childbirth, resulting in a large number of father-headed families. The difference today is that one-parent families are primarily headed by the mother and, in some cases, this is because of child custody being awarded to the mother. In other cases, it is due to large increases in teenage pregnancies and because many single women of child-bearing age are now making a conscious choice to have children outside of marriage (Hartley 1995).

These changes have also had an impact on child-rearing practices, and thus on the role of women. With 62% of Australian women in the paid workforce, which is only slightly higher than in most other industrialised countries, approximately half to three-quarters of all families with young children use some combination of formal and informal child care services. Most involve family carers, particularly grandmothers, some of whom are themselves engaged in at least part-time employment of their own (ABS 1993a; ABS 1996; Castaglia 1994).

In addition to employment, control over fertility and subsequent decreased fertility rates have changed mothering from being *all* of a woman's life to being only *part* of a woman's life. In industrialised nations such as Korea and Japan, birth rates are among the lowest in the world. In Thailand, Indonesia and China, birth rates are declining sharply. In Malaysia, the Philippines and India the rates are also declining but more slowly. This incipient population decline has led to the conclusion that the family can no longer be seen as a reproductive unit (Halsey 1993).

Fertility rates are currently rising in the US and in Scandinavian countries, albeit more slowly than in Australasian countries. Population researchers explain that this does not represent another baby boom, but may be due to a delay in births in the mid-1980s. In all Western European countries, fertility rates are below replacement levels, despite differences between countries and a diversity of family types (Chesnais 1996). An overly simplistic explanation for these variable fertility rates revolves around the negative relationship between women's status and child-bearing. Women of low status or low education have traditionally been expected to have high rates of child-bearing. However, bearing children today may be more appropriately related to a constellation of factors such as government support for child care, gender relations, and family and community support. Paradoxically, in Sweden where women have attained a high level of equality, generous social support from both government and family sources has allowed *all* women to balance career and family responsibilities. Women have responded to this level of support by continuing to have children regardless of status. This exemplifies the importance of empowerment and healthy policies in sustaining the future of the community (Chesnais 1996).

Healthy families

The health of families is a function of the same influences as those discussed in relation to other groups of individuals (see figure 9.1). Any prescription for healthy families, whether structural, functional or developmental, represents the ideal. In reality, families comprise individuals with their human frailties who are confronted with conditions of life that evoke less than ideal responses. To promote family health it is important to recognise some of the risk factors that compromise family health.

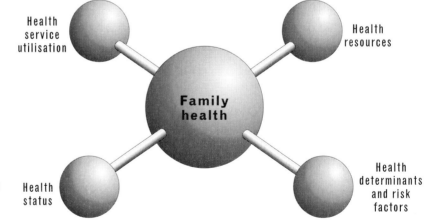

Figure 9.1
The interrelationship of factors influencing the health of families

Health determinants and risk factors

One of the most important determinants of family health is the physical and mental health of family members. Many families live with a member's illness or disability, which can create risk for the other members.

Families and illness

In many families, at least one member has a chronic illness and must be cared for at home. The number of these caregiving families has increased dramatically in recent years, for several reasons. The first is related to the ageing of the population. As fertility rates have fallen, the number of older persons in our midst has become proportionately higher (WHO 1996). In addition, medical knowledge and technology keep many people alive longer than in the past, so in general we all live longer today, including those among us with chronic illnesses or varying degrees of disablement. Economic factors have also contributed to the burden of family care giving. We live in an era of 'drive-through' medicine, where the cost of caring for people in hospital has proven prohibitive for all but the most critically ill. This, coupled with recognition of the risk of *nosocomial* or hospital-induced infections, has led to the conclusion that hospitals are generally neither cost-effective nor conducive to rehabilitation. So today the trend is increasingly toward home and community care. As a result, the family home has become the venue for treating larger numbers of people with illness, and for treating illnesses of greater acuity than in the past.

The move toward home care has had a profound impact on families. One Australian study revealed that only 17% of people with a severe or profound handicap who needed assistance or supervision with personal daily activities lived in institutions. For people beyond age eighty, 58% of those with a severe or profound handicap lived in households, cared for by relatives or others, with or without formal assistance. Equally large proportions of family members and relatives regularly provide care for ill or disabled persons in other cultures, particularly those of the Asian and European continents (ABS 1993b; Goode 1996; Lorensen 1992; McKeever 1994; Mistiaen et al. 1997).

One of the most challenging aspects of caring for a family member with a chronic illness is ensuring that the person's condition is maintained without the occurrence of a crisis. This is often an onerous task in that the family member with epilepsy, diabetes, asthma or a cardiac condition may be prone to intermittent, acute episodes of their illness. Although health professionals attempt to provide sufficient information and support to family caregivers, research studies have revealed that they often overestimate family members' health-related knowledge, underestimate the ill person's functional status, have poor understanding of the family's cultural needs and are sometimes insensitive to the family's intergenerational needs

(Castiglia 1994; Jackson 1994; Morrow-Howell et al. 1996; Reiley et al. 1996). As a result, family members may be left to deal with medical crises, symptom management and other maintenance issues with less than adequate professional backup, relying primarily on their own judgement, wisdom and resourcefulness.

Caring for a chronically ill person is thus a stressful undertaking and, although the effects may differ in different families, caregiver stress has been known to cause physical and/or emotional illness in the caregiver(s) (Turner-Henson, Holaday & Swan 1992). Caregivers also forego predictability and long-term planning for their own lives. They are often not able to make career changes, relocate or implement retirement plans (Fink 1995). The stress of caring for a chronically ill person also places considerable strain on family harmony and social functioning, in some cases precipitating abuse of the ill or elderly (Fink 1995). Research has shown that in some cases the heavy burdens and constraints of caring for chronically ill children, for example, significantly affect parenting behaviours as well as limiting opportunities for family interaction. This, of course, compromises the capacity of the family for healthy functioning (Turner-Henson, Holaday & Swan 1992).

An additional pressure that may be created by family care giving is a sense of social isolation. In some cases, the family may become isolated either by the desire of the ill person to remain out of public view, or by the altruistic desire to manage the situation as well as possible (Sanders 1995). In some cases, the caregiver gets caught up in a cycle of caring without respite, becoming exhausted to the point of emotional breakdown. Whether this occurs because of a lack of available resources or an unwillingness to seek assistance, it is a dysfunctional state for both the caregiver and the rest of the family. All families need co-operation and support from others, mutual caring and a sense of control, especially those who are called upon to assist with such an important task as managing another's illness. The challenge for health advocates is to recognise the bi-directional impact of family care giving and to help families in this situation develop the resources and support mechanisms to ensure that the health of all members is preserved and sustainable (Sanders 1995).

Separation and divorce

Most couples marry or cohabit in the expectation that they will become a family unit, regardless of whether or not they intend to have children. However, as we have come to realise, this situation does not always endure for close to 40% of couples in Australia, and 50% of those in the US and in Scandinavian countries. Divorce rates in England, Wales and Canada fall somewhere between these two, with Mediterranean countries like Greece and Italy having the lowest rates (ABS 1993a; Goode 1995; US Bureau of Census 1990). The divorce rate is even higher for second marriages and, perhaps as a consequence, the rate of second marriages has been steadily declining for the past decade. The number of children affected by divorce has also declined somewhat, with 54% experiencing divorce, compared with 60% a decade ago (ABS 1996; US Bureau of Census 1990).

In the not-too-distant past, divorcing families were stigmatised on the basis of not conforming to societal expectations. In some cases it was healthier for all family members to disengage themselves from a highly con-flicted environment. However, divorced women especially were seen in a less favourable light than, for example, widows. The children of divorce were also somewhat stigmatised and any child behaviour that failed to conform to normal expectations was blamed on the fact that the child had come from a 'broken home'. Researchers of the 1970s tended to also blame the disruptive carry-over effects of divorce for the social and academic performance of children in school (Eastman 1989).

Early studies on the effect of divorce on the children pointed toward children's resilience and allayed the fears of many separating parents that their actions would have adverse effects on their children (Wallerstein & Kelly 1980). However, more recent studies of children over longer periods have concluded that children do suffer enormously from separation and divorce. Today the focus is not so much on laying blame as on emphasising the importance of parental support networks, which are seen as fundamen-tal to healthy social and cognitive development in children (Melson, Ladd & Hsu 1993; Wallerstein & Blakeslee 1990). This signals a more balanced view of both adult and child behaviour with respect to divorce. It signifies that family separation may be due to any one or a combination of factors, including the environment. Societal attitudes are thus shifting toward acknowledging *variability* rather than *conformity* in families' behaviours, attitudes, beliefs and values.

Attitudes toward parenting from outside, as well as inside the family home, are also changing. In the past, the conflicts between separating par-ents often interfered with positive parenting. Many of these were related to custody of children. With an increasing body of research into post-divorce parenting, the role of both parents in child-rearing, regardless of residence, has been acknowledged. This has become legitimised in the 1996 changes to the Australian Family Law Act. The new legislation has seen the language of separation and divorce changed to reflect the fact that *custody* of children is no longer the most important issue. Instead, the emphasis is on allowing all children *access* to parents, rather than the other way around.

The changes have also followed the lead set by the British Family Law Act of 1992, which mandated a parenting plan to be devised at the time of divorce. This ensures that the rights of the child supersede the rights of either parent. Parenting plans represent one of the most important contemporary initiatives in helping families adjust to divorce. They are designed to document both parents' negotiated goals and intentions to ensure safety, physical and emotional care, education and legal responsibilities throughout childhood; although they are not legal documents, they provide a means to clarify the roles and responsibilities of both parents. Development of a parenting plan also helps to separate the processes of resolving money and property disputes from those involving the children. It is expected that humanising the approach to planning for the children's wellbeing after separation in this way will help to counter the effect of emotionally intense legal negotiations that often interfere with rational decision-making.

Although many people survive the emotional trauma of marital separation, it is one of the most stressful events in any person's life, and one that continues for varying periods of time. The risks to health are most evident in the period immediately following separation, particularly where no support system is available. The most enduring effect of separation and divorce is related to economic status and the interactive effects between poverty and health. For at least the initial years following marital separation, both sides of the family are worse off financially. Women who become the head of a separated household tend to be affected most and thus have become entrenched in what some writers have called the *feminisation of poverty*. This term refers to the large number of women who have become poverty-stricken by the circumstances of their lives, including divorce. A report on childhood in Norway describes this as the *pauperisation of motherhood*, placing the emphasis on outcomes for the mother (Frones, Jensen & Solberg, cited in Edgar 1992). The poverty of mothers raising children alone has been documented throughout the world, and is not only an issue for the women themselves but, as many researchers have discovered, the most significant predictor of child outcomes (Pearson & Thoennes 1990).

Demographic, economic and social trends

Geographic mobility for both the family and its adult members is typical of today's family. In general, families tend to move location many more times in their lifetime than in the past. This may be due to unemployment and increased migration, as migrants tend to move several times in the first few years after arriving in a country (ABS 1992; ABS 1993; McDonald 1995). The experience of multiple relocations, particularly in the context of migration, presents a stressful risk to family stability. In many cases, young families make the transition to both parenthood and a new country at the same time. This increases the complexity of the transition, which has an effect on subsequent patterns of family development. Sometimes the transition is made easier by migrating to a place where there is an enclave of people sharing the same ethnic identity, but this is not always the case. Adaptation to the new environment may also be affected by economic capacity and pre-migration experiences. In some cases, migrant families have also had to endure trauma, combat, displacement from home and community, physical injury from war, torture, rape, famine and separation from family members, as well as the loss of familiar social roles and kinship systems (Foss 1996).

The key to healthy immigration is the quality of the marital relationship, particularly in the first stage when the new couple has little knowledge of the available resources. The post-migration environment is also an important element in helping such families work through their adjustment. Essential elements in this process include the presence or absence of cultural and religious traditions, accessible educational and health care resources, social support and a political environment in their resettlement country that is amenable to peace and stability (Foss 1996).

Changing economic trends have also had a profound effect on the social milieu of families. In the past, children left home when they became adults, but today's financial uncertainties see more children leaving and returning several times, depending on education and employment opportunities. This creates multiple transitions and adjustments for all family members as well as a sense of unpredictability. Financial constraints have also increased the proportion of young, dual-income, child-rearing families. With both parents employed, the responsibility for parenting shifts from the exclusive domain of the family to social institutions such as child care centres and schools (Baker 1994). As a result, there is increased reliance on the advice of outside experts and little opportunity to parent intuitively. This has had a considerable impact on parenting styles.

New parents attempt to squeeze copious amounts of information into the immediate period following the birth of their child before parental leave expires, causing a steep learning curve characterised by anxiety and fearfulness. During this period they are also bombarded by consumerism, which creates media images of 'the good mother' designed to manipulate her position as the chief family buyer (Rieger 1991). Such media manipulation tends to disempower young couples with a false sense of free choice, and this is worse where the family is isolated from friends or family, who would help create a balance between consumer pressure and sensible decision-making.

Technology also creates a certain consumerist vulnerability for the family. Not only is there all manner of expensive high tech gear for babies, but even before the child is born, young parents are confronted with multiple ultrasounds (sometimes administered for reasons other than diagnosis), alphafetoprotein tests at the slightest provocation, and a host of defensive medical procedures. These often prove to be unnecessarily intimidating and frightening. Rather than pacifying the expectant parents, many of the tests tend to provoke anxiety and a checklist mentality of ruling out *negatives* rather than capitalising on *positives* related to the pregnancy. So by the time the baby is born, the couple have a portfolio of exclusions rather than expectations.

Another concern is, of course, not having paid employment to sustain the family. We are currently witnessing an epidemic of male unemployment, which has had dramatic effects on the families of many nations. In the US, the restructuring of the economy in the 1970s had an important impact on family structure, especially for the urban underclass. Male joblessness expanded rapidly, resulting in a growth of female-headed families. Many women decided to delay or decline from marriage rather than marry an unemployed male. One researcher explored the impact that these changes in the economy had on the structure of the American family (Wilson 1987).

▶ CASE STUDY

Economic transformation and family structure

The widespread economic reform of the 1970s resulted in the loss of many manufacturing industries in the cities of the American northeast and midwest. These were replaced by service industries such as finance and real estate. In contrast, the sunbelt cities of the south and west experienced gains in both types of industries, and this trend continued until the 1980s. As a result of the erosion of the manufacturing base in the cities of the northeast and midwest, there were fewer low-skilled, highly paid manufacturing jobs and more low-skilled, low-paying or high-skilled, high-paying jobs in the service industries. This spatial mismatch (a mismatch between the types of jobs and people with the appropriate skills in those areas) created the impetus for young people to seek training and education beyond high school, in order to secure the service jobs.

Subsequently, two types of jobs were created. The first included high-wage jobs in high tech fields such as insurance, real estate and finance, and the second resulted in low-wage jobs in the service industry, such as fast food and retail employment. Because the former low-skills, high-wage earners in the cities were usually not able to migrate to jobs elsewhere, they remained in the cities, unemployed. Those with the educational preparation and resources to move to where the jobs were, relocated. As a result, the large cities now have a disproportionate number of males, many of them black, from the lower class, with no well-paying jobs, opportunities or positive role models. This has created what is now referred to as an urban underclass, or ghetto poor. Unfortunately, the term *urban underclass* has also come to be associated not only with high unemployment but also with deviant social behaviours, high crime rates and low status. Many of these men now are considered less-than-desirable marriage partners. The demographic pattern of many of these inner city areas now reveals a trend toward never-married or female-headed families, primarily because of divorce. This has led to a cycle of entrenched, intergenerational poverty, as the women tend to be also unemployed or in low-paying jobs and cannot afford a better life for their children.

This case illustrates the relationship between economic factors and health. Some of the families described will live their entire lives without productive work, and this is of increasing concern to society.

The family unit today is diverse and dynamic in its composition, perceptions and performance. It continues to be redefined in terms of the wider influences of both the larger society and its members (Scanzoni & Marsiglio 1991; Sparling 1991). For some families, having a wider range of choices has enhanced the quality of members' lives, while in others the result has been family dissatisfaction and disharmony. Industrialisation has played havoc with family expectations in the developed world. In the former USSR the collective family is no more (Imbrogno 1986; Shlapentokh 1991). In modern Japanese and German families, traditional values are being eroded (Morioka 1990; Rueschmeyer 1988). Even in countries like Spain and the Caribbean, where there has always existed a strong religious tradition, there are great changes in structures and values (Gonzalez 1987; Halsey 1993; Sharma 1986). In the face of such unremitting change, families will need the support of societal structures and policies and the commitment and guidance of all health professionals to ensure sustainability into the next century.

Goals for healthy families

The goals for healthy families are aimed at providing:
■ physical, emotional and cultural support for all families
■ access to the means for economic sustainability
■ a common bond from which to relate to the outside world
■ a sense of heritage and continuity.

Strategies for assisting families in meeting health goals must be linked to the wider social and cultural context of their lives.

Building healthy public policy

An ecological view of families must address the family and its children as a public resource and a public responsibility (Edgar 1993). Community services for families must be seen as a social investment rather than a public expense, and integral to the economic processes of a nation (Cass 1994a). This means that we must reconsider our family assistance practices and the stigmatising effect of requiring families to demonstrate their inadequacy before any public assistance is provided. This could be redressed by creating formal support systems that strengthen informal support systems, for families at all stages of the developmental continuum (Bronfenbrenner 1982).

One of the goals of the International Year of the Family in 1994 was to put the family at the centre of public policy. To a large extent this has been less than optimal, although some governments did institute a variety of family-friendly policies. In Australia, several such initiatives have begun. One will raise the tax-free threshold for families with dependent children, another will develop a national planning framework for child care, and others will address youth homelessness, youth suicide and the need for extra marriage and relationship services (CDCSH 1997). These policies suggest political acknowledgement of the family's place in the development of society.

In addition to existing policies, we must also confront the issue of variable family definitions. The way a family is defined sets boundaries for inclusion and exclusion when funding allocations are made. For example, government programs that fund programs for ageing families on the basis of such criteria as age and frailty fail to recognise that in doing so they may sever a vital relationship between ageing family members. Government policies must therefore be developed in consultation with the community and the families who reside there. The basis for defining the family must be what people regard as their family, and public policy must be responsive to them (Bateman 1997). The special needs of migrant families, those with extended family households, indigenous people, and those whose family of definition is based on sexual preference must also be addressed within a family-friendly context.

Public policies must also recognise the difficulties of separated families, and the effect of long work hours on families struggling to survive. The need for respite is essential, for young working mothers who come home to the responsibilities of child care, and for family caregivers, who often need encouragement to seek respite care. This may require a shift from thinking of family benefits in the workplace as an industrial relations issue, to seeing it as a social issue. From a social perspective, policies can be developed to support effective choices in supporting employment and family care combinations (Cass 1994b).

Urie Bronfenbrenner (1982, p. 112), who has written extensively about the need for a family ecology, sums up the public responsibility in creating and sustaining human development through caring for our young:

> *The involvement of one or more adults in care and joint activity in support of child rearing requires public policies and practices that provide opportunity, status, resources, encouragement, example, stability, and above all, time for parenthood, primarily by parents, but also by other adults in the child's environment, both within and outside the home.*

Policies must also be responsive to the vital need to create employment for successive generations of young people. This is particularly acute with an ageing society who will require care and economic support for many years to come. An unemployed generation can develop neither the skills nor the experience necessary to provide infrastructure for an ageing society unless there are job-creation programs. This is a complex issue, particularly in a society where the national capacity to employ young people is prohibited by schemes that ensure that their wages achieve parity with older workers. Such a system leads to higher wages for a few, but fewer jobs for the majority. Our family-friendly policies must therefore revolve around the ways in which political decisions, finances, child care, family relationships, school, workplace training, domestic violence, aged care and other issues affect the ability of families to create and sustain health (Hartley & McDonald 1994).

Creating supportive environments

One of the most important elements of helping families is to convey a sense of non-judgemental support. Often the language we use to describe single mothers or divorcees or those who have chosen single parenthood is less than supportive. In some cases our expressions are actually discriminatory, as we refer to 'single-parent families' where the family actually has two parents but is headed by one adult in the home. In this case, the term 'separated family' may be more appropriate and less dismissive of the parent who lives outside the family home. Similarly, our language needs to reflect various forms of families, including gay and lesbian couples with or without children.

Non-judgemental support is also required in the way we respond to people's need to balance the conventions of their culture with the circumstances of their lives. For example, it is unacceptable in some communities to be divorced, yet violence against women is tolerated. This presents a conflict for health professionals advocating for equality in marriage and the family, when the inclination may be to encourage a wife to leave her husband. We can all assist families by becoming knowledgeable about other cultures and developing mutually supportive systems with cultural sensitivity. This means shifting our own values to acknowledge different families' sense of history, heritage and rituals (Campbell 1991) and developing strategies for incorporating this knowledge into our plans for assisting them.

Strengthening community action

Advocacy means acknowledging family competence and preferences. The key to strengthening community action is family empowerment. As health professionals our role is to allow families to own their own problems rather than telling them what to do, and to provide the information and guidance that will assist with self-management and self-empowerment. We must therefore ensure that families are aware of the influences in society that affect their functioning and development. Our role is to filter health-related information, conveying the results of our research to them without engineering their strategies for change. This is particularly important in this information age, when the sheer volume of information is bewildering to most people. As Edgar (1993, p. 24) suggests, 'parental confidence has been undermined by public confusion about what it means to be "successful", either as a parent or a child'. Families need to experience success with minimal intervention and maximum support.

Consolidation of family issues is crucial for the development of society. We must do our part in helping bring about widespread change to the allocation of health resources to support families in all their geographic, cultural, social and developmental configurations. This is a highly political undertaking and counter to historical views of family advocacy, which assumed that families needed only to have social welfare needs met. The communications media has awakened us to the large number of hidden facets of family issues and sparked a debate over the public versus private nature of the family. Relationships between men and women, the rights and responsibilities of parents and children and the issue of sexuality are often highly contested areas of family life (Hartley 1995). Yet the collective morality of communities is increasingly on the public agenda. Reports have proliferated on abuses of young, old and disabled family members that would once have been suppressed. One writer, commenting on the James Bulger trial in the UK, suggests that a return to privatisation of the family as in days gone by would signal the end to morality in our society (Roberts 1994). We must therefore help families keep issues of concern to them at the centre of public focus.

Developing personal skills

We have a duty of care to help educate all family members, and this can be done in many ways. We must draw societal attention to the relationship between the education of women and the subsequent health of the family, and the relationship between environmental issues and the family's health agenda. The challenge is to balance resources and responsibility for community support with fostering individual responsibility and individual choice, so that family members gain mastery over their lives. We must also help families to understand the interconnections linking its members. When the family is seen as a foundation of community development, the relational aspects of family life are validated, effectively negating the notion that the family is little more than a holding environment.

As advocates for health and wellbeing in the family, we can enable that process through respect, understanding and therapeutic engagement with the family in ways that allow them to access our knowledge and our nurturing. This can occur within the context of a mobilising episode of care giving, or in the ongoing dialogue we maintain as members of society. At times, this means that we must learn to engage families through a social rather than professional perspective, an approach that requires self-understanding and a transformation of consciousness (Gibson 1991). A social approach will also help us to appreciate the plight of family caregivers, who often enter therapeutic relationships with family members with inadequate support. It is our responsibility as health professionals to ensure that they are not disadvantaged by becoming the unwitting guinea pigs in our economic rationalising of health care. Our models of integrated (home and community) care must take their needs into consideration and recognise the need for resources to support family care giving in all its forms.

Reorienting health services

We have a responsibility to connect the needs of families entrusted to our care with the wider global agenda. Thus, once again we must think global and act local. We have a social responsibility to contribute to the equitable rationalisation of resources, especially in light of major demographic changes to fertility rates, ageing, migration, wars and employment patterns. However, we also have a responsibility to ensure that regional needs are identified and become part of the local as well as larger health agenda.

As health professionals we can become therapeutically engaged with the family in a multitude of ways: in our high-technology, high-touch care, in our nurturing of young people and their parents, in our understanding of society and the way in which social forces help and hinder the family's attempts to define itself to achieve health, wellbeing and happiness. Of course, this demands research, reflection and an attitude of tolerance. Family research must address the impact of public policies, the interface of families and the legal, religious and health care system, the impact of societal events such as economic downturns, natural disasters, wars, and changes in cultural values and attitudes (Ganong 1995).

Our research must continue to respond to the challenges of evolving family forms. At this time in history, we must redirect at least some research efforts towards the divorcing family, investigating ways of assisting people undergoing marital separation to understand their situation and to explore ways of redressing any negative influences on individual family members. We must also reorient our research strategies from focusing on problems, to examining the distinguishing features of remarriages and stepfamilies, particularly with respect to cultivating effective, rather than ineffective, functioning (Ganong 1995).

THINKING CRITICALLY

Family health

....

▶ Identify three major ways in which the family influences the health of society.

▶ Identify five characteristics of contemporary families and how each of these influences the health of a community.

▶ Describe four risk factors for family health and wellness.

▶ Conduct an analysis of a family you know using one of the theoretical orientations provided in this chapter.

▶ Examine one social policy with which you are familiar in terms of its historical precedents, responsiveness to family health needs, and effect on family health.

▶ Describe three strategies for empowering separated families.

REFERENCES

Australian Bureau of Statistics 1992, *Survey of Families in Australia Mar–May 1992*, ABS, Canberra.

Australian Bureau of Statistics 1993a, *Australia's Families: Selected Findings from the Survey of Families in Australia* (catalogue no. 4418.0), ABS, Canberra.

Australian Bureau of Statistics 1993b, *Survey of Disability, Ageing and Carers*, ABS, Canberra.

Australian Bureau of Statistics 1996, *Population Census*, AGPS, Canberra.

Baker, C. 1994, 'School health: policy issues', *Nursing and Health Care*, vol. 15, no. 4, pp. 178–84.

Bateman, G. 1997, 'Defining families for policy making', paper presented at Australian Institute for Family Studies conference, Melbourne, May 15, 1997.

Brady, M. 1995, 'Culture in treatment. Culture as treatment. A critical appraisement of developments in addictions programs for indigenous North Americans and Australians', *Social Science and Medicine*, vol. 41, no. 11, pp. 1487–98.

Bronfenbrenner, U. 1982, 'Children and families: the silent revolution', *Australian Journal of Sex, Marriage and Family*, vol. 3, no. 3, pp. 111–23.

Campbell, D. 1991, 'Family paradigm theory and family rituals: implications for child and family health', *Nurse Practitioner*, vol. 16, no. 2, pp. 22–31.

Cass, B. 1994a, '*Connecting the public and the private: a lasting legacy of the International Year of the Family in Australia*', Edith Cowan University Public Lecture, Perth.

Cass, B. 1994b, 'Integrating private and social responsibilities: better partnerships between families, governments and communities', *Family Matters*, vol. 37, pp. 20–7.

Castiglia, P. 1994, 'Grandparenting: benefits and problems', *Journal of Pediatric Health Care*, vol. 8, pp. 79–91.

Chesnais, J. 1996, 'Fertility, family, and social policy in contemporary Western Europe', *Population and Development Review*, vol. 22, no. 4, pp. 729–39.

Commonwealth Department of Community Services and Health 1997, '*Strengthening Australian Families*', media release, 23 April, Canberra.

DeVaus, D. & Wolcott, I. (eds) 1997, *Australian Family Profiles: Social and Demographic Patterns*, Australian Institute of Family Studies, Melbourne.

Duvall, E. 1977, *Marriage and Family Relationships*, 5th edn, Lippincott, Philadelphia.

Duvall, E. & Miller, B. 1985, *Marriage and Family Development*, 6th edn, Harper & Row, New York.

Eastman, M. 1989, *Family: The Vital Factor*, Collins Dove, Melbourne.

Edgar, D. 1992, 'Childhood in its social context', *Family Matters*, vol. 33, pp. 32–5.

Edgar, D. 1993, 'The development of competence', *Family Matters*, vol. 36, pp. 21–5.

Fink, S. 1995, 'The influence of family resources and family demands on the strains and wellbeing of caregiving families', *Nursing Research*, vol. 44, no. 3, pp. 139–46.

Foss, G. 1996, 'A conceptual model for studying parenting behaviors in immigrant populations', *Advances in Nursing Science*, vol. 19, no. 2, pp. 74–87.

Franks, P., Campbell, T. & Shields, C. 1992, 'Social relationships and health: the relative roles of family functioning and social support', *Social Science and Medicine*, vol. 34, no. 7, pp. 779–88.

Friedman, M. 1986, *Family Nursing: Theory and Assessment*, 2nd edn, Appleton-Lange, Norwalk, Connecticut.

Ganong, L. 1995, 'Current trends and issues in family nursing research', *Journal of Family Nursing*, vol. 1, no. 2, pp. 171–206.

Gibson, C. 1991, 'A concept analysis of empowerment', *Journal of Advanced Nursing*, vol. 16, pp. 354–61.

Gonzalez, P. 1987, 'The sociological analysis of value judgements by families', *Bodajoz: Cuadernor de Realidades Sociales*, vol. 29–30, pp. 71–90.

Goode, J. 1996, 'Comparing family systems in Europe and Asia: are there different sets of rules?', *Population and Development Review*, vol. 22, no. 1, pp. 1–20.

Halsey, A. 1993, 'Changes in the family', *Children and Society*, vol. 7, no. 2, pp. 125–36.

Hartley, R. (ed.) 1995, *Families and Cultural Diversity in Australia*, Allen & Unwin, Sydney.

Hartley, R. & McDonald, P. 1994, 'The many faces of families', *Family Matters*, vol. 37, pp. 7–12.

Imbrogno, S. 1986, 'Marriage and the family in the USSR: Changes are emerging', *Social Casework*, vol. 67, no. 2, pp. 90–100.

Jackson, M. 1994, 'Discharge planning: issues and challenges for gerontological nursing: a critique of the literature', *Journal of Advanced Nursing*, vol. 19, pp. 492–502.

Johnston, G. 1995, *The Transformation of American Families: Employment Dislocation and the Growth of Female-headed Families*, Population Research Institute, Department of Sociology, Pennsylvania State University.

Lorensen, M. 1992, 'Health and social support of elderly families in developed countries', *Journal of Gerontological Nursing*, June, pp. 25–32.

Lynch, I. & Tiedje, L. 1991, 'Working with multiproblem families: an intervention model for community health nurses', *Public Health Nursing*, vol. 8, no. 3, pp. 147–53.

Matseoane, S. 1997, 'South African health-care system at the crossroads', *Journal of the National Medical Association*, vol. 89, no. 5, pp. 350–5.

McDonald, P. 1995, *Families in Australia—a Socio-demographic Perspective*, Australian Institute of Family Studies, Melbourne.

McKeever, P. 1994, 'Between women: nurses and family caregivers', *Canadian Journal of Nursing Research*, vol. 26, no. 4, pp. 15–21.

Melson, G., Ladd, G. & Hsu, H. 1993, 'Maternal support networks, maternal cognitions, and young children's social and cognitive development', *Child Development*, vol. 64, pp. 1401–17.

Mistiaen, P., Duijnhouwer, E., Wijkel, D., de Bont, M. & Veeger, A. 1997, 'The problems of elderly people at home one week after discharge from an acute care setting', *Journal of Advanced Nursing*, vol. 25, pp. 1233–40.

Morioka, K. 1990, 'Demographic family changes in contemporary Japan', *International Social Science Journal*, vol. 42, no. 4, pp. 511–22.

Morrow-Howell, N., Chadiha, L., Proctor, E., Hourd-Bryant, M. & Dore, P. 1996, 'Racial differences in discharge planning', *Health and Social Work*, vol. 21, no. 2, pp. 131–9.

Pearson, J. & Thoennes, N. 1990, 'Custody after divorce: demographic and attitudinal patterns', *American Journal of Orthopsychiatry*, vol. 60, no. 2, pp. 233–49.

Peplau, H. 1994, 'Quality of life: an interpersonal perspective', *Nursing Science Quarterly*, vol. 7, no. 1, pp. 10–15.

Reiley, P., Iessoni, L., Phillips, R., Davis, R., Tuchin, L. et al. 1996, 'Discharge planning: comparison of patients' and nurses' perceptions of patients following hospital discharge, *Image: Journal of Nursing Scholarship*, vol. 28, no. 2, pp. 143–7.

Reuschmeyer, M. 1988, 'New family forms in a State Socialist Society: the German Democratic Republic', *Journal of Family Issues*, vol. 9, no. 3, pp. 354–71.

Rieger, K. 1991, *Effects of child care on young children: forty years of research*, Australian Institute of Family Studies, Melbourne.

Roberts, V. 1994, 'Teaching children to be bad', *Health Visitor*, vol. 67, no. 1, pp. 11–12.

Sanders, M. (ed.) 1995, *Healthy Families, Healthy Nation*, Australian Academic Press, Brisbane.

Scanzoni, J. & Marsiglio, W. 1993, 'New action theory and contemporary families', *Journal of Family Issues*, vol. 14, no. 1, pp. 105–32.

Schlapentokh, V. 1991, 'The Soviet family in the period of the decay of Socialism', *Journal of Comparative Family Studies*, vol. 22, no. 2, pp. 267–80.

Sharma, K. 1986, 'Changing forms of East Indian marriage and family in the Carribean', *Journal of Sociological Studies*, vol. 5, pp. 20–58.

Sparling, J. 1991, 'The cultural definition of the family', *Physical and Occupational Therapy in Pediatrics*, vol. 11, no. 4, pp. 17–29.

Sweeting, H. & West, P. 1995, 'Family life and health in adolescence: a role for culture in the health inequalities debate?', *Social Science and Medicine*, vol. 40, no. 2, pp. 163–75.

Turner-Henson, A., Holaday, B. & Swan, J. 1992, 'When parenting becomes care giving: caring for the chronically ill child', *Family Community Health*, vol. 15, no. 2, pp. 19–30.

US Bureau of Census 1990, *Current population reports: marital status and living arrangements*, US Department of Commerce, Washington.

Wallerstein, J. & Blakeslee, S. 1990, *Second Chances: Men, Women and Children a Decade after Divorce*, Tickner & Fields, New York.

Wallerstein, J. & Kelly, J. 1980, 'Effects of divorce on the visiting father-child relationship', *American Journal of Psychiatry*, vol. 137, no. 12, pp. 1534–9.

Wellard, S. 1997, 'Constructions of family nursing: a critical exploration', *Contemporary Nursing*, vol. 6, no. 2, pp. 78–84.

Wilson, W. 1987, *The Truly Disadvantaged: the Inner city, the Underclass and Public Policy*, University of Chicago Press, Chicago.

World Health Organization 1996, *The World Health Report 1996. Fighting Disease, Fostering Development*, WHO, Geneva.

Wright, L & Leahy, M. 1987, *Families and Chronic Illness*, Springhouse Corp, Pittsburgh.

10 Health and gender: healthy women, healthy men

Gender relations have an enormous impact on the economic, political, environmental and sociocultural aspects of our society, and thus on our capacity to for health. Inequalities between women and men persist even in societies where equity and affirmative action policies exist. To some extent, these inequalities are related to differential access to, and control over, resources, education, credit, technology, services and decision-making processes. The consumer movement, the women's movement of the 1970s and 1980s, and the men's movement of the 1990s have all helped create an awareness of the importance of disparities in health status, health risk behaviour, health care provision and patterns of utilisation for women and men. The most important outcome of these grass-roots movements has been a convergence of interest in the relationship between gender and health. This chapter examines women's health and men's health from the perspective of primary health care principles, in order to illustrate the linkages between gendered social relations and the creation and sustainability of health.

Objectives

By the end of this chapter you will be able to:

• *describe the social construction of health*

• *explain the central issues related to gender and health*

• *identify three important influences on the creation of men's health and women's health*

• *identify four high-risk behaviours that compromise the health of women and men respectively*

• *develop a community strategy for improving the health of women and the health of men.*

The social construction of health

As discussed previously in this book, health is created within the context of the social environment. Our genetic makeup and hereditary predispositions provide only a template for the construction of healthy lives. Personal choices in health-related matters are embedded in the social, cultural and economic conditions of family and community life. Gender, race and class are among the most important personal characteristics that we bring to our social world. All three have been described as major influences in the extent to which we are healthy, our patterns of service utilisation and the way we respond to health challenges. In fact, the strongest risk factors for poor health status are those that show the greatest gender differences (Verbrugge 1988). From a population perspective, gender issues and the interaction between gender, race and socioeconomic class are therefore important indicators of community health (Ruzek, Olesen & Clarke 1997; Thorne, McCormick & Carty 1997).

Gender is an important determinant of health for reasons that are not only biological, but related to community rules and roles (Goldner et al. 1990). In some cases the respective influence of biology and social and cultural norms is clearly evident, but there are also some situations where the effect of gender on health is a function of the complex interplay between biology and the way in which male or female roles are enacted. For example, women live longer on average than men, and this may be related to a combination of biological hardiness and the fact that they are more inclined to use preventive services. It may be also that their lives are extended because they seek help more readily, especially when reproductive issues bring them into health care more frequently. Women also have more chronic illnesses and disabilities than men but, again, this may be a function of their longer lifespan (Bergman-Evans & Walker 1996; Thorne, McCormick & Carty 1997).

Another gender-related difference relates to economic status. Because of the way society structures women's economic dependency, a larger number of women than men live in poverty, particularly those in mother-headed households. Many women who live in these conditions have also been shown to be at risk for ill health and injuries (Macran, Clarke & Joshi 1996). Where there is illness or disability, family caregivers are typically mothers, daughters and wives rather than fathers, sons and husbands, and this increases the role strain of women, leaving them susceptible to illness (McKeever 1995). One of the dilemmas of family care giving is learning to balance the responsibilities of caring for others with the freedom to make decisions for oneself. This causes many women psychological distress, which often exacerbates illness (Smith 1995).

One of the difficulties facing women arises where women are engaged in the paid workforce, as they are often relegated to lower-status and lower-paying jobs, sometimes because of child care or family care obligations. This leaves them with little time to attend to their own health needs and with fewer opportunities for self-improvement.

Migrant women in the workforce are at particular risk of ill health and injury. Studies of non-English-speaking-background women migrating to Australia have shown that many of these women arrive in their new country with a superior health status relative to Australian women. However, after arrival they show a marked decline in health status directly proportional to the length of residence in Australia. Compared with Australian-born women they also experience higher rates of work-related illnesses and injuries and a greater incidence of poor mental and emotional health, a finding that has been confirmed in research on migrant women in other countries (Meleis et al. 1996; Spurlock 1995; Young 1996).

The plight of these women clearly illustrates the link between health and social conditions. They tend to work in dangerous, dirty, and low-status occupations. They suffer from the role strain of dual careers in paid and unpaid work with the additional stress of migration to unfamiliar surroundings. In addition, many have moved away from the support of extended families, and encounter many obstacles related to not being able to speak English, many of which are related to essential social support services such as housing, transport, child care and health care (Alcorso & Schofield 1992).

Women in higher levels of the workforce also are placed at risk for ill health by the compound stress of dual roles. Even those who attain management positions are in many cases still expected to undertake the majority of household tasks once they return home. Despite the fact that participation in paid economic activity is generally beneficial to women, for many the added responsibility of the 'second shift'—that is, the work at home—is a health hazard. Scandinavian researchers have found a definite difference between the sexes in relation to the 'unwinding' period at the end of a day's work. They conclude that, despite having made gains in reducing workplace inequities, women suffer from greater stress than men once they return home in the evening (Bergman, Carlsson & Wright 1996; Elstad 1996). This may also explain why marriage seems to have a more positive health effect on men than on women (Oakley 1994; Umberson 1992).

Specific health issues and gender

Biologically, some health issues are distinctly female or distinctly male, the most obvious being testicular and breast cancer. However, the role of biology in determining health and illness has for many years been fraught with ambiguities, as is clearly illustrated in the case of heart disease. Historically, medical researchers have considered cardiovascular disease a disease of males. Many have systematically excluded females from their studies, perhaps in ignorance of the fact that cardiovascular disease causes ten times more deaths in women than breast cancer (Beery 1995; Moser 1997; Thorne, McCormick & Carty 1997). In some cases, biomedical researchers have intentionally excluded women or selected only male data for analysis. This has been done on the basis of either sample size, or the desire for homogeneous, or 'cleaner' results, uncontaminated by hormonal fluctuations. Still others have excluded female subjects to exclude the chance of causing harm to a developing or potentially developing foetus (Narrigan et al. 1997).

Many diagnostic tests for cardiovascular disease have thus been developed from the results of male-only studies and this calls into question their sensitivity to female patients. Certain cardiac scans have been accepted as the norm, and yet they may be inaccurate for females because of the need to scan through breast tissue, or because of distortions related to women's biochemistry (Beery 1995). Another difference is related to treatment. Women hospitalised for cardiac disease tend to have fewer diagnostic procedures while hospitalised. It is unknown whether this relates to a greater valuing of males, the willingness of women to make lifestyle changes (and thus the lesser need for dramatic interventions), or the dilution of medical concerns about women because of their frequency of contact with the health care system (Beery 1995). Even the system of costing various health care procedures has recently shown gender bias in the disproportionately low valuing of procedures conducted on women compared with men (Harer 1996).

The exclusion of women from research, diagnosis and treatment protocols is problematic for several reasons. One is that there are few studies of the ways in which women's symptoms differ from men's, yet preliminary data suggest there may be serious differences. For example, one study revealed that 46% of women first seen with an acute myocardial infarction presented with shortness of breath or epigastric pain, yet the male norm for diagnosis is a presentation of chest pain (Beery 1995). It is important for community health that health care professionals be made aware of the differences in epidemiology, risk factors, intervention and treatment of disease between women and men in order to ensure equity of access to members of both groups (Flitcraft 1996).

Women's health risks

The most important women's health issues of our time are related to reproductive health and illness, diseases such as breast, lung and colorectal cancer, societal influences on women's health (norms, roles and poverty), violence against women, and the need for women's voices to be heard in the health care policy arena (Chesney & Ozner 1995; Rozenberg et al. 1996).

Reproductive risk

Because of women's unique physiology and their place in society, they carry a special group of risks associated with reproduction. Social norms influence women's reproductive health by controlling women's literacy and education. Women who have had access to formal education tend to marry at a later age than uneducated women, have smaller families, use family planning methods and make better use of antenatal and delivery care (Varkevisser 1995). Yet in many countries, such as India, where 40% of female school children do not attend school, unequal access to education clearly perpetuates discrimination against women and thus poorer health status for the next generation (UNICEF 1996).

Another aspect of reproductive health relates to infertility and abortion. Women often carry the burden for involuntary childlessness in the family, undergoing harsh and difficult infertility treatments, even when responsibility for the infertility rests with the male (Mahowald, Levinson & Cassel 1996). The antithetical situation is the right to choose to discontinue a pregnancy. Powerful sociocultural norms, often reinforced by religious and judicial sanctions, exert societal control over when women should give birth, when they should not, and to whom the fruits of their womb belong (Varkevisser 1995). For many women, the fact that they have little control over their reproductive choices is a cause of extraordinary stress, matched only by the danger and emotional conflicts surrounding the act of abortion itself. In China, where there is a family limitation policy, abortion is part of the politics of survival, a fact of life to which Chinese women must accommodate. In that country, safe abortions are readily available to all women (Rigdon 1996). But this is not the case in many other places in the world, where complications from unsafe abortions account for approximately 40% of maternal deaths worldwide. Most of these occur among the poor and illiterate of Asian, African and Latin American countries and the Caribbean (Kabira, Gachukia & Matiangi 1997; Timpson 1996; Varkevisser 1995).

Reproductive risks are primarily related to menstruation, pregnancy and menopause and, despite years of research, many myths prevail about each of these. For example, menopause still remains poorly differentiated from the effects of ageing in women, and this continues to cause confusion about how it should be managed. The debate over whether or not to encourage women to take hormone replacement therapy during menopause is still unequivocal (Utian 1996). In many cases, the lack of clarity on reproductive issues arises from decisions that surround the interactions between biological factors and economic conditions. Governments are hesitant to fund mass screening programs or research into areas that have not proved to be effective for large numbers of people, and this is reflected in public health goals. As a result, a large number of women at low risk for reproductive cancers, for example, have a large number of pap smears and many at high risk have none (Bonnar 1996). Some public health decisions that are gender-biased or based on inaccurate information fail to provide equity of access and, as a result, adversely affect women's health.

Women's workplaces provide a good example of an area overlooked by government policies and resources. In industrialised nations, few workplaces are woman-friendly. Workstation design, equipment and production schedules and levels of chemicals or toxins are hazards common to all workers, but are magnified in pregnancy or when a woman's energies are depleted by child care responsibilities. In some types of employment where women outnumber men, such as nursing, hairdressing, cleaning, factory and clerical work, there are hazards such as back strain, eyestrain and repetitive strain injuries and exposure to a plethora of chemical agents (Bryant 1996; Macran, Clarke & Joshi 1996). Because many of these chemical agents can affect the production and metabolism of oestrogen within the body, the health of women may be more at risk than that of men. Recent research has shown that many toxins are stored in fat and may reside in the body for long periods and, because women tend to have more body fat than men, they may experience a greater residual effect. Women also endure hormonal changes during pregnancy, lactation and menopause that mobilise internal stores of pollutants, and these may affect their health years after exposure. This has caused widespread concern at a time when rates of breast cancer, for example, are on the rise, especially for women who work in or live near chemical facilities (Bryant 1996).

Rural women's work carries with it even greater risks, especially in developing countries. This is even worse in places where there has been mass environmental degradation (Agarwal 1996). In many countries such as China and India, women's traditional and culturally defined roles include maintaining household sanitation and water supply, food preparation, and the care and education of children. Many of these tasks are performed after putting in a full day at paid work. These women spend their day collecting fuel wood, fodder and water to meet household needs and then proceed to cook over wood stoves in poorly ventilated rooms. As a result, they are exposed to more carbon monoxide and benzopyrene than chain smokers or people working in the most polluted cities of the world (Agarwal 1996). Yet despite these enormous health hazards to women themselves, most health programs in developing countries focus on the woman's role in maintaining infant and child health. This clearly defines women's role in the society but fails to value her personal health as integral to the health of the community (Bhullar 1996; Wang, Burris & Ping 1996; Wong et al. 1995).

Women and cancers

Breast cancer is one of the most insidious threats to women's health. The incidence of breast cancer is increasing rapidly, and today approximately one in eight women in industrialised societies will develop breast cancer, with the ratio even greater among women of colour (Grisso & Ness 1996; Rozenberg 1996). About 25% of the risk can be attributed to known risk factors. The web of causation includes such things as family history, previous breast disease of some other type, a prolonged oestrogen climate throughout life (early onset of menarche and late menopause), childlessness or a late first pregnancy, increased fat and alcohol consumption, and a mutation in a single gene, such as BRCA1 or BRCA2 (Rozenberg et al. 1996).

Lung cancer is another disease that is increasing among women. American women's rate of lung cancer mortality now surpasses that of breast cancer. This has been directly attributed to a rise in smoking and exposure to environmental tobacco smoke (Kendrick & Merritt 1996). The increased incidence of lung cancer may also be related to the fact that women today start smoking at a younger age, and tend to smoke a larger number of 'heavy' brands and inhale the smoke (Rozenberg et al. 1996). Smoking is the most serious public health problem of our time, but for women the risks are even greater than for men. Smoking among women who use contraceptives increases their risk for cardiovascular disease. Smoking also has been associated with ectopic pregnancy, spontaneous abortion, and maternal complications such as placenta previa and abruptio placentae. In addition, pregnant women who smoke have twice the risk of infant mortality from all causes, and from sudden infant death syndrome in particular (Kendrick & Merritt 1996). Obviously, the health problems common to women require intervention programs that combine individual health education with system-wide or societal change.

Societal attitudes and norms

An important aspect of women's health is related to women's status and constraints on their ability for self-determinism. Many women are disenfranchised in society by factors such as race, a lack of education, low socioeconomic status or cultural conventions. Others are victims of societal attitudes that disempower females by setting unrealistic standards for behaviour or appearance. In many contemporary societies, women are under societal pressure to look good. Researchers have known for years that people who are considered beautiful or handsome are more likely to be seen as good and as more desirable as friends or partners, and tend to gain better jobs than others. Those considered unattractive receive less attention as infants, are evaluated more harshly in school and earn less than their attractive counterparts (Zones 1997). This has a much more powerful impact on women than on men, whose personal appearance is not governed by the strict norms seen in all forms of public media.

One of the biggest problems with societal expectation of attractiveness is the pervasive effect of the media on young women's perceptions of themselves and, subsequently, on their self-esteem. In her expose of the beauty industry, Naomi Wolf (1991) drew attention to the way these perceptions are politically and economically entrenched in our society. She contends that the focus on, and demand for, beauty has become more intense as women have achieved success in many areas. The 'Beauty Myth'—that is, the belief in an objective quality called *beauty*—keeps male dominance intact by perpetuating women's insecurity about their appearance. Women are deceived by advertising and peer pressure to believe that beauty, elusive as it may be, defines womanhood, and whether or not a woman will be desired by men. The beauty myth has important implications for the empowerment and thus the health of women. When young women are continually questioning the adequacy of their appearance, they are distracted from more worthwhile and confidence-building pursuits (Zones 1997).

One of the most dramatic effects of the beauty myth is the current epidemic of eating disorders among young women, as was discussed in chapter 6. Although anorexia nervosa and other eating disorders have existed since the nineteenth century, the prevalence of such disorders is today seen to be linked with women's search for social acceptance. Theorists contend that anorexia is symptomatic of women's attempt to deny their basic biology in a world where the body has become a public representation of the self. By succeeding in remaining thin, they are able to demonstrate their strong-willed victory over their physiology (Bemporad 1996). This is a sad indictment of social norms that continue to create unrealistic images as a model of womanhood. The fact that these images are so prevalent is a signal that it is a problem of concern to public health. Perhaps it is now time to respond to the issue within healthy public policies that more closely monitor advertising codes and encourage empowerment of women in ways that are more substantial and healthful.

Women and AIDS

Women's experiences related to HIV infection and AIDS also exemplify the impact of contemporary societal attitudes and norms, for these women experience many forms of oppression and discrimination, primarily related to gender, race, sexuality and socioeconomic status. Being a female, poor and a member of a racial minority can be stigmatising itself, but when AIDS is involved, there is an additional stigma related to the assumption of promiscuity, which is better tolerated in males than in females (Bunting 1996). With AIDS increasing in prevalence among women, sexual inequality in the diagnosis and treatment of AIDS has become life-threatening. In societies where a man is considered to have exclusive rights to his wife's womb, a woman cannot refuse to have sexual intercourse with her husband, even if he has been unfaithful to her. Neither can she demand that he use condoms. Many women with sole responsibility for child care do not see leaving their husbands as an option, particularly where his promiscuity is related to male labour migration caused by the family's economic condition. So most remain for the sake of status, honour, love, or the children. Such women have found few resources to help them break free from what is an ongoing cycle of despair (Varkevisser 1995; Zierler & Krieger 1997).

AIDS is a classic case of a disease that has been viewed by the general public as a moral, rather than a public health, problem. When a woman succumbs to AIDS she often loses her ability to care for her children, so the disease creates vulnerability not only for her but for the rest of the family. The victims are blamed for their sexual activities that caused the transmission of the virus and for the risk to innocent unborn children. Yet a large number of cases of AIDS are now the result of heterosexual transmission, where wives are the unwitting victims of male sexual activity outside the home (Bunting 1996; Zierler & Krieger 1997).

In many industrialised countries where the incidence of AIDS among women is increasing rapidly, women, especially poor black women, are trying to overcome not only the reality of AIDS but the multiple risks of living in neighbourhoods burdened by poverty, racism, crack cocaine, heroin and violence (Zierler & Krieger 1997). In addition, many women with HIV have endured a dismissive attitude by the health professions. Because the disease was originally seen to be a disease of gay men, women's symptoms went unnoticed, or worse, were ignored. Several female journalists and female medical researchers tried to draw attention to women's HIV-related symptoms in the early 1980s. After a protracted struggle that also enlisted feminist nurses and emergency department medical doctors, gynaecological symptoms of HIV infection were finally included in diagnostic guidelines for AIDS in 1993. But even today, women continue to be seen as vectors of the disease rather than as victims. Despite the devastation caused to women by AIDS, 'there is no quilt for women, there are no candlelight services... and they do not have the cameraderie, the loving network that has been created for gay men' (Bunting 1996, p. 72).

Violence against women

Violence against women is another risk to women's health that is closely interlinked with women's roles in society. One of the worst forms of violence against women is rape. Rape can be a form of political violence, when in wartime the rape of women is used as a deliberate strategy to brutalise the enemy. Rape on this level, which is usually sanctioned by political leaders, has devastating consequences for the community in that it disrupts the type of social and community bonds so important for post-war reconstruction (Flitcraft 1996). Away from civil conflicts, rape is still a major cause of injury to women, one from which many women never psychologically recover, even after their bodies heal. It is also a crime that is rapidly increasing in prevalence in so-called civilised societies. It is estimated that over 12 million adult women in the US have been victims of at least one forcible rape, the legacy of which is often rape-related post-traumatic stress disorder (Schafran 1996).

By far the most pervasive form of violence against women is that perpetrated by an intimate spouse or partner. Domestic violence or domestic abuse, which is now the leading cause of injuries among women, consists of a pattern of coercive control usually designed to isolate the victim. It may be physical, sexual and/or psychological in nature and, sadly, this type of behaviour usually becomes a pattern from one generation to the next (Grisso et al. 1996; Hadley et al. 1995; Robbe et al. 1996; Short, Lezin & Zook 1995). It is a major public health problem, yet seldom is it referred to as such in the popular press or other media.

The women's movement has helped to heighten awareness of the prevalence and problems of domestic abuse, with general agreement that it is related to power and control. A simplistic view of family violence sees men as abusing their power, and women as colluding in their own victimisation by not leaving. But this view casts men as tyrants and women as masochists, which obscures the many complexities of family interactions within which the violence occurs (Goldner et al. 1990). Many acts of violence are perpetrated by wives and girlfriends against husbands or boyfriends, and the literature contains heated arguments about gender symmetry in spousal violence (Morse 1995; Sorenson, Upchurch & Shen 1996). In many violent relationships, both partners engage in assaults against the other, but irrespective of who strikes whom, the danger for women is that men strike harder, so women are more often injured (Morse 1995).

The continuum of violence against women ranges from workplace harassment to mortal acts of personal violence. Sexual harassment can be verbal, physical, visual or written, ranging from a disparaging remark to rape. In the US, even a work environment that creates a climate hostile to women can be considered sexual harassment (Britton 1997). The problem is related to workplace politics. The woman being harassed is typically at the mercy of a workplace superior, and thus risks advancement in her work once the act is reported. Many refrain from reporting acts of sexual harassment on the basis that, like women in rape cases, they will be the ones under suspicion and charged with demonstrating that they did not provoke the incident. Harassment of any kind is more often perpetrated against women of colour, single mothers, working-class women, older women, lesbians, feminists and those with disabilities (Britton 1997).

One of the greatest frustrations in dealing with victims of violence is the lack of trust between health care professionals and the person needing assistance. Health care workers have been known to treat victims of abuse with little sensitivity, especially if she has been in the system previously. Another problem is related to classifying an abused woman's injuries according to standard medical terminology. This often obscures the underlying circumstances surrounding the injury, and may prevent early detection of the problem (Richardson & Feder 1996). Many nurses, doctors, police officers or ambulance attendants simply fail to understand why a woman who has been repeatedly abused doesn't just up and leave. Yet the problems with leaving are many and complex. In most cases, abused women are caught between maintaining their spousal attachment, economic survival, and their partner and children's wellbeing on one side, and their own physical and emotional wellbeing on the other (Campbell 1992; Vazquez 1996). For rural women, leaving is even more difficult as they often suffer from geographical isolation and lack of resources (Dimmitt 1995).

As health professionals our first challenge is to understand, and then lend non-judgemental support to all victims of violence. At a societal level, however, we must use the principles of primary health care to raise aware-ness of equity and empowerment issues. Our role as advocates includes becoming actively engaged in changing the social and cultural institutions that have given rise to notions of masculine entitlement and all those influ-ences that shape society's attitudes towards women (Goodman et al. 1993). The following case study exemplifies one group of health professionals' attempts to provide a sensitive and helpful climate for assisting victims of spousal violence (Hadley et al, 1995).

> ## CASE STUDY

WomanKind: a response to domestic abuse

WomanKind was established in Minnesota in the US to provide a unique community service that would respond to the issue of domestic abuse. It is a non-profit organisation that operates from three hospital sites to integrate case management and advocacy services for victims of domestic abuse, and to provide education and consultative support for health professionals. The health care staff and volunteers work toward empowering women to make positive decisions to help discover their own strengths and thus be better prepared to live in an environment free of violence. The process begins in the hospital when a victim of trauma is admitted through the emergency department. From here the case is co-ordinated so that the program acts as a bridge between hospital and the world outside.

WomanKind volunteers provide on-call advocates at all hours and are trained to maintain comprehensive networks of local community services for referral purposes. Their approach is one of respecting each woman's process, her timetable and her decisions, so each worker can be supportive of her needs rather than simply try to solve her problems by telling her what to do. Because the program also targets health personnel working in hospitals and community agencies, standardised protocols have been developed for all women upon entry to hospital. The protocol includes a question relevant to domestic abuse being included in the normal health screening procedure. Each woman is asked 'Are you now or have you ever been in a relationship in which you have been abused physically, emotionally, or sexually?' This provides her with the opportunity to choose whether she wishes to discuss information related to her situation. Providing the opportunity to do so is a means of helping the woman become empowered to make her own decisions.

One of the features of the program is the WomanKind Professional Reference Card, a pocket-sized card that provides tips on assessment and identification for health care workers. It includes certain signals and subtle signs, intervention techniques with questions/responses, documentation procedures, do's and dont's, and resources for victims of abuse. Another card has been developed for community members such as friends, neighbours, relatives or co-workers to help guide them in communicating with someone who has been abused.

The program is unique in targeting not only the women, but health professionals and others in her social network as well. It has been so well accepted in Minnesota that there are plans to introduce it to other centres.

Men's health risks

Like women, men have numerous risks to health and, at all ages, men's mortality rates exceed those of women. Men's life expectancy is therefore considerably less than that of women, a trend that is not improving (Huggins 1995). The greatest public health problems experienced by men include coronary heart disease, lung and several other cancers, accidents at work or on the road, suicide and other forms of violent death. Each of these is influenced by the same social conditions that influence women's health: gender, culture, socioeconomic status, age and geographic residence (McMillan 1995).

Men are also at greater risk than women for contracting HIV infection, primarily because of the high prevalence among the gay male population. In addition, men are more likely than women to die from injuries. Epidemiological data reveal an injury rate among 15–24 year old Australian males nearly three times that of females in this age group (Huggins 1995). As was discussed in chapter 5, rates of male suicide throughout the world are considerably higher than for females.

In the older age groups the picture is equally grim. Older men die at a rate nearly twice that of older women from heart and lung disease. They die from lung cancer at nearly five times the rate of women. The type of work they do places them at risk of higher rates of workplace injury (Huggins 1995). To date, health planners have not been able to construct a satisfactory equation to predict the relative effects of men's biology, lifestyle and social factors. It has been suggested, however, that their participation in risky behaviours is up to 300% greater than that of females. Risk taking and hesitancy to seek help for illnesses are therefore considered the two most likely causes of increased rates of injury and poor illness outcomes.

Men are more likely to engage in health-damaging behaviours such as over-indulging in alcohol consumption, smoking, dangerous driving and unsafe sexual practices. Men also respond differently than women to stress. Some react to the pressures of their lives with aggressive acts, which has been used to explain their high rate of suicide, but this may also be a function of the social acceptability of men using firearms, which prove more lethal than some other methods of self-destruction.

Some men react to stress by ignoring or denying its presence, and tend to disregard bodily changes or symptoms of illness. While women have biological stages to force them into awareness (menstruation, maternity, menopause), men have no such stages (Arndt 1995). Their view of masculinity can also be a health hazard. Many men see 'maleness' in terms of strength and sexual function only, rather than in terms of their whole body. Narrowly defined ideas of masculinity are more common among working-class men, those who live in rural areas, and Aboriginal males. Unfortunately, it is among these groups of men that rates of alcohol and tobacco consumption and road accidents, especially in rural areas, are higher than their urban counterparts (Huggins 1995, 1996).

Men are the most infrequent users of all health services, and only rarely utilise community-based health services. Although boys use outpatient clinics 38% more than girls, a rapid decline in health service utilisation occurs during adolescence, a trend that continues to age 50 (Huggins 1995). Male patients visiting a medical practitioner tend to take longer to unravel some of their medical and personal issues, perhaps because they are not as expressive as women. Where standard consultation rates prevail, they may be inadequately served by the health service (Huggins 1995). Another explanation for their low utilisation rates, especially for mental health services, is that men find it difficult to admit the existence of a problem. They fear the type of emotional intimacy required to discuss such things as their mental health, and are hesitant to ask for help (Huggins 1995). Men have also been hesitant to complain about health care or health services. Consequently, the health care system has been slow to respond to their unique needs (Fletcher 1995).

Men's social and emotional health outcomes are of increasing concern to health planners and health professionals. The recent men's movement has drawn attention to the emotional impoverishment of men and the need for men to engage in more self-caring and self-valuing. This runs contrary to the status quo, where, in most societies, men continue to abide by traditional masculine roles only marginally dissimilar to that of their forebears. There is evidence to suggest that males who adopt a traditional masculine role are more inclined to adopt risky behaviours and are less receptive to health promotion messages (Pilbara Public Health Unit 1994). This is predictive of morbidity and mortality in places like Australia and New Zealand, where the dominant model of masculinity is associated with excessive alcohol and tobacco consumption, fast driving, being dominant, competitive, preoccupied with work, and always needing to be in control (Huggins 1995).

Traditional male behaviour is a product of the socialisation of young men and women. The process differs for each gender, but the socialisation of males has a profound effect on both men and women in adulthood.

The women's movement made visible the oppression of women by a male-dominated society. Societal responses to these women's voices have included a number of changes to social structures and processes, including equal opportunity legislation, affirmative action in the workplace and attempts to reframe the images of young girls in our educational curricula. The men's movement is attempting to show how men are victims of their own masculine socialisation, yet few changes have occurred in recent times (Huggins 1995).

An Australian activist for the men's movement, Steve Biddulph, has written prolifically about the effects of socialisation on boys. He contends that many of men's health risks—violence, accidents, heart attacks, lung cancer and addictive behaviours—are sub-suicidal actions taken out of a deep sense of misery and a lack of meaning or purpose. To some extent, men's unhealthy risk patterns can be attributed to a lack of fathering. In the burgeoning number of families where there is no father to provide role modelling and male bonding, young males may be left to construct their masculine roles from television, from stereotypes, and from the equally inept pretences of their peer group. What they need is meaningful interaction beyond the few minutes a day most boys have with their fathers. This, according to Biddulph, may be the key to masculine mental health (Biddulph 1995).

The lack of fathers in the home is a pressing social problem, and one that, in a climate of unprecedented divorce rates, represents a crisis of parenthood. Family trends see many more men than in the past attempting to share child-rearing responsibilities, but being poorly equipped from their own childhood socialisation for this important task. Paradoxically, one of the social conditions that jeopardises health, namely male unemployment, has increased the number of fathers now involved in child care. This is leading to a renewed interest in men's contribution to parenting. A further trend for a small number of divorcing couples is for the children to remain in their father's home. However, this is still far from the norm; for most divorcing fathers, moving away from the children has a profound impact on their parenting role.

Fathers who live outside the home confront an enormous number of obstacles in their attempt to remain involved with the children's upbringing. These men are beset by the financial constraints that both partners to a divorce encounter, yet, due to societal expectations, they are still expected to be the family financier. Because of their financial position, some find it difficult to compete with the parent in the home for their children's attention. Many feel disempowered by their inability to adequately provide for their children or establish a new relationship (McMurray & Blackmore 1993).

Contrary to the myth of the 'deadbeat dad' who abandons his family for more interesting pursuits, most males who live outside the marital home wish for *more*, not *less*, contact with their children (McMurray & Blackmore 1993). Yet stereotyped gender roles seem to be entrenched within the legal and welfare systems, and this runs counter to effective parenting. It is interesting that despite the gains of the women's movement in drawing society's attention to gender inequalities, many of our social mores and roles have remained unchanged. The instrumental role of the male as breadwinner and the role of the female as primary child carer have changed little over the years.

Goals relevant to gender issues in health

The problems of gender bias in our society are more than a war between the sexes. Inequalities in opportunity and all forms of discrimination represent risks to personal health, in some cases actually causing illness and injury. These problems are also a major risk to community health, which can only be secured on a basis of harmonious enactment of gender roles. The Beijing Conference on Women held in 1995 was aimed at raising awareness of gender issues and their effect on health. The conference focused primarily on inequities in relation to women, but these issues are equally relevant to men's health as they affect the whole of society. They include the following as a guide to the development of public health goals.

■ poverty and its result on women and men:
■ unequal access to education for women and men
■ inequalities in health care
■ inequalities in human rights
■ family violence
■ effects of armed conflict on women and men
■ equitable economic structures, policies and access to resources
■ gender inequality in power and decision-making
■ discrimination and violation of the rights of girls
■ socialisation of males
(INR 1996; Huggins 1995).

To counter gender bias in health care, a whole-of-community approach is needed.

Building healthy public policy

One of the major recommendations of the Beijing Conference on Women and the many conferences that are now being held on men's health is that governments must confront the issue of poverty and its effect on health. States must ensure food security, support female-headed households, recognise the needs of migrants, ensure access to financial services for both males and females, create gender sensitivity in economic policy making, and examine the relationship between unremunerated work and poverty (International Nursing Review 1996). Male unemployment is a major issue for both men and women and must be dealt with sensitively and comprehensively from an economic, as well as social, standpoint.

Overcoming poverty must also address the inequities surfacing in the area of international aid programs. International development projects affect community life, but especially the daily lives of women. Sometimes these effects are not understood by those granting aid, yet they must be addressed within the life of any given project. For example, a project that provided piped water in Zambia reduced the time taken to fetch and carry water, but this left women with more time for other work, and thus *increased*, rather than *decreased*, their workload (Manderson & Mark 1997). Many economic development programs create a plethora of health hazards for local people, who are so destitute that they will accept work that puts them at risk of exposure to chemical pesticides and other industrial hazards. This is particularly the case for women in developing countries, who also relinquish the property they are given due to social and cultural pressure. This defeats the intention of empowering their lives (Cox 1997).

In the industrialised nations, one obstacle to healthy public policies and practices for both women's and men's health has been the preoccupation with illness and illness treatments at the expense of wellness and of illness prevention. The emphasis on market metaphors (health expenditures) reflects short-term political decisions to deploy resources in favour of such things as gene mapping and cost-effective outcome indicators of health care rather than understanding how social and behavioural factors lead to preventive health practices. This leaves few resources for critical social investments that promote health, such as education, job training, environmental safety and housing (Ruzek, Olesen & Clarke 1997).

Another obstacle to achieving women's health has been the contradictions purveyed by some aspects of feminism. The focus of feminist teaching is 'woman-centredness', and this has sometimes obscured the fact that women are a heterogeneous population engaging in a wide array of complex interactions with their communities in ways that are not always predictable. In the early days of the feminist movement, women's health issues were argued from a monolithic focus on gender, and women were urged to unite in voicing their concerns on the basis of gender uniqueness. But as the movement was joined by women of many ethnic origins and varied perspectives, the base of examination was broadened from sex differences in health and health-seeking behaviour to the interactions between such things as race, class and cultural experiences (Ruzek, Olesen & Clarke 1997). This more closely reflects today's quest by women of many diverse backgrounds and in a wide variety of situations to address the issues that will assist them in securing health for themselves, and for their families and communities.

A contemporary view of women's health thus places emphasis on the social conditions affecting health, and this must also be the case for men. Our policies for community health must address the following:

- roles in separated families
- overcrowding, homelessness and urban deterioration
- migration patterns
- rapid technological developments, particularly as they affect women's reproductive processes and choices for women, and men's employment
- the resource requirements of a rapidly ageing population and policies governing the private sector controlling these
- variable patterns of utilisation of services
- health care costs.

It is important that gender discrepancies in medical research, diagnosis and treatment be addressed, and this is currently the focus of community pressure from the grass-roots feminist movement (Geary 1995; King & Paul 1996). Research into differential conditions and responses for males and females is likely to gather momentum as the number of women's health advocates in the competition for research funds increases. This will also occur as their research findings increase public awareness of historical omissions in the research agenda. Gender balance in the research agenda would help dispel the notion that women's health issues are related predominantly to gynaecology and child care. Similarly, a more balanced agenda would incorporate more than physical health problems in researching men's health, so that the root causes of such things as male violence and suicide would become visible. Researching the social conditions peculiar to both genders, the economic disparities in health that create advantages or disadvantages for families, and factors related to understanding environmental issues are crucial for the development of all healthy public policies.

Research resources must be directed toward illuminating issues related to the education of women, preserving the physical and social environment that will enhance women's economic status and allow them to better support their families within safe living and working conditions. Women everywhere have welcomed the surge in interest and research funding into breast cancer research, for example, but we must guard against the 'novel technologies' approach of most medically dominated funding bodies, and this applies equally to research on male cancers (Narrigan et al. 1997). Priorities for funding research studies must also include environmental and behavioural factors and the ways in which women's and men's social and culturally embedded meanings and issues of access lead to preventive behaviour. This is particularly urgent in research related to HIV sexual risk reduction (Wingood & DiClemente 1996). Medical researchers must therefore be encouraged to extend the traditional methods of research to those offered by social scientists so that we can examine people's actual experiences of health and illness, their preferences in health care and views of appropriate treatment interventions, and their roles as both carer and recipient of care.

Government policies must address the decriminalisation of abortion issue and the right to choose family planning strategies. In addition, women must be protected by law from such unhealthy cultural practices as female genital mutilation, infanticide and dowry-related violence (International Nursing Review 1996). Other forms of violence must be overcome through a combination of community efforts and government initiatives. The current movement to eliminate land mines is a major global initiative against violence, and it is a mark of its importance that the international director of the movement has received a Nobel Peace Prize. One of the most important measures that can be taken to reduce conflict-related violence is to encourage all governments to examine excessive military spending and to balance spending with that intended to protect, assist and train refugees and displaced persons. Culturally appropriate shelters, health care, legal aid and other necessary services should be provided for all victims of violence.

Family-friendly policies should be designed to eliminate or reduce family violence. One such act is the Violence Against Women Act, introduced in the US Senate in 1991 with the intention of identifying gender-motivated acts of violence as civil rights violations (Goodman et al. 1993). Along with such legal initiatives, further research should be conducted into gender-based violence and male power as a basis for educational programs for young people. Other research agendas must address issues of gender in both epidemiological and policy studies, including the special needs of gay males contracting HIV infection. Woman-friendly policies include job protection and training programs that promote women's self-reliance, facilitate their access to resources and create flexible work environments. Male-friendly policies address workplace illness and injury, unemployment and men's socialisation and lifestyle issues.

Creating supportive environments

Within our society, many things influence the health of women and the health of men. Most of these (social, cultural, demographic and environmental factors) are the same influences mentioned in conjunction with the creation of health for all people. The most powerful influence specific to women's health is equal opportunity, which encompasses the primary health care principles of equity, access, cultural sensitivity, empowerment and self-determinism. Women in all communities will only achieve and sustain health where they have the opportunity to do so. This will only be possible where a society's institutionalised policies and processes provide access to health information and health care, equal consideration and provision of culturally appropriate health resources, the means to design and administer those resources by women themselves, and acknowledgement that *all* members of the community help create and sustain health. Men will only shift their gendered roles when the community normalises the changes by supporting these roles.

Supportive environments for men must begin at birth, with the way we raise our male children. In the absence of fathers in the home, there must be more community programs instituted to provide male role models for young boys. The social environment within which young males are nurtured must allow them to balance traditional notions of masculinity with their need for emotional support. In turn, we must provide support to those parents attempting to raise children and provide for their emotional growth. In today's society there remains little time for parents to share their concerns. For separated families this is particularly acute, as there is little respite from the duties of child care. Community-based information and support centres for parents can help provide a climate of concern so that individuals do not get swallowed up in the task of parenting, and have resources for personal growth. One of the most important vehicles for changing existing stereotypes and allowing both women and men a sense of possibilities is the mass media. By becoming involved with the local media we can ensure that culturally appropriate human rights information is disseminated and that non-stereotyped, balanced and diverse images of women and men are portrayed as models for the next generations.

Strengthening community action

Many social conditions that perpetuate gender bias can be addressed through balanced education programs for the young. In Africa and many other countries, women's health is influenced by a myriad of factors that have nothing to do with women themselves. These include a lack of educational facilities and training for girls, and ignorance coupled with cultural and societal attitudes that discriminate against women and generally undervalue the girl-child (Kabira, Gachukia & Matiangi 1997). Investing in community health means investing in strategies to counter such societal stereotyping. Community intervention programs may be directed at individual issues, but must also focus on the community itself and the societal conditions that undermine familial competence. Included are discriminatory practices and those that encourage violence or other forms of human rights violations.

Community members must be encouraged to develop person-to-person support in times of crisis and mechanisms for sharing problems and solutions. This involves healthy neighbourhood initiatives. Unhealthy, high-risk neighbourhoods can be the setting for activities such as parent groups, job retraining and collective action designed to empower community residents to deal with stress and risk factors, provide education, social support and tangible resources for family life to allow positive family interactions (Bowers Andrews 1994).

Developing personal skills

Government interventions and community action can provide a foundation for the empowerment of individuals, although healthy choices are a matter of personal knowledge and skills. Women need to be encouraged to overcome the vulnerability that results from being brought up to depend on males for social and personal esteem. Men, in turn, need to recognise the need for a balanced lifestyle. Young people of both sexes need to see understand the need for intimacy and closeness, but from a perspective of equal power and decision-making in relationships.

Young women need to see how reproductive health and overall health both reflect and affect each other (Magrane & McIntyre-Seltman 1996).

Women of all ages need to be encouraged to learn how decisions are made so that they can participate in public health decisions. This requires literacy programs. For those communities where high rates of illiteracy exist, health information must be provided through radio and television, workshops and seminars, drama and community festivals, posters and leaflets (M'Jamtu-sie 1996). To deal with the problem of domestic abuse, person-centred and problem-focused interventions are essential. These entail programs to help people, especially young couples, develop personal coping skills and self-esteem by nurturing them through ways of accepting ownership for critical life functions. Such programs are based on the belief that all people must be able to speak for themselves, that empowerment is the entitlement of all people, and that respect for personal dignity is integral to health, not just an 'add-on'. As health professionals we must advocate symbolic empowerment of people at the policy level, and demonstrate practical examples of empowering others by relinquishing control over health-related decisions that could easily be assumed by community members.

Reorienting health services

The notion of health risk must balance individual choices with institutionalised hazards. For example, women are often the target of pervasive advertising by the food, alcohol and tobacco industries, and many live in violent circumstances or work in circumstances of economic or sexual exploitation. Risk reduction must therefore begin with the contextual issues that govern women's and men's individual behaviour. This is often problematic in a society dominated by individualist thinking, where efforts to impose 'passive controls', such as gun control regulations, advertising restrictions and severe penalties for drink driving, are often rejected (Ruzek 1997). But society must also provide women and men with individual resources to modify their behaviour. Lack of assertiveness is a risk factor for many things that compromise women's health: sexual harassment, economic exploitation, rape and domestic abuse. The emphasis of health promotion programs for women must be on empowerment skills such as assertiveness training, personal defence, stress management and other skills that help women gain control over things within their personal realm of influence and control (Ruzek 1997). In turn these must be balanced with services for men that respond to their mental health and physical needs.

One of the ways in which our health care of women can be improved relates to victims of violence. We have done little to overcome the revolving door syndrome for victims of domestic abuse. One way of dealing with this is to depathologise victims' responses by re-examining our treatment of such women. Often we tend to engage in subtle victim-blaming when a women is admitted into care on repeated occasions. By reframing the incident in terms of normal responses to abnormal events we may see a slightly different perspective on her condition (Browne 1993).

Another way of addressing inequities in health services for migrant women in particular is to ensure cultural sensitivity in services for women. Many women migrants find the services of their host country ethnocentric and alienating. Given that it is the woman in many of these families who must choose health services for all family members, particular attention must be paid to removing communication barriers. This involves provision of language services in health service agencies, bilingual and bicultural health workers and the participation of women of non-English-speaking backgrounds in health planning, data collection and service evaluation (Alcorso & Schofield 1992). Specialist services that sometimes separate women's services from children's services must be reconsidered. Many women from developing countries find it impossible to navigate the maze of specialised services, and need a place to receive health information and treatment that can simultaneously address their own and their children's needs for a range of health concerns (AbouZahr, Vlassoff & Kumar 1996).

It is also important for all health professionals to be attuned to the need of some women to be attended by female carers. Most health care services are male-centred, and many women from cultures unfamiliar to the service providers find they must explain their cultural context, their cultural perspective regarding health care, and the role of women within that culture before they can secure culturally appropriate services (Taylor & Dower 1997). They may hesitate to demand such services, and be left with inadequate treatment. This is not quite as much of an issue for males, as in many countries female physicians are the norm.

The challenge of women's health and, indeed, men's health is thus to conceptualise their respective health issues from an *inclusive*, rather than *exclusive*, perspective. This type of approach will mobilise social forces for caring, curing and concern in a direction that will contribute to women's health and men's health as individuals and, within social relations, as members of communities (Ruzek, Olesen & Clarke 1997). This type of approach is illustrated in the following case study (Danguilan & Verzosa 1996).

▶ CASE STUDY

The Philippine POPCOM experience

The Philippine Population Commission (POPCOM) undertook to reorient population policies and programs to make population workers more gender-responsive. Their strategies included forming a critical mass of various community groups to demand policy shifts, encouraging women, development, and environmental non-governmental organisations to identify allies in government and international organisations, to engage in regular dialogues between health care workers and the government's central planning agency, and to use the media to promote their initiatives within the community.

The program was based on the recognition that there was differential access to and control over resources, credit, technology, training and services, with disparities evident in labour force and political participation rates. An historical emphasis on fertility and family planning needed to be broadened to include concerns about family formation, the status of women, maternal and child health, child survival, morbidity and mortality, population distribution and urbanisation, internal and international migration and population structure.

The group formed an interagency advisory committee, which conducted a survey revealing that POPCOM board members, staff and population officers were generally not aware of the concept of gender, or its implication for development. Most people held the assumption that population growth was a major concern as a threat to the environment, and a major cause of poverty and resource depletion. Once the level of awareness was understood, POPCOM began a gender-sensitising program, wherein policy and training groups were developed. The policy framework was designed to guide selected

projects in key regions of the country to test certain approaches and mechanisms in promoting gender and reproductive health policies and programs. This included assessing the pre-marriage counselling program, integrating gender and reproductive health and rights in training, analysing community information projects from a gender perspective, mobilising youth councils to advocate for gender and reproductive health and rights, and mainstreaming gender and reproductive health concerns in the family welfare industry program. The overall objective of these initiatives was to serve as the basis for legislative reforms.

The program confronts the state machinery that governs gender issues. Far from the 'add women and stir' approach, which grafts women onto all policies and programs, it is committed to questioning the basic assumptions upon which the ideology of family planning rests. It challenges the status quo by addressing gender relations within the household, across classes, and within the wider economic, political, environmental and sociocultural spheres. It questions the ways in which existing values and norms entrench gender bias into the governance of the system. The group's thorough approach to their task has yielded a set of principles around which all future policies will revolve. These include autonomy, self-determination, equity, social justice, pluralism, participation, responsibility and accountability. The overarching goal is to enable men and women to live self-determined, productive, satisfying and fulfilled lives. To accomplish this is it acknowledged that both women and men must be able to exercise their capacities to achieve and sustain knowledge and skills to deal with issues that potentially compromise the quality of their lives.

THINKING CRITICALLY

Health and gender

▶ Give four reasons why gender issues are important to community health.

▶ Identify three health risks of females and three health risks of males related to gender issues.

▶ Discuss three political, cultural or social issues related to reproductive health from the perspective of gender equity.

▶ What five strategies would you recommend for an HIV health education program for young males and females?

▶ Devise one public policy and three strategies for implementation related to gender, to respond to a community health problem.

REFERENCES

AbuZahr, C., Vlassoff, C. & Kumar, A. 1996, 'Quality health care for women: a global challenge', *Health Care for Women International*, vol. 17, pp. 449–67.

Agarwal, A. 1996, 'The health and environment interface', *Promotion and Education*, vol. 111, no. 1, pp. 15–42.

Alcorso, C. & Schofield, T. 1992, 'Redirecting the agenda. The National NESB Women's Health Strategy', *Migration Action*, April, pp. 15–19.

Arndt, B. 1995, '*Why masculinity is a health hazard*', Proceedings of the National Men's Health Conference, AGPS, Canberra, pp. 87–90.

Beery, T. 1995, 'Diagnosis and treatment of cardiac disease', *Heart and Lung*, vol. 24, no. 6, pp. 427–35.

Bemporad, J. 1996, 'Self-starvation through the ages: reflections on the pre-history of anorexia nervosa', *International Journal of Eating Disorders*, vol. 19, no. 3, pp. 217–37.

Bergman, B., Carlsson, S. & Wright, I. 1996, 'Women's work experiences and health in a male-dominated industry', *Journal of Occupational and Environmental Medicine*, vol. 38, no. 7, pp. 663–72.

Bergman-Evans, B. & Walker, S. 1996, 'The prevalence of clinical preventive services utilization by older women', *Nurse Practitioner*, vol. 21, no. 4, pp. 88–106.

Bhullar, S. 1996, 'Working women and health problems', *The Nursing Journal of India*, vol. 87, no. 1, pp. 1–2.

Biddulph, S. 1995, 'Healthy masculinity starts in boyhood', *Australian Family Physician*, vol. 24, no. 11, pp. 2047–52.

Bonnar, J. 1996, 'Issues in women's health', *South African Medical Journal*, vol. 86, no. 6, pp. 707–8.

Bowers Andrews, A. 1994, 'Developing community systems for the primary prevention of family violence', *Family Community Health*, vol. 16, no. 4, pp. 1–9.

Britton, B. 1997, 'Sexual harassment', in *Women's Health: Complexities and Differences*, eds S. Ruzek, V. Olesen & A. Clarke, Ohio State University Press, Columbus, pp. 510–19.

Browne, A. 1993, 'Violence against women by male partners', *American Psychologist*, vol. 48, no. 10, pp. 1077–87.

Bryant, K. 1996, 'Impact of air pollution on women's health', *Otolaryngology, Head and Neck Surgery*, vol. 114, no. 2, pp. 267–70.

Bunting, S. 1996, 'Sources of stigma associated with women with HIV', *Advances in Nursing Science*, vol. 19, no. 2, pp. 64–73.

Campbell, J. 1992, 'Ways of teaching, learning and knowing about violence against women', *Nursing and Health Care*, vol. 13, no. 9, pp. 464–70.

Chesney, M. & Ozner, E. 1995, 'Women and health: in search of a paradigm', *Women's Health: Research on Gender, Behavior, and Policy*, vol. 1, pp. 3–26.

Cox, C. 1997, 'Medical education, women's status, and medical issues' effect on women's health in the Caribbean', *Health Care for Women International*, vol. 18, pp. 383–93.

Danguilan, M. & Verzosa, E. 1996, 'Making women and men matter: the Philippine Popcom experience', *Health Care for Women International*, vol. 17, pp. 487–503.

Dimmitt, J. 1995, 'Self-concept and woman abuse: a rural and cultural perspective', *Issues in Mental Health Nursing*, vol. 16, pp. 567–81.

Elstad, J. 1996, 'Inequalities in health related to women's marital, parental, and employment status—a comparison between the early 70's and the late 80's, Norway', *Social Science and Medicine*, vol. 41, no. 1, pp. 75–89.

Fletcher, R. 1995, 'An outbreak of men's health—the history of a welcome epidemic', *Proceedings of the National Men's Health Conference*, AGPS, Canberra, pp. 26–31.

Flitcraft, A. 1996, 'Synergy: violence prevention, intervention, and women's health', *Journal of the American Medical Women's Association*, vol. 51, no. 3, pp. 75–6.

Goldner, V., Penn, P., Sheinberg, M. & Walker, G. 1990, 'Love and violence: gender paradoxes in volatile attachments', *Family Process*, vol. 29, no. 4, pp. 343–64.

Goodman, L., Koss, M., Fitzgerald, L., Felipe Russo, N. & Puryear Keita, G. 1993, 'Male violence against women', *American Psychologist*, vol. 48, no. 10, pp. 1054–8.

Grisso, J. & Ness, R. 1996, 'Update in women's health', *Annals of Internal Medicine*, vol. 125, pp. 213–20.

Grisso, J., Schwarz, D., Miles, C. & Holmes, J. 1996, 'Injuries among inner-city minority women: a population-based longitudinal study', *American Journal of Public Health*, vol. 86, no. 1, pp. 67–70.

Hadley, S., Short, L., Lezin, N. & Zook, E. 1995, 'WomanKind: an innovative model of health care response to domestic abuse', *Women's Health Issues*, vol. 5, no. 4, pp. 189–98.

Harer, W. 1996, 'Gender bias in health care services valuations', *Obstetrics and Gynecology*, vol. 87, no. 3, pp. 453–4.

Huggins, A. 1995, *The Australian Male: Illness, Injury and Death by Socialisation*, Men's Health Teaching and Research Unit, Curtin University, Western Australia.

Huggins, A. 1996, *A Report on Men's Health in Western Australia*, Men's Health Teaching and Research Unit, Curtin University, Western Australia.

Hurst, D. 1995, 'Men's violence and men's health: some recent worldwide trends', *Proceedings of the National Men's Health Conference*, pp. 100–11.

International Nursing Review 1996, 'Women's health: how it scored in Beijing', *International Nursing Review*, vol. 43, no. 2, pp. 59–63.

Kabria, W., Gachukia, E. & Mataiangi, F. 1997, 'The effect of women's role on health: the paradox', *International Journal of Gynecology and Obstetrics*, vol. 58, pp. 23–34.

Kendrick, J. & Merritt, R. 1996, 'Women and smoking: an update for the 1990s', *American Journal of Obstetrics and Gynecology*, vol. 175, pp. 528–35.

King, K. & Paul, P. 1996, 'A historical review of the depiction of women in cardiovascular literature', *Western Journal of Nursing Research*, vol. 18, no. 1, pp. 89–101.

Macran, S., Clarke, L. & Joshi, H. 1996, 'Women's health: dimensions and differentials', *Social Science and Medicine*, vol. 42, no. 9, pp. 1203–16.

Magrane, D. & McIntyre-Seltman, K. 1996, 'Women's health care issues for medical students: an educational proposal', *Women's Health Issues*, vol. 6, no. 4, pp. 183–91.

Mahowald, M., Levinson, D. & Cassel, C. 1996, 'The new genetics and women', *Milbank Quarterly*, vol. 74, no. 2, pp. 239–83.

Manderson, L. & Mark, T. 1997, 'Empowering women: participatory approaches in women's health and development projects', *Health Care for Women International*, vol. 18, pp. 17–30.

McKeever, P. 1995, 'Between women: nurses and family caregivers', *Canadian Journal of Nursing Research*, vol. 26, no. 4, pp. 15–21.

McMillan, I. 1995, 'Men's health: their own worst enemy', *Nursing Times*, vol. 91, no. 48, pp. 25–8.

McMurray, A. & Blackmore, A. 1993, 'Influences on parent-child relationships in non-custodial fathers', *Australian Journal of Marriage and Family*, vol. 14, no. 3, pp. 151–9.

Meleis, A., Douglas, M., Eribes, C., Shih, F. & Messias, D. 1996, 'Employed Mexican women as mothers and partners: valued, empowered and overloaded', *Journal of Advanced Nursing*, vol. 23, pp. 82–90.

M'Jamtu-sie, N. 1996, 'Health information for the grass roots', *World Health Forum*, vol. 17, pp. 277–82.

Morse, B. 1995, 'Beyond the conflict tactics scale: assessing gender differences in partner violence', *Violence and Victims*, vol. 10, no. 4, pp. 251–72.

Moser, D. 1997, 'Correcting misconceptions about women and heart disease', *American Journal of Nursing*, vol. 97, no. 4, pp. 26–9.

Narrigan, D. Zones, J. & Worcester, N. 1997, 'Research to improve women's health: An agenda for equity', in *Women's Health: Complexities and Differences*, eds S. Ruzek, V. Olesen & A. Clarke, Ohio State Univeristy Press, Columbus, pp. 551–79.

Oakley, A. 1994, 'Who cares for health? Social relations, gender, and the public health', *Journal of Epidemiology and Public Health*, vol. 48, pp. 427–34.

Pilbara Public Health Unit 1994, *Men's Health Project Report*, Health Department of Western Australia, Geraldton, WA.

Richardson, J. & Feder, G. 1996, 'Domestic violence: a hidden problem for general practice', *British Journal of General Practice*, April, pp. 239–42.

Rigdon, S. 1996, 'Abortion law and practice in China: an overview with comparisons to the United States', *Social Science and Medicine*, vol. 42, no. 4, pp. 543–60.

Robbe, M., March, L., Vinen, J., Horner, D., & Roberts, G. 1996, 'Prevalence of domestic violence among patients attending a hospital emergency department', *Australian and New Zealand Journal of Public Health*, vol. 20, no. 4, pp. 364–8.

Rozenberg, S., Liebens, F., Kroll, M. & Vandromme, J. 1996, 'Principal cancers among women: breast, lung and colorectal', *International Journal of Fertility*, vol. 41, no. 2, pp. 166–71.

Ruzek, S. 1997, 'Women, personal health behavior and health promotion', in *Women's Health: Complexities and Differences*, eds S. Ruzek, V. Olesen & A. Clarke, Ohio State University Press, Columbus, pp. 118–53.

Ruzek, S., Olesen, V. & Clarke, A. 1997, *Women's Health: Complexities and Differences*, Ohio State University Press, Columbus.

Schafran, L. 1996, 'Topics for our times: rape is a major public health issue', *American Journal of Public Health*, vol. 86, no. 1, pp. 15–16.

Smith, A. 1995, 'An analysis of altruism: a concept of caring', *Journal of Advanced Nursing*, vol. 22, pp. 785–90.

Sorenson, S., Upchurch, D. & Shen, H. 1996, 'Violence and injury in marital arguments: risk patterns and gender differences', *American Journal of Public Health*, vol. 86, no. 1, pp. 35–40.

Spurlock, J. 1995, 'Multiple roles of women and role strains', *Health Care for Women International*, vol. 16, pp. 501–8.

Taylor, D. & Dower, C. 1997, 'Toward a women-centered health care system: women's experiences, women's voices, women's needs', *Health Care for Women International*, vol. 18, pp. 407–22.

Thorne, S., McCormick, J. & Carty, E. 1997, 'Deconstructing the gender neutrality of chronic illness and disability', *Health Care For Women International*, vol. 18, pp. 1–16.

Timpson, J. 1996, 'Abortion: the antithesis of womanhood?', *Journal of Advanced Nursing*, vol. 23, pp. 776–85.

Umberson, D. 1992, 'Gender, marital status and the social control of health behavior', *Social Science and Medicine*, vol. 34, no. 8, pp. 907–17.

UNICEF 1996, *Human Development Report*, UNICEF, New York.

Utian, W. 1996, 'Direction, misdirection and misconception in menopause research and management', *British Journal of Obstetrics and Gynaecology*, vol. 103, pp. 736–9.

Varkevisser, C. 1995, 'Women's health in a changing world', *Tropical and Geographical Medicine*, vol. 47, no. 5, pp. 186–92.

Vazquez, C. 1996, 'Spousal abuse and violence against women: the significance of understanding attachment', *Annals of the New York Academy of Science*, vol. 789, pp. 119–28.

Verbrugge, L. 1988, 'Unveiling higher morbidity for men: the story', in *Social Structures and Human Lives*, ed. E. Riley, Sage, Newbury Park, CA.

Wang, C., Burris, M. & Ping, X. 1996, 'Chinese village women as visual anthropologists: a participatory approach to reaching policymakers', *Social Science and Medicine*, vol. 42, no. 10, pp. 1391–400.

Wingood, G. & DiClemente, R. 1996, 'HIV sexual risk reduction interventions for women: a review', *American Journal of Preventive Medicine*, vol. 12, no. 3, pp. 209–17.

Wolf, N. 1991, *The Beauty Myth: How Images of Beauty Are Used Against Women*, William Morrow, New York.

Wong, G., Li, V., Burris, M. & Xiang, Y. 1995, 'Seeking women's voices: setting the context for women's health interventions in two rural counties in Yunnan, China', *Social Science and Medicine*, vol. 41, no. 8, pp. 1147–57.

Young, R. 1996, 'The household context for women's health care decisions: impacts of UK policy changes', *Social Science and Medicine*, vol. 42, no. 6, pp. 949–63.

Zierler, S. & Krieger, N. 1997, 'Reframing women's risk: social inequalities and HIV infection', *Annual Review of Public Health*, vol. 18, pp. 401–36.

Zones, J. 1997, 'Beauty myths and realities and their impact on women's health', in *Women's Health: Complexities and Differences*, eds S. Ruzek, V. Olesen & A. Clarke, Ohio State University Press, Columbus, pp. 249–75.

Healthy Aboriginal people

11

Culture is a type of blueprint for living that is handed down within a particular society (Eckermann et al. 1992). It encompasses the way people organise and think about life: their values and beliefs, traditions, customs and rituals (Spradley & Allender 1996). Cultural traditions vary widely. Some cultures tend to value large family gatherings, festivals and general sociability, while others may be slightly more private. Certain cultures place great value on religion and spirituality, whereas others do not. Although there are also variations within cultures, group beliefs and traditions often determine people's views about health-related issues. Cultural norms often prescribe diet and eating habits, child-rearing practices, reactions to pain, stress and death, a sense of past, present and future, and responses to health care services and practitioners. These views, in turn, may have an effect on survival rates among the population or on whether preventive measures such as immunisation are undertaken. Culture and cultural customs are therefore instrumental in creating and sustaining health.

The culture, and thus the health, of Aboriginal people is of particular concern to those of us advocating for community health and development. For many years, Aboriginal people have experienced considerably poorer health status than other groups in society. This is thought to be linked to their sub-standard economic and social conditions relative to the non-Aboriginal population, which may in turn be linked to their history of colonisation and oppression by other groups (MacMillan et al. 1996). This chapter addresses historical, social, economic and situational factors that influence the health of Aboriginal people. It is aimed at examining the inter-relationships between Aboriginal people's culture, their health and the health of their communities.

Objectives

By the end of this chapter you will be able to:

- *explain the influence of historical factors on the creation of health among Aboriginal people*

- *explain the link between health and social justice for indigenous people*

- *identify three risk factors for ill health among indigenous people*

- *explain the importance of cultural knowledge in developing health promotion strategies*

- *devise health promotion strategies to counter risk among Aboriginal people.*

Understanding culture

Cultural groups are bound together by many things: art, customs, habits, language, roles, rules, shared meanings about the world, and a sense of history. Culture is usually tacit in people's behaviours, an unconscious predisposition rather than a deliberate attempt to be distinctive. From an ecological perspective, culture prescribes the way people tend to interact with the environment and, in turn, the way their social organisation and cultural values are influenced by that environment (Eckermann et al. 1992). Because this is a dynamic process, cultures change, adapting somewhat as they interact with their own environment and that of others. In some cases, this is of mutual benefit. For example, in multicultural societies, people of different cultures learn from one another, often enjoying one another's foods and ways of cooking, lifestyles and folk-ways such as festivals and celebrations. In some cases where two cultures attempt to interact within the same environment, there is the potential for culture conflict, particularly if one group has power over the other. Culture conflict can cause disharmony in the community, when members of the conflicting groups close ranks and withdraw from each other rather than co-operating to build a system of mutual community support. Without mutual support mechanisms, there is little chance of the community meeting its common goals or achieving health and a quality lifestyle for its residents.

Aboriginal culture and health

The term *Aboriginal* refers to the initial, or earliest, inhabitants of a place. They may also be described as *First Nations*, or *indigenous*, people. However, membership in an Aboriginal group does not imply homogeneity, for, like other cultures, Aboriginal people have diverse subcultures. Aboriginal groups live in a spectrum of ecological zones, speak many different languages, and have varying religious and healing practices, diets, family traditions, community and economic structures (Reid & Trompf 1991). But despite diversity in affiliations and lifestyles, most Aboriginal people have in common a history of colonisation that has left them disempowered in relation to other population groups. The history of Australia, New Zealand, Canada and the US reveals a belief by their white European conquerors in their superiority over the native people. In most cases, this view was so extreme that the early explorers dismissed the very presence of Aboriginal people as irrelevant because they failed to use the land in a way that would be expected in a civilised country. The colonisers thus declared the respective countries *Terra Nullius*—a land belonging to nobody (ACAR 1994; Eckermann et al. 1992).

As the white colonialists developed the land, predictably, conflicts ensued between the European and native people. In Australia, once the presence of indigenous people was acknowledged, the newcomers considered the Aboriginal people treacherous, barbarous, lazy or mentally inferior. As a result, laws were passed that considered Aborigines wards of the Government and therefore without proper citizenship (Eckermann et al. 1992). This situation effectively created an institutionalised form of racism that resulted in mass undermining of the Aboriginal people's social organisation. Geographic groupings were dispersed, Aboriginal women were captured and alcohol was introduced to their culture. Their religious and spiritual beliefs were undermined by religious missionaries. Because they no longer had the right to use the land they had previously inhabited, their food supply was disrupted. The new landlords then upset the balance of nature through over-grazing and the destruction of grasslands and forest, with its edible seeds, roots and fauna (Eckermann et al. 1992). The social, economic, political and physical environment of their culture was thereby almost completely subjugated by the dominant white colonialists in what has been called 'pacification by force' (Bush & van Holst Pellekan 1995, p. 223).

In those early days of white colonialism, institutionalised racism was supplanted with scientific racism, which contended that Aboriginal people were so low on the human scale that they deserved only subhuman treatment. No recognition was given for 'their powers of observation, memory, concepts and calculation of distance, knowledge of the natural world and athletic competence, because these abilities were used for different skills in a life style governed by different priorities' (Bush & van Holst Pellekan 1995). Few attempts were made to understand or preserve Aboriginal culture. Instead these First Nations were almost exterminated by disease and war, dehumanised through alcoholism, sexual abuse and economic exploitation, and then blamed for being demoralised and living in squalor—a classic case of what we now call 'victim blaming' (Eckermann et al. 1992).

Over time, and as a sense of social consciousness developed among colonial governments, eventually the European people began to work toward protecting the Aborigines. Attempts were made to assimilate them into white culture. This saw many young children removed from their parents so that they could be sent to white schools to gain what was considered to be 'appropriate' educational preparation. As the civil rights movement gained momentum in the developed world, the injustice of this practice was recognised and attempts were made to make amends. Today, the notion of empowerment and self-determination for Aboriginal people has gradually become accepted by the majority of the non-Aboriginal population. What remains to be addressed in this current era is recognition by non-Aboriginal people of the residual effects of the past discriminatory practices. Then a commitment must be made by all governments to assisting Aboriginal people develop the skills and resources for self-determinism and self-management (Eckermann et al. 1992). Without this commitment there cannot be social justice.

Among the indigenous people of Canada, the US and New Zealand, the most devastating and prolonged effect of colonisation is the depressed economic and social circumstances of their lives (MacMillan et al. 1996; Saggers & Gray 1994). A cycle of risk clouds their future. First, financial and social impoverishment creates dependency, limits self-expression and leads to people accepting sub-standard community infrastructures (Tookenay 1996). As poor people, they live in sub-standard housing and have an inadequate diet and lifestyle, which predisposes them to ill health. A combination of illness, socioeconomic status and geographic inaccessibility constrains their educational performance, which then limits employment opportunities, completing a cycle of poverty. Prejudice and discriminatory attitudes and values compound their low status in society. As economic fortunes among the whole of society declines, their means of support and roles are further compromised, leaving many in a situation of social disintegration. Social disintegration destroys opportunities for self-improvement and continuity of employment, creating a loss of values and social networks (Saggers & Gray 1994). As a result, indigenous people develop feelings of cultural exclusion accompanied by stress and anxiety.

For some, cultural exclusion becomes a self-fulfilling prophecy. They either withdraw or, as many young people have done, lash out in violent episodes, causing further discrimination and marginalisation from the wider society (Eckermann et al. 1992). The latter response causes a considerable number to become incarcerated, which further adds to their feelings of hopelessness. Feeling trapped in the cycle of risk and hopelessness, some choose to end their lives in custody, a situation that occurs with alarming frequency. This cycle is illustrated in figure 11.1.

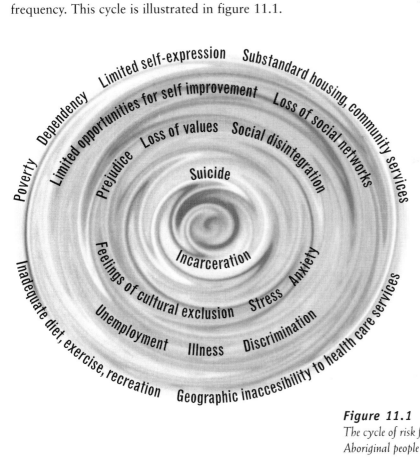

Figure 11.1
The cycle of risk for Aboriginal people

In 1987, an Australian Royal Commission was established to investigate the phenomenon of Aboriginal deaths in custody. The findings revealed inequities in education, cultural awareness, research, resources and Aboriginal input into policies governing their people (Johnston 1991). Despite the report's recommendations that a comprehensive strategy be but in place to address the problem, there remains a rate of suicide in custody that far excels that of the white population. This has led to general discouragement among Aboriginal people, particularly surviving family members where there has been a death in custody. They tend to see government inaction and the lack of meaningful initiatives as reflecting a lack of commitment to their need for self-empowerment and cultural valuing.

The indigenous people of Canada and the US have also suffered from the effects of colonisation, with similar morbidities to those experienced by Australian Aborigines and New Zealand Maori (Brady 1995). The First Nations people of North America have, however, a longer history of negotiating their rights with their colonisers. This has left them with marginally more power over their affairs, and slightly better health status, than the indigenous people of the South Pacific and Polynesia (Brady 1995).

In New Zealand, the history of the Maori people shows that their culture and health status have also suffered from colonisation despite the fact that they have enjoyed the protection and rights and privileges of British citizenship. Their citizenship status is enshrined in the Treaty of Waitangi, the Maori people's founding document and a statement of their cultural need (NCNZ 1996). Like that of the Australian Aborigines, the health status of Maori people has been eroded by civil and colonial wars, introduced diseases, geographic isolation, land deprivation and a user-pays Victorian health system. Since the 1940s, mortality rates among the Maori have declined due to improved public health screening and treatment (Pool 1991). These gains have, however, been somewhat disproportionate to those experienced by non-Maori New Zealanders and, as with other indigenous people, this can be attributed to continued poverty and other social factors. For the past decade, there has been renewed Government commitment to the Treaty of Waitangi, with an emphasis on educational goals that would encourage responsiveness to Maori issues (NCNZ 1996). Embedded in all these educational programs, including those preparing health care professionals, is the concept of cultural safety.

Cultural safety

The concept of cultural safety was first described in New Zealand in 1988 by the Hui Waimanawa (Ramsden, in Eckermann et al. 1992). The concept revolves around recognition of the social, physical and economic elements required by those belonging to the Maori culture, and their rights to partnership, participation and protection (Shipley 1996). Cultural safety encompasses a holistic reflection of the person within the context of family and community and the customs, attitudes, beliefs and preferred ways of doing things that comprise that system (Eckermann et al. 1992). Unsafe cultural practice is any action that diminishes, demeans or disempowers the cultural identity and wellbeing of an individual (NCNZ 1992).

The first step in achieving cultural safety is *cultural awareness*. This includes recognising the fact that any health care relationship is unique, power-laden and culturally dyadic. Once there is recognition of the inherent nature of cultural difference, *cultural sensitivity* can be developed. People can be expected to develop cultural sensitivity once they engage in some form of self-exploration of their own life experience and realities, and the impact this may have on others. The final stage is a commitment to ensuring preservation and protection of others' cultures. Cultural safety is advocacy informed by a recognition of self, the rights of others and the legitimacy of difference (NCNZ 1996).

The principles of cultural safety are similar to the principles of primary health care in that the focus is on social justice. In a socially just and thus healthy environment, the relationship between health professionals and the community is one of partnership and mutual exploration of need, rather than one where there is a power differential of provider and consumer. People are free to choose the pathways to health that best suit their needs and customs. All cultures are seen to be equally valid, and both personal and collective views are valued. Both cultural safety and primary health care are not as much about *what* is done by health professionals to promote health and reduce risks, but about *how* this is done (Johnson 1997).

Like primary health care, the cultural safety approach also encourages examination of political processes as they affect health. The overall aim is to empower all people to gain autonomy over decisions affecting their health and health services. The primary goals are to improve health and access to services for all people, irrespective of age, gender, sexual orientation, occupation or socioeconomic status, ethnic origin or migrant experience, religious or spiritual belief, or disability (NCNZ 1996). This can only be accomplished with an understanding that equality means having a right to be *different*, not just a right to be the *same* (Houston 1993).

The major strategy for achieving cultural safety in any community is education. Health professionals must be educated within an ethos of cultural relativism; that is, they must learn to understand and value diversity in cultures, history, attitudes and life experiences. Dowd and Johnson (1996) provide an example of this in their illustration of the health care professional who believes an indigenous person who sleeps in the desert to be sick because he lives in the dirt surrounded by germs. Cultural beliefs, on the other hand, may attribute his illness to the fact that he failed to look after his land. When we fail to gain this type of cultural understanding, our attempts at helping indigenous people or those of any other culture are doomed to failure. Professional ignorance may be seen as professional arrogance, and this interferes with our attempts to advocate for health as a *partner* rather than a *provider*. The role of the health professional is therefore to understand how power imbalances impede health and how an equitable helping role can be negotiated and changed to provide effective, efficient and acceptable services (NCNZ 1996). Our educational processes must be developed accordingly.

Health risks of Aboriginality

The concept of health risk is somewhat ambiguous when applied to Aboriginal people, for their notion of health, and thus risk to health, is broader than the usual definitions proposed by health professionals. When Aboriginal people speak of health, they usually refer to the context of wellbeing. Health and wellbeing means integrity and harmony in the interrelationships among all things that constitute people's life-ways. Central to wellbeing is self-determination, and central to self-determination are land rights and the right to their own laws and customs. To sustain health and wellbeing, Aboriginal people must have territorial security, and this involves having a dignified and meaningful place for all community members, and control over natural resources (NAACHO 1993).

Because of this holistic view of health, and the inextricable links between health and the environment, including the land and sea, citing health status and health service statistics based on white people's definitions of illnesses has only limited usefulness. Aboriginal people feel that their health needs are poorly understood within non-Aboriginal epidemiological definitions. Health departments do not usually couch their needs in terms of a 'whole-of-life' approach, as would be done by lay community members. Service structures are often inappropriate and difficult to negotiate (NACCHO 1993). Health professionals discuss compliance with treatment regimes, yet there is little motivation to comply with prescribed treatments they cannot comprehend because of culturally inappropriate frames of reference. Aboriginal people see their health problems not in terms of epidemiological cause and effect data, but in terms of a disharmony between what they define as health and wellbeing and the choices that have been imposed upon them by people outside their culture (NACCHO 1993).

The health of Aboriginal people is cause for alarm among those seeking to prevent, treat or reduce illness and promote a consistent level of community health and wellness. From an epidemiological perspective, Aboriginal people in all countries tend to have higher rates of illness and injury than the rest of the population. The risk of diabetes mellitus, circulatory and renal disease and many cancers is far greater among the Aboriginal populations of Australia, New Zealand, Canada and the US, than their non-Aboriginal counterparts (AIHW 1996; MacMillan et al. 1996; NCNZ 1996). For women in both Canadian and Australian Aboriginal communities, cervical cancer is a major problem, causing disproportionately higher rates of mortality among their population than that experienced by non-Aboriginal women (MacMillan et al. 1996; Mak & Straton 1997). Respiratory diseases are also many times more prevalent in Aboriginal people than non-Aborigines, and include high rates of tuberculosis among adults, asthma, and more severe and frequent upper respiratory infections among young children (AIHW 1996; Hanna et al. 1997; MacMillan et al. 1996).

High rates of many other infectious and non-infectious diseases have been reported among Aboriginal people. These are believed to be related to the risk factors characteristic of indigenous people, namely nutritional problems, genetic factors, poverty and crowding, and environmental pollutants such as tobacco and wood smoke (Lee 1996; MacMillan et al. 1996; Saggers & Gray 1994). With widespread environmental pollution in today's world, those Aboriginal people who follow a traditional lifestyle are also at risk of ingesting trace metals and a range of environmental pollutants through traditional food sources (MacMillan et al. 1996).

Improving Aboriginal health

Improving Aboriginal health status is a far from simple matter. Effective health promotion approaches must include comprehensive and multilayered strategies that seek to redress social inequities in all aspects of life, including education, employment, the administration of legal processes and land rights. Health education must be presented in forms, structures, settings and language that local Aboriginal community members can identify with (NACCHO 1993). This process must begin with an understanding of Aboriginal culture, and community-defined goals that may or may not always correspond to those suggested by the wider community.

Aboriginal people unfamiliar with the need for preventive screening or, in some cases, for treating illnesses and injuries, often neglect their personal health. Without role models who are part of the culture and who share common beliefs and behaviours, many do not see the credibility of health education messages. In traditional communities, the older members had elevated status and their role was to guide the young, to ensure that justice was served and that the traditions were handed down from generation to generation. Since Aboriginal assimilation, older members of the community have lost their previous elevated status among the people. This is decried by many families attempting to maintain cultural identity while trying to teach their young to conform to the laws and customs of the wider society to ensure that their lives and health are not placed in jeopardy. For example, diseases of modern society, such as HIV infection, require that all people take precautionary action. Because AIDS is a new epidemic, traditional teachings must be supplanted with modern health education messages that teach safe sexual practices and encourage screening where necessary, without diminishing cultural beliefs (NACCHO 1993).

The AIDS epidemic is increasing at an alarming rate among Aboriginal people (DuBois, Brassard & Smeja 1996; Mill & Desjardins 1996). Other lifestyle illnesses also compromise the health of Aboriginal people. Tobacco use is a major problem. Canadian researchers recently reported that as many as 60% of Aboriginal Canadians smoke regularly, and the figure is nearly as high among Australian Aborigines (AIHW 1996; MacMillan et al. 1996). Young people especially are at risk of smoking and alcohol and drug overuse despite the proliferation of health education messages to the contrary. In the long term, these are known threats to health, but in the short term they are also hazardous in heightening the risk of accidents, injuries and family disruptions, and in bringing young people into contact with the police (Gray et al. 1997). Smoking, caffeine and alcohol consumption are also threats to maternal health, with the added danger of perpetuating a cycle of disadvantage and disempowerment among the next generation (MacMillan et al. 1996).

Another problem threatening Aboriginal communities is that of youth suicide. Researchers have looked for explanations for the high rates of suicide and self-harm, especially among the young, identifying risk factors as social change, poverty, alcohol abuse, family violence and access to firearms (Malchu et al. 1997). Some of these factors are illustrated in figure 11.1. An alternative explanation for the high rate of suicide among Aboriginal young people is that cultural differences may lead to different manifestations of depression and suicidal tendencies, one of which is to shy away from help-seeking, especially where the victim has been feeling socially isolated (Mock et al. 1996).

The health problems of Aboriginal people can be segregated into various constellations of symptoms and underlying causes. However, Saggers and Gray (1991) contend that the high levels of ill health among these people are directly attributable to their dispossession, their marginalisation and their dependence on a variety of government and welfare services. Governments have attempted to mobilise public resources to respond to their health needs, but none have been able to significantly alter existing power relations between Aboriginal and non-Aboriginal people. Until they do, the problems that lead to ill health will persist (Saggers & Gray 1991).

Government agencies have been established in many countries to empower Aboriginal people to meet culturally specific needs. However, some are beset by bureaucratic problems, inadequate placement of Aboriginal professionals or managers, misunderstanding of group identity, language difficulties, a lack of co-ordinated information systems or geographic isolation (Newbold 1997; Tookenay 1996). One of the first things that must be addressed is variable provision and utilisation of services. Jurisdictional disputes between state or provincial and federal governments sometimes create inconsistencies in services or confusion among those needing the services about where to seek help. Clearly, the way to counter rampant illness and sub-optimal health among Aboriginal people is within a culturally sensitive political structure. Aboriginal people must become empowered for self-determinism through enhanced educational and economic opportunities that reconcile the past, present and future. As health professionals, we must do our part to heighten awareness of the interrelationships between history, health, place and culture to ensure that the primary health care principles of access, equity and self-determinism are achieved.

Aboriginal reconciliation

In recognition of the link between dispossession and the health and wellbeing of Aboriginal people, many governments have undertaken measures aimed at reconciliation between indigenous people and non-indigenous residents of their nations. In Australia, the Australian Council for Aboriginal Reconciliation was established as a statutory authority in 1991. The Australian Council's Bill for Aboriginal Reconciliation was passed that same year as an Act of Parliament (ACAR 1994). The key issues identified as crucial to reconciliation are as follows:

- understanding country—that is, the importance of land and sea in Aboriginal and Torres Strait Islander societies
- improving relationships between indigenous Australians and the wider community
- valuing cultures as part of the Australian heritage
- sharing histories for shared ownership of the country
- addressing disadvantage to create awareness of its causes
- responding to custody levels to address the underlying issues related to Aboriginal deaths in custody
- agreeing to a document to chart the course of reconciliation
- controlling destinies with greater opportunities for Aboriginal people.

Despite broad political support for the process of reconciliation there remain many hurdles before widespread public acceptance can occur. The Australian legal, political and social systems are working toward satisfactory resolution of the Native Title Act of 1993, which was intended to restore the fundamental rights of Aboriginal and Torres Strait Islander people to their native land. The Act changed the face of land rights issues from one of social welfare to one of recognition of legal title to land, a measure which had the capacity to reap large gains in the process of reconciliation (ACAR 1994). Interpretation of the Act has, however, been beset with controversy in that it has polarised public opinion into pro-development (retain the land to create jobs) versus empowerment of native people by restoring their lands. Once again, an overly simplistic equation threatens the course of social justice. The issues are complex, and it is the expectation of the Reconciliation Council that with considerable effort in communicating all sides of the issues, public understanding will prevail, leading to changes in federal legislation that allow both Aboriginal people and non-Aboriginal people to coexist in harmony.

South Africa

South Africa has also sought reconciliation in a way similar to Australia. Despite a different history that included blatant segregation of black and white people through apartheid, South Africans have been able to negotiate a form of power-sharing and a deconstruction of oppressive laws and institutions that was formerly thought inconceivable. Since coming into power in 1994, the African National Congress (ANC) has established the Government of National Unity (GNU), which has developed an interim constitution with reconciliation as its central theme. The government has been working toward a negotiated solution to Afrikaner self-determination, establishing a 'Volkstaat', or Afrikaner homeland, and has been attempting to end civil conflict in that country. One contentious issue has been the establishment of the 'Truth and Reconciliation Commission', which has been received with mixed reactions, some believing it to be a legitimised form of revenge, and others maintaining their faith in the process of reconciling the past with the present (ACAR 1994).

Canada

The colonisation of indigenous people in Canada was accomplished without the warfare and civil conflict that has occurred in South Africa and Australia. Native title has been recognised in Canada since 1973. There have been numerous treaties and land claim negotiations between the Aboriginal and non-Aboriginal people, and some have been the subject of protracted dispute. The Canadian constitution was amended in 1982 to recognise the status and treaty rights of indigenous people. However, its implementation and thus the process of reconciliation has not always run smoothly. The treaties have sometimes been devised with insufficient input from the indigenous people and have been the subject of numerous grievances (ACAR 1994; Brady 1995).

Another contentious issue is the right of the federal government, enshrined in The Indian Act of 1867, to define who is Indian and who is not, and to legislate over Indian people and the lands reserved for them. As a result, indigenous people have always been stratified according to whether they are 'status' Indians (those living on Indian reserves or Crown land), 'non-status' Indians (non-treaty or non-reserve Indians) or Inuit. Status Indians have attracted the majority of federal government resources and have greater rights to self-government within their Indian bands than either the non-status or Inuit people. One of the effects of this has been to create a second and third layer of discrimination for non-status Indians and Inuit, who sometimes are marginalised by their own people through circumstances not always under their control, such as their place of residence.

Tripartite negotiations between the federal and provincial governments and the Indian people are continuing, with the ultimate aim of Aboriginal self-government grounded in the constitution. At present, some limited forms of self-government exist through negotiation between various Indian bands and the government. The most notable of these is the largest land claim of any indigenous people: the establishment of the community of Nunavut in the Eastern Arctic Region which, in the year 1999, will see the Inuit people achieve self-government (ACAR 1994). In a gesture of reconciliation, in 1998 the Canadian Federal Government offered an apology to all First Nations people for past injustices.

The United States

The American situation is unique in the level of power and authority vested in that country's indigenous people. The early days of the US saw many bloody conflicts between indigenous and non-indigenous people. At the time of independence, the federal government assumed full responsibility for Indian affairs to protect the native people from the settlers. However, since two landmark decisions in the 1830s, which granted nation status to two tribes, the Indian people have existed as sovereign, self-governing entities, subject to federal laws and administrative arrangements (ACAR 1994).

The 1970s saw the beginning of a trend to recognise Indian rights to self-determination and self-governance, and many gains have been won. Indian tribal courts now have extensive civil and criminal jurisdictions over matters involving Indians arising on Indian lands. Tribal laws predominate on Indian lands, and the tribal courts have exclusive jurisdiction over minor crimes where both victim and perpetrator are Indian, and concurrent jurisdiction over major crimes committed against Indian people. In Alaska, a state-wide land claims settlement has launched a new era of political negotiation between indigenous and state governments, with discussions currently focusing on environmental management, ecologically sustainable development and indigenous cultural autonomy (ACAR 1994).

New Zealand

New Zealand was founded on the Treaty of Waitangi, written in both languages and signed by both the Crown and Maori tribal chiefs in 1840. Since then, securing Maori land rights and self-determination has been an arduous process, primarily because of differing interpretations of each version of the Treaty. Both versions were incorporated into statute law by the Treaty of Waitangi Act of 1975 and despite considerable initial litigation over the implications of the Act, it required each party to act towards the other in good faith.

In recent years, the trend toward litigation between the two groups has been replaced with negotiation, and this has resulted in some satisfactory fisheries and minerals claims. One area of contention has been a government-imposed deadline on land claims which, according to the Maori Congress (a non-statutory body representing tribes), is contrary to the spirit of shared rights exemplified by the Treaty. Although it is only entrenched in domestic law, the Treaty of Waitangi has been extremely influential in its effect on the position and perception of Maori people in New Zealand. The most visible effect of the 150-year tradition of sharing the two cultures in that country is the pervasiveness of Maori language, symbols and customs in the wider community. However, as with other indigenous people, their economic and social status remains far below that of the non-indigenous people (ACAR 1994; Brady 1995).

Goals for Aboriginal health

Each of these First Nations has endured years of oppression in a range of areas. Each has had to struggle to retain indigenous customs, laws, political processes and resources. In each case, enormous progress has been made in reconciling their culture with that of the rest of society and with heightening public awareness of their plight. As health professionals, it is imperative that we continue to articulate the need for Aboriginal empowerment as the way toward health and wellbeing. This can be done by continuing to lobby for equity, access, self-determination and self-management and, above all, reconciliation with the past so that all nations can move on to the future.

To address Aboriginal health needs, the following goals are important:
■ access and equity in health care
■ cultural sensitivity and cultural safety in all health care practices
■ community self-determinism and self-empowerment

■ public recognition of the unique needs of Aboriginal people

■ reconciliation with other people of the world.

Building healthy public policy

The health of indigenous people is essentially a political minefield. Government policies have attempted to resource Aboriginal health strategies, but have had only modest success in reducing mortality and morbidity rates. As a result, few claims can be made for self-determinism, empowerment of indigenous people, or cultural safety. It is an indictment on non-indigenous policy-makers that the most pressing problems have not been addressed. Government funding for Aboriginal health must ensure access to culturally appropriate health services and to the community infrastructure that determines health, including housing and clean water. This can only be done with the participation of Aboriginal people at all levels of government policy so that there is careful integration of physical, emotional, social, spiritual, environmental, political and cultural needs (Golds et al. 1997). Segregating Aboriginal health into one policy or separating individual needs from the whole perpetuates fragmentation of services and destroys understanding of the dynamic interrelationships necessary for achieving health and wellbeing.

Health goals and strategies for Aboriginal people must include broad, comprehensive notions of equity. Equity is a two-dimensional concept that consists of horizontal equity (the equal treatment of equal people) and vertical equity, which refers to unequal, but equitable, treatment of people who may not have equal requirements or preferences (Jan & Wiseman 1996). This is closely aligned with the contention that true equity incorporates the right to *difference*, not *sameness*. Equity involves equality of access to and use of health care, without coercion to use one or another service. So there are situations where top-down provision of equitable services may actually be inequitable to indigenous people on the basis of cultural preferences and holistic, traditional definitions of health. Similarly, setting equal goals for health (horizontal equity) may not achieve intended outcomes, especially if there are disparate needs (Jan & Wiseman 1996).

Creating supportive environments

The most important elements of a supportive environment are understanding and communication (Arriaga 1994). To understand another culture requires understanding of our own beliefs and attitudes first, then a concerted effort to understand those of the other culture. It is important to know the symbols of the culture and how members of the culture see our symbols. For example, when the health professional is seen as a bona fide community member, a different message is conveyed than when the helper is simply flown in to treat an illness or collect information on the community. Another issue in assessing the need for support is to know how illness is perceived and how its causes and cures are framed within the cultural context. Having at least a cursory grasp of the language is also important to ensure that communication is appropriate.

When members of some cultures are ill, specific facilities may be required to accommodate religious or other beliefs. Sometimes these may be related to the need for special religious observances, hygiene, diet and bodily contact (Ashkam 1996). Young families may have special needs related to child-rearing, such as the need for a hospitalised child to always feel the security of family members, or the need to consult a traditional healer (Bushy & van Holst Pellekan 1995). The family may need to deal with social beliefs about the causes of the problem that may be unfamiliar to the health professional, or to formulate priorities for treatment based on family, rather than patient need (Bushy & van Holst Pellekaan 1995; Kaona, Siziya & Mushanga 1990). Supporting families in these cases requires cultural sensitivity and patience to ensure that appropriate assessment is done and then acted upon.

One of the most pressing challenges for health carers lies in meeting mental health needs. The problem of alcohol abuse, for example, is poorly understood. Alcohol abuse is one of the most destructive influences on Aboriginal family life (Brady 1995 1997; Gray et al. 1997). Restricting supply is one tactic being used, and another is stricter policing at the point of sale. While these may be justified in some cases, they are also regarded as heavy-handed, top-down approaches and have attracted conflicting views.

Some see excessive sanctions on the availability or distribution of alcohol as aligned with white colonialist approaches (Kelso Townsend & de Vries 1995). Alternative approaches, where Aboriginal people them-selves participate in developing community plans to address the problem, are usually more widely accepted and thus more effective (Brady 1995). Treatments for alcohol-related disorders, including counselling strategies, must be designed from knowledge of the conditions that precipitated drink-ing, and based on an understanding of Aboriginal culture (Kelso Townsend & de Vries 1995). One widely held misconception is that excessive drink-ing is socially embedded in Aboriginal culture, yet the reasons why people of any culture drink are many and varied (Brady 1997). To assess preven-tion and rehabilitation needs effectively, the health professional must be receptive to information provided by the person and other family and community members (Kelso Townsend & de Vries 1995).

Another very important issue to young Aboriginal people is the growing incidence of HIV infection. To counter the spread of the disease, an approach is needed that capitalises on appropriate and credible role models, is embedded within the cultural context, is sensitive to the needs and behaviours of young people, and is compatible with the communal environment. One such program is described in the following case study (Mill & Desjardins 1996).

▶ CASE STUDY

The Feather of Hope

The Feather of Hope is a peer support program for Canadian indigenous people diagnosed with HIV infection. It was developed by a group of community workers in a small Aboriginal community in northern Alberta, Canada. In the first stage of the program, discussions were held within the community to plan an approach that would be culturally and developmentally appropriate to those who most needed help. The participants identified the need to have an Aboriginal Elder provide a linkage between the older generation and the new. As there was no nominated Elder, an ageing (96-year-old) member of the community was recruited to help plan and oversee implementation of the program. Once the local community of AIDS sufferers were made aware of the program and its focus on Aboriginal culture, a process of guidance and support was begun.

The program's approach is as follows. Each day begins with a traditional Sweet Grass ceremony and prayers to the Creator and Sacred Spirits. The emphasis is first on developing cultural insight into the social, economic and health issues faced by Aboriginal communities and how these are related to development of HIV infection. The educational presentations include an explanation of the ways in which traditional methods (healing circles, retreats, sweat lodges and traditional healers) can be used

to support people who are HIV positive. The next part of the program focuses on the development of presentation skills by group participants so that they can all participate in a self-help process and perpetuate the cycle of helping.

All aspects of the program are culturally sensitive. Staff of Aboriginal ancestry have been hired as both staff and board members, to enhance credibility among the community. Because these are local people, they are expected to carry out the local, traditional ceremonies. The philosophy of the program revolves around the belief that disease is a product of both biological and social factors. The illness is viewed as a lesson, not in the sense of a retribution but as a spiritual teaching. The program is based on mutual support and non-interference, wherein the thoughts, beliefs and decision-making abilities of individuals are honoured. The strategy for learning and understanding is modelling rather than coercion and persuasion, so the older and more experienced people are valued as they are called upon to discuss cultural issues or demonstrate desired behaviours. The most attractive aspect of the program is its basis in empowering the community to develop its potential; it is an example of a client-focused, culturally sensitive approach to health promotion.

Strengthening community action

Community action in many Aboriginal groups involves any activity designed to encourage self-empowerment. An empowered community has equitable resources, the capacity to identify and solve problems, participate in community activities, develop self-confidence and influence social change (Herbert 1996). The role of the health advocate involves enhancing the community's sense of self-empowerment by consulting with them on their need for housing, sanitation, jobs, education, transportation and health care. To perform this role adequately, it is important to become familiar with their problems and needs from an insider's perspective, rather than from the stereotypical assumptions of non-Aboriginal groups.

To understand Aboriginal culture with respect to health matters is to recognise that Aboriginal people often interpret health issues in terms of relationships between people rather than in terms of medical signs and symptoms (Bushy & van Holst Pellekan 1995; Eckermann & Dowd 1991). Health-related behaviour change is therefore embedded in the relationships among friends, family members and health care workers. The role of the health advocate is to enhance interaction between people. The objective of these interactions is the development of social integration—a sense of belonging and sharing, and mutual problem-solving (Eng, Salmon & Mullan 1992).

One misconception that persists among policy makers is that simply adding more resources will fix the problems that conspire to keep Aboriginal people in deprived economic and social conditions. Education is the key to strengthening community action, and indigenous people throughout the world are attempting to upgrade their education in a number of ways. The most visible of these is the education of young people to increase their employment opportunities. Other aspects of education that should be addressed relate to environmental issues. Environmental pollution is a major problem in many indigenous communities. Air pollution, land degradation and organochlorines in the food chain are becoming all too familiar to many Aboriginal people, who are dealing not only with the ensuing illnesses, but the cultural insult of pollution of sacred lands (Colomeda 1996). We have a responsibility to help heal these communities by blending information from current research with that of traditional wisdom to work toward a healthier environment for all cultures.

Developing personal skills

One of the greatest truths in public health is the link between educational attainment and health, for to be illiterate is to be powerless and unable to seek assistance in improving one's lot in life. In order to encourage self-determinism among Aboriginal people, they must be provided with culturally relevant, easily accessible training and development opportunities (Tsey 1997). However, ambiguities exist among Aboriginal and non-Aboriginal people concerning the extent to which education for the young must be wholly embedded in culture. Some believe non-Aboriginal education will destroy the culture; but unless young Aboriginal people become articulate and able to argue among professionals, bureaucrats and politicians at any level, they will not attain equitable social and health outcomes (Tsey 1997). This type of education can be supplanted with indigenous educational programs. Such an approach is currently gaining widespread acceptance throughout New Zealand, where primary school children now have access to immersion programs that teach the Maori culture and languages (ACAR 1994).

Indigenous people must be helped to deal with the past before any sense of the future can be anticipated. Many Aboriginal families harbour continuous loss and grief from episodes in their histories that have been part of the colonial processes of dispossession, institutionalisation and control. Their concept of health, particularly community health, must be framed within this context, and we must acknowledge their quest to restore harmony between body, land and spirit (Golds et al. 1997). As health professionals we have a responsibility to adopt a conciliatory approach to their needs by acknowledging the importance of family, community and spiritual resources to their health and wellbeing.

Reorienting health services

The most important consideration in attempting to reorient health services toward indigenous communities is to recognise the primacy of community participation (Golds et al. 1997). Self-care is central to community participation and occurs when people are empowered to choose their own combination of health treatments and services. These may be exclusively traditional healing practices, or a combination of cultural rituals, remedies and folk-medicine with more contemporary medical treatments (Borins 1995). When health professionals attempt to learn about traditional folk practices and their origins, there is a capacity for building trust within the community and this sends a clear message to the community that self-determinism is valued (Bushy 1992).

Accepting folk-ways and folk remedies for self-care also provides an opportunity to acknowledge the importance of social roles in the culture, particularly those that revolve around the member of the community who may have the responsibility for healing community members. Without knowledge of these practices, a complete assessment of health needs is impossible.

Similarly, encouraging people of other cultures to discuss their beliefs about spiritual elements of healing will help us learn more about the things that they believe will and will not work, and in some cases this becomes a self-fulfilling prophecy. If we are inattentive to their ideas, our health education information may be seen as incompatible with traditional beliefs and thus rejected (Bushy 1992; Brady 1995). By sharing information, a foundation of mutual respect is established and the health professional may then be able to exchange ideas for preventive actions or assist members of the culture to recognise the need for such things as health screening or immunisation. It is also important to understand how the medical knowledge systems of family, community and traditional healers intersect, particularly in the face of continuing developments in health care and medicine and evolving indigenous belief systems (Cavender 1991; Lane & Millar 1987).

Indigenous health workers in many countries of the world have played an instrumental role in extending modern health services to their local communities (Tsey 1996). These health workers are usually the most effective means of delivering information to families on child care, immunisation, elder care and a range of other issues. However, in some cases, the local community health workers hesitate to become involved with intimate 'women's business', such as pap smears. This is usually related to complex kinship networks and the need to separate 'women's business' from 'men's business'. Program planners must therefore consider the gendered context of all health programs and services, and this can only be done with the participation of community members who can act as guardians of cultural interests.

It is not enough to evaluate health and other social investments among Aboriginal people solely in terms of program reach and expected health outcomes (Tsey 1997). It is also important to examine the linkage effects of programs in terms of tangible benefits, such as employment, and intangible benefits, such as wellbeing and social opportunities. By making these outcomes visible, they may serve as incentives for young people to aspire to improving their educational status and thus being better prepared to ensure ongoing preservation of their culture.

THINKING CRITICALLY
Aboriginal health

▶ Identify five factors related to colonisation that predispose indigenous people to ill health.

▶ Describe three government actions designed to guarantee social justice for Aboriginal and non-Aboriginal people.

▶ Identify the four areas of greatest health risk to young Aboriginal people.

▶ For each of the above factors, devise a health promotion strategy that is culturally appropriate.

▶ Explain four cultural practices common to urban-dwelling Aboriginal people.

REFERENCES

Arriaga, R. 1994, 'Risk management: cross-cultural considerations', *Rehabilitation Management*, vol. 99, Aug.–Sep., p. 131.

Ashkam, J. 1996, 'Ageing in black and ethnic minorities: a challenge to service provision', *British Journal of Hospital Medicine*, vol. 56, no. 11, pp. 602–4.

Australian Council for Aboriginal Reconciliation 1994, *Walking Together: The First Steps*, Report of the Australian Council for Aboriginal Reconciliation, AGPS, Canberra.

Australian Institute of Health and Welfare 1996, *Australia's Health 1996*, AGPS, Canberra.

Borins, M. 1995, 'Native healing traditions must be protected and preserved for future generations', *Canadian Medical Association Journal*, vol. 153, no. 9, pp. 1356–7.

Brady, M. 1995, 'Culture in treatment, culture as treatment. A critical appraisal of developments in addictions programs for indigenous North Americans and Australians', *Social Science and Medicine*, vol. 41, no. 11, pp. 1487–98.

Brady, M. 1997, 'Aboriginal drug and alcohol use: recent developments and trends', *Australian and New Zealand Journal of Public Health*, vol. 21, no. 1, pp. 3–4.

Bushy, A. 1992, 'Cultural considerations for primary health care: where do self-care and folk medicine fit?', *Holistic Nursing Practice*, vol. 6, no. 3, pp. 10–18.

Bushy, A. & van Holst Pellekan, S. 1995, 'Footprints, a trail to survival', in *Issues in Australian Nursing 4*, eds G. Gray & R. Pratt, Churchill-Livingstone, Melbourne, pp. 219–33.

Cavender, A. 1991, 'Traditional medicine and an inclusive model of health-seeking behaviour in Zimbabwe', *Central African Journal of Medicine*, vol. 37, no. 11, pp. 362–9.

Colomeda, L. 1996, *Through the Northern Looking Glass*, National League for Nursing Press, New York.

Dowd, T. & Johnson, S. 1996, *Aboriginal Cultural Awareness Program*, Northern Territory Health Services and Institute for Aboriginal Development, Alice Springs, NT.

DuBois, M., Brassard, P., & Smeja, C. 1996, 'Survey of Montreal's Aboriginal population's knowledge, attitudes and behaviour regarding HIV/AIDS', *Canadian Journal of Public Health*, vol. 87, no. 1, pp. 37–9.

Eckermann, A. & Dowd, T. 1991, 'Strengthening the role of primary health care in health promotion by bridging cultures in Aboriginal health', *Australian Journal of Advanced Nursing*, vol. 9, no. 2, pp. 16–20.

Eckermann, A., Dowd, T., Martin, M., Nixon, L., Gray, R. et al. 1992, Binan Goonj: *Bridging Cultures in Aboriginal Health*, University of New England Press, Armidale, New South Wales.

Eng, E., Salmon, M. & Mullan, F. 1992, 'Community empowerment: the critical base for primary health care', *Family Community Health*, vol. 15, no. 1, pp. 1–12.

Golds, M, King, R., Mieklejohn, B., Campion, S. & Wise, M. 1997, 'Healthy Aboriginal communities', *Australian and New Zealand Journal of Public Health*, vol. 21, no. 4, pp. 386–90.

Gray, D., Morfitt, B., Ryan, K. & Williams, S. 1997, 'The use of tobacco, alcohol and other drugs by young Aboriginal people in Albany, Western Australia', *Australian and New Zealand Journal of Public Health*, vol. 21, no. 1, pp. 71–6.

Hanna, J., Gratten, M., Tiley, S., Brookes, D. & Bapty, G. 1997, 'Pneumococcal vaccination: an important strategy to prevent pneumonia in Aboriginal and Torres Strait Island adults', *Australian and New Zealand Journal of Public Health*, vol. 21, no. 3, pp. 281–92.

Herbert, C. 1996, 'Community-based research as a tool for empowerment: the Haida Gwaii diabetes project example', *Canadian Journal of Public Health*, vol. 87, no. 2, pp. 109–12.

Houston, S. 1993, opening address, Council of Remote Area Nurses of Australia National Conference, Broome, Western Australia.

Jan, S. & Wiseman, V. 1996, 'Equity in health care: some conceptual and practical issues', *Australian and New Zealand Journal of Public Health*, vol. 20, no. 1, pp. 9–11.

Johnston, E. 1991, *National Report, Royal Commission into Aboriginal Deaths in Custody*, AGPS, Canberra.

Johnson, S. 1997, 'Cultural safety: from risk to respect', unpublished paper, Australian Council of Remote Area Nurses of Australia, Alice Springs, NT.

Kaona, F., Siziya, S. & Mushanga, M. 1990, 'The problems of a social survey in epidemiology: an experience from a Zambian rural community', *African Journal of Medicine and Medical Science* vol. 19, pp. 219–24.

Kelso Townsend, J. & de Vries, N. 1995, 'Aboriginal mental health: a personal view', in *Issues in Australian Nursing 5*, eds G. Gray & R. Pratt, Churchill-Livingstone, Melbourne.

Lane, S. & Millar, M. 1987, 'The "hierarchy of resort" re-examined: status and class differentials as determinants of therapy for eye disease in the Egyptian Delta', *Urban Anthropology*, vol. 16, no. 2, pp. 151–82.

Lee, A. 1996, 'The transition of Australian Aboriginal diet and nutritional health', *World Review of Nutrition and Diet*, vol. 79, pp. 1–52.

MacMillan, H., MacMillan, A., Offord, D. & Dingle, J. 1996, 'Aboriginal health', *Canadian Medical Association Journal*, vol. 155, no. 11, pp. 1569–626.

Mak, D. & Straton, J. 1997, 'Effects and sustainability of a cervical screening program in remote Aboriginal Australia', *Australian and New Zealand Journal of Public Health*, vol. 21, no. 1, pp. 67–70.

Malchy, B., Enns, M., Young, T. & Cox, B. 1997, 'Suicide among Manitoba's Aboriginal people 1988 to 1994', *Canadian Medical Association Journal*, vol. 156, no. 8, pp. 1133–8.

Mill, J. & Desjardins, D. 1996, 'The feather of hope: Aboriginal AIDS prevention society: a community approach to HIV/AIDS prevention', *Canadian Journal of Public Health*, vol. 87, no. 4, pp. 268–71.

Mock, C., Grossman, D., Mulder, D., Stewart, C. & Koepsell, T. 1996, 'Health care utilization as a marker for suicidal behavior on an American Indian reservation', *Journal of General Internal Medicine*, vol. 11, pp. 519–24.

National Aboriginal Community Controlled Health Organisation 1993, *Manifesto on Aboriginal Well-Being*, NACCHO, Brisbane.

Newbold, K. 1997, 'Aboriginal physician use in Canada: location, orientation and identity', *Health Economics*, vol. 6, pp. 197–207.

Nursing Council of New Zealand 1992, *Standards for Registration of Comprehensive Nurses from Polytechnic Courses*, NCNZ, Wellington.

Nursing Council of New Zealand 1996, *Guidelines for Cultural Safety in Nursing and Midwifery Education*, NCNZ, Wellington.

Pool, I. 1991, *Te Iwi Maori, New Zealand Population, Past Present and Projected*, Auckland University Press, Auckland.

Reid, J. & Trompf, P. (eds) 1991, *The Health of Aboriginal Australia*, Harcourt Brace Jovanovich, Sydney.

Saggers, S. & Gray, D. 1991, *Aboriginal Health and Society*, Allen and Unwin, Sydney.

Saggers, S. & Gray, D. 1994, 'Aboriginal ill health: the harvest of injustice', in *Just Health. Inequality in Illness, Care and Prevention*, eds C. Waddell & A. Petersen, Churchill-Livingstone, Melbourne, pp. 119–33.

Shipley, J. 1996, *Policy Guidelines for Maori Health 1996–1997*, Ministry of Health, Wellington, New Zealand.

Spradley, B. & Allender, J. 1996, *Community Health Nursing: Concepts and Practice*, 4th edn, Lippincott, Philadelphia.

Tookenay, V. 1996, 'Improving the health status of aboriginal people in Canada: new directions, new responsibilities', *Canadian Medical Association Journal*, vol. 155, no. 11, pp. 1581–3.

Tsey, K. 1996, 'Aboriginal health workers: agents of change?', *Australian and New Zealand Journal of Public Health*, vol. 20, no. 3, pp. 227–8.

Tsey, K. 1997, 'Aboriginal self-determination, education and health: towards a radical change in attitudes to education', *Australian and New Zealand Journal of Public Health*, vol. 21, no. 1, pp. 77–83.

Healthy settings:

promoting health and wellness in context

Introduction

Part three of this book moves to a discussion of strategies for promoting health among the population groups described in part two. Its central thesis is that, to be effective, health promotion must be situated within the context of people's lives and appropriate to their preferences and goals for health and wellness. This approach reverses the traditional approach to health promotion, which was aimed at disseminating health messages to as many people as possible on the assumption that information was the key to changing people's health-related behaviours. Today there is widespread recognition that resources are more important than instruction in helping people achieve sustainable health. Another change from the past is the recognition that health promotion strategies must also take account of people's relationship with their environment. This includes the places where people work, play and engage in the activities of their daily lives. Thus the setting is fundamental to whether people will take notice of health education and whether this will provide the supportive mechanisms necessary for health.

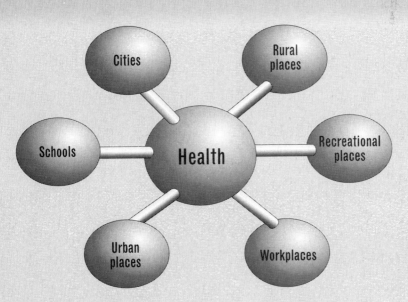

Chapter 12 extends the discussion of the foundations of health promotion introduced in part one of this book. This chapter provides an in-depth examination of the conceptual ideas that have guided the development of health education and health promotion. It addresses the ways in which our thinking about health promotion has been shaped by both public attitudes and prevailing approaches to health care.

Chapter 13 explains the integral relationship between people and the places important to their lives. The discussion revolves around the linkages between health and place, and therefore the appropriateness of situating health promotion activities in the places where people work, live and play. Dispossession of place, and the risks to health of both rural and urban living, are addressed. The chapter is designed to set the stage for the student to analyse the features of healthy cities, healthy schools, healthy workplaces and healthy recreational areas that make them particularly influential on people's choices for illness prevention and health promotion.

Chapters 14 and 15 provide examples of the two most important settings for health promotion: schools and workplaces. Chapter 14 discusses the capacity of schools to ensure health-enhancing attitudes and behaviours in young people. The links between health and education are discussed from the perspective of their mutual health-promoting functions. Components of comprehensive school health promotion programs are addressed, and an example is provided of a response to the need for school-based violence-prevention programs.

Chapter 15 describes the historical development of occupational health and safety services, culminating in the contemporary perspective of the need for comprehensive, integrated workplace health programs. The workplace is described as an ecosystem within the wider environment of the community. Work is discussed as integral to community development, and therefore to fulfilment of public health goals. Gaps in our research knowledge and the need for better dissemination of workplace-related information are identified. The chapter culminates in a discussion of the need for healthy workplaces and healthy policies that will sustain these.

Conceptual models for health education and promotion

12

A s mentioned in chapter 1, health promotion encompasses all activities that enable and facilitate health, including planned interventions aimed at the voluntary actions people can take to look after their health or the health of others. Health promotion programs may also encompass health education interventions and programs or actions taken to encourage early detection of illness or its precursors (Sindall 1992). This chapter takes a closer look at the factors that influence people in making decisions for health and wellness. Our discussion of health promotion will examine the ways in which the field of health promotion has evolved throughout the past century on the premise that previous experience with helping people develop healthy lifestyles can be used to inform strategies for the future.

Objectives

By the end of this chapter you will be able to:

- explain the genesis of contemporary health promotion approaches

- plan a health promotion intervention guided by a conceptual model

- explain the merit of a settings approach to health promotion

- analyse the differences between the Ottawa Charter for Health Promotion and the Jakarta Declaration on Health Promotion into the 21st Century

- develop a comprehensive strategy for promoting health in a defined population group.

Developments in the approach to health promotion

The way in which health promotion has been conceptualised by the health professions has changed dramatically over the years. The most significant change has been a shift in focus from teaching people how to manage their health (the 'top-down' model) to a more socially embedded approach that capitalises on the inherent capacity of community members to establish their own goals, strategies and priorities for health (the 'bottom-up' model). As mentioned in part one, this is a socioecological, community development approach to community health. It is based on the premise that if community members are provided with structural resources and information appropriate to their cultural, social and physical needs, they will make informed choices to improve their health and the health of their environment. A healthy environment, in turn, provides the situation within which health can be sustained. Sustainable community health is therefore a product of all the factors that promote healthy interactions between people and their environment. The role of the health professional in this model of health promotion is not to persuade people to undertake certain behaviours because it will be 'good for them', but to help people recognise the personal, social and structural influences and elements of their lives and their environment that have a health-enhancing potential (Mitchell & Wright 1992). Recognition of these factors is the first step toward community development.

The most important aim of community development is community self-reliance. This does not imply that the community is *self-contained*. Instead, it suggests a community in which people are able to capitalise on the resources within their own environment that can be used to improve health and reduce the risk of illness. A self-reliant community is also able to identify community needs, establish local goals and objectives for health, and identify what additional resources will be necessary to meet those goals. Encouraging self-reliance among community members is fundamental to the principles of primary health care and social justice. However, communities must also have access to epidemiological information as a basis for illness prevention and treatment.

Epidemiological knowledge has developed only during the past one hundred years. At the turn of the past century, health was promoted on the basis of current medical knowledge, and the opinions of medical experts were accepted without question. This created enormous pressure on scientists to advance the field of biomedical investigation and, to a large extent, this was undertaken in medical laboratories. But laboratory medicine was only partially able to explain why some people became ill with the prevalent conditions of the time, while others thrived. Obviously, factors outside the biological sphere, and in the context of people's lives, exerted some effect on health outcomes. One of the first medical experts to pursue this thesis was John Snow, a physician in London. His research into the causes of cholera in the residents of London was a signal event, in that it led to an important, if somewhat primitive, understanding of the links between people and their environment.

▶ CASE STUDY

Epidemiology as a basis for health promotion

For many years scientists have attempted to find plausible explanations for the causes of disease. Some explanations have emerged through Biblical myths and folklore, while others have been the product of careful observation and investigation. In the 1850s, John Snow, a London physician began piecing together the likely reasons for a cluster of cholera cases. For months he treated numerous people for the dreaded disease, systematically recording aspects of his patients' lives that might indicate a common cause. He was aided by the advent of quantitative measures of recording disease frequency, called rates (Valanis 1986). Snow carefully compiled rates of infection among his patients, relating these to a wide variety of factors. Because those with the illness were of all ages and of widely varying general health status, he began to look beyond characteristics of the individual to those in the physical environment. As it turned out, the common thread in this cluster of cases was a water pump in the centre of town shared by all those who became ill.

Once his documentation indicated a strong enough link between the pattern of using town water from the pump and development of the disease, Snow removed the pump handle to prevent further usage. He continued to record what would later be described as incidence and prevalence data related to the cholera cases. From his careful documentation, he was able to build an explanatory framework to be used for educating the local residents on preventive measures they should take to avoid contracting the infection. He recruited the local community leaders from the church and schools to help explain to their families, neighbours and friends how the disease could be contracted from the water pump, and how to dispose of contaminated waste from those already infected. Although it was later found to be the cholera vibrio rather than the water itself that caused the disease, his work was a landmark in furthering our knowledge of health and disease (Valanis 1986).

Snow's epidemiological research heralded the beginning of a movement to provide a rational basis for health promotion. However, the intention of teaching people the causes of disease was to justify their compliance with expert advice. For many years this was the basis of health promotion. The health educator, usually the medical doctor, was expected to provide instruction to the public on what they should and should not do. In most cases, the scientific principles informing this expert opinion were considered beyond the comprehension of the public and thus not shared with them. This created a sense of medical mystique, which heightened with the rapid expansion of medical and epidemiological knowledge resulting from developments in biomedical and communications technology.

By the 1920s the so-called 'golden age of medicine' was born, where medical doctors were considered privy to fascinating information inaccessible to the general public (Emanuel & Emanuel 1996). In this era, health promotion was health instruction, dominated by the medical profession, usually without public scrutiny. With the onset of the information age in the 1960s, medical and health information became readily available to all, and the public began to demand greater responsiveness from medical science. The information age ushered in an age of consumerism, which advanced the cause of community involvement and thus community development.

Consumerism: health as a marketable commodity

The information revolution of the 1960s and 1970s transformed the world into a global village, where communities began to share ideas and to have a greater say over the conditions that affected their lives. Greater access to information led to greater critical awareness in many realms, including health, the environment and the politics of health care. The consumer movement was a product of this explosion of information. As active consumers (rather than passive recipients) of government policies and strategies, people began to exert their right to greater participation in matters concerning their health and the conditions of their lives.

Concomitant with the consumer movement was the growth of public advertising in the 1960s, reflecting in part most people's access to television. The field of marketing experienced unprecedented growth. By the 1970s, health began to be seen as a product, and health educators borrowed strategies from the marketing specialists, subsequently engaging in what was called *social marketing*. Social marketing uses the system of developing the right *product*, backed by the right *promotion*, put in the right *place* at the right *price* (Kotler 1975). The formula conceptualises health education messages as an almost tangible product that has some cost benefit to the consumer. Proponents of this approach were attracted to the idea of promoting health using public media campaigns, primarily because it allowed access to large numbers of the population, an outcome that is today called 'product reach'.

The major goal of the public health promotion era of the 1970s was to prevent people from adopting high-risk lifestyles (Kickbusch, cited in Chu 1994). The underlying assumption informed by the advertising specialists was that if people heard a message often enough, behaviour change would follow. The scientific and professional basis for health promotion campaigns was a combination of behavioural epidemiology, preventive medicine and health education. In contrast to the medicalised 'old public health' (top-down) approach, it focused on 'individualised cultural patterns by concentrating on disease categories and risk factor causation principles (heart disease/high blood pressure/health behaviour change)' (Kickbusch, cited in Chu 1994, p. 3).

The field of health promotion burgeoned from the mid 1970s to the 1980s. Health educators used information from psychology and marketing to systematise the process of social marketing. They developed persuasive techniques for behaviour change, targeted to specific goals such as smoking cessation, reducing fat intake and increasing exercise. Although some health promotion programs were carefully conceived and researched, many were poorly evaluated, making it difficult to compare what was working with what was not. In addition, they were usually costly and, as government-funded programs, carried the additional challenge of having to demonstrate visible results within the time frame of a particular term in office.

The most effective health promotion campaigns used a community organisation approach, where the community was targeted in campaigns to heighten awareness and encourage behavioural change. Included were several large-scale, longitudinal studies of health-related behaviour change in the US (Maccoby & Solomon 1981; Lassater, Carleton & LeFebre 1988), Finland (McAlister et al. 1981), Wales (Nutbeam & Catford 1987) and the North Coast of NSW, Australia (Egger et al. 1990). Each of these studies reported substantial improvements in a range of lifestyle factors, with the largest gains evident in the extent to which community attitudes became more attuned to health issues. As community-wide programs, each was impressive from the perspective of general population awareness. Many health professionals (including this author) were attracted to the idea of widespread preventive programs, and we witnessed first-hand the way in which community members accepted the 'healthy lifestyle' messages with almost evangelical zeal (Esler-McMurray 1980). However, by the 1990s, the mass media campaign approach to health promotion had drawn considerable criticism.

Some criticised the mass health promotion approach on the basis that it was directed at the average, or 'typical' person. The problem with this was that few campaigns were directed toward encouraging healthy lifestyles among the various sub-populations, segmented by different ages and cultural backgrounds (Young et al. 1996). Another criticism was that mass health promotion campaigns did not incorporate a view of health issues in terms of social relations and their interdependence with the environment (Kickbusch, in Chu 1994). Trying to reach large numbers of people using the media was seen to represent an attempt at cost-containment by health administrators seeking cheaper ways to provide health services (Grace 1991). Even today, health promotion policies are criticised on the basis that they resonate with the cost-constrained nature of health care delivery (Iannantuono & Eyles 1997).

In the area of environmental issues, mass media coverage, primarily via television, has generally focused on dramatic visual opportunities, controversial health risk information, blaming someone (or some group) for the situation, and political conflict (Greenberg & Wartenberg, in Labonte 1994). As a result, many people tend to accept as truth, information that is biased and seemingly 'scientific'. The single-issue focus that is portrayed in many of these television messages leads many to conclude that solutions are beyond their control, and that in time, the scientists will solve the problems. As a result, many are discouraged from seeking community solutions or engaging in local participatory networks (Labonte 1994).

Despite these problems, the mass media have been useful in contributing to positive health education outcomes. An analysis of the research examining the influence of the mass media reveals the following (from Labonte 1994):

- Campaigns combining media messages and securing 'commitment' such as pledges obtained in a door-to-door survey have produced significant behaviour changes.
- Mass media campaigns without community participatory or 'pledging' functions have produced poor and cost-ineffective changes.
- Media appeals that were personalised and which modelled specific behaviour changes were more effective than general, non-role-modelling approaches.
- Feedback has been shown to be essential in reinforcing and improving behaviour change.
- Specific, often financial, rewards or penalty-avoidance were associated with behaviour change that was maintained over time.

The health promotion rhetoric of the 1970s and 1980s has also been the subject of criticism by those advocating for the poor and other marginal groups. For those with few resources, the lifestyle approach wherein all people were urged to take up jogging, eat more vegetables and ensure more leisure time, may have also exacerbated inequalities in health (Chu 1994). Members of various consumer movements, such as the women's health movement, challenged the genuineness of health promotion campaigns. Women especially were attempting to articulate new forms of social and political relations with respect to health and healing. This meant regaining control over their bodies, their children's health and birthing practices. On the one hand they were hearing the rhetoric of empowerment, and on the other were being urged to change their behaviour (Grace 1991).

The dichotomy between individual and social responsibility for health was also debated in the health promotion literature of the time. The debate argued for a social model of health that would relieve the individual of exclusive responsibility for outcomes (Labonte 1986). For example, when a problem such as driving under the influence of alcohol is viewed from an individual perspective, the victim is blamed. Strategies to address the problem involve changing personal attitudes and what is presumed to be irresponsible behaviour. A social model of health includes a broader rearrangement of the environment within which the high-risk behaviour occurs, including alcohol advertising, liquor licensing laws, road conditions, public transport, hours of work and automobile design (Sindall 1992). This places the onus for health as much on structural conditions in the environment as on individual choices. Grace (1991) suggests that little changed from the 1980s to the 1990s. In her view, health promotion initiatives continue to be infiltrated by a contradictory logic wherein there is a promise of creating conditions for empowerment, yet health professionals continue to preach and control, simply in more subtle ways than previously.

Health for all

As early as 1974, Canada's Lalonde Report reflected a growing awareness among politicians and health planners as well as the general community that many health promotion campaigns were too narrowly defined and had only limited effectiveness. The central tenet of the report was that, to be effective, health promotion must change from a focus on using educational strategies to promote individual changes, to creating favourable environments within which health could be created (Hancock 1992). The rhetoric of the Lalonde Report met with general approval from health promotion specialists, especially for its emphasis on the *creation* of health, and the importance of the *environment* in allowing health to be created.

The WHO saw this new approach as the key to tackling the problems of the twenty-first century, and in the 'Global Strategy of Health for All by Year 2000' document, health promotion was viewed as a process of enabling people to increase control over, and improve, their health. Health was no longer seen as a goal; instead, it was a resource for living, and potentially available to all (Ashton & Seymour, cited in Iannantuono & Eyles 1997). This changed the emphasis from the provision of and access to health services, to a focus on accessing *health*, effectively shifting from service *input* to *output*. Being healthy therefore was seen to have less to do with the actual consumption of services than with the choices made to lead healthy lives.

The shift to a more global, outcome-focused construct of how health is created gradually gained wide acceptance among the health promotion community. Health researchers began to adjust their models of documenting and measuring the achievement of specific health goals, to incorporate a wider range of factors influencing health, including the environment and other situational factors. The ultimate aim of health was seen not as increasing longevity, but as enhancing quality of life. Evans & Stoddart (1990) described the key elements in quality of life outcomes within a framework that included culture, healthy public policies and economic activities that would shape people's social and physical environments. Individual responses were seen as a product of those social and physical environments which, in conjunction with appropriate health care services, could be expected to improve health status (Evans & Stoddart 1990). Promoting health within this framework includes different combinations of strategies that could include any or all of the following (from Sindall 1992):

- legislative change (compulsory wearing of seat-belts)
- organisational change (parental leave for early child care)
- sociocultural change (restricting smoking in public places)
- environmental change (reducing automobile emissions or pesticide use in food)
- behavioural change (safe sexual practices)
- technological change (introduction of lead-free petrol)
- economic change (removing subsidies for tobacco producers).

Another product of this health promotion era was the PRECEDE-PROCEED model (Green & Kreuter 1991). Like the approach of Evans and Stoddart, Green and Kreuter's model integrated individual and environmental elements into a set of specific factors.

The PRECEDE-PROCEED model

Green and Kreuter's model was based on the premise that health promotion must adopt a systematic approach and be based on epidemiological evidence and local needs assessment. The model revolves around establishing goals for improving the health of community members. Before the goals can be defined or achieved, a rigorous assessment of existing influences on health must be conducted so that a program of intervention can be adapted accordingly. The assessment begins with a diagnosis of the community's educational needs.

The first stage of needs assessment is called the *social* diagnosis. Assessment at this stage includes such social variables as level of educational attainment, crime, population density and unemployment. This is followed by an *epidemiological* diagnosis, which is intended to reveal rates of morbidity, mortality, disability and fertility, complete with dimensions of each, such as incidence and prevalence. Next, a *behavioural* and *environmental* diagnosis is undertaken. Behavioural indicators include such elements as consumption patterns (healthy diet), preventive actions (safe sexual practices), self-care indicators and coping skills (stress management practices).

Green and Kreuter's model was the first to include environmental factors as equally important influences on health. Environmental aspects were explained in the model as economic indicators (a community's productivity), geographic features (potable water, sewage) and services (health care and preventive services). Analysis of these factors is complemented by analysing those elements in the social environment that would be predictive of a community's inclination to change. This phase of the model includes an *educational* and *organisational* diagnosis, which is aimed at identifying predisposing, reinforcing and enabling factors that could lead to behavioural and environmental change. Predisposing factors include individual knowledge, attitudes, values and perceptions that may hinder or facilitate motivation for change. Reinforcing factors include the attitudes and behaviours of others. Enabling factors are those skills, resources or barriers that could help or hinder the desired changes, including environmental factors. Following this phase, an *administrative* and *policy* diagnosis is conducted to examine organisational and administrative capabilities and resources available to respond to identified needs. These elements include such things as current government policies and organisational or workplace trends.

Once these diagnostic phases have been completed, implementation can begin. The implementation program and its constituent strategies are developed to correspond to all issues identified in the diagnostic phases. Once the strategies have been implemented, each aspect is evaluated to compare the extent to which the program's objectives were met (Green & Kreuter 1991). Figure 12.1 is a representation of the PRECEDE-PROCEED model.

PRECEDE

PHASE 5	PHASE 4	PHASE 3	PHASE 2	PHASE 1
Administrative and policy diagnosis	Educational and organisational development	Behavioural and environmental diagnosis	Epidemiological diagnosis	Social diagnosis

Health promotion

Health education

Policy regulation organisation

Predisposing factors

Reinforcing factors

Enabling factors

Behaviour and lifestyle

Environment

Health

Quality of life

PHASE 6	PHASE 7	PHASE 8	PHASE 9
Implementation	Process evaluation	Impact evaluation	Outcome evaluation

PROCEED

Figure 12.1 The PRECEDE-PROCEED model for health promotion planning and evaluation (From Health Promotion Planning: An Educational and Environmental Approach, 2nd edn, by L. W. Green & M. W. Kreuter. Copyright © Mayfield Publishing Company. Reprinted by permission of the publisher.)

The PRECEDE-PROCEED model has gained wide acceptance, as it guides careful evaluation of activities taken to promote health. Since its inception there have been more than 300 public applications of the model (Green et al. 1994). But it has also come under criticism for its academic orientation, primarily in its use of behavioural and social science jargon (Grace 1991; Green et al. 1994). One of its co-authors has subsequently developed a slightly more user-friendly model to illustrate the application of the theories and procedures underlying the PRECEDE-PROCEED model. The new model is called PATCH (Kreuter 1992).

The PATCH model

PATCH refers to the Planned Approach to Community Health. It is based on the assumption that a competent community is fundamental to community development. When a community is competent to manage and sustain its own structures and processes for sustaining health and a quality life for its residents, it is considered competent. However, again this does not imply self-containment. Instead, the competent community relies on horizontal and vertical coalitions (Green et al. 1994; Kreuter 1992). A horizontal coalition could be such a group-to-group link as a men's or women's health group linking up with other similar groups for the purpose of sharing ideas, strategies or resources. At the government level, horizontal linkages could involve several departments of a state government collaborating to improve a community service. Transportation may join with education, health and recreational services, for example, to improve facilities for underprivileged youth. Vertical coalitions involve linkages between various levels of government (local, state and federal) or various levels of health services.

The primary goal of PATCH is to create a practical mechanism for effective community health education to respond to local level health priorities. In this respect, the model is sensitive to the importance of the context in which health decisions are made. A second goal of the program is to offer a practical, skills-based approach of technical assistance to local people to develop health education programs. Like its predecessor, (PRECEDE-PROCEED) the model emphasises community participation and rigorous evaluation of information. Its basic concept is that of local ownership and this is based on the premise that decisions for social change affecting lifestyle issues can best be made 'collectively, as close as possible to the homes and workplaces of those affected' (Kreuter 1992, p. 136).

PATCH and, to a slightly lesser extent, the PRECEDE-PROCEED model have both been influenced by the community development approach in that they are designed to empower local residents to make health-enhancing choices. Both models acknowledge the importance of the environment or context, within which community choices and community development occur. PATCH also signals the importance of the setting in community health and development, foreshadowing the current model proposed by the WHO.

Health promotion as an investment: the settings approach

From the 1990s, the WHO has adopted an approach to health promotion that places the emphasis on health-promoting environments. It is based on the assumption that health is an indication of the extent to which people are able on the one hand to develop aspirations and satisfy needs, and on the other hand to change or cope with the environment (Kickbusch 1997). It is built on three premises. The first is the fundamental question of Antonovsky (cited in Kickbusch 1997): *what creates health*? Good health is a product of coherent interactions between people and their environments in the course of everyday life. Within this model, the most important strategies for health promotion are those that strengthen people's sense of coherence, and this can be achieved by supporting their environments: their schools, hospitals and workplaces (Kickbusch 1997).

The second element of this model is the public health premise: *which investment creates the largest health gain*? From a public health perspective, health is seen as an investment. Practically, it is achieved through community development, participation and partnership. The key resource questions revolve around the relationship between health investments and outcomes. Health policies address the ways in which resources can be deployed to lead to optimal health outcomes for the population. Health is seen to be created from a pattern of factors related to living and working, social support, genetic makeup and individual behaviour. Community health gains are made possible from public investments in areas other than health, such as cities, islands, villages, market places, workplaces and school. This is currently referred to as the *settings* approach to health promotion (Kickbusch 1997).

The practical premise is the third aspect of the health-promoting environments approach, and this involves *community development and organisational development*. Developing community potential can be fostered through a series of community-defined strategies to be implemented across a range of settings (Kickbusch 1997). The settings approach to health promotion broadens the aim of establishing goals for health promotion from the population level, to the level of organisations and systems (Harris & Wills 1997). Healthy organisations are assumed to be integral to community health, and are also predictive of a community's capacity for sustainability. Such organisations are able to accommodate change by responding to health needs at the environmental or service level (Kickbusch 1997). For example, where there is a constant influx of new populations into the community, a healthy system of assisting the newcomers with the myriad of transitions would include providing assistance with language, education and workplace services, and culturally appropriate health care in the settings of their daily lives.

The settings of people's lives are considered ideal for promoting health as they are organised for more deeply binding reasons than health. Neighbourhoods, schools, workplaces and health care sites are characterised by frequent and sustained patterns of communication and interaction and therefore have the capacity to facilitate healthful choices (Mullen et al. 1995). Partnerships between community residents and health professionals, and between community groups, are more readily established and maintained in the ordinary settings of people's lives. Particular settings often reach populations differentiated by age, stage, socioeconomic status and other circumstances, and this makes it easier to deploy resources and evaluate outcomes appropriately as well as encourage community participation.

The advantages of settings as the site of health promotion are summarised in the table below (from Mullen et al. 1995).

Advantages of healthy settings

They provide channels for delivering health promotion.

They represent units of identity, such as school or work.

Diffusion of ideas occurs in and is facilitated by settings.

They provide access to gatekeepers.

Policies can be readily implemented in a particular structure.

They provide access to specific populations.

Funding categories for health promotion usually specify settings.

They contain unique practice and/or training traditions.

Professional identities are linked to settings.

The settings approach is exemplified within the Jakarta Declaration on Health Promotion Into the 21st Century (WHO 1997). As mentioned in chapter 2, Jakarta, Indonesia was the site of the 4th International Conference on Health Promotion, the first to be held in a developing country. The Declaration extends a decade of work in refining health promotion strategies and illustrates the shift in emphasis toward the social, economic and environmental conditions that determine health. The strategies of the

Ottawa Charter for Health Promotion are acknowledged in the Jakarta Declaration in that there is encouragement for an approach that would integrate all five strategies of the Ottawa Charter in all settings where health is to be promoted. Community education and participation are seen as the core elements in achieving community health, and these rely on partnerships between governments, non-government organisations and all public and private sectors of society (WHO 1997). The Jakarta Declaration is reproduced below.

Jakarta Declaration on Health Promotion Into the 21st Century

1 Promote social responsibility for health

Decision makers must be firmly committed to social responsibility. Both the public and private sectors should promote health by pursuing policies and practices that:
- avoid harming the health of other individuals
- protect the environment and ensure sustainable use of resources
- restrict production and trade in inherently harmful goods and substances such as tobacco and armaments, as well as unhealthy marketing practices
- safeguard both the citizen in the marketplace and the individual in the workplace
- include equity-focused health impact assessments as an integral part of policy development.

2 Increase investments for health development

In many countries, current investment in health is inadequate and often ineffective. Increasing investment for health development requires a truly multi-sectoral approach, including additional resources to education, housing as well as the health sector. Greater investment for health, and reorientation of existing investments—both within and between countries—has the potential to significantly advance human development, health and quality of life. Investments in health should reflect the needs of certain groups such as women, children, older people, indigenous, poor and marginalised populations.

3 Consolidate and expand partnerships for health

Health promotion requires partnerships for health and social development between the different sectors at all levels of governance and society. Existing partnerships need to be strengthened and the potential for new partnerships must be explored. Partnerships offer mutual benefit for health through the sharing of expertise, skills and resources. Each partnership must be transparent and accountable and be based on agreed ethical principles, mutual understanding and respect. WHO guidelines should be adhered to.

4 Increase community capacity and empower the individual

Health promotion is carried out by and *with* people, not on or to people. It improves the ability of individuals to take action, and the capacity of groups, organisations or communities to influence the determinants of health. Improving the capacity of communities for health promotion requires practical education, leadership training, and access to resources. Empowering individuals demands more consistent, reliable access to the decision-making process and the skills and knowledge essential to effect change. Both traditional communication and the new information media support this process. Social, cultural and spiritual resources need to be harnessed in innovative ways.

5 Secure an infrastructure for health promotion

To secure an infrastructure for health promotion, new mechanisms of funding it locally, nationally and globally must be found. Incentives should be developed to influence the actions of governments, non-governmental organisations, educational institutions and the private sector to make sure that resource mobilisation for health promotion is maximised.

'Settings for health' represent the organisational base of the infrastructure required for health promotion. New health challenges mean that new and diverse networks need to be created to achieve intersectoral collaboration. Such networks should provide mutual assistance within and between countries and facilitate exchange of information on which strategies are effective in which settings.

Training and practice of local leadership skills should be encouraged to support health promotion activities. Documentation of experiences in health promotion through research and project reporting should be enhanced to improve planning, implementation and evaluation.

All countries should develop the appropriate political, legal, educational, social and economic environments required to support health promotion.

Community health education

The Jakarta Declaration represents the vanguard of health promotion into the next millenium. The statement is firmly grounded in the principles of primary health care and social justice, with a clear focus on community empowerment and self-determinism. It is the culmination of a century of thinking about health promotion and includes a synthesis of conceptual approaches that revolve around integrating the principles of the Ottawa Charter and ensuring that appropriate environmental resources are available and mobilised for promoting community health. Although the statement has a strong emphasis on maintaining the infrastructure and conditions within which people can make healthful choices, there remains a need to develop the skills to make these choices.

Principles of health education

The health promotion approaches that preceded the Jakarta Declaration produced a body of knowledge that today can be used to empower individuals with the skills and knowledge essential to effect change. Community health education involves planned, consistent, integrated learning opportunities aimed at providing this type of support (Green & Ottoson 1994). The process is guided by the following principles (from Green & Ottoson 1994):

1 *Principle of cumulative learning*

Because behaviour is the sum of a lifetime of personal and cultural experience, social, economic and environmental circumstances and genetic inheritance, behaviour change requires a planned sequence of experiences and activities over time, tailored to individual needs and prior experiences to the extent allowed by available resources.

2 *Principle of multiple targets*

To achieve population-level objectives a health education program must consider both the characteristics of the population, and the social systems within the setting that enable the behaviour.

3 *Principle of aggregating educational targets*

A community health education program must be flexible and broad enough to accommodate varied personal histories and circumstances.

4 *Principle of participation*

The early involvement of the community provides greater opportunities to establish and meet relevant and realistic goals, using acceptable methods.

5 *Principle of situational specificity*

The selection of health education methods should be tailored to the needs of the population and the circumstances.

6 *Principle of intermediate targets*

Health education may be directed at a range of intermediate goals. It may be aimed at changes in knowledge, attitudes, beliefs, values and perceptions. It may reinforce behaviour by strengthening social support. It can enable or facilitate behaviour through changes in community resources, skill development and referrals.

7 Principle of multiple methods

No single educational input can be expected to have significant, lasting impact on health behaviour unless it is supported by other educational input. Strategies should be cumulative and mutually supportive of all factors conducive to health.

8 Principle of diversity

Educational methods within programs should vary according to the audience's characteristics and circumstances.

9 Principle of health promotion

Health education cannot be expected to accomplish more than voluntary behaviour change. The success of health education may be impaired by organisational, legal or economic factors that must be addressed within the larger health promotion strategy.

10 Principle of administration

The educational component should have the following:
- the education plan incorporated into a broader health program plan
- a clear designation of the individual responsible for co-ordination
- specific people designated to each educational intervention
- a budget for personnel, materials and other costs.

As health educators and health advocates we know that, despite national goals and targets for healthy lifestyles, and widespread public information on high risk behaviours, people continue to smoke, eat too much dietary fat and undertake too little exercise. In Australia, for example, tobacco consumption has halved since 1960 (Chapman 1997). Yet, for those who continue to smoke, the severity of outcome may be greater in the 1990s when the risk of smoking is combined with air pollution and other environmental co-factors for respiratory disease. Smoking cessation therefore remains a major challenge.

Research into what works in health education reveals that continual bombardment by the media urging people to quit smoking has minimal impact on many smokers. They know smoking is unhealthy for them and their children yet it may be their only source of stress relief (Beeber 1996).

The key to helping them to quit or remove their children from the smoke environment lies in understanding the principles of specificity, the value of multiple methods, and the diverse nature of personal motivation.

It is also helpful to understand the need to set intermediate goals. Fewer than 20% of people with a less-than-ideal behaviour pattern are prepared to change at any one time (Wechsler et al. 1996). Even when they are prepared to do so, only one in five who try to change their health-related behaviour succeed the first time. Smokers take an average of three to four attempts before they successfully quit, with weight loss being the hardest change of all. For those with chronic diseases like diabetes, making lifestyle changes while trying to live a normal and fulfilling life is a constant balancing act (Susman & Helseth 1997). As advocates for change we need to guide people away from unrealistic goals and help them understand the merits of a phased-in approach to change.

The principle of participation directs us toward incorporating cultural views in our health education strategies. When people are encouraged to help plan programs that will ultimately provide them with the skills for change, there is greater opportunity to achieve cultural appropriateness. Encouraging participation also helps counter incongruities between the expectations of health professionals and those receiving the messages. Research over the past decade is unequivocal in directing us toward recognising differences in conceptions and understandings of health, health needs and expected outcomes (Cegala, Socha McGee & McNeilis 1996; Folden 1993; Hall, Roter & Katz 1988; Strickland & Strickland 1996).

Tailoring the language of health education to the needs of particular groups or aggregates is also important. As health educators, we often assume our written messages are understood, but this has not always been found to be the case (Hobbie 1995). We must also recognise that a health education message falls within a sequence of accumulated experience. Adopting new ideas or a change is seldom an impulse decision, but part of a process that culminates in healthier living (Lewis 1996). Messages must be tailored to individual needs to ensure both knowledge transfer and prolonged retention (Lewis 1996).

Educating children requires additional knowledge and skills. Likewise, adolescents require particular attentiveness to their social stage of development. To encourage change among this group, the principles of health education direct us to listen carefully to the ways they choose to participate in the change process. It is also important to be attuned to their emotional state and level of motivation. The social environment within which change will occur is extremely important for this group. Multiple approaches will also ensure that individual needs are met and varying levels of participation are valued. By using the principles as a guideline, adolescents can be encouraged to develop critical thinking skills for decision-making and problem-solving (Elias & Kress 1994). These are the most essential tools for lifelong health and wellness.

THINKING CRITICALLY
Health promotion

▶ Identify four developmental phases that signalled a change in the way health promotion has been conceptualised.

▶ Using Green and Kreuter's health promotion model, devise a planned strategy for increasing physical activity among the ageing population.

▶ Identify four important features of the health settings approach.

▶ Compare and contrast the Ottawa Charter and the Jakarta Declaration, identifying three distinct elements of difference.

▶ Construct a health promotion plan for enhancing the health of migrant women in an urban environment.

REFERENCES

Beeber, S. 1996, 'Parental smoking and childhood asthma', *Journal of Pediatric Health Care*, vol. 10, no. 2, pp. 58–62.

Cegala, D., Socha McGee, D. & McNeilis, K. 1996, 'A study of doctors and patients' perceptions of communication competence during a primary care medical interview', *Health Communication*, vol. 8, pp. 1–26.

Chapman, S. 1997, 'Simon Chapman honoured by WHO for tobacco control', *In Touch*, vol. 14, no. 8, pp. 1.

Chu, C. 1994, 'Integrating health and environment: the key to an ecological public debate', in *Ecological Public Health: From Vision to Practice*, eds C. Chu & R. Simpson, Institute of Applied Environmental Research, Brisbane, pp. 1–10.

Egger, G., Fitzgerald, W., Frape, G., Monaem, A., Rubinstein, P., et al. 1983, 'Results of a large scale media anti-smoking campaign in Australia: the North Coast Healthy Lifestyle Program', *British Medical Journal*, vol. 287, pp. 1125–87.

Elias, M. & Kress, J. 1994, 'Social decision-making and life skills development: a critical thinking approach to health promotion in the middle school', *Journal of School Health*, vol. 64, no. 2, pp. 62–6.

Emanuel, E. & Emanuel, O. 1996, 'What is accountability in health care?', *Annals of Internal Medicine*, vol. 124, pp. 129–39.

Esler-McMurray, A. 1980, 'The body shop: marketing a healthy lifestyle', *The Canadian Nurse*, vol. 76, no. 4, pp. 46–8.

Evans, R. & Stoddart, G. 1990, 'Producing health, consuming health care', *Social Science and Medicine*, vol. 31, no. 12, pp. 1347–63.

Folden, S. 1993, 'Definitions of health and health goals of participants in a community-based pulmonary rehabilitation program', *Public Health Nursing*, vol. 10, no. 1, pp. 313–35.

Grace, V. 1991, 'The marketing of empowerment and the construction of the health consumer: a critique of health promotion', *International Journal of Health Services*, vol. 21, no. 2, pp. 329–43.

Green, L. & Kreuter, M. 1991, *Health Promotion Planning: An Educational and Environmental Approach*, Mayfield Publishing Co. Mountain View, CA.

Green, L. & Ottoson, J. 1994, *Community Health*, 7th edn, Mosby, St Louis.

Green, L., Glanz, K., Hochbaum, G., Kok, G., Kreuter, M. et al. 1994, 'Can we build on, or must we replace, the theories and models in health education?' *Health Education Research*, vol. 9, no. 3, pp. 397–404.

Hall, J., Roter, D. & Katz, N. 1988, 'Meta-analysis of correlates of provider behavior in medical encounters', *Medical Care*, vol. 26, pp. 657–72.

Hancock, T. 1992, 'The Healthy City: Utopias and realities', in *Healthy Cities*, ed. J. Ashton, Milton Keynes, Philadelphia, pp. 22–9.

Harris, E. & Wills, J. 1997, 'Developing healthy local communities at local government level: lessons from the past decade', *Australian and New Zealand Journal of Public Health*, vol. 21, no. 4, pp. 403–12.

Hobbie, C. 1995, 'Maximizing healthy communication: readability of parent educational materials', *Journal of Pediatric Health Care*, vol. 9, pp. 92–3.

Iannantuono, A. & Eyles, J. 1997, 'Meanings in policy: a textual analysis of Canada's "Achieving Health for All" document', *Social Science and Medicine*, vol. 44, no. 11, pp. 1611–21.

Kickbush, I. 1997, 'Health promoting environments: the next step', *Australian and New Zealand Journal of Public Health*, vol. 21, no. 4, pp. 431–4.

Kotler, P. 1975, *Marketing for Non-profit Organisations*, Prentice-Hall, Englewood Cliffs, NJ.

Kreuter, M. 1992, 'PATCH: its origin, basic concepts, and links to contemporary public health policy', *Journal of Health Education*, vol. 23, no. 3, pp. 135–9.

Labonte, R. 1986, 'Social inequality and healthy public policy', *Health Promotion*, vol. 1, no. 3, pp. 341–51.

Labonte, R. 1994, '"See me, hear me, touch me, feel me." Lessons on environmental health information for bureaucratic activists', in *Ecological Public Health: From Vision to Practice*, eds C. Chu & R. Simpson, Institute of Applied Environmental Research, Brisbane, pp. 269–76.

Lasater, T., Carleton, R. & LeFebre, R. 1988, 'The Pawtucket heart health program: utilizing community resources for primary prevention', *Rhode Island Medical Journal*, vol. 71, pp. 63–7.

Lewis, D. 1996, 'Computer-based patient education: use by diabetes educators', *The Diabetes Educator*, vol. 22, no. 2, pp. 140–5.

Maccoby, N. & Solomon, D. 1981, 'The Stanford community studies in heart disease prevention', in *Public Communication Campaigns*, eds R. Rice & W. Paisley, Sage, Beverley Hills.

McAlister, A. 1981, 'Anti-smoking campaigns: progress in developing effective communications', in *Public Communication Campaigns*, eds R. Rice & W. Paisley, Sage, Beverley Hills.

Mitchell, S. & Wright, M. 1992, 'Creating some confusion for professionals in the community health setting, in *Community Health Policy and Practice in Australia*, eds F. Baum, D. Fry & I. Lennie, Pluto Press in association with the Community Health Association of Australia, Sydney, pp. 249–63.

Mullen, P., Forster, J., Gottlieb, N., Kreuter, M., Moon, R. et al. 1995, 'Settings as an important dimension in health education/promotion policy, programs, and research', *Health Education Quarterly*, vol. 22, no. 3, pp. 329–45.

Nutbeam, D. & Catford, J. 1987, 'The Welsh heart program evaluation strategy: progress, plans and possibilities', *Health Promotion*, vol. 2, no. 1, pp. 5–18.

Sindall, C. 1992, 'Health promotion and community health in Australia: An overview of theory and practice', in *Community Health Policy and Practice in Australia*, eds F. Baum, D. Fry & I. Lennie, pp. 277–95.

Strickland, W. & Strickland, D. 1996, 'Partnership building with special populations', *Family Community Health*, vol. 19, pp. 19–24.

Valanis, B. 1986, *Epidemiology in Nursing and Health Care*, Appleton-Century Crofts, Norwalk.

Wechsler, H., Lovine, S., Idelson, R., Schor, E. & Coakley, E. 1996, 'The physician's role in health promotion revisited—a survey of primary care practitioners', *New England Journal of Medicine*, vol. 334, no. 15, pp. 996–8.

World Health Organization 1997, *The Jakarta Declaration on Health Promotion into the 21st Century*, WHO, Jakarta.

Young, D., Haskell, W., Barr Taylor, C. & Fortmann, S. 1996, 'Effect of community health education on physical activity knowledge, attitudes and behavior', *American Journal of Epidemiology*, vol. 144, no. 3, pp. 264–74.

13 Healthy places

People are social creatures who come to know themselves through their connection with the wider community to which they belong (Shotter 1985). Developing healthy communities is therefore a function of helping people develop coherent interactions with their environments. Feeling comfortable in a community and recognising its opportunities and resources helps promote a sense of personal equilibrium and harmony, and this is fundamental to health and wellness. At the community level, a sense of comfort or harmony is not simply the collective experiences of individuals who have decided to lead a healthy lifestyle. Healthy communities are a product of healthy organisations, including healthy governments, healthy cities, islands, villages, market places, workplaces and schools (Kickbusch 1997).

Within healthy organisations are opportunities for people to interact with one another, where they work, play, suffer, worship, celebrate and engage in commercial exchange. This chapter takes a closer look at the way in which healthy places can be created and sustained, and provide the background and the reinforcement for healthy individual choices. In the discussion to follow we will examine the links between health and place from the perspective of people's territorial identification and the way in which this contributes to the overall health of the community.

Objectives

By the end of this chapter you will be able to:

- *explain the links between health and place*

- *identify four major influences on community health that arise from urban living*

- *identify three factors influencing community development in rural areas*

- *discuss the implications for health promotion for those dispossessed of their place*

- *develop a strategic plan to address environmental issues in a defined geographic community.*

The concept of place

As social beings, we inhabit many places, some physical, others conceptualised in terms of our relationships with others. The concept of *place* provides a way to understand these literal and metaphorical geographies peculiar to each of us (Hudson-Rodd 1997). Our beliefs, interests and commitments are shaped within the context of our lives, and constantly shared through interaction with others in the places we live, work and play (Cutchin 1997). In each place we inhabit, unique mixtures of local and wider circles of social relations accumulate. At the community level, this cumulative set of relations is often referred to as the community's *social capital* (Hudson-Rodd 1997). Through interactions, we become valued participants in the community, and this can have a health-enhancing effect on our lives. Interaction with others also provides us with the empowering potential of the collective voice to lobby for the structures and processes necessary to sustain health in the community.

The social capital of a community is also important to those beyond our particular place. Historically, the anthropocentric approach to nature of many Western nations has been blamed for much of the environmental destruction and exploitation of the world's human and natural resources (Hudson-Rodd 1997). Fortunately for future generations, this type of environmental ruthlessness is no longer tolerated, as health advocates recognise the importance of intersectoral commitment to securing safe and healthy places for communities to develop. The environmental movement has provided a rallying point for *globalism*, based on ideals of sharing, common interests and long-term perspectives (Petersen & Lupton 1996). In this era of globalisation, the world is connected through telecommunications, rapid transportation and migration patterns. This provides an opportunity for greater sharing, through porous local, regional and international boundaries. The world has therefore become a global network where inter-connections meld (Hudson-Rodd 1997). As a result, and irrespective of our geographic, social or cultural origins, over time we evolve in ways that are linked to the dynamic 'life-and-place' interactions of all communities (Cutchin 1997; Hudson-Rodd 1997).

Individuals are linked to their place through three key psychological processes: attachment, familiarity and identity (Thompson Fullilove 1996). Attachment to others in the context of a familiar place is fundamental to the development of self, particularly in cultivating human intimacy and other types of relationships (Cutchin 1997; Goffman 1995). The theory of attachment suggests that we each have a personal environment that serves as an ' "outer ring" of life-sustaining systems complementary to the "inner ring" of systems that maintain physiological homeostasis' (Bowlby 1973, p. 150). Attachment to our outer ring is synonymous with place attachment, which is important to our sense of identity, safety and satisfaction with life (Thompson Fullilove 1996). Attachment to home is the core of successively wider attachments, including neighbourhood, region and country. People who are dispossessed of their homes and community therefore lose an important aspect of their self (Thompson Fullilove 1996).

The loss of place also represents a loss of important aspects of culture, which is embedded in the context of people's lives. For the indigenous peoples of the world, a deep and spiritual sense of belonging to the land is central to their identity and creates a bond between successive generations (Hudson-Rodd 1997). Indigenous people cultivate a strong sense of place for functional as well as cultural reasons. For example, Australian Aborigines consider going 'out bush' as a solution to such things as substance abuse problems. The land is understood to nurture and heal those who live upon it and who partake of its resources (Brady 1995). This is related to Aboriginal practices and beliefs which are 'intimately bound up with features of the landscape which were made in the creative "Dreaming" by mythical ancestors' (Brady 1995, p. 1494). Bush food and the smoke from special fires are important for purification and healing. Mother Earth provides a means of articulating a spiritual connection, which is open to all of Aboriginal 'blood' who feel for the land in an Indigenous way (Swain, in Brady 1995). The land also provides an opportunity for co-operative planning and the formation and maintenance of economic relations with other indigenous groups. Indigenous knowledge of geography and of nature is therefore fundamental to life, and has ensured the survival of many peoples living in fragile habitats, from the nomadic pastoralists of West Africa to the Inuit of the frigid Arctic regions (Hudson-Rodd 1997).

Place and health

Place is important to health for many reasons. The most essential link between health and place is the biological imperative that people have access to food, water, safe shelter, appropriate waste disposal and minimal toxic substances. This is inextricably linked to socioeconomic as well as geographic factors. In addition, people need to understand the effects of their particular life spaces on personal health. As we mentioned previously, women in developing countries are prone to respiratory illness because they must cook in small, closed homes over wood fires with little ventilation. Similarly, many urban dwellers in the 1990s suffer from 'sick building' syndrome. This is a situation where, paradoxically, systems of conserving energy (shutting out as much outdoor air as possible) create opportunities for illness-producing micro-organisms to thrive in the chemical contamination of indoor heating or air conditioning (Laird 1994).

Healthy places also extend beyond location, to experience (Gesler, Thorburn Bird & Oljeski 1997). Place represents 'the nodes of the life biography, which is itself a unique web of situated life episodes' (Paasi, cited in Thompson Fullilove 1996, p. 1517). A place of residence acts as a repository of meanings, which are in turn important to the balance between physical, psychological and spiritual health. At a social level, preservation of place is fundamental to developing and sustaining this balance. The dislocation caused by war, homelessness, decolonisation, epidemics, natural disasters and institutionalisation for prolonged periods poses a threat to community mental health (Thompson Fullilove 1996). The frequency of these events in poor countries has devastated the capacity for many people to lead healthy lives free of fear or anxiety. Years of community destruction through urban renewal, segregation, imprisonment, isolation, forced resettlement, out-of-home placement, sudden fame or wealth and disaster have had a powerful, negative effect on the health of people in the industrialised world (Thompson Fullilove 1996).

Rural places

People who live in rural communities have distinct sociocultural, occupational and ecological characteristics (Puskar, Tusaie-Mumford & Boneysteele 1996). Rural sociocultural issues include a value system that prefers the relative autonomy of rural life compared with the complex interdependencies of urban life. Most rural people have a visible affinity for their place. Those who farm the land, or provide services for agricultural communities, tend to see their lives as interwoven with features of the land and its life-sustaining capacity. Rural life is closely integrated with rural work, so rural people tend to assess their health and quality of life in relation to work role and work activities (Long & Weinert 1989). For many, a good life is a good house, good husbandry, hard work and blessed rain (at the right time!).

Many rural families believe their hard-working lifestyles to be healthier than that of urban dwellers. Farmers especially tend to show a high level of acceptance of injury and disease, preferring to be seen as 'hardy' rather than as succumbing to a sick role (Strasser, Harvey & Burley 1994). From an ecological perspective, rural places are not always as hardy as their residents perceive them to be. Many rural areas revolve around a single industry such as farming or mining. As the industry declines, the outflow of resources occurs at great cost to the rural population. The decline in opportunities for productive work leads to a decline in financial resources and a concomitant decline in young role models for the next generation. This often causes people to lose optimism and become dispirited. Loneliness is a problem in young people especially, and this is exacerbated by the fact that adolescence is a time when their need for emotional support is acute (Puskar, Tusaie-Mumford & Boneysteele 1996).

To those unfamiliar with rural life, the image of rural peace and serenity can be misleading. Although rural places do not suffer from the crowding and pollution of large cities, they do hold many risks to health and safety. Rates of unintended injuries are higher in rural and remote areas, particularly for males, and health services are fewer than in the city, so injuries are often fatal (Long & Weinert 1989; Strasser, Harvey & Burley 1994). The rate of motor vehicle traffic deaths is much higher for rural people than for urban residents, primarily as a function of the environment. Rural people must travel greater distances for services, on roads of lower standard, in older automobiles, and often by a driver under the influence of alcohol (AIHW 1996). Because of their work role, rural males are susceptible to injuries involving machinery, or falling objects such as ladders or scaffolding. The latter type of injury occurs because of the self-reliance of rural dwellers, who do not have the range of outside expertise available in the city (AIHW 1996; Long & Weinert 1989).

In all countries of the world, the rural decline of the 1980s has had a profound impact on health (Gay, Herriot & May 1995; Shouls, Congdon & Curtis 1996). During this period, rural communities throughout the world suffered from selective subsidisation of certain competitive goods, falling commodity prices and decreased global reliance on traditional primary industries (Gay, Herriot & May 1995). As a result, many farming families without the resources to diversify into industries that would maintain their rural lifestyle have been forced to leave their family farms. Some have remained with a severely diminished lifestyle and this has been particularly stressful for older people, who are now over-represented in farming communities (Schmidt, Brandt & Norris 1995). Ironically, the financial hardships of the rural economy have created a downward spiral of disadvantage by successive losses of hospitals and other social support services so important to the health of this ageing population (Rosenberg & Hanlon 1996).

The demographic constitution of rural communities is likely to change as young people leave the country for urban centres in search of employment. For many of these young people, their dislocation has met with simply a different kind of unemployment. As a result, they tend to experience a downward *social drift* (LeClair & Innes 1997). They find themselves in areas of low socioeconomic status and then are exposed to a new set of social problems such as disenchantment, poverty, inequality, and lack of access to housing and education. Many end up suffering from the stresses familiar to other disadvantaged urban young people, the extreme extent of which is a dual loss of place: the transient place of the city and their place of origin in the country (Gay, Herriot & May 1995).

Urban places

From the time of the industrial revolution, a strong demographic trend has been a mass exodus away from rural areas to seek the employment and social interaction of the cities. This trend increased following the two World Wars. Factories thrived and, despite improving people's financial status, presented numerous threats to health. These went relatively unnoticed, as the industrialised world concentrated more on increased productivity and innovation than on the potential for industry-related ill-health (Craig 1995).

Today, after more than half a century of growth in the industrial sector, the hazards accompanying urban living have become a matter of concern to all members of the public. Urban population density, brought about by those seeking the financial and social resources of cities, has intensified air and water pollution, and waste management problems, and resulted in competition for scarce natural resources (Craig 1995). Even resource-rich nations have had to deal with the fact that rates of production and consumption are too high to sustain.

Resource inequities have led to variable efforts to renew natural resources, and to reverse environmental destruction (Craig 1995). The careless consumption of overpopulated cities has been allowed to continue by many governments seeking short-term political gain, rather than long-term optimisation of resources (Craig 1995). The WHO has been lobbying all member countries to work toward attaining lifestyles and undertaking consumption patterns consistent with ecological sustainability (WHO 1993). As the new century nears, campaigns led by consumer groups are also attempting to redress a legacy of ill-fated political decision-making by heightening public awareness of environmental issues and ensuring these issues remain high on the political agenda.

The Kyoto conference of 1997 represented the culmination of environmental lobbies from many countries. The conference in Kyoto, Japan, was instigated by the worldwide threat of global warming caused by air pollution from six major 'greenhouse gases' gradually destroying the air quality in all industrialised nations. The greenhouse effect is a result of carbon dioxide and other gases generated by human agriculture and industry, trapping the sun's heat (Lemonick 1997). The ultimate environmental outcome of this destructive force has yet to be defined, but some researchers contend that worst-case scenarios will be dangerously rising seas, more powerful storms, floods, droughts, drastically altered weather patterns and outbreaks of tropical diseases in places where they have not previously been seen (Lemonick 1997; McMichael & Hales 1997). Climate change would also have a severe influence on regional agricultural productivity, causing population displacement and unemployment (McMichael & Hales 1997).

The major outcome from the Kyoto conference was a commitment by all industrialised nations to reduce emissions of six different 'greenhouse' gases by 5.2% below the levels that existed in the air in 1990, by the year 2012 (Lemonick 1997). To achieve these quotas, all consumers will have to make a commitment to change consumption patterns. Industries will have to become more energy efficient, changing from dirty fuels like coal and oil to cleaner natural gas, which generates far less carbon dioxide. Drivers will have to switch to fuel-efficient cars that run at least partly on fuel cells, batteries and other non-polluting power sources. Home-owners will have to generate their own emission-free electricity by such means as installing solar cells on their roofs to capture the energy of the sun. Electric utilities will have to rely more on wind, solar, hydroelectric and other renewable energy sources. Householders will have to begin buying devices that consume less energy than at present, like compact fluorescent bulbs and energy-efficient appliances (Lemonick 1997).

The major conclusion drawn by those analysing the Kyoto conference is that there must be heightened awareness by all people of the world, of the need to create healthier cities (Lemonick 1997). The ideal of the healthy city is an unpolluted, safe environment. The built environment, particularly housing, is of high quality. The city itself is supported by, and contributes to, a stable and sustainable ecosystem. Social life is rich, and political participation highly developed. Human relations are reciprocal, with no exploitation. Decisions are reached only after widespread public debate, thereby creating community empowerment (Curtice, in Petersen & Lupton 1996). Although this may seem a bit utopic, it exemplifies the idealistic goals of primary health care: equity, access, self-determinism and community empowerment, all achieved in the context of a healthy environment.

At present, more than one thousand cities are working toward improving urban environments under the healthy cities principles, which are also being extended to healthy villages, healthy towns and healthy islands. 'Healthy marketplaces' is an extension of this movement, designed to mobilise all sectors of cities in the developing nations to focus on food safety and hygiene, which is a major threat to health in these countries (Kickbusch 1997). The key to success in creating healthy cities, healthy villages and healthy marketplaces is community participation. Together, people can participate in long-term planning for health that goes beyond the instrumental act of achieving a defined outcome (Cooke 1995; Kickbusch 1997).

The healthy cities movement is a prime example of a grass-roots movement to improve the places where people live. As mentioned in chapter 2, the healthy city, town or shire is one in which many members of the community establish health goals relevant to their particular needs, then work collectively toward achieving these goals (Chapman & Davey 1997). In Australia, as in many other nations, the focus of this work is on developing co-operative, local urban management plans. One approach being used to guide the healthy cities concepts in several shires in Australia is illustrated in Chapman's (1995) framework (see figure 13.1). The framework guides health professionals to foster collaborative partnerships between government and non-government sectors, community groups and individuals. In the process, people are encouraged to express their preferred options for a healthier place. Using a participative approach achieves two major goals: it mobilises all community residents to help with community development, and it enhances people's understanding of the linkages between health and place. Ultimately, this could be expected to lead to greater efforts at preserving and sustaining the natural environment.

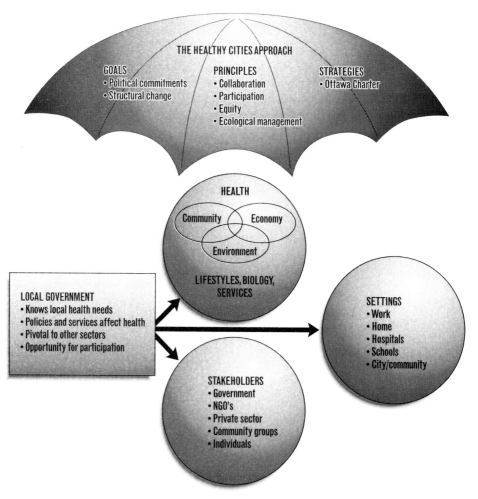

Figure 13.1 *Planning healthy communities within a healthy cities and shires framework (from Chapman 1995, reproduced with permission)*

> CASE STUDY

Health and place in the urban sectors of developing countries

In developing countries such as Kenya, the population migrating from rural to urban areas is burgeoning, creating a health crisis of unprecedented proportions. From the time of Alma Ata, the emphasis in developing countries was on implementing primary health care in rural areas. However, increasing population pressure in those areas has created shortages of land, food and employment opportunities. Africa and other developing countries have seen mass population movements into the cities, and it is estimated that by the year 2000, approximately 40% of the sub-Saharan Africa population will be urban; 60% of these will be living in slum areas or illegal settlements. At present, the poor living in slums have no access to adequate health services. They have experienced epidemics of communicable diseases such as cholera, and their children are in poor health from malnourishment and a lack of immunisation. Although environmental pollution affects all people in the cities, because of their living circumstances, the poor tend to be exposed to a greater extent than others to air and water pollution.

For those living in illegal settlements the problems are intensified by the lack of access to any services. These people, like the fringe dwellers of other countries, tend to live near industrialised areas, in open spaces by poorly drained marshes or rivers, in degraded and unclean environments. They are exposed to a range of wastes and disease vectors such as mosquitoes. They have little or no access to health services, which are overburdened by the rising number of urban migrants. The increased demands have limited both quantity and quality of care, as staff attempt to respond to the needs of legal and illegal residents.

Because health planning has been done with projections more heavily weighted toward rural health, financial resources for urban programs are incapable of meeting the needs of urban dwellers. Those who live legally in the cities are indirectly subsidising their rural neighbours as well as those living illegally, who pay no taxes that would help alleviate the situation. Planning is problematic as no precedent exists for such unexpected growth in the urban areas. The major question health authorities are having to deal with is how to support a sustainable health system for an expanding population.

The country is adopting strategies to address the problem using the principles of primary health care. Their plan for healthy cities includes health education, food supply and proper nutrition, safe water and basic sanitation, maternal and child health care, immunisation, prevention of endemic diseases, treatment of common diseases and injuries, and provision of essential medications. Primary health care models, previously adopted for the rural areas, are being tailored to the needs of cities. Strategies include intersectoral action for housing, education, transportation, nutrition, environmental sanitation and community development.

In order to reorient the health services to meet people's needs, community members are working at the political and social levels. One of the dilemmas of reorientation is that while absolute numbers increase rapidly, regional (sector) revenues decrease, mandating a rise in taxes. This has the potential to create a cycle of diminished capacity for development in certain areas, leading to the need for greater central management of health resources. The communities are lobbying for a change to the laws to de-illegalise the settlements of the urban poor so that they will be charted on maps, and thus provided with services. They are also working toward redistributing the taxation base to achieve access and equity for all members of the population. Finally, and within the context of these political and economic strategies, they are attempting to improve the country's health care system (Wang'Ombe 1995).

This case illustrates the interrelationship between the myriad issues affecting place and health. Without knowledge of geography, migration trends, population composition and the law, the health goals of a community cannot be adequately achieved. It is yet another way in which the social, political and geographic environment are inextricably linked to the health of a population.

People's health status is only a surface manifestation of underlying social forces, which are numerous and powerful in either facilitating or constraining health. Health, illness and treatment are social constructions, mediated by the institutions and practices of society (Gesler, Thorburn Bird & Oljeski 1997). It is only recently that we have begun to realise the influence of healthy institutions on population health. People are disadvantaged when they live in close proximity to conflict, or when they have inadequate housing, work, transportation or health care (Gesler, Thorburn Bird & Oljeski 1997; Rosenberg & Hanlon 1996). On the other hand, their health is enhanced when the places in which they interact are designed to be health promoting.

Social change and economic instability have become major challenges to planning for health promotion (Chapman & Davey 1997). One of the most difficult challenges for the future will be to maintain health promotion services at a time when only bare essentials are available from shrinking health care budgets. Integrating health promotion within the settings of people's lives provides an attractive and financially viable alternative to the segmented health promotion services of the past. Within a settings approach, we can imbue people's places of residence, whether village, town or city, with structures and policies to promote health, creativity and human interaction (Thompson Fullilove 1996). In addition, we can encourage empowered collaboration, helping communities develop and re-develop by re-establishing familiarity, repairing their attachments, and helping them become stabilised within their environment (Thompson Fullilove 1996).

To date, participative programs have included such things as community land care programs, where community residents plant trees and adopt strategies to prevent erosion and improve water quality (Gay, Herriot & May 1995). Similarly, with assistance and advocacy for co-operative planning, those formerly displaced can be encouraged to build friendship networks with neighbours and contribute to the caretaking of both personal and shared portions of their place (Thompson Fullilove 1996). These grass-roots efforts must also be backed up by public policy and resources.

Hancock (1994) suggests a set of criteria to guide public policy towards healthy and sustainable communities. He identifies six qualities that are necessary determinants to achieve health in the socioecological context as follows:

- *conviviality*—people living well together
- *viability*—remaining within ecological limits and maintaining species diversity
- *adequate prosperity*—consuming less but with sufficiency and creative alternatives to economic production
- *liveability*—healthy natural and built environments to assist living
- *sustainability*—sufficient development without threatening viability
- *equity*—equal opportunity for the development of human potential.

These goals can be accomplished by using the Ottawa Charter for Health Promotion as a framework for change. For example, healthy public policies need to include housing policies that are responsive to the need for all people to achieve all of these goals. Supportive environments must include both places and processes that acknowledge the linkages between people and their place, and the interrelationships between place and health. Recreational settings and hospitals, schools and workplaces must become more integrated with one another, and focused on personal development as a way to achieve health.

Community action must be participative and oriented toward community definitions of need, so that healthy places are not defined by those who will not inhabit them. To encourage participation, most people will require a considerable level of new knowledge. Those interested in health are usually uninformed about the processes of conservation, regeneration, land and waste management, and transportation. A whole-of-community, multigenerational approach will ensure that children at school and their parents and grandparents are all being exposed to similar information relevant to preserving places for them, and for subsequent generations. Health care services will also need to become reoriented toward helping people learn, work, play and heal in the context of everyday life rather than only in designated institutions.

Healthy places provide the template for the creation of health. For young children, healthy schools set the stage for a balanced life of industriousness, play and social interchange. In healthy occupational settings, adults can develop the skills to maintain a healthy work life free of injury or occupational illness. At play on healthy golf courses, beaches or ski slopes, healthy patterns of interactions with others are developed in safe environments conducive to physical and psychological wellbeing. Healthy hospitals strive for illness prevention rather than focusing only on illness, and they ensure that the refuse produced in treating illness does not perpetuate the decline of our environment. In the chapters to follow, we will examine two of these healthy settings in-depth, as exemplars for how we can work toward healthy places and thus healthy lives.

THINKING CRITICALLY

Healthy places

▶ Identify four ways in which *your* geographical place influences your personal health.

▶ What steps would need to be taken in your city or town to ensure it met the healthy cities criteria? *(See also chapter 2.)*

▶ Conduct an inventory of environmental issues affecting your city or town. Devise one strategy to overcome each of these.

▶ Identify three characteristics of a healthy recreational facility.

▶ Develop a five-point plan to educate pre-primary school children about preserving their place.

REFERENCES

Australian Institute of Health and Welfare, 1996, *Australia's Health 1996*, AGPS, Canberra.

Bowlby, J. 1973, *Attachment and Loss, vol. 11, Separation: Anxiety and Anger*, Basic Books, New York.

Brady, M. 1995, 'Culture in treatment, culture as treatment. A critical appraisal of developments in addictions programs for indigenous North Americans and Australians', *Social Science and Medicine*, vol. 41, no. 11, pp. 1487–98.

Chapman, P. 1995, 'A model for planning for healthy and sustainable communities in Queensland', unpublished manuscript, Griffith University, Brisbane.

Chapman, P. & Davey, P. 1997, 'Working "with" communities, not "on" them: a changing focus for local government health planning in Queensland', *Australian Journal of Primary Health—Interchange*, vol. 3, no. 1, pp. 82–91.

Cooke, R. 1995, 'Two healthy cities in South Australia', in *Health for All: The South Australian Experience*, ed. F. Baum, Wakefield Press, Kent Town, SA, pp. 93–116.

Craig, B. 1995, 'Urban planning and health', in *Health for All: The South Australian Experience*, ed. F. Baum, Wakefield Press, Kent Town, SA, pp. 193–214.

Cutchin, M. 1997, 'Community and self: concepts for rural physician integration and retention', *Social Science and Medicine*, vol. 44, no. 11, pp. 1661–74.

Gay, J., Herriot, M. & May, A. 1995, 'Primary health care beyond the city', in *Health for All: The South Australian Experience*, ed. F. Baum, Wakefield Press, Kent Town, SA, pp. 375–92.

Gesler, W., Thorburn Bird, S. & Oljeski, S. 1997, 'Disease ecology and a reformist alternative: the case of infant mortality', *Social Science and Medicine,* vol. 44, no. 5, pp. 657–71.

Goffman, E. 1995, 'The insanity of place', in *Health and Disease: A Reader*, 2nd edn, eds B. Davey, A. Gray & C. Seale, Open University Press, Buckingham, pp. 72–8.

Hancock, T. 1994, 'A healthy and sustainable community: the view from 2020', in *Ecological Public Health: From Vision to Practice*, eds C. Chu & R. Simpson, Institute of Applied Environmental Research, Griffith University, Brisbane, pp. 245–53.

Hudson-Rodd, N. 1997, 'Geographical knowledge', in *Encyclopaedia of the History of Science, Technology and Medicine in Non-Western Cultures*, ed. H. Selin, Kluwer Publishers, Dordrecht, pp. 347–51.

Kickbusch, I. 1997, 'Health-promoting environments: the next step', *Australian and New Zealand Journal of Health Promotion*, vol. 21, no. 4, pp. 431–4.

Laird, R. 1994, 'Sick of the system?', *Occupational Health and Safety*, Sep., pp. 54–68.

LeClair, J. & Innes, F. 1997, 'Urban ecological structure and perceived child and adolescent psychological disorder', *Social Science and Medicine*, vol. 44, no. 11, pp. 1649–59.

Lemonick, M. 1997, 'Turning down the heat', *Time*, Dec. 22, pp. 18–21.

Long, K. & Weinert, C. 1989, 'Rural nursing: Developing the theory base', *Scholarly Inquiry for Nursing Practice*, vol. 3, pp. 113–27.

McMichael, A. & Hales, S. 1997, 'Global health promotion: looking back to the future', *Australian and New Zealand Journal of Public Health*, vol. 21, no. 4, pp. 425–8

Peterson, A. & Lupton, D. 1996, 'The "healthy" city', in *The New Public Health. Health and Self in the Age of Risk*, eds A. Petesen & D. Lupton, Sage Publications, London, pp. 120–45.

Puskar, K. Tusaie-Mumford, K. & Boneysteele, G. 1996, 'Rurality and advanced practice nurses', *Journal of Multicultural Nursing and Health*, vol. 2, no. 4, pp. 32–47.

Rosenberg, R. & Hanlon, N. 1996, 'Access and utilization: a continuum of health service environments', *Social Science and Medicine*, vol. 43, no. 6, pp. 975–83.

Schmidt, L., Brandt, J. & Norris, K. 1995, 'The advanced registered nurse practitioner in rural practice', *The Kansas Nurse*, vol. 70, no. 9, pp. 1–2.

Shotter, J. 1985, 'Accounting for place and space', *Environment and Planning, volume D, Society and Space*, vol. 3, pp. 447–60.

Shouls, S., Congdon, P. & Curtis, S. 1996, 'Modelling inequality in reported long-term illness in the UK: combining individual and area characteristics', *Journal of Epidemiology and Community Health*, vol. 50, pp. 366–76.

Strasser, R. Harvey, D. & Burley, M. 1994, 'The health service needs of small rural communities', *Australian Journal of Rural Health*, vol. 2, no. 2, pp. 7–13.

Thompson Fullilove, M. 1996, 'Psychiatric implications of displacement: contributions from the psychology of place', *American Journal of Psychiatry*, vol. 153, no. 12, pp. 1516–22.

Wang'Ombe, J. 1995, 'Public health crises of cities in developing countries', *Social Science and Medicine*, vol. 41, no. 6, pp. 857–62.

World Health Organization 1993, *Implementation of the Global Strategy of Health for All by the Year 2000. Second Evaluation, Vol. 1, Global Review*, WHO, Geneva.

14 *Healthy schools*

Health in the 1990s is conceptualised as a resource for living. To gain maximum benefit from this resource, patterns for healthy living should be established early in life. Families, neighbours and community members all play a role in encouraging young people to adopt healthy lifestyles; however, schools offer a unique setting for reinforcing their messages. Schools are a constant in most young people's lives. They provide a forum for the exchange of ideas, attitudes and values, and they represent a setting that is comfortable, creative, supportive and conducive to change.

Worldwide, schools reach approximately 1000 million young people and, through them, their families and communities. Schools are therefore 'the world's broadest and deepest channel for putting information at the disposal of its citizens' (Nakajima 1996, p. 3). In addition to information, healthy school environments can build health potential, create buffers between young people and their wider social networks, create intermediary support for them to develop into healthy adults, strengthen the community's protective factors and, in the context of developing skills for lifelong learning, reduce the effect of social gradients (WHO 1997). This chapter examines the global trend toward promoting health in the school setting and provides an overview of issues that influence the creation of health in schools.

Objectives

By the end of this chapter you will be able to:

- *discuss the capacity of schools to improve the health of young people*

- *explain the links between education and health*

- *discuss three advantages of comprehensive school health programs*

- *identify three barriers to school health promotion*

- *design a school-based program to respond to the physical, social and emotional needs of youth.*

The global initiative for school health

In recognition of the importance of schools in health promotion, in 1995 the WHO established the Global School Health Initiative. This program was to serve as a unifying framework for all countries of the world to work towards strengthening school health promotion activities (O'Byrne et al. 1996). Its basic premise is that health is inextricably linked to educational achievement, quality of life and economic productivity. If the appropriate environment for learning and for the development of healthy lifestyles can be provided early in a person's development, there is a greater likelihood of sustaining health throughout their lifespan. The WHO initiative involves three broad strategies for encouraging health promotion in the schools. These include developing the resource materials to advocate for school health programs, mobilising public and private resources through the WHO regional networks, and strengthening national capacities for school health by bringing member nations together to learn from one another (O'Byrne et al. 1996).

Health and education

The link between health and education has been demonstrated in numerous ways. Creating opportunities for health at school has an important effect on learning. Young people who are ill or injured, or who suffer from mental health problems, hunger, pregnancy, the effects of alcohol and drug use, or those who fear violence are less likely to learn, irrespective of educational processes (Kolbe, Collins & Cortese 1997). In the case of nutrition, even moderate under-nutrition can have lasting effects on children's cognitive development and school performance. When children are hungry or undernourished they are less likely to resist infection and thus may become ill and miss school; they may become irritable and have difficulty concentrating, and their low energy may compromise physical fitness (Centre for Disease Control 1997a).

Providing opportunities for schooling is in itself a powerful way to influence health, especially for those who are destined to become family caretakers. For example, literate women have a greater potential to achieve maternal and child health. They tend to marry later and are more likely to use family planning methods. Women with only one year of schooling take better care of their babies than those without any formal education, and are more likely to seek medical care for their children and to have them immunised (Nakajima 1996). By acquiring health-related knowledge, all children are better placed to pursue a healthy life and to work as agents of change to improve the health of their families and communities (Patil et al. 1996). Schools therefore play an important role in supporting basic human rights as well as in raising the social status of women and girls (Nakajima 1996; Nutbeam 1997). Achieving literacy for all is thus central to achieving economic and social development and, as such, is an important public health goal (Nutbeam 1997; CDHSH 1995).

The evolution of school health services

Throughout this past century, the value of school-based health services has been increasingly acknowledged. School health centres were originally established to respond to a broadening of the concept of schooling beyond vocational training to encompass the provision of social services (Sedlak 1997). Prior to the era of professionalisation (the early part of the twentieth century), most services beyond the traditional teaching functions in schools were provided by community volunteers. With the development of discrete professions, the number of participants in school health services proliferated; however, their arrival also signalled a fragmentation of function. Health teaching was predominantly relegated to the health or physical education teacher, while the school nurse was primarily concerned with conducting screening tests and responding to playground injuries with first aid services (Leavy et al. 1995). School psychologists, guidance officers and social workers were also considered an important part of school health services, in their role as advocates for positive emotional student health.

During the 1920s to the 1970s, school-based health promotion focused on the provision of information primarily related to hygiene and bodily functions. Little attention was given to environmental or contextual factors beyond the influence of the family. Once research studies began to systematically evaluate these programs, predictably, health-related information being provided in schools was found to have little or no effect on behaviours such as smoking, eating and physical activity (Stone 1996). Gradually, it became clear that healthy behaviours, such as a child's eating habits, were found to be influenced by the interaction between the child and her/his social and physical environments, not simply on knowledge of the healthfulness of foods (Nicklas et al. 1997).

As the research data accumulated, the characteristics of an effective health promotion program became clear. These included programs based on research evidence, those that included developmentally appropriate, culturally sensitive information presented in a gender-sensitive way (especially for diet-related issues), provided by well-prepared teachers, on the basis of clinical data from health screening, with adequate guidance, reinforcement and follow-up (DeMuth Allensworth & Bradley 1996; Dusenbury & Falco 1995; Fardy et al. 1996).

During the community health promotion era of the 1970s and 1980s the focus of school health expanded to include a more holistic approach with input from all involved in children's educational experiences. A more concerted approach was also timely because of the increasing numbers of medically fragile students and those with chronic health problems (Magyary & Brandt 1996). The role of the school nurse expanded to include medication administration, specialised health care procedures, implementation of HIV infection policies, provision of health education and counselling to students and staff, and participation in the school health promotion team (Bradley 1997; Leavy Small et al. 1995; McClowry et al. 1996).

School health promotion campaigns of this time were thus developed as a team effort, and many reported successes in improving health knowledge, attitudes and behaviours; for example in reducing high sexual risk behaviours (Mullen et al. 1995). American, Australian, Canadian, New Zealand and Swedish research studies from this era concluded that school-based programs can serve as a catalyst for broader, societal change (Mullen et al. 1995). Programs aimed at preventing eating disorders, maintaining cardiovascular health and healthy sexual behaviour, and educating young people about tobacco were found to be more effective when enhanced by targeted community-wide programs that address the role and resources of families, community organisations, related policies (including anti-tobacco advertising), and other elements in the social environment (Beaglehole 1991; Chapman et al. 1994; Mackie & Oickle 1997; Mullen et al. 1995; Neumark-Sztainer 1996; Nutbeam 1997; Resnicow, Robinson & Frank 1996). Including adolescents in planning such programs and encouraging peer support was also identified as a predictor of success (Komro et al. 1996).

In conjunction with the cumulative body of research evidence, a broader approach to school health promotion was spawned by a growing awareness that the physical, mental and social health needs of adolescents were often not being met by an increasingly complex, costly and fragmented health care system (Brindis & Sanghvi 1997). Health promotion experts agreed that comprehensive, well co-ordinated, school-based health promotion programs were the best way to meet the needs of adolescents in a way that could provide confidentiality, respond to their need for spontaneous services, overcome transportation needs, and eliminate their loss of study time and even loss of work time for families where, increasingly, both parents were in full-time employment (Brindis & Sanghvi 1997; Resnicow & Allensworth 1996).

Today there is widespread acceptance of the necessity for a comprehensive, integrated approach to school health promotion (Adelman & Taylor 1997; Hinton Walker et al. 1996; Kolbe, Collins & Cortese 1997; Mackie & Oickle 1997; Ryan, Jones & Weitzman 1996). Comprehensive programs of community health for young people that are situated in the context of their lives are seen as an effective 'medical home' for young people (Schlitt et al. 1995, p. 71). Integrating health education with other educational and developmental influences enhances access to appropriate services, enables young people to be responsible decision-makers in promoting their own health, and improves the ability of health professionals to manage their health care needs and co-ordinate resources (Adelman & Taylor 1997; Schlitt et al. 1995). This approach to school health is rapidly expanding in the US and Canada and, through the work of the WHO, the comprehensive, integrated model is being introduced to other countries throughout the world (O'Byrne et al. 1996). Some are attempting to introduce the notion of a school-linked 'one stop shop' that would provide a family service or resource centre, established at or near a school with an array of medical, mental health and social services. These services have the potential to draw together all members of the community health team in a location accessible to all family members (Adelman & Taylor 1997).

This type of approach is consonant with the principles of primary health care in that it is has increased the community's capacity to be self-determined and collaborative across sectors. Schools also have an ideal opportunity to enhance access, equity and cultural sensitivity.

Health-promoting schools

A health-promoting school is defined as one that is 'constantly strengthening its capacity as a healthy setting for living, learning and working' (O'Byrne et al. 1996, p. 5). According to the WHO Expert Committee on Comprehensive School Health Education and Promotion, a health-promoting school is one that:

■ engages health and education officials, teachers, students, parents and community leaders in efforts to make the school a healthy place

■ implements policies, practices and measures that encourage self-esteem, provide multiple opportunities for success, and acknowledge good efforts and intentions as well as personal achievement

■ strives to provide a healthy environment, school health education and school health services along with school/community health projects and outreach, health promotion programs for staff, nutrition and food safety programs, opportunities for physical education and recreation, and programs for counselling, social support and mental health promotion

■ strives to improve the health of school personnel, families and community members as well as pupils; and works with community leaders to help them understand how the community contributes to, or undermines, health and education
(O'Byrne et al. 1996, p. 5).

An ideal health-promoting school exemplifies the principles of primary health care. It is an environment in which the social and physical environment are considered to be equally important to health, one where pupils, teachers, administrators, family members and others in the community collaborate to develop policies and practices that reduce all forms of violence and adversity, increase equity, respect, caring, self-esteem and opportunities for success in the classroom, the playground and the community. Most importantly, it is a school that is the hub of health promotion, where many sectors (health, recreation, social services, law enforcement, transport, food and commerce) come together to maximise the health, education and development needs of young people (Kickbusch & Jones 1996; Mackie & Oickle 1997).

Comprehensive school health programs

The most significant problems of today's society are to a great extent caused by behavioural patterns established during adolescence. The physical and mental problems experienced by adolescents are problematic because they tend to persist into adulthood. One of the reasons for this is the hesitancy of many young people to utilise traditional health care services (Keyl et al. 1996; Walter et al. 1995). Confidentiality is a major issue for all adolescents, particularly those in rural areas, where local health providers are often neighbours or family friends (Rickert et al. 1997). In some cases, cultural norms prevent school-age children or adolescents from seeking information or preventive services that would be discouraged within the family context (Soon, Chan & Goh 1995).

Although it would be unreasonable to expect that schools could solve society's health and social problems, comprehensive school health programs are today being attributed with widespread changes in the health behaviours of young people (Mackie & Oickle 1997; Nutbeam 1997). To a large extent this is a function of careful design. The most powerful programs target the most significant problems of youth within the context of a healthy organisation: the school. Successful school health programs are therefore designed within health-promoting schools. They represent an integrated and mutually reinforcing set of experiences for young people that are compatible with the school's educational goals and values (Nutbeam 1997). They include the social influence of members of the school community and are developed to respond to community-wide public health goals (Villalbi 1997). Fundamental to the success of all school health promotion programs is an understanding of the problems of youth.

Six categories of behaviour cause most of the major health problems of young people, and most are preventable. These include: behaviours that cause unintentional or intentional injuries; drug and alcohol abuse; sexual behaviours that cause sexually transmitted diseases, including HIV infection and unintended pregnancies; tobacco use; inadequate physical activity; and dietary patterns that cause disease (Kolbe, Collins & Cortese 1997). Many of these behaviours are interrelated and contribute simultaneously to poor health outcomes, poor education outcomes and poor social outcomes.

The most effective comprehensive school health programs are designed to address these behaviours through eight interactive components (Allensworth & Kolbe 1987) as follows:

- health services
- psychological, counselling and social services
- health education
- nutrition services
- physical education and other physical activities
- the psychosocial and biophysical environment
- health programs for faculty and staff
- integrated efforts of schools, families and communities to improve the health of students and staff.

Integration of all eight components means that the school develops as a healthy organisation within a healthy community, with the full participation of students, teachers, parents and others. It also involves ensuring that all teachers are prepared to link their teaching with the development of personal skills to ensure healthy lifestyles. The school environment must be conducive to health and safety, and students must be provided with access to appropriate health services that recognise mental health as well as physical health needs (Nutbeam 1997). Because young people are among the most vulnerable and powerless in society, other forms of action must also be taken to ensure they can utilise their learning in a safe and healthy environment, with opportunities to overcome the limitations of social and/or economic disadvantage. Healthy communities external to the school, guided by healthy public policies such as those governing tobacco and alcohol distribution, are imperative to reinforce the school-based program (Nutbeam 1997).

Evaluating the success of comprehensive school health promotion

Pilot studies of school-based clinics providing comprehensive services reveal that they do contribute to improvements in health status of students and in reducing some risk-taking behaviours. One study found that students who were enrolled in the school clinic were twice as likely to stay in school than non-enrolled students, and another demonstrated their influence on increasing contraceptive use (Brindis & Sanghvi 1997). Another pilot study evaluated school-based mental health services, reporting decreased depression and improved self-concept (Flaherty, Weist & Warner 1996), and another indicated their usefulness in preventing substance abuse (Shope et al. 1996). However, further studies are necessary before definitive conclusions can be drawn on the long-term value of mental health outcomes (Flaherty, Weist & Warner 1996). Evaluation of mental health services is complicated by the fact that children rarely seek such services for themselves, and are dependent on parents, teachers or other adults to recognise the need (Armbruster, Gerstein & Fallon 1997). Because of the confidential nature of most mental health consultations, most researchers conclude that schools represent the most attractive situation for community-based services in providing a single point of access to services in a familiar, non-threatening atmosphere (Anglin, Naylor & Kaplan 1996; Weist et al. 1996).

To be comprehensive, school health promotion services must integrate mental health services along a continuum of care with other services. Holistic and developmental perspectives must focus on individuals, families and the environment, and range from primary prevention and early intervention, through treatment and rehabilitation in the school, community and home environment (Adelman & Taylor 1996). Many components of comprehensive programs require multi-disciplinary teamwork, especially in sensitive areas such as suicide prevention. A review of the relevant research reveals that there remains insufficient evidence to support prevention programs based primarily on curriculum components, indicating a need to ensure that these programs are designed with the right 'mix' of input from health professionals (Ploeg et al. 1996).

Evaluation of comprehensive school health programs in Canada has identified four factors that contribute to successful implementation of Healthy Schools programs. These include: school readiness, as indicated by a visionary Healthy School Committee; support by the principal, who acts as gatekeeper for the program; community outreach, including the involvement of school councils or home and school groups, community organisations and local businesses; and staff development for public health nurses co-ordinating the programs (Mitchell, Laforet-Fliesser & Camiletti 1997).

In the US, most evaluation studies have provided strong evidence for health gains, and some school-based services have also shown cost savings. However, it is unknown whether this is actual cost-effectiveness or simply cost shifting (Brindis & Sanghvi 1997; Flaherty, Weist & Warner 1996). The costing issue is contentious, because health goals for young people may actually include bringing them into contact with more, rather than fewer, services. One group of researchers reported increased use of primary care services, while use of emergency rooms and hospital services declined.

These were seen as successful outcomes in shifting the focus to prevention (Santelli, Kouzis & Newcomer 1996). Another research group found that visit rates in the comprehensive school-based program significantly exceeded visit rates on a national basis (Anglin, Naylor & Kaplan 1996). These early studies show a promising trend, but further research on patterns of utilisation is needed to identify the nature of services used in relation to the goal of encouraging young people to use more preventive services.

Obstacles to success of school health promotion

Despite encouraging reports from comprehensive school health promotion strategies, some barriers remain to be overcome. In the past, one of the most important obstacles to success in school health promotion has been a lack of government policies mandating school health. Even today, when policies have been put in place to encourage comprehensive programs, there is insufficient awareness of their existence and a lack of clarity about the respective roles of individual team members (Small et al. 1995). One study in Australia found that, despite Commonwealth policy indicated endorsement for a multi-disciplinary approach to school health promotion, teachers were unaware of the concept of a health-promoting school, or their roles in implementing health promotion programs (Thyer 1996). Similarly, in the US, many schools have yet to translate health promotion ideals into positive classroom experiences. This may require better resourcing of schools, better inservicing of teachers and a shift in the curriculum from a focus on anatomy and physiology to an emphasis on health and health education (Williams 1996). One approach may be to ensure that health education subjects are reinforced by infusing a health promotion orientation into all other subjects. In this way, such important issues as safe sexual behaviour, violence and injury prevention can be interwoven into more than one component of the curriculum (Collins et al. 1995).

Another issue that needs to be addressed is the need for crisis response mechanisms in schools. Unfortunately, the escalating level of violence in society is mirrored in the school setting, and few schools are adequately prepared to manage crisis situations. This must be redressed to maintain staff and student morale in times of crisis, and so that children's unresolved reactions to violence at school do not create a downward spiral of poor academic performance (Fiester et al. 1995).

Another barrier to effective school health promotion is related to the typically highly structured and under-resourced nature of school systems. Without staff, space and industrial policies that value health promotion, school-based services will be less than optimal (Nicklas et al. 1997). Geographic location may also be a constraint in school health promotion, particularly for schools with little indoor space for physical activities.

The concept of a school-linked community health centre will bear close consideration, particularly for its capacity to bring together many sectors of society interested in community health. Such developments will require horizontal co-operative resourcing arrangements at the school and community level as well as vertical co-operative arrangements to ensure that the various bureaucratic obstacles to service delivery can be overcome (Adelman & Taylor 1997). Members of the school community need to be familiar with the local, external community and its health goals to ensure collaborative input and student participation (Landis & Janes 1995).

Another potential barrier to success in comprehensive school health programs is related to the attitudes of either staff or administrators. Endorsement of initiatives by the school principal is crucial (Hazell et al. 1995). Because of a lack of understanding or a lack of valuing, opportunities for consolidating health promotion messages may be scheduled during times considered 'expendable', such as in place of physical or health education classes, which are already declining in many places. Similarly, changes in food preparation may be thwarted by staff who have entrenched ways of running school cafeterias (Nicklas et al. 1997). Some of these obstacles may be overcome by: sensitive approaches to training existing staff; ensuring that appropriate information and materials are disseminated to teachers, administrators and food service staff; maintaining consistency in applying policies and practices; providing motivating health education programs for teachers and ensuring they have the time for development, delivery and evaluation of the content (Nicklas et al. 1997; Ross et al. 1995; Tappe, Galer-Unti & Bailey 1995).

Despite utilisation data indicating the success of comprehensive school-based clinics in providing greater access to adolescents, there is a need for research focusing on clinical outcomes (Walter et al. 1995). Some studies indicate that high-risk students have found school-based services favourable, although longitudinal morbidity and mortality data demonstrating a reduction in unmet need are not yet available (Walter et al. 1995). One study in Canada found that a co-ordinated approach had little or no value in enhancing programs for heart and mental health in children (McIntyre et al. 1996). This type of research needs to be carefully examined from the standpoint of appropriate use of limited resources.

School-based violence prevention is one example of an important social issue that is currently being addressed in a number of communities. Research to date reveals that consistent exposure to violence can harm children's cognitive abilities, physiological functioning and ability to form close attachments (Fiester et al. 1996). School-based mental health and violence prevention projects are dependent on appropriate location and space, customised services, effective referral mechanisms, and confidentiality. The success of such programs within a comprehensive school health team service will therefore rely on involvement of all team members. Such involvement builds a project's legitimacy, facilitates referrals, increases the likelihood of the program being continued and reduces the burden of maintenance on health staff (Fiester et al. 1996). The following case study (from Embry et al. 1996) provides an example of one school-based violence prevention program that has adopted this type of team and community approach to overcoming the problem.

▶ CASE STUDY

PeaceBuilders: school-based violence prevention

PeaceBuilders was devised as a school-wide violence prevention program for early primary school children (years 1–5) in Arizona in the US. It is aimed at encouraging staff and students to work together to change the school climate and promote social behaviour. The approach is behavioural, based on the theory that youth violence can be reduced by initiating prevention early in childhood, by increasing children's resilience and reinforcing positive (non-violent) behaviours.

The theoretical foundation for the program contends that children at risk for violent behaviour are cognitively, socially and imitatively different from their non-violent peers. They tend to be suspicious of others, have difficulty reading non-verbal cues, and often misinterpret ambiguous events as hostile. Children in the 'at risk' group tend to insult their peers, disrupt

classroom activities and engage in higher rates of physical and verbal aggression than socially competent children. They tend to gravitate toward antisocial behaviours, and are often at risk for both victimisation and perpetration of violence.

Children participating in the PeaceBuilders program are taught five simple principles: to praise people, avoid put-downs, seek wise people as advisors and friends, notice and correct hurts caused by them, and right wrongs. Teachers, community volunteers and school administrators are familiarised with these tenets and provided with a set of support materials to encourage their participation in the program.

The school is seen as the ideal setting for the program as it is the setting for many daily antecedent events, behaviours by students (and teachers), and rewards (consequences) for positive actions. The school-based program capitalises on the daily rituals and language of the program. The expressions 'Peace Builders', 'Peace Cards', 'Peace Circle', 'Praise Notes' are all intended to foster a sense of belonging, cues and symbols that can be applied to diverse community settings. They also represent specific prompts that can be transferred between places, people, behaviours and time. In addition, new materials or strategies are introduced for times and circumstances when behaviour might otherwise decay.

The language of the program develops community 'norms'. Stories, models and environmental clues model positive behaviours. Role plays increase the range of potential responses and 'new way replays' allow the children to rehearse positive solutions after negative events. True to the behavioural model, response costs are incurred as punishment for negative behaviour. Group and individual rewards are provided to strengthen positive behaviour. Threat reduction is used to reduce reactivity to situations. Self and peer monitoring are used as reinforcers and generalisation promotion is used to promote maintenance of change across time, places and people.

The children are encouraged to spend time, perhaps lunch with a 'wise person' in their friendship network. This could be a family relative or a local business owner. The children also mentor one another, with older ones reading to younger ones from a newsletter they produce monthly. They are also given the opportunity to highlight their accomplishments by having their 'praise notes' featured on the school bulletin board, or in the local community TV station.

These aspects of behaviour change are intended to have a combined effect of changing the everyday interactions of students, staff and families. Teachers provide coaching by integrating the concepts of PeaceBuilding into their interactions and teaching strategies. Students participate in formal activities including such things as a 'PeaceBuilder Pledge' at the start of the day, or a 'Peace Circle' in which they compliment one another for various acts of helpfulness. They are taught to coach one another and to teach other family members about such things as praising one another. Parents are supplied with materials to help reinforce the appropriate behaviours. Staff and community volunteers attend training workshops so that they can help make PeaceBuilders a way of life at the school.

The PeaceBuilders program is currently the subject of intensive research, but early indications suggest wide acceptance by students, staff and community, and the value of community reinforcement for school-based interventions. This type of program is reliant on community involvement, and for this reason may not be appropriate in all settings or in other cultures. However, it does represent a prototype for refinement that could be adapted in other ways to other settings.

Using the school as the setting for health promotion shows enormous potential, especially in view of the fact that approximately 95% of all youth ages between 5 and 17 are enrolled in school (Centre for Disease Control 1997b). Schools therefore represent the major socialising environment in which children's attitudes toward health can be moulded (Nicklas et al. 1997). Integrating comprehensive health services into a school health program with wide environmental support may be an ideal way to meet the objectives of the Ottawa Charter for Health Promotion.

First, there must be healthy public policies that extend a commitment to funding health-promoting schools. Next, there must be widespread community support to provide an environment amenable to healthy schools. Community attitudes need to be evaluated in relation to the extent to which people will endorse the opportunity cost of increasing health education during school time. Wide consultation is required to ensure that culturally appropriate curricula match community and family values. Collaboration with all sectors of the community must be undertaken to strengthen community action. Time and resources must be allocated to developing the personal and professional skills of health care personnel, teachers, parents, and school administrators. In addition, there must be commitment by the health services industries to reorient delivery mechanisms to the school setting. This may require some shifting in expectations from traditional time lines for expected improvements in clinical outcomes to those that are synchronous with school systems. Most importantly, there must be further research to evaluate health promotion outcomes in the school setting. Numerous studies are necessary to extend existing research, to investigate refinements in costing school health services, to examine staffing issues relevant to outcomes and to conduct controlled trials of comparative approaches to health education in the school.

THINKING CRITICALLY
School health promotion

▶ Explain three ways in which education and health are interlinked.

▶ List five factors that influenced the development of comprehensive school health programs.

▶ Describe four ways in which the school setting can influence health behaviours.

▶ Describe the facilitating factors and barriers to developing a health-promoting school in your community.

▶ Identify the essential components of a school-based program to prevent drug and alcohol misuse.

REFERENCES

Adelman, H. & Taylor, L. 1997, 'Addressing barriers to learning: beyond school-linked services and full service schools', *American Journal of Orthopsychiatry*, vol. 67, no. 3, pp. 408–21.

Allensworth, D. & Kolbe, L. 1987, 'The comprehensive school health program. Exploring an expanded concept', *Journal of School Health*, vol. 57, pp. 409–73.

Anglin, T., Naylor, K. & Kaplan, D. 1996, 'Comprehensive school-based health care: high school students' use of medical, mental health, and substance abuse services', *Pediatrics*, vol. 97, no. 3, pp. 318–30.

Armbruster, P., Gerstein, S. & Fallon, T. 1997, 'Bridging the gap between service need and service utilization: A school-based mental health program', *Community Mental Health Journal*, vol. 33, no. 3, pp. 199–211.

Beaglehole, R. 1991, 'Science, advocacy, and health policy: lessons from the New Zealand tobacco wars', *Journal of Public Health Policy*, vol. 22, no. 30, pp. 175–83.

Bradley, B. 1997, 'The school nurse as health educator', *Journal of School Health*, vol. 67, no. 1, pp. 3–8.

Brindis, C. & Sanghvi, R. 1997, 'School-based health clinics: Remaining viable in a changing health care delivery system', *Annual Review of Public Health*, vol. 18, pp. 567–87.

Centre for Disease Control 1997a, 'Guidelines for school health programs to promote lifelong healthy eating', *Morbidity and Mortality Weekly Report*, vol. 45, no. RR-9, pp. 1–40.

Centre for Disease Control 1997b, 'School-based HIV prevention education—United States 1994', *Journal of School Health*, vol. 67, no. 3, pp. 103–5.

Chapman, S., King, M., Andrews, B., McKay, E., Markham, P. et al. 1994, 'Effects of publicity and a warning letter on illegal cigarette sales to minors', *Australian Journal of Public Health*, vol. 18, no. 1, pp. 31–42.

Collins, J., Leavy Small, M., Kann, L., Collins Pateman, B., Gold, R. et al. 1995, 'School health education', *Journal of School Health*, vol. 65, no. 8, pp. 302–11.

Commonwealth Department of Human Services and Health 1995, *The health of young Australians: a national health policy for children and young people*, AGPS, Canberra.

DeMuth Allensworth, D. & Bradley, B. 1996, 'Guidelines for adolescent preventive services: a role for the school nurse', *Journal of School Health*, vol. 66, no. 8, pp. 281–5.

Dusenbury, L. & Falco, M. 1995, 'Eleven components of effective drug abuse prevention curricula', *Journal of School Health*, vol. 65, no. 10, pp. 420–5.

Embry, D., Flannery, D., Vazsonyi, A., Powell, K. & Atha, H. 1996, 'PeaceBuilders: A theoretically driven, school-based model for early violence prevention', *American Journal of Preventive Medicine*, vol. 12, no. 5, pp. 91–100.

Fardy, P., White, R. Haltiwanger-Schmitz, K., Magel, J., McDermott, K. et al. 1996, 'Coronary disease risk factor reduction and behavior modification in minority adolescents: the PATH program', *Journal of Adolescent Health*, vol. 18, pp. 247–53.

Fiester, L., Nathanson, S., Visser, L. & Martin, J. 1996, 'Lessons learned from three violence prevention projects', *Journal of School Health*, vol. 66, no. 9, pp. 344–6.

Flaherty, L., Weist, M. & Warner, B. 1996, 'School-based mental health services in the United States: History, current models and need', *Community Mental Health Journal*, vol. 32, no. 4, pp. 341–52.

Hazell, J., Henry, R., Francis, J. & Halliday, J. 1995, 'Teacher-initiated improvement of asthma policy in schools', *Journal of Paediatric Child Health*, vol. 31, pp. 519–22.

Hinton Walker, P., Bowllan, N., Chevalier, N., Gullo, S. & Lawrence, L. 1996, 'School-based care: clinical challenges and research opportunities', *Journal of School and Pediatric Nursing*, vol. 1, no. 2, pp. 64–74.

Keyl, P., Hurtado, M., Barber, M. & Borton, J. 1996, 'School-based health centers', *Archives of Pediatric Adolescent Medicine*, vol. 150, pp. 175–80.

Kickbusch, I. & Jones, J. 1996, 'A health-promoting school starts with imagination', *World Health*, vol. 4 (July–Aug.), p. 4.

Kline, M., Schonfeld, D. & Lichtenstein, R. 1995, 'Benefits and challenges of school-based crisis response teams', *Journal of School Health*, vol. 65, no. 7, pp. 245–9.

Kolbe, L., Collins, J. & Cortese, P. 1997, 'Building the capacity of schools to improve the health of the nation', *American Psychologist*, vol. 52, no. 3. pp. 256–65.

Komro, K., Perry, C., Murray, D., Veblen-Mortenson, S., Williams, C. et al. 1996, 'Peer-planned social activities for preventing alcohol use among adolescents', *Journal of School Health*, vol. 66, no. 9, pp. 328–34.

Landis, S. & Janes, C. 1995, 'The Claxton elementary school health program: merging perceptions and behaviors to identify problems', *Journal of School Health*, vol. 65, no. 7, pp. 250–4.

Leavy Small, M., Smith Majer, L., Allensworth, D., Farquhar, B., Kann, L. et al. 1995, 'School health services', *Journal of School Health*, vol. 65, no. 8, pp. 319–26.

Mackie, J. & Oickle, P. 1997, 'School-based health promotion: the physician as advocate', *Canadian Medical Association Journal*, vol. 156, no. 9, pp. 1301–5.

Magyary, D. & Brandt, P. 1996, 'A school-based self-management program for youth with chronic health conditions and their parents', *Canadian Journal of Nursing Research*, vol. 28, no. 4, pp. 57–77.

McClowry, S., Galehouse, P., Hartnagle, W., Kaufman, H., Just, B. et al. 1996, 'A comprehensive school-based clinic: University and community partnership', *Journal of the Society of Pediatric Nursing*, vol. 1, no. 1, pp. 19–26.

McIntyre, L., Belzer, E., Manchester, L., Blanchard, W., Officer, S. et al. 1996, 'The Dartmouth health promotion study: a failed quest for synergy in school health promotion', *Journal of School Health*, vol. 66, no. 4, pp. 132–7.

Mitchell, I., Laforet-Fliesser, Y. & Camiletti, Y. 1997, 'Use of the healthy school profile in the Middlesex-London, Ontario, Schools', *Journal of School Health*, vol. 67, no. 4, pp. 154–6.

Mullen, P., Evans, D., Forster, J., Gottlieb, N., Kreuter, M. et al. 1995, 'Settings as an important dimension in health education/promotion policy, programs, and research', *Health Education Quarterly*, vol. 22, no. 3, pp. 329–45.

Nakajima, H. 1996, 'Health-promoting schools', *World Health*, vol. 4 (Jul.–Aug.), p. 3.

Neumark-Sztainer, D. 1996, 'School-based programs for preventing eating disturbances', *Journal of School Health*, vol. 66, no. 2, pp. 64–71.

Nicklas, T., Johnson, C., Webber, L. & Berenson, G. 1997, 'School-based programs for health risk-reduction', *Annals of the New York Academy of Sciences*, pp. 208–24.

Nutbeam, D. 1997, 'Promoting health and preventing disease: an international perspective on youth health promotion', *Journal of Adolescent Health*, vol. 20, pp. 396–402.

O'Byrne, D., Jones, J., Sen-Hai, Y. & Macdonald, H. 1996, 'WHO's global school health initiative', *World Health*, vol. 4 (Jul.–Aug.), pp. 5–6.

Patil, V., Solanki, M., Kowli, S., Naik, V., Bhalerao, V. et al. 1996, 'Long-term follow-up of school health education programmes', *World Health Forum*, vol. 17, pp. 81–2.

Ploeg, J., Ciliska, D., Dobbins, M., Hayward, S., Thomas, H. et al. 1996, 'A systematic overview of adolescent suicide prevention programs', *Canadian Journal of Public Health*, Sep.–Oct., pp. 319–24.

Resnicow, K. & Allensworth, D. 1996, 'Conducting a comprehensive school health program', *Journal of School Health*, vol. 66, no. 2, pp. 59–63.

Resnicow, K., Robinson, T. & Frank, E. 1996, 'Advances and future directions for school-based health promotion research: commentary on the CATCH intervention trial', *Preventive Medicine*, vol. 25, pp. 378–83.

Rickert, V., Davis, S., Riley, A. & Ryan, S. 1997, 'Rural school-based clinics: are adolescents willing to use them and what services do they want?', *Journal of School Health*, vol. 67, no. 4, pp. 144–8.

Ross, J., Einhaus, K., Hohenemser, L., Greene, B., Kann, L. et al. 1995, 'School health policies prohibiting tobacco use, alcohol and other drug use, and violence', *Journal of School Health*, vol. 65, no. 8, pp. 333–8.

Ryan, S., Jones, M. & Weitzman, M. 1996, 'School-based health services', *Current Opinion in Pediatrics*, vol. 8, pp. 453–8.

Santelli, J., Kouzis, A. & Newcomer, S. 1996, 'School-based health centers and adolescent use of primary care and hospital care', *Journal of Adolescent Health*, vol. 19, pp. 267–75.

Schlitt, J., Rickett, K., Montgomery, L. & Lear, J. 1995, ' State initiatives to support school-based health centers: a national survey', *Journal of Adolescent Health*, vol. 17, pp. 68–76.

Sedlak, M. 1997, 'The uneasy alliance of mental health services and the schools: an historical perspective', *American Journal of Orthopsychiatry*, vol. 67, no. 3, pp. 349–62.

Shope, J., Copeland, R., Marcoux, B. & Kamp, M. 1996, 'Effectiveness of a school-based substance abuse prevention program', *Journal of Drug Education*, vol. 26, no. 40, pp. 323–37.

Soon, T., Chan, R. & Goh, C. 1995, 'Project youth inform—a school-based sexually trans-mitted disease/Acquired Immune Deficiency Syndrome education programme', *Annals of Academic Medicine of Singapore*, vol. 24, pp. 541–6.

Stone, E. 1996, 'Can school health education programs make a difference?', *Preventive Medicine*, vol. 25, pp. 54–5.

Thyer, S. 1996, 'The "Health-promoting schools" Strategy: implications for nursing and allied health professionals', *Collegian*, vol. 3, no. 2, pp. 13–24.

Villalbi, J. 1997, 'The prevention of substance abuse in schools: a process evaluation of the effect of a standardised education module', *Promotion and Education*, vol 4, no. 1, pp. 15–19.

Walter, H., Vaughan, R., Armstrong, B., Krakoff, R., Tiezzi, L. et al. 1995, 'School-based health care for urban minority junior high school students', *Archives of Pediatric Adolescent Medicine*, vol. 149, pp. 1221–5.

Weist, M., Paskewitz, D., Warner, B. & Flaherty, L. 1996, 'Treatment outcome of school-based mental health services for urban teenagers', *Community Mental Health Journal*, vol. 32, no. 2, pp. 149–57.

Williams, J. 1996, 'The school environment and health', *Promotion and Education*, vol. 3, no. 1, pp. 10–13.

World Health Organization 1997, *Report of the World Health Organization Expert Committee on Comprehensive School Health Education and Promotion*, WHO, Geneva.

Healthy workplaces

15

Healthy workplaces represent an exemplary model for community health. From an ecological perspective, the workplace can be seen as an ecosystem, with the worker its biological core (McEvoy 1997). Because workplaces attract a large and captive audience with the opportunity for prevention of illness and injury, they are ideal settings in which public health goals can be achieved (Pearse 1997). Sustaining health and wellbeing is important to all workers—those who employ, those who are employed, and those in both paid and unpaid work. At a personal level, being healthy at work is fundamental to self-development. It allows socioeconomic gain, maintenance of skills, education and creative abilities, fulfilment of personal goals and, to some extent, a self-determined lifestyle. These personal accomplishments also help to fulfil family lifestyles and goals, provide continuity with the past, a link to the future, and a sense of communal belonging, particularly for those from diverse cultures. At the community level, healthy workers and healthy industries contribute to a community's socioeconomic capacity and interrelatedness with the wider global community.

This chapter examines the workplace and workplace health promotion as an important element of community health. It provides an overview of the historical developments leading up to the current emphasis on the workplace as an ideal setting for health promotion, and examines the links between healthy and sustainable workplaces, and the health and sustainability of the wider environment.

Objectives

By the end of this chapter you will be able to

- *explain the ecological aspects of workplace health and safety*

- *discuss the links between work and health*

- *describe the health potential of comprehensive workplace health promotion programs*

- *explain the role of healthy public policies in maintaining healthy workplaces*

- *design a comprehensive workplace health promotion program to respond to the needs of employers, employees and the industry.*

The evolution of workplace health and safety

The field of workplace, or occupational, health and safety is concerned with preserving and protecting the health of workers. Occupational health and safety services in the workplace have traditionally been an adjunct to work processes. They vary in the extent of services provided, from simple first aid to such protective services as hearing conservation, to general health promotion. Since the age of industrialisation, the field has evolved in tandem with increasing knowledge of workplace risk. Many occupational health and safety services have developed from a highly specialised and somewhat fragmented function of protecting a specific type of worker in a designated industry, to a more comprehensive approach, encompassing a philosophical view of work, workers and the workplace, in terms of their contribution to the common good.

In the early days of the industrial era, people accepted difficult working conditions—dust, heat, fumes and long hours—as part of industrialisation (Spradley & Allender 1996). In the US, Americans believed science and technology were the key to an orderly, productive life. The worker's body was considered an appendage of the machine, designed for economic gain, and accidents a necessary evil (McEvoy 1997). Workers were seen as mindless cogs who, under supervision, could perform their jobs as scripted, measured and ordered (Rest 1996). Following several disastrous and well publicised accidents, public pressure was brought to bear on the politics of the day, and factory laws and workers' compensation laws were enacted. This signalled the birth of the labour movement and the beginning of systematic research into occupational health and safety factors that was aimed at improving the conditions of work (McEvoy 1997; Spradley & Allender 1996).

In the 1900s the first studies of dust conditions were conducted in the mining, cement manufacturing and stone-cutting industries, and the incidence of lead poisoning was found to be as high as 22% in pottery workers (Spradley & Allender 1996). In 1914, also in the US, a study of garment workers showed a high incidence of tuberculosis related to poor ventilation, overcrowding and unsanitary working conditions. Following this, a proliferation of studies of hazardous conditions followed in other industries, and in other countries. This research interest has continued to the present time (Spradley & Allender 1996).

The growth of technology has been a mixed blessing for the worker. Technological innovations have streamlined many work processes, yet made them more labour intensive (Quinlan & Bohle 1991). Information technology has enabled scientific information and knowledge of the world of work to be shared between industries and between governments, creating a mechanism for sharing workplace standards and practices. This burgeoning field of knowledge includes: specific data relating to the structure and function of work as well as the materials and processes used; appropriate strategies for ensuring adequate and consistent education and training for employees; identification of the biophysical and psychosocial needs of workers, and management practices related to hazardous chemicals and industrial waste. Occupational health and safety practice today has evolved as a synthesis of healthy public policies, management accountability, employee understanding, and fair industrial relations (Pearse 1997; Quinlan & Boyle 1991).

Today, occupational health and safety is seen as integral to healthy communities and healthy societies. Labour is seen as 'more than economic activity controlled by impersonal market forces; it is the manifestation of the worker's life force, the expression of which makes human life distinctively human' (McEvoy 1997, p. 8). The health and safety of the working public is of increasing concern to all members of society. Of particular concern to public health are the statistics on workplace illness and injury. Seventeen million work-related injuries or illnesses and 99,000 work-related deaths occur in the US each year (US Statistical Abstracts 1994). Equally high rates of injury occur in other developed countries such as Canada (Sass 1996).

It is interesting that although Australia has comparable rates of injuries, the rate of fatalities is more than double that of the US and more than three times the rate in Britain, Sweden and Japan (Quinlan & Bohle 1991). Adjusted for population, this works out to at least 500 work-related accidental deaths per year, and 2000 deaths annually related to hazardous substances (Chu, Driscoll & Dwyer 1997; Couch 1994). Accident and injury prevention are therefore considered areas of high priority in Australian public health initiatives, as they are in other industrialised countries (AIHW 1996; Spradley & Allender 1996; Walters 1997).

Workplace health and community development

At the community level, a healthy workforce increases productivity and sustainable employment, thereby contributing to the achievement of economic goals. On the other hand, work accidents constitute a major example of both the costs and opportunities related to technological development. Workplace relations provide an opportunity to achieve equity and cross-cultural social exchange, contributing to public consciousness of the social order (McEvoy 1997). The workplace, and workplace health and safety initiatives, are therefore at the centre of a community's socioeconomic capability. The workplace is instrumental to sustainable development for the following reasons (from Pearse 1997):

■ Preventing accidents, injuries and diseases conserves precious human resources.

■ Safe working environments use the safest, low-energy, low-emission, low-waste technology and the best production technology and process management to avoid unnecessary loss of energy and materials.

■ Occupational identification of harmful environmental hazards can be done before they are exposed to the wider environment. The workplace thus provides an early warning system and the place to develop preventive action.

■ A healthy, productive and well-motivated workforce is the key agent for overall socioeconomic development.

■ Employment provides a place to sustain people and their families.

Although workplaces vary in many ways, five environmental risk factors are common to many. These are discussed here.

Physical factors

Physical hazards of work include structural aspects of the workplace that influence worker health and productivity. In some industries these can be electro-physical agents such as microwaves, lasers, ultra-sound or X-rays. Work space, temperature, lighting, noise, vibration, colour and pressure are also physical hazards. Physical conditions that create high risk for workers include: buildings and equipment that are unsound; exposure to ultra-violet radiation from the sun such as that experienced by migrant field workers, farmers, construction crews and, in hot climates, physical education teachers; and the unnatural pressure to which deep-sea divers or those working at high altitudes or in tunnels are exposed. Working in temperature extremes, or the confined spaces of chemical plants or refineries presents another physical hazard. In the agricultural services, manufacturing or transportation industries a worker may be exposed to improper gas exchange and tissue damage. Any of these may cause physical damage by affecting a worker's ears, sinuses and teeth. For health care workers, exposure to blood-borne pathogens such as hepatitis B and HIV provide another type of physical risk (Quinlan & Bohle 1991, Spradley & Allender 1996).

Chemical factors

Chemical factors are usually the first that come to mind in discussions of workplace health and safety risk. Chemicals may be gases, solvents, mists, vapours, dusts or solids. A range of chemicals are used in most production processes involving raw materials, in the daily operations of industries and businesses such as dry cleaners, painters, food companies, photographers, automobile manufacturers, plastics factories, farms, pharmaceutical companies, and hospitals. More than five million chemicals are registered and about 25,000 are added to the list each year. In the US, the petroleum and chemical industries subjects workers to several hundred untested new compounds per year (Spradley & Allender 1996). Countries like Australia import many of these (approximately 20,000 per year) and manufacture many more. Identification of their harmful effects lags far behind development, as only 2% of chemicals commonly used are accompanied by a summary analysis of their risk intended to inform all those handling the material (Material Safety Data Sheets). Only a fraction of these are subject to government regulation (Quinlan & Bohle 1991).

Chemicals can cause harm through burning the skin or other tissue, by irritating skin or the respiratory system, or through a sensitising effect which leads to long-term skin, lung or allergic complaints. The use of chemicals is also accompanied by risks related to their explosiveness or flammability (Spradley & Allender 1996). The adverse health effects of many chemicals may be exacerbated by other hazards, including physical and organisational ones. Communication problems are a classic example, especially in workers from a non-English-speaking background (Quinlan & Bohle 1991). Pregnant women may also be at increased risk from dangerous chemicals, as some of these (such as benzene and other compounds used in the plastics industries) may cause damage to the unborn foetus (Quinlan & Bohle 1991).

The most important aspect of working with chemicals involves understanding the toxicity and associated risks and making sure this information is widely disseminated. It is important to know: the threshold limit value (TLV, the amount of chemical exposure that produces toxicity); the routes by which chemicals enter the body; and the appropriate actions and personal protection that workers must take to prevent contamination. However, some have criticised the explication of TLV's in implying that there is a harmless level of exposure that can be practically distinguished from a harmful one. Because no *harmless* level exists, the employer must be clear that the issue is related to *acceptable levels*, not an *absence* of risk (Quinlan & Bohle 1991).

Biological factors

Biological workplace hazards include organisms and potential contaminants found in the work environment. Many of these place health care, child care and food preparation workers at risk, but they may also be hazardous to people working in other industries where work is undertaken outdoors or where there is food prepared. The hazards include bacteria, viruses, rickettsiae, moulds, fungi, parasites, insects, animals or toxic plants. Biological hazards may also be found in contaminated water or insects, improper waste or sewage disposal, unsanitary work environments, improper food handling, or unsanitary personal practices (Spradley & Allender 1996).

Ergonomic factors

Ergonomic problems in the workplace are the result of a mismatch between human and job factors. As a field, ergonomics is the study of human abilities and limitations and the application of this information to the design of the fabricated environment. An ergonomically appropriate workplace is one where workplaces, tools and tasks have been designed to match the physiological, anatomical and psychological characteristics and capabilities of the worker (Stobbe 1996). Besides mechanical features, these can include customs, laws, design, expectations of the work itself, physiological, anatomical and psychological demands of the job, and other workplace stressors that can cause anxiety (Faucett 1997; Quinlan & Bohle 1991; Stobbe 1996; Spradley & Allender 1996).

The rise of new work technologies has created a proliferation of ergonomically related hazards. Technological innovations have been responsible for the introduction of micro-electronic equipment into office work which entails specialised, and sometimes rapid, repetitive tasks. The ease of work afforded by the new technology is, however, accompanied by an increased risk of strain injuries and other health problems (Quinlan & Bohle 1991). Advanced mechanisation of the workplace has also increased the opportunity for a greater rate of injury. Technology has also increased the speed and spread of work so that today there is a larger number of people engaging in shift work and night work, which is known to be hazardous because of worker fatigue (Quinlan & Bohle 1991).

Many workplace illnesses and injuries are related to ergonomic problems. The most prevalent of these are cumulative trauma disorders (CTD) related to inadequate ergonomic design. The most familiar of these are back injuries and other musculoskeletal strains that occur in occupations where there is a large amount of manual handling required, and repetitive strain injuries, which affect many women clerical workers (Hatch 1996; Stobbe 1996). Manual handling guidelines have been developed as part of occupational health and safety regulations. These address a number of factors that contribute to back injuries, including specific conditions of the work, and guidelines for workers (Stobbe 1996). The guidelines cover such things as the weight and frequency of load (in lifting) and posture, lighting and pace of repetitive tasks involved in clerical work (Hatch 1996).

One of the reasons for the persistence of ergonomic injury is that, historically, the approach has been to design a workplace and then try to fit the workers into it through training, worker selection and other administrative schemes. With the rapid rise in CTD disorders, ergonomists are now trying to get employers to consider the worker at all stages of the design process, including the design of tools, equipment, lighting and ventilation (Stobbe 1996). This represents a more inclusive approach to workplace health and safety that is consultative and based on the experience of all involved in the process of work, rather than relying on external expertise.

Psychosocial factors

The responses and behaviours that workers exhibit on the job can also be a workplace hazard (Spradley & Allender 1996). Responses to work demands are the product of personal attitudes and values, but also represent work-site norms. For example, some employees have a fatalistic approach to work because of their perception of powerlessness. Workers who feel there is no real protection against risk because employers' priorities rest with productivity rather than safety are often deterred from taking individual precautions even when they are urged to do so by employers (Holmes & Gifford 1997).

Another psychosocial issue is related to the fact that certain types of work may be experienced differently by different people, so boring work may evoke agitation in some, calm in others. Working conditions that are time sensitive or conflict with personal values may cause stress that compromises health as well as performance of the job. Ethical dilemmas such as selling or promoting a product or service that might be injurious to others may also create undue stress in employees, as may peer pressure, labour disputes or unrealistic personal expectations. Stressors may also arise as a combination of personal and work stress, and may ultimately compromise work safety (Quinlan & Bohle 1991; Spradley & Allender 1996).

Organisational variables are another potential source of stress (Cooper, in Quinlan & Bohle 1991). These include factors intrinsic to the job, such as work overload or underload, physical danger, or a general lack of fit between workers' psychosocial characteristics and the work environment. Relationships at work are also a major cause of stress for many workers. For some, their role in the organisation may be problematic if there is role ambiguity, conflict with others, or responsibility for others' work practices. Workers may also be disadvantaged by organisational practices that may not be conducive to self-fulfilment or career development. Those who find themselves in an inappropriate status because they have been over-promoted or under-promoted, those who experience career blockages or who lack job security, tend to suffer most. Career blockages and the lack of congruence between status and skills tend to be particular problems for women, who may have come late to the workplace because of child care responsibilities. Some suffer subtle discrimination for their need to fulfil both workplace and home duties (Cooper, in Quinlan & Bohle 1991; Hatch 1996).

Work trends

In addition to the factors already mentioned, certain prevailing work trends present an additional burden on workers. To some extent, rapid technological changes have contributed to the decline of workplaces, to unemployment, segmentation of work processes and the density of work (increased tasks to be completed per hour) (Wenzel 1994). Despite the expectation that new technologies would ease the work burden, there is today increasingly intensive use of labour at a time of inadequate and inconsistent regulatory controls. Workers engaging in increasingly complex interactions with their equipment or machinery may suffer from the compound stress of working during non-standard working hours and working with new machinery. They may also be at risk in workplaces containing new chemicals and potentially harmful substances, or tending machinery that generate glare, noise, heat or cold, vibration, fumes and air-borne contaminants.

The 1990s have also seen a growth in self-employment and subcontracting, which carries its own peculiar group of risk factors (Quinlan & Bohle 1991). The construction industry, for example, is characterised by episodic involvement, changing and unpredictable worksites, rapid contractor turnover, and the use of subcontractors, which tends to sidestep legislative and union-based regulation (Quinlan & Bohle 1991; Ringen & Stafford 1996). Subcontracting is used where there is intense competition for goods and services which are labour intensive. The competition drives down returns and provides an incentive to complete tasks cheaply (Ringen & Stafford 1996). The ensuing work intensification to meet deadlines and economic targets can lead to hazardous work practices. In the building industry, workers may fail to erect proper scaffolding, reinforce trenches or use 'over-the-hand' brick-laying techniques. If injury occurs, they may ignore or delay treatment (Quinlan & Bohle 1991).

Identifying and communicating workplace risk

Although some workplace hazards fit into one or another risk category, workplace injury is best understood as the culmination of industrial, organisation, technical and human error processes rather than in terms of individualised and technical processes (Frye 1997). Many occupational factors are part of an interactive effect between individuals and the tools of their trade. For example, smoking and exposure to workplace chemicals is a lethal carcinogenic combination of risk factors. Known carcinogens (asbestos and vinyl chloride) continue to threaten the health of workers who may not take adequate protection (Quinlan & Bohle 1991). This may be related to their personal choice, or to a lack of information, which is an important element in ensuring safe workplaces.

Inadequate or ambiguous information can be hazardous not only to the worker, but to others in the work environment. The governments of most countries in the world have enacted legislation guiding work practices and workplace hazards that compels employers to identify and communicate workplace risk to the employees (Baker, Israel & Schurman 1996; Sass 1996; Walters 1997). In the US, where workplace health and safety is considered to be at an advanced level, the General Duty Clause, as set down by the Occupational Safety and Health Authority (OSHA), describes a hazard as something that is recognisably dangerous if it is known to be so by either the employee, the employer, or others belonging to the same industrial sector (Baram 1996; Christenson 1995). This level of ambiguity leaves the interpretation of risk open to exploitation, and is not helpful to workers or companies (Baram 1996). A similar situation occurs in other countries, where the interpretation of the employer's duty of care to the employee is not always clear.

One effect of the increasing bureaucratisation of occupational health and safety services has been a lack of information-sharing between the scientific community, employers, and government and non-government agencies (Schurman 1996). The impact of this can be lethal, as we have learned in the case of asbestos-related diseases. In Canada, for example, insurance companies refused to provide cover for asbestos workers as early as 1904; yet in other countries, production of asbestos products escalated, with regulatory controls being introduced only in the 1970s. Researchers working on epidemiological studies in Australia have now linked a range of respiratory diseases, including mesothelioma to asbestos used in the mining industry in the 1950s (Hobbs et al., in Quinlan & Bohle 1991). As a result of this research, it is now recognised that there is no safe level of asbestos exposure, a fact of extreme importance to Australians, who have the highest rate of asbestos-related mesotheliomas in the world (Quinlan & Bohle 1991).

Government bodies have also failed in their attempt to direct the occupational research agenda in a concerted way. In the mid-1970s the research into occupational health promotion paralleled that in the broader field, by concentrating on factors influencing worker behaviour (the present author, apologetically, included) (Esler-McMurray 1978). The context of work was not included in many of the studies undertaken and, even today, some studies adopt the 'victim blaming' approach of the previous era, attributing accidental injuries to the victim's accident-proneness (Salminen & Heiskanen 1997).

To some extent, this shortcoming in the occupational health and safety research agenda is a failure of the national research-funding bodies to incorporate workplace issues as an integral part of their public health research profile, a situation that persists today. One recent study in the US found that the majority of local health departments across the country have little knowledge of occupational health and safety. Instead, these issues and problems appear to be nested deeply within other priorities (Christenson 1995). Only scant information filters down to the level of general practice, creating a difficulty for workers in receiving appropriate medical attention. One study of GPs in the UK found that as recently as 1996, few British GPs had any knowledge of occupational health and safety and most believed that the relevant legislation was irrelevant to them (Osborne 1997).

Political events have also constrained the occupational health and safety research agenda. With the economic decline of the 1980s, the occupational health and safety movements have also stalled. Regulatory agencies are reticent in responding to workers' rights to know, to participate and to refuse dangerous work. In North America, neo-conservative policies have been intensified by the North American Free Trade Agreement (NAFTA) and the General Agreement on Tariffs and Trade (GATT), resulting in the globalisation of capital and labour. So instead of these political events facilitating expansion of workplace health and safety initiatives, they have had a directly opposite effect (Sass 1996).

Researching occupational health

Contemporary research trends reveal that occupational researchers are using a range of techniques, including occupational epidemiology, to establish distribution and determinants of conditions and causal relationships between work factors and illness (Chu, Driscoll & Dwyer 1997; Frye 1997; Quinlan & Bohle 1991; Thacker et al. 1996). Epidemiological data provide information on dose–response or safe limits of substances used in industrial processes. Through case control studies, such as the one that defined the link between asbestos and mesothelioma, they are able to compare outcomes in one area or one group that were exposed to a harmful substance, with another that may not have been exposed (Quinlan & Bohle 1991).

Another extension of this type of research uses a hazard–exposure–outcome axis to show complementary information on the hazard, the exposure history, and the health outcomes (Thacker et al. 1996). Researchers using these techniques expect that their surveillance data will detect epidemics, and clusters of specific birth defects from newly emerging conditions (toxic shock syndrome). This information can inform those developing guidelines on various levels of risk as a basis for prioritising control activities (Thacker et al. 1996).

Despite the contribution to knowledge of workplace health and safety made by occupational epidemiologists, there is a need to broaden the research agenda. Some researchers claim that the type of studies being conducted in the work environment, which are primarily medical and technical, has retarded meaningful workforce reforms. Many studies have been considered an intrusion into workers' experiences in the work environment, and have failed to inform employer practices, particularly relating to education of the workers (Sass 1996). Occupational health activists understand that education goes beyond information, to understanding of workers' traditions and goals. Research must therefore examine the actual situations of work, including how workers experience the environment—dizziness, nausea, irritability, menstrual problems—rather than how the statute and regulations define working conditions (Sass 1996).

Gender issues

One of the factors impeding progress in identifying work-related diseases has been the lack of research on women workers. Gender-biased differentiation of work is a universal phenomenon. Women make up roughly half the workforce but their numbers are not widely distributed across occupations and industries (Hatch 1996). With the exception of visual terminal display (VDT) use, most hazards common to female-dominated industries have been virtually ignored. During the World Wars, two cohorts of women were studied extensively. During the First World War, those exposed to radium in the course of painting radium dials on wrist watches were part of an investigation into radiation-related illness, and during the Second World War, women testing asbestos masks in Britain were subjects in studies of asbestos-related disease (Hatch 1996).

The first group added to our knowledge of head, neck and bone sarcomas related to radium, and to our understanding of the concept of *dose–response*—that is, the amount of radium that causes harmful reactions. The second group, many of whom developed mesotheliomas, added to our knowledge of lung cancer and asbestos-related aetiology. These studies raise ethical questions, even in the present, with research on women workers still in its infancy. The ethics of employing women for a certain job without sufficient data on the health implications of the work is a major concern. Those currently involved in researching women at work suggest that we need careful documentation of all cases of chemical-related illnesses and gender-oriented exposure registries, especially with so many women entering traditional male occupations (Hatch 1996).

In addition to workplace illnesses, there is a need for careful examination of injuries peculiar to women, with respect to social factors. One study of female aerospace workers found that those with young children were at a two- to five-fold increased risk of on-the-job injury compared to women without children. The researchers were unable to conclude whether this reflected fatigue or the preoccupation arising from household responsibilities (Hatch 1996). Children must also be included in the occupational research agenda as they also are the victims of occupational accidents, primarily in relation to agricultural work or as bystanders to work and, in the case of adolescents, as newcomers to the workforce (Mandryk & Harrison 1995).

Injuries and illness in the workplace need also to be examined in the context of labour market segmentation. Vulnerable groups such as women, migrants and the disabled have been disadvantaged by restricted employment opportunities. As a result, they often hesitate to report problems at work. This needs to be addressed by formal differentiation in legislation, in workplace design, and in the subtle and complex processes that affect the origin, reporting and treatment of illnesses and injuries (Frye 1997). Workers also need to be involved in the processes of collecting and analysing data to ensure that problems are both framed and investigated in such a way as to eliminate ambiguity and any suspicion of exploitation (Baram 1996; Sass 1996).

Another approach to examining the workplace that has thus far been overlooked is the ecological context of work. Environmental approaches to workplace research emphasise context and contingency, describing the connections between workers and the tangible instruments of work (technology) (McEvoy 1996). This type of approach re-frames industrial development in terms of social organisation, allowing us to look at how ecology, political economy and consciousness interact with each other over time. In today's climate of conservation, there is a need to examine closely interactions between the worker's body and its maintenance, the productive processes that draw on the worker's energy, and the law and ideology that guide them (McEvoy 1996).

In addition, there needs to be a concerted effort to integrate research information on workplace health and safety. We need surveillance systems for certain occupations or industries, or for specific occupational disorders. Individual employers need to maintain information networks to communicate the importance of workplace health promotion and the process by which it can be achieved (Baker, Israel & Schurman 1996; Chu, Driscoll & Dwyer 1997). This would assist in globalisation of workplace health and safety information by providing a national data bank of diagnostic and evaluative information with which to evaluate workplace health profiles and to assess and compare various workplaces (Chu, Driscoll & Dwyer 1997). These could be developed to include information on the wider social, political, economic and cultural environment of work, which would help to avoid linear and polarised (the worker or the system) explanations for accident causation and occupational illness (Couch 1994; Holmes & Gifford 1997).

Health-promoting workplaces

Reducing risk involves a multifaced approach that includes engineering, administrative, behavioural and regulatory mechanisms (Faucett 1997). Most occupational health programs that have been instituted this century have focused primarily on prevention (eliminating hazardous substances or conditions) and protection of the worker. These programs have used a range of techniques including job analysis, pre-placement examinations to ensure a good 'fit' between the worker and the job, hazard communication, materials handling and training, and various forms of health surveillance. They have attempted to educate and support workers, provide treatment and guidance for occupational and non-occupational illnesses and injuries, and institute rehabilitation programs for those requiring them (Quinlan & Bohle 1991).

One of the problems with these occupational health and safety programs has been an over-reliance on medical information. Workplace physicians have traditionally been responsible for determining a worker's fitness to pursue a particular work role (Couch 1994; Quinlan & Bohle 1991).

In the 1970s, at the height of the health promotion era, workplace health promotion programs were also established, usually in addition to, rather than as a part of, occupational health and safety initiatives. Just like the general public, workers were encouraged to participate in programs designed to teach them to eat well, quit smoking and get fit. Delivering these messages in the workplace was based on the premise that it was the appropriate setting for behaviour change, particularly with a captive audience, and because the programs were generally well accepted by both labour unions and employers (Frye 1997).

Under the guidance of professionals skilled in health education and health promotion, worksite health promotion programs flourished. In the US, for example, the National Survey of Worksite Health Promotion Activities in 1989 found that approximately two-thirds of companies with more than fifty employees have some sort of health promotion programs, most aimed at individual behaviour change with some social and environmental support (Quinlan & Bohle 1991).

After two decades of experience with these programs, a new, comprehensive and integrated approach is being advocated. As with other health promotion strategies of the 1970s, personal lifestyle changes were seen to be only part of the problem, and these programs were criticised as blaming the victim (Chu, Driscoll & Dwyer 1997). At the same time, workplace medical screening was losing favour, on the basis that such practices may be exploitative if the information was used to deny workers' compensation or to circumvent the employer making structural changes in the workplace (Quinlan & Bohle 1991). It was also recognised that mass employee screening had failed to prove cost effective in terms of either worker health or employer goals (Labonte 1994).

Today there is widespread recognition that in order to create a healthy workplace, it is necessary to understand the nature of social relationships and their contribution to health. Worker satisfaction is a function of social integration or isolation, social network structure, relational content, demands or conflicts, and social and organisational regulation (Quinlan & Bohle 1991). To create a healthy workplace therefore requires strengthening social support and examining organisational policies, especially those (such as forced overtime) that compromise family life (Quinlan & Bohle 1991).

Today's health promoters advocate a systemic approach that acknowledges the interdependence of structural, environmental, organisational and individual factors at work and in the community (Chu, Driscoll & Dwyer 1997).

The organisation of labour, the distribution of power and influence, relation-ships between employers and employees, and aspects of the overall social structure of a society are all now recognised as influencing personal health and wellbeing (Rest 1996; Wenzel 1994). The labour structure represents applica-tion of societal values, belief systems, economic, social and cultural dimensions in a materialistic way. In order to empower workers, all aspects of work, including health and safety, need to be incorporated into comprehensive goals for healthy living and healthy working (Wenzel 1994). To achieve these goals an integrated, interdisciplinary team approach is necessary so that the exper-tise of many areas is included and mutual influence of multiple strategies and influences can be acknowledged (Quinlan & Bohle 1991).

The comprehensive workplace health promotion program

Workplace health promotion (WHP) is defined as:

> *Those educational, organisational or economic activities in the workplace that are designed to improve the health of workers and therefore the community at large. This type of health promotion involves workers and management participation on a voluntary basis in the implementation of jointly agreed programs which utilise the workplace as a setting for promoting better health (National Steering Committee on Health Promotion in the Workplace, in Chu 1994, p. 185).*

A comprehensive approach to workplace health promotion extends the occupational health and safety approach to the application of public health principles. This is accomplished by including health in corporate policy, cre-ating a safe working environment, enabling workers to be represented on health and safety committees, developing health skills through education, and placing the emphasis on prevention rather than cure (Australasian College of Occupational Medicine, in Chu 1994). This exemplifies a com-munity development approach in the workplace.

Guidelines for establishing a comprehensive WHP program include the following (from Chu & Forrester 1992, p. 61):

■ WHP must be made an integral part of a corporate culture. Programs should be comprehensive, address both individual and broader environ-mental and structural issues and have ongoing and long-term managerial commitment.

- WHP that aim to improve workers' health by addressing individual risk factors should also consider the underlying workplace structures and practices that bring about exposure to such hazards and how improvements can be made that can result in better health.
- A community development approach emphasising grass-roots participation, self-determination and empowerment should be adopted as an essential WHP strategy to involve workers in the planning, decision making, organisation, and implementation of WHP programs.
- WHP must be an activity shared by both employees and employers, with health professionals acting as facilitating and mediating agents.

As with all community development approaches, community participation is the key to success. Real participation involves workers having a say on meaningful issues and being involved in negotiation, problem-solving and decision-making (Rest 1996). Workers may be asked to participate in waste management decisions, practices that increase service or productive capacity, improved efficiency and enhancement of quality processes, including health and safety (Rest 1996). In order to participate at this level, workers also need information and participatory training techniques. This may be rewarding in itself, in that it helps cultivate further marketable skills.

Worker participation illustrates the constant interplay between working conditions and work-health-related patterns of behaviour and action. Wenzel (1994) calls this *workstyles*; these symbolise the reservoir of shared and normative values within and between professional groups. The main objective of health programs for the working world should be the development of workstyles conducive to health. Collective workstyles are socially, culturally, historically, technologically, politically and economically developed patterns of actions related to specific occupations, developed during vocational training and the first years of occupational socialisation.

The development of workstyles is always related to structural features of the work environment and workplace, or industrial goals. This diminishes the potential for conflict in worker and workplace values. As Wenzel (1994, p. 176) suggests, 'it is a contradiction *per se* to develop lifestyles conducive to health in a society which produces unhealthy products and environments'. Workers who are included in the life and mission of the workplace can make a substantial contribution to the process of broadening workplace health and safety to a more comprehensive program for health in the workplace. In addition, they need the support of healthy workplace policies.

Healthy workplace policies

In the US, the National Occupational Safety and Health Authority is engaged in ongoing workplace reform (Baram 1996). In Canada all thirteen jurisdictions have legislated three basic workers' rights: the right to know about chemicals in work environment; the right to participate in joint health and safety committees with a role of surveillance and monitoring the work environment; and the right to refuse dangerous work (Sass 1996).

In the European region, the integrated approach that combines structural as well as personal factors has played a far more prominent role in worksite health promotion than in the non-European developed world. The humanisation of work—the interplay between trade unions and employers to improve working conditions—has been adopted as government policy for a number of years, especially in the Scandinavian countries (Wenzel 1994). In Scandinavia, work is seem as a meaningful and enriching aspect of the human environment (Rest 1996).

The European Union's Framework Directive of 1989 made implicit the integration of preventive functions in occupational health and safety, to broaden the concept of occupational medicine to occupational health (Walters 1997). Many large enterprises or well-resourced group services have now complied with legislation as well as involving workers and their representatives in the appointment and oversight of the operation of workplace health and safety services. In the Scandinavian countries, worker participation is paramount. Joint health and safety committees have a substantial role in decision-making on the implementation of workplace health and safety services. As well as improving legislation, the Netherlands, Sweden, Denmark and Finland have improved quality, integration, accountability and adaptability of preventive services (Walters 1997).

Not all European countries have succeeded in securing the level of worker participation that is seen in Scandinavia, but most southern European countries have introduced or significantly improved provisions for preventive services. These are somewhat less in France, Belgium and Germany, where the medical model still dominates (Walters 1997). In Britain and Ireland there remains a lack of specific legislative requirements to encourage either comprehensive workplace health promotion or greater participation by workers. Management of Health and Safety at Work Regulations (1994) is only slowly being taken on board within the NHS in Britain (Aziz 1996). The number and breadth of programs have fallen with cuts in public expenditure during the 1990s and a decline in trade union membership. This shows the importance of trade union support for worker representation in occupational health and safety education and training and its integration with other services in the workplace (Walters 1997).

In Japan, the trend persists toward occupational health and fitness programs. Of 395 companies that participated in a survey of WHP programs, 70% said they had health guidance and fitness programs (Muto et al. 1996). Japan has regulatory mechanisms, the Industrial Safety and Health Law, for providing employees with adequate occupational health services. Budgetary restrictions and lack of facilities are governed by the attitudes of corporate management toward health promotion policy. Although data showing the results of WHP programs are considered the best way of convincing others to follow suit, few have been evaluated (Muto et al. 1996).

In Australia, the Australian National Steering Committee on Health Promotion in the Workplace has recommended the following measures, guided by the four principles of prevention, participation, equity and access, and responsibility (from Chu, Driscoll & Dwyer 1997):

■ including health issues on planning agendas—that is, corporate plans
■ creating a safe environment that supports people's health
■ enabling people to act in the interests of their health by participation in health and safety committees
■ developing personal health skills through education
■ emphasising prevention rather than cure.

Despite these worthy goals, there remain variable legislation and variable implementation of policies between Australian States (Quinlan & Bohle 1991).

In this era of cost containment it is important to gain value for investment. This can be accomplished by capitalising on the health potential of work. As a first step, we need to ensure better information gathering and dissemination. The next step is to investigate best practice models of creating healthy workplaces. Finally, workplace health and safety must continue to be at the centre of political activities aimed at sustaining community development. An ecological view of health dictates that the health of the working population must be seen as part of the harmonious interaction with the political, economical and social elements necessary for society to thrive in the next century and beyond.

► CASE STUDY

Worker participation in a manufacturing industry

The case study described here is a true account of the author's involvement in a workplace health and safety program at a biscuit manufacturing plant in Canada in the 1970s. It was one of the most enjoyable roles of my professional career, not only because of the bonus jelly beans and chocolate biscuits that I received each pay day, but because of what I learned from the world of factory work about multicultural, industrial and human relations.

The company was situated in an inner-city industrial area and had been there for many years. The owners had resisted several offers to purchase the land, despite the potential for considerable profit. One of the reasons for this was that its location was accessible to the majority of workers, most of whom lived in the neighbourhood and walked to work. The factory was also a landmark, a source of pride sitting in the middle of the city. The owners rejected another element of progress—worker unionisation. They boasted a 'plant committee' which, although it sounded innocuous, turned out to be a very powerful, participatory force, contributing to a relatively contented workforce.

My role in the company was as occupational health nurse. I had been appointed to conduct pre-placement and periodic physical examinations, to render first aid, to process illness-oriented absentee forms and to refer to the visiting physician any ongoing or serious health problems. It was an interesting challenge, particularly as a large proportion of the workforce, mostly young women, were newly arrived immigrants, and just learning to speak English.

After I had been working at the plant for approximately two months, I couldn't help but notice an extraordinary number of cases of tenosynovitis (which today would be called repetitive strain injury), among young female packers. None would remove themselves from

the workforce, even temporarily, so I would bandage them and send them back to work. Although the individual cases seen in the health service were confidential, it was my responsibility to report aggregated information on matters that seemed relevant to the manufacturing supervisors. Armed with statistical data, I contacted the plant manager, who listened to my concerns, and then attempted to dissuade me from pursuing the issue further. He explained that my vigilance might jeopardise the workers because if their problems persisted, they may be replaced on the 'packing line'. The packing line happened to be a difficult area for new employees to break into, because the offer of bonuses for increased production made it attractive as a place to work. There was a waiting list to shift to the packing line, and those working the line guarded their jobs zealously. I left the plant manager's office in a quandary and decided to discuss my concerns with others in different areas of the plant.

I approached a group of senior workers who I knew to be active participants in the plant committee. This group were the long-standing employees (all males), who ran the candy-making operations on a floor separate to where the young women worked. Having previously established a relationship of mutual trust with these men, I asked them for help. My questions revolved around the ergonomic design of the packing area. I asked if anyone had looked at the design of the conveyor belts, or attempted to work out why the packers were experiencing such pain. Their replies were cautious, and a bit dismissive. They appreciated my concern, as they knew the rest of the employees would, but they refused to take the matter to the plant committee.

My next step was to try to catch up with some of the young women after work to discuss their perceptions of the cause. This was necessary because when they visited the health centre, their time off the job was clocked to what was expected as a minimum absence from the line. This precluded any in-depth interview that would have shed light on the problem. Unfortunately, the women were hesitant to share any information relating to their jobs with me outside the treatment room. I thought it strange, but decided to not break their trust by pressing them for further information.

Over the next two months, I continued to collect information about the women's strain injuries and also noted signs of extreme psychological stress in all those who visited the health centre. After this amount of time had passed, I felt it was time for further action. My discussion with the plant physician was singularly unrewarding. 'Don't worry about it,' was his response. 'These are immigrant girls who want desperately to stay here.' I left his office wondering if he was talking about staying 'here' in the plant, or 'here' in the country. The plot thickened. Next, I visited the general manager and finally found a sympathetic ear. He walked me through the entire production process, explaining the work at each stage. He, too, wanted to keep a healthy workforce and was particularly unhappy with the thought of either increased turnover among his employees, or the threat of the plant committee becoming militant. I received permission from him to 'work the line' for a week, a move that, despite vehement opposition by the line supervisor and the plant manager, eventuated the following week.

It took one shift to work out what was happening on the assembly line. The conveyor belt began each morning at a pre-set speed. An hour or so into the shift, the belt supervisor would surreptitiously swing her knee over the control dial and speed up the belt unexpectedly. The women would pack faster. Their movements were made difficult by the fact that the supervisor was tall, and had set the height of the belt accordingly.

Most of the workers were from the Mediterranean areas, and were under five feet in height. To reach the belt they had to assume an awkward angle. To pack meant sustained forearm movements at that angle. When the speed of the belt was varied, they were continually making adjustments to their movements with no recovery time. In addition, they were forbidden by the belt manager to talk during the work, so the tension mounted and, with increasing arm pain, they developed tense posture, holding their neck and shoulders rigid in an attempt to keep up.

Having witnessed a situation one could only describe as inhumane, my task was clear. I requested a meeting with the belt supervisor to discuss the problem. Of course, her reaction was that production processes had nothing to do with my role or the health and safety of the workers. Over the next two weeks, I had several discussions with her and tried to draw her attention to the outcomes of what she described as scheduling decisions. In the end, my persistence paid off, and fortuitously, while she herself was away on sick leave, the plant committee took up the matter with the general manager.

The general manager was extremely helpful for reasons that I chose to view as compassionate rather than economical. As a result of his interventions, the following policies were put in place. Workers were allowed to talk during production. The belt speed was to be constant during each shift, with workers being informed of the production schedule and their expected role in fulfilling it. The belt was lowered to accommodate the majority of the workers. Those who had been suffering severe strain were given sick leave with a guarantee of their job when they returned. Education sessions were conducted to explain the mechanical processes of the work to workers, and to people such as myself, who needed a deeper understanding of the work. During these sessions, I attempted to teach the workers a few things that they needed to know about their health and wellbeing but more importantly, I learned of the stress and anxiety that accompanies migration to a new country and then the transition to a new workplace.

I was also invited to participate in the plant committee as a fully fledged member rather than as someone peripheral to the operation of the plant. This proved to be invaluable, as other issues emerged that had been confined to one or another work group. With increased interaction, the work groups seemed to gain a greater coherence and a sense of pride in their company. Slowly, the occupational health service that had begun to react to the health problems of the workforce shifted to a stronger emphasis on prevention and protection.

This experience taught me to never exclude a single element of human behaviour in seeking to promote health. What people do in their daily lives is fundamental to the creation of health. For those of us who are charged with helping them sustain this, it is an important lesson.

THINKING CRITICALLY

Healthy workplaces

▶ Give three reasons why occupational health and safety is important to community development.

▶ Explain how the workplace can be seen as an ecosystem.

▶ Identify four main features of healthy workplace policy.

▶ In an occupational health setting of your choice, discuss the interaction between organisational features, physical and demographic characteristics of the workers, and health and safety hazards in the workplace.

▶ Devise a comprehensive workplace health and safety program for a widget manufacturing company of 500 employees.

REFERENCES

Australian Institute of Health and Welfare 1996, *Australia's Health 1996*, AGPS, Canberra.

Aziz, B. 1996, 'Developing good policies for the health of pregnant workers', *Nursing Times*, vol. 92, no. 47, pp. 32–3.

Baker, E., Israel, B. & Schurman, S. 1996, 'The integrated model: implications for worksite health promotion and occupational health and safety practice', *Health Education Quarterly*, vol. 23, no. 2, pp. 175–90.

Baram, M. 1996, 'Generic strategies for protecting worker health and safety', *Occupational Medicine*, vol. 11, no. 1, pp. 69–77.

Christenson, G. 1995, 'Application of core function concepts to local health department occupational safety and health initiatives', *American Journal of Preventive Medicine*, vol. 11, no. 6, pp. 45–50.

Chu, C. 1994, 'An integrated approach to workplace health promotion', in *Ecological Public Health: From Vision to Practice*, eds C. Chu & R. Simpson, Institute of Applied Environmental Research, Brisbane, pp. 182–94.

Chu, C. & Forrester, C. 1992, *Workplace Health Promotion in Queensland*, Ministry for Health, Housing and Community Services, Brisbane.

Chu, S., Driscoll, T. & Dwyer, S. 1997, 'The health-promoting workplace: an integrative perspective', *Australian and New Zealand Journal of Public Health*, vol. 21, no. 4, pp. 377–85.

Couch, M. 1994, 'Health impacts of work: the case of Broken Hill miners', in *Just Health: Inequality in Illness, Care and Prevention*, eds C. Waddell & A. Petersen, Churchill-Livingstone, Melbourne, pp. 73–86.

Esler-McMurray A. 1978, 'Attitude change in an industrial hearing conservation program', *Occupational Health Nursing*, vol. 26, no. 1, pp. 15–20.

Faucett, J. 1997, 'The ergonomics of women's work', in *Women's Health Complexities and Differences*, eds S. Ruzek, V. Olesen & A. Clarke, Ohio State University Press, Columbus, pp. 154–72.

Frye, L. 1997, 'Occupational health surveillance', *American Association of Occupational Health Nurses Journal*, vol. 45, no. 4, pp. 184–7.

Hatch, M. 1996, 'Women's work and women's health', *Epidemiology Prevention*, vol. 20, pp. 176–9.

Holmes, N. & Gifford, S. 1997, 'Narratives of risk in occupational health and safety: why the "good" boss blames his tradesman and the "good" tradesman blames his tools', *Australian and New Zealand Journal of Public Health*, vol. 21, no. 1, pp. 11–16.

Labonte, R. 1994, '"See me, hear me, touch me, feel me": lessons on environmental health information for bureaucratic activists', in *Ecological Public Health: From Vision to Practice*, eds C. Chu & R. Simpson, Institute of Applied Environmental Research, Brisbane, pp. 269–76.

Mandryk, J. & Harrison, J. 1995, 'Work-related deaths of children and adolescents in Australia 1982 to 1984', *Australian Journal of Public Health*, vol. 19, no. 1, pp. 46–9.

McEvoy, A. 1997, 'Working environments: An ecological approach to industrial health and safety', *Clio Medica*, vol. 41, pp. 59–89.

Muto, T., Kikuchi, S., Tomita, M., Fujita, Y., Kurita, M. et al. 1996, 'Status of health promotion program implementation and future tasks in Japanese companies', *Industrial Health*, vol. 34, pp. 101–11.

Osborne, K. 1997, 'General practices and health and safety at work', *British Journal of General Practice*, vol. 47, pp. 103–4.

Pearse, W. 1997, 'Occupational health and safety: a model for public health', *Australian and New Zealand Journal of Public Health*, vol. 21, no. 1, pp. 9–10.

Quinlan, M. & Bohle, P. 1991, *Managing Occupational Health and Safety in Australia: A Multidisciplinary Approach*, MacMillan, Melbourne.

Rest, K. 1996, 'Worker participation in occupational health programs', *American Association of Occupational Health Nursing Journal*, vol. 44, no. 5, pp. 221–5.

Ringen, K. & Stafford, E. 1996, 'Intervention research in occupational safety and health: examples from construction', *American Journal of Industrial Medicine*, vol. 29, pp. 314–20.

Salminen, S. & Heiskanen, M. 1997, 'Correlations between traffic, occupational, sports, and home accidents', *Accident Analysis and Prevention*, vol. 29, no. 1, pp. 33–6.

Sass, R. 1996, 'A strategic response to the occupational health establishment', *International Journal of Health Services*, vol. 26, no. 2, pp. 355–70.

Schurman, S. 1996, 'Making the "New American Workplace" safe and healthy: a joint labor–management–researcher approach', *American Journal of Industrial Medicine*, vol. 29, pp. 373–7.

Spradley, B. & Allender, J. 1996, *Community Health Nursing: Concepts and Practice*, 4th edn, Lippincott, Philadelphia.

Stobbe, T. 1996, 'Occupational ergonomics and injury prevention', *Occupational Medicine*, vol. 11, no. 3, pp. 531–43.

Thacker, S., Stroup, D., Gibson Parrish, R. & Anderson, H. 1996, 'Surveillance in environmental public health: issues, systems and sources', *American Journal of Public Health*, vol. 86, no. 5, pp. 633–7.

US Government 1994, *US Statistical Abstracts 1994*, 114th edn, US Government Printing Office, Washington.

Walters, D. 1997, 'Preventive services in occupational health and safety in Europe: developments and trends in the 1990s', *International Journal of Health Services*, vol. 27, no. 2, pp. 247–71.

Wenzel, E. 1994, 'Conceptual issues in worksite health promotion', in *Ecological Public Health: From Vision to Practice,* eds C. Chu & R. Simpson, Institute of Applied Environmental Research, Brisbane, pp. 172–81.

Community health issues:

a global approach

Introduction

Part four of this book addresses issues common to all communities seeking to create and sustain health. The most important of these is the organisation of health care, and this is the subject of chapter 16. In all countries, the health care system represents the formalisation of government commitment to the health and wellbeing of the community and its capacity to provide the infrastructure for health and health services. In order to operationalise this commitment, it is essential that the health care system itself be a healthy organisation.

Like other healthy organisations, the health care system must be efficient and effective in its management, ethical in its conduct, equitable and accessible to all members of the community, strategic in its endeavours to meet the needs of current and future communities, transparent in communicating its goals and capabilities, oriented toward empowering its members to make informed choices, and resourced to the extent that it can support those choices. These elements of the health care system will be discussed in the context of an international comparison of health care systems and their efforts toward the organisation and delivery of health care.

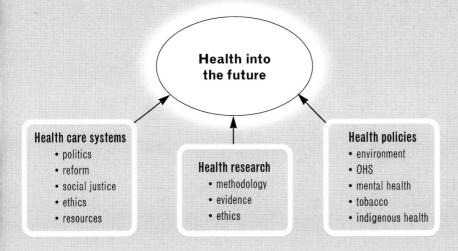

Health care systems are also part of the wider political agenda, which has enormous influence on the creation and sustainability of health. One of the ways in which this is communicated to people is through research into issues that inform community health policy and practices. The research agenda is thus an important aspect of public commitment to continuous improvement of community health. Despite the rhetoric of process and outcome evaluation in health services, evidence-based health care practice, and quality improvement, many questions remain to be addressed in today's health care environments. These must be incorporated into the culture of health care and health services as integral to improving organisational processes. This does not mean that all practitioners and all administrators need to become researchers, but it implies that the mechanisms and outcomes of the health care system are transparent and therefore open to inspection. It also means that resources need to be deployed to those with the commitment and the expertise to contribute to the scientific foundations for improving community health. These research issues are discussed in chapter 17.

Chapter 18 provides an analysis of healthy public policies for the future, the most pressing issues that must be drawn to the attention of policy makers in order to create a climate for sustainable change. This chapter provides a nexus for discussion of health promotion into the twenty-first century, for without healthy public policy, there can be no healthy cities, villages, schools or workplaces. The discussion of healthy public policies embodies a vision for the future that will help us achieve successive generations of healthy people with a self-determined quality of life, living harmoniously in healthy places that will preserve and sustain the ecosystem and its inhabitants.

Health care systems

16

Among the health care systems of the world, there is no paragon of excellence. Systems of health care have been constructed on the premise that they will be responsive to the needs of people, within the resource capabilities of those that govern their administration and the distribution of services. Although funding for health care varies between countries, most health care systems consist of discrete branches or departments designated to the treatment of illness and/or injury prevention and protection, health promotion and public health. In many cases, these functions are also categorised according to population groups such as children, adults, the elderly, rural or indigenous people. An alternative categorisation scheme is the program approach, wherein a program is linked to a health issue (immunisation, for example), and a department is responsible for all activities related to that issue.

The allocation of resources is central to the functioning of health care systems. Governments have a finite pool of resources to service the needs of their constituents. Health care is one area where strict market forces cannot operate effectively as, in the case of illness, each of us would like the maximum treatment possible. Similarly, we would all like to think that we have access to the best available preventive and protective services and information. This poses a set of important ethical issues, primarily revolving around the equitable distribution of resources, and ways in which access to health care can be achieved for all people. This chapter provides an overview of how the health care systems of several countries have attempted to meet the health needs of their populations within a framework that adheres to the principles of ethics and social justice.

Objectives

By the end of this chapter you will be able to:

• compare the health care systems of at least four different countries on the basis of equity, access and adherence to ethical principles

• discuss the issues that must be considered in planning health services that are responsive to the needs of indigenous people

• identify the most pressing global problems related to health care services

• explain current trends in the organisation of health services

• devise a set of strategies to reorient health care systems toward prevention rather than treatment.

The politics of health care

Although all health care systems have in common the goal of creating and sustaining the greatest good for the largest proportion of people, there is wide variability in the extent to which this goal is achieved. Political processes determine the flow of strategic activities in the health care system on the basis that these are resource intensive, and represent only one element in the political agenda. Numerous programs compete for government funds and, since the advent of the consumer movement, public lobby groups tend to create pressure on political decision-makers to act in favour of their interests. In the area of health care, especially where health care improvements can be made, there is considerable political mileage to be gained from responding to vocal, public interests, particularly if these relate to current, high-profile issues, such as HIV, the environment, or health care for the elderly.

Political tradition also plays a part in the way health care systems are shaped. In some countries, the concept of entrepreneurial health care would be rejected outright, for cultural and historical reasons, whereas in others it is readily accepted. For example, two extremes are represented in the health care systems of the UK and the US. In the UK, the national health services model is characterised by a government financed and operated system. The US has an entrepreneurial/market model where the private sector, rather than the government, controls health care. Most health care systems do, however, have some degree of privatisation, and the extent to which they are privatised represents another political element. Commercial partners in the delivery of health care seek returns on their investments. The goals of these vested interests sometimes compete with those of health professionals, but their contribution to goal-setting is also important if only to ensure their continued supplementation of government resources.

Health professionals also have vested interests in the conduct of a health care system. Medical practitioners, especially, spend long years of educational preparation in the expectation of practising in the geographic location, and specialty of their choice. Political decisions that limit either intakes into medical education programs, or the employment of graduates, therefore have the potential to create tensions within the labour force. Similarly, decisions that regulate policies related to reimbursing medical practitioners, or that pave the way for the reimbursement of more cost-effective health care providers, challenge the tradition of medical dominance that has existed for many years. Because medical practitioners represent a power elite in health care, any challenge to their role as gate-keepers to the system is a major source of political tension.

Another area of contention in the political arena is related to political decisions to favour or discontinue one or another program or service. Elected policy-makers are sometimes transient and may be intent on fulfilling their personal political visions rather than undertaking innovative and unproven approaches to health care. In addition, evaluative data that would support innovations or changes to health care delivery are gathered slowly and systematically, and thus often extend beyond the tenure of a political party or faction. When there is a change in the political party in power, the process of maintaining programs may be left to the vagaries of residual mechanisms, causing uncertainty about whether or not a service will continue. It is important then, in any health advocacy role, to recognise the inherently political nature of health care. The discussion to follow explains the urgency and intensity of developing efficient, effective structures and processes to meet health care needs.

The need for health care

The organisation of health care services is of vital interest to all proponents of improving health. Demographic trends indicate the need for all health care systems to prepare for an ageing population. The WHO informs us that not only will services need to expand to meet the needs of the elderly with chronic illness and/or disability but, as we approach the end of this century, up to half the world's people (5.72 billion) are at risk of many endemic diseases, and strategies must be developed to counter these (WHO 1996). After a temporary abatement, malaria and tuberculosis are returning in epidemic proportions. In South Africa, for example, tuberculosis is rampant, accounting for 80% of the reportable communicable disease, and is associated with higher rates of HIV infection and the emergence of drug-resistant tuberculosis strains (Matseoane 1997). This and other diseases are spreading because of people's hesitancy to report symptoms and their poor understanding of disease processes, and because of social conditions such as inadequate housing, poor nutrition, inadequate immunity, and the lack of user-friendly health care (WHO 1996).

The role of infectious agents in the development of many types of cancer is also becoming more evident. Many unknown viruses are emerging. There is a rapid spread of pathogens resistant to antibiotics and disease-carrying insects resistant to insecticides. Some of our most powerful antibiotics have been rendered impotent and few are being developed to replace them. To break the chains of transmission will require vigilance and intervention by all health care systems throughout the world (WHO 1996).

At a global level, the organisation of health care is understood to be inextricably linked to socioeconomic conditions, which are not always favourable to health. More than one-fifth of the world's population live in extreme poverty. Almost one-third of all children are undernourished. Half the people in the world lack regular access to the most needed essential drugs. Millions of city dwellers live in crowded and unhygienic conditions because of population growth and the failure of governments to adequately meet their health needs (WHO 1996).

The health needs of those living in an overpopulated world are also intertwined with efforts to preserve the environment. Ninety per cent of expected population growth in the coming decades will be in the developing regions of Africa, Asia and Latin America—the areas of richest biological diversity. Not only does this compromise the natural environment that would sustain people in the future, but humans encroaching on tropical forests have little or no disease resistance against insects carrying infectious diseases (WHO 1996). Expanding areas of human habitation have put millions of people at risk from previously rare pathogens, and these are increasing and spreading to other geographical areas because of climatic changes. It is of particular concern that so little is known about the disease potential of these environments, as the health systems in many countries are unable to cope with the need for either information or treatment (WHO 1996).

Wars, civil turmoil and natural disasters have also provided fertile breeding ground for infectious diseases, and many disease-producing organisms have been transported by increases in international travel. Global communications and changes in global food trade have also created an environment for infections to flourish. Fragmented, uncoordinated approaches to infectious disease control and the inadequate exchange of epidemiological information have prevented worldwide monitoring, leaving the primary response to the resources of one or another health care system (WHO 1996).

Changes in patterns of human behaviour have also changed health care requirements. In many places, economic constraints have led to an increased need for day care for children and the elderly, which places clusters of people at risk of hepatitis B and C infection (WHO 1996). Because of changes in human sexual behaviour, almost a million people a day contract sexually transmitted diseases. The nature of some epidemics is also evolving in conjunction with changing standards of behaviour. In many African nations, for example, AIDS is transmitted through normal, heterosexual sexual relations (approximately 60%), whereas in the past it was commonly thought to be a disease predominantly affecting the homosexual population. Because only about 10% of AIDS cases are reported, there is a need for efficient surveillance mechanisms to prevent the rates from escalating (Matseoane 1997). Increasingly, the drug problem is pervading the incidence and prevalence of AIDS, as the number of people contracting the disease through needle sharing is surpassing the number who contract the disease through sexual behaviour (WHO 1996).

Despite the ongoing threats to health, health care systems have also effected some improvements to health. Taken as a global aggregate, there is evidence of rising, sustainable economic growth, decreasing birth and death rates, an overall increase in life expectancy, slowing growth of urban populations, improvement in literacy rates (although there remains a need to improve the literacy rates of African, Asian, and Latin American women), decrease in fertility rates and an increase in contraceptive practices in the most populated countries (WHO 1996). These improvements are related to socioeconomic improvements, the growing body of health knowledge and improvements in the delivery of health care. However, the need for continuous improvement in health care services is ongoing and has led to system-wide reform in many places.

Health care reform

In all countries of the world, health and population trends have evoked unprecedented alarm, for reasons of both human and financial resource capacity. Government response to the health 'report card' has typically been to institute a number of reforms aimed at redressing the cost-inefficiencies of existing health care systems, with a view toward projecting future needs. Although there are substantial differences in the way health care reform is being approached in different countries, Ham (1997) categorises three distinct types: *big bang* reform, which has characterised sweeping changes to health care in places like the UK and New Zealand; *incremental* reform, which has been set in motion in the Netherlands and Germany; and *bottom-up* reform, which is a feature of the Swedish response. The health care system changes in the US have been called 'reform without reform' (Ham 1997), but at present the US is engaged in introducing incremental measures to revamp their extremely costly health care system. This slow but steady approach is being taken as an alternative to the sweeping reforms that were previously recommended, but rejected by the American Congress (Kearney & Engh 1997).

The health care reforms of all countries represent a response to escalating health care costs, and the gradual recognition that health care should not be driven by system capability, but by people's needs. Yet this is difficult to define. What the reforms have in common is a renewed emphasis on efficiency, greater attention to quality, and changes in the relationship between service providers and community members. Some of the changes have been welcomed as positive steps toward empowering people to make health care decisions, but the full distributional effects are unknown because of the absence thus far of systematic evaluation (Ham 1997). For example, in England and Wales and other parts of Europe, 'free' health care has had little impact on balancing social class inequalities in health or health services use (Najman 1994). It may be that our services are not always utilised by those who need them the most.

In the UK, where a government-funded National Health Service has been in place for many years, decentralisation in the form of regionalisation has occurred, and this is also the case in many other countries. Regionalisation in the UK has devolved responsibility for service provision to collective health insurance funds situated in regional trusts, some of which have included GPs in their membership (Ham 1997). This model of devolving authority is similar to the case in Sweden, where, despite some national initiatives, local health councils have been given the authority to decide which policies will be pursued. Similarly, in Canada, Australia and a number of other countries, local area or regional health authorities have been given increased responsibility over the mechanisms that operationalise health care delivery. In these countries, however, central regulatory control over key policy objectives remains, and this includes such things as patient waiting times, expansion of health insurance providers or adjustments to the education or licensing of health care providers (Barer, Lomas & Sanmartin 1997; Ham 1997).

In most of the European countries, North America, New Zealand and Australia, consumer choice, and thus equity, has become a key objective of the changes to health care. In the UK, the Netherlands, Germany, Sweden, Australia and New Zealand, there has been a shift from the integrated model of health services, where employees of the health department provided services, to the contract model, which outsources many services in order to effect cost savings. This has been accompanied by the use of market-like mechanisms, and the deployment of a range of budgetary incentives to improve provider performance (Ham 1997).

One of the features of contracting has been to separate purchasing and provider services. The health care systems of Canada, Australia, New Zealand and the UK have adopted this approach, with the intention of shifting accountability. The purchasing arm of a health board, department or authority is accountable for cost-effective purchasing of health care services for their residents in line with national goals and targets and assessment of local health needs. It is a financial contract, distinct from any obligation to account for clinical outcomes, which is relegated to the providers (Pollock 1997).

For the public, many of whom equate good health care with good physician care, the commercialisation of health care has been difficult to accept, and this indicates the importance of the vocabulary of reform (Attenborough 1997; Ham 1997). Public disenchantment with market-oriented solutions to human problems has been evoked by words such as 'competition', 'purchasers' and 'contracts'. In response, the UK and the Netherlands have shifted their rhetoric to focus on 'collaboration', 'commissioners' and 'service agreements' (Ham 1997). This is also occurring in places like Australia and New Zealand, where the emphasis is increasingly on partnerships and collaborative participation (Ashton 1996; Minichiello 1995).

In all countries, there is a search for a synthesis of different approaches, primarily focused on accountability, public health and primary care, which would incorporate health promotion, as an alternative to hospital based medicine (Ham 1997). But there are widespread variations in clinical standards, practice and outcomes (Pollock 1997).

The Canadian health care system has been grappling with reform in a number of ways. Although Canadians have been reported to be among those most satisfied with their health care system, fiscal concerns have placed the system under scrutiny (Blendon et al. 1997). Canada's contribution to health care is 9.9 % of its gross domestic product (GDP), which is less than the 14% of that of the US, but more than that of other nations such as Sweden and Japan (6 to 7%), all of whom have equally good or better population health statistics (Barer, Lomas & Sanmartin 1997; DeBois Inglis & Kjervik 1993). Health care reform in Canada is characterised by regionalisation and a shift from acute to community and residential care, controlling medical school enrolments, regulated reimbursement for care providers and benchmarking services between provinces (Attenborough 1997; Barer, Lomas & Sanmartin 1997).

Another reform currently being trialled in the US and Canada is capitation (Barer, Lomas & Sanmartin 1997). Capitation, a system whereby the health provider is reimbursed on the basis of a certain population of people under his or her care, has always been a part of the British health care system. Under capitation agreements, a formula is constructed to guide the allocation of resources to districts (Pollock 1997). Another important change to health services has been the emergence of primary managed care organisations in which GPs work within a designated budget to either provide or procure the necessary medical services for their patients. This is done within a framework of health promotion guidelines and incentives for providing cost-effective services (Ham 1997).

Managed care is a controversial topic in health care reform, and is mainly a feature of the American health care system. The system in the US is one where private insurance schemes predominate, with two forms of health assistance (Medicare and Medicaid) available to provide health care to the poor and those who are not otherwise insured (Kearney & Engh 1997). Until 1983, fee-for-service arrangements prevailed. This resulted in overutilisation of services, primarily by those who were insured, as hospitals and other providers took maximum advantage of the financial opportunities inherent in what was essentially a commercialised system.

Hospital stays were extended, many radiological and laboratory procedures were used, and there was overuse of some pharmaceuticals (Evans 1997).

In 1983, diagnostic related groupings (DRG) reimbursement was introduced in the US, and created about 470 diagnostic categories of illness, each with a price tag. Hospitals were paid prospectively for a patient's care, on the basis of the estimated cost of caring for a typical case in that category. The DRG system seemed effective in reducing health care costs, so in the late 1980s, large insurance companies began to adopt a DRG-like arrangement with hospitals. This led to a per diem arrangement, where the insurance company paid a flat rate per day regardless of what type of care a person received. This led to a system of private capitation, wherein people enrolled in a health insurance scheme that provided hospitals with a certain rate of reimbursement per enrolled member (Evans 1997).

Managed care is essentially a capitation system in which the insuring organisation either requires or encourages persons to obtain insured services through a network of participating providers. It is designed to reduce inefficiencies and improve access, but it has been widely criticised on the basis that it may underservice those most in need by disparate access and treatment policies designed to reduce costs (Rosenbaum et al. 1997). Discrimination against vulnerable groups whose health needs are substantial (and thus more costly than others) can occur as a function of point-of-entry practices. These include denying staff privileges to physicians who accept public patients, locating services in places that are inaccessible to the poor or minority groups, or biasing enrolment in services by failing to advertise the extent of services to these groups (Rosenbaum et al. 1997).

Managed care schemes have also been criticised on the basis of disadvantaging the working poor. In the US, a feature of most workplaces is that health insurance funds are part of a person's employment package, either partly or wholly funded by the employer. A current trend is for the employer to contract directly with health care providers to effect cost savings for employees and themselves. This has resulted in large-scale mergers between providers, who then become part of the contracting scheme on a capitated basis (Thorpe 1997). Employers, who are the purchasers of services, have increased the price of fee-for-service relative to managed care plans to encourage people to join managed care schemes. As a result, there is a transfer of risk to the employee.

Under the old fee-for-service arrangements, purchasers (employers and employees) largely financed annual increases in health care costs through increased premiums. Capitation is negotiated as a fixed cost, thus moving financial risk downstream to provider groups. In response, networks of physicians and pharmaceutical firms have developed 'disease management' services where the management of asthma, diabetes, hypertension, depression, AIDS and cancer, for example, is sold as a service directly to purchasers (Thorpe 1997). At first glance, this sounds ideal as a vehicle for health promotion and preventive services, but in its implementation it is paternalistic and perpetuates inequities between those who are participants in a workplace-based scheme, and the millions of people in the US without health benefits, including the unemployed (Kearney & Engh 1997).

Some large industrial corporations have now also joined the ranks of health service provision, establishing organised systems of care, which combine both the financing and delivery of care (England 1997). They oversee the full continuum of care from birth to long-term care, at delivery sites that range from the technically complex to an individual's home. Their rhetoric reveals a distinctive difference from other health service delivery models by offering accountability, integration, patient-centred care, and continuous improvement by ensuring that all management strategies are systematically evaluated (England 1997).

New Zealand is also in the midst of changes to the health care system, as part of that country's overall social reform. The reforms have seen a general trend towards greater reliance on market mechanisms (Ashton 1996). The health care system is predominantly public, but approximately half the population also have private health insurance. In 1992, a new regime of user charges was introduced to direct funding away from universal subsidies and thus free up funding for low-income groups; however, this has not been successful in improving access for these people. The lag in throughput of surgical services, and thus patient waiting lists, continues to increase (Ashton 1996). Perhaps more importantly, the most vulnerable in that society, including Maori and Pacific Islanders, continue to be underrepresented in their use of health care services (Bullen & Beaglehole 1997).

In South Africa, the problems surrounding health care reform have been complicated by that country's reliance on political and economic stabilisation for adequate health services (Matseoane 1997). Since 1994, there has been a national health insurance plan that operates through capitation with a fee-for-service component. Special groups, such as pregnant women and children under six years of age, receive free care under this plan, but there remains great disparity between services for blacks and those for whites. Fewer than 20% of South Africans, mostly privileged whites, have insurance that provides first-class health care. The remainder depend on state-supported services, provided in overcrowded, under-funded clinics and hospitals (Matseoane 1997).

South Africa spends only 6% of its GDP on health care, but the richest 10% earn more than half the national income and consume more than 50% of the national health budget (Matseoane 1997). About one-third of all South African households and more than half of the children (mostly black) live in poverty. With a rapidly expanding population, unemployment among blacks has increased their vulnerability in terms of education, health and social cohesion. Social disintegration is seen through family breakdown, single parenthood, rising divorce and separation rates, high teenage pregnancy rates, high unemployment and unemployability, lower performance at school, high rates of alcohol and substance abuse, and high rates of crime and endemic violence within families and among neighbours (Matseoane 1997).

As part of the quest for cost-containment, many health care systems are focusing on health technology assessment and evidence-based practice. In most countries, the expenditure-related justification for various health technologies is now integrated with clinical planning exercises and attempts to eliminate ineffective service provision (Ham 1997). In the Netherlands, the framework revolves around four criteria: whether the service or treatment is necessary from the community's point of view; whether it is effective; whether it is efficient; and whether it can be left to personal responsibility. In Sweden, reform is guided by three principles: human dignity, need or solidarity, and efficiency (Ham 1997).

Evidence-based practice is now a worldwide movement that seeks to require research evidence for all clinical as well as system innovations (Bero & Rennie 1995). It is based on the contention that without evidence there may be system wastage, and this applies also to the need for discretion in clinical treatment. Recent research in North America reveals that physician practice style is as important as population health needs in directing the health care system. In all countries, to be poor is to have poor health status and spend more days in hospital, and, especially in countries like Canada, where there is universal health coverage, to have more contact with physicians (Roos & Mustard 1997).

Research has also shown that the rate of discretionary procedures such as laminectomy have been shown to be sensitive to new neurosurgeons moving into an area (Deyo 1995). The supply of specialists does not, however, affect those in the lower socioeconomic groups to the same extent as those in the middle and higher groups (Roos & Mustard 1997). This seems to be linked to the fact that people of higher socioeconomic status are better able to: negotiate the health care system; communicate (and be believed) when there is a problem requiring surgical treatment; be aware of surgical treatments and ask for a referral to a specialist; and make and keep appointments because of work and/or child care arrangements (Roos & Mustard 1997). This indicates a need for some type of regulatory mechanisms to ensure equity of access.

Closer monitoring of surgical practice is particularly important, because of the high rates of surgical care especially among middle and higher socioeconomic groups. However, monitoring must be conducted within the context of cultural considerations. In Japan, people almost have an aversion to surgery (a quarter the US rate), yet Japan has made the most dramatic gains in life expectancy over the last several decades to become the country with the healthiest people in the world. This is, however, not related to physician behaviour, because Japan's medical community continues to focus on the hospital (most of which are private) as the physician's sanctuary. Because of widespread public insurance, Japanese people can choose their service providers, but there is a convergence of patients at certain hospitals, causing inefficiencies in health care access. A stable economy, high education of women and a comprehensive health care system have led to the improvements, which include the lowest perinatal, neonatal and maternal death rates in the world (Nishida 1997).

Rationing of health care services

Rationing of health services has always existed in the form of withholding potentially beneficial treatments from some group, and is inevitable when there are insufficient resources to meet need. However, the processes of rationing should be undertaken with accountability by the decision-makers, community consultation and systematic evaluation of outcomes. When this does not occur, there is the opportunity for clinically cloaked political decisions that are simple exercises in cost shifting, rather than cost savings. Many of these approaches simply transfer the cost of care to the individual (Pollock 1997). Those who carry the burden of such redistribution exercises are typically people in social and long-term care, the poor, the sick and the elderly. Paradoxically, excluding individuals from care to reduce costs may actually bring about decreased benefits for the population as a whole, because more resources will be needed to achieve favourable population-based clinical outcomes (Pollock 1997). This situation has arisen in a number of countries where care remains inefficient, hospital-centred, highly specialised, and urban-based. The politics of health care reform may therefore be more important than any other aspect, especially in its capacity to mobilise resources in the right (or wrong) direction (Ham 1997).

The impact of population ageing has received wide attention in political circles in the past few years. The cost of institutional care is escalating, and projections indicate that expenditure on the aged will increase by more than 50% in real terms between the years 2001 and 2021 (Minichiello 1995). A current debate centres on whether responsibilities for community services, particularly for the elderly, should lie in the hands of the public or the private sector. This has caused suspicion surrounding the attempts of politicians to increase community care provision, which to a large extent places undue burden on family caregivers.

Family caregivers, especially unpaid women, care at great personal, social and financial cost. Services need to be made available to families on the basis of a broad approach that does not disadvantage certain families on the basis of social criteria. In a truly participative system, older people need to have a say over services and help plan implementation strategies. The research agenda also needs to include critical examination of the effects of aged care reform on those who receive and provide care (Minichiello 1995).

Ethical issues in health care

The paradoxes of health care rationing, discussed above, crystallise the need to maintain ethical practices in health care administration, especially in the wake of widespread reform. The allocation of resources is fraught with ethical dilemmas, some related to the potential for power relations to prevail over issues of access and equity, and others related to social and/or cultural appropriateness. The very act of coming into care may lead to vulnerabilities for certain patients, in the 'power and authority structures and discourses that organise and control health care' (Liaschenko 1997, p. 48). The medicalisation of health and wellbeing through paternalistic language and diagnostic labelling can be disempowering for many people (Engelhardt 1996). In addition, there is a risk of exploitation by virtue of the fact that patient care is not the primary goal in all situations. A more subtle form of exploitation may also occur in the homogenisation of identity that is a feature of aggregated or public health objectives (Liaschenko 1997).

Cultural issues in health care delivery

In planning culturally appropriate health services, most countries face the dilemma of whether to integrate cultural information into existing services, or to create parallel services that would be acceptable to indigenous people. This is not an easy dilemma to resolve, given the resource and equity implications that accompany either choice. Some health planners advocate parallel services on the basis that Western medicine is incapable of encompassing the knowledge and methods necessary to understand suffering in others' cultural terms (Campbell et al. 1997).

Indigenous knowledge such as is embodied in the laws of Tapu for the New Zealand Maori, the Dreaming for Australian Aboriginal people, and a range of sources of tribal knowledge of many African and South American nations, emerge from non-secular, spiritual beliefs. Any attempts to provide guidance in health matters must therefore be couched in these cultural beliefs (Campbell et al. 1997; Kasanene 1994). Native Americans and Canadians also maintain a variety of spiritual and healing practices and have attempted to incorporate these into treatment programs. However, experience has shown that, in the example of young people in treatment for alcohol problems, embracing their culture while drawing from the techniques of Western medicine is more helpful than one or another approach alone (Brady 1995).

In Australia, responses of government health agencies to Aboriginal health issues have been to enhance existing mainstream public health programs and to also lend support to a non-government system of Aboriginal health services (Aboriginal Medical Services). However, this approach has claimed few successes, as Australia's indigenous people continue to experience significantly higher rates of infectious diseases, and morbidity and mortality from a range of causes than non-Aboriginal people. Any health improvements that have occurred have been attributed to improvements in their standard of living rather than the organisation of health services (Gray & Saggers 1994).

Similarly, New Zealand's Maori have a lower life expectancy, lower average incomes, higher unemployment and generally poorer health than non-Maori for much the same reasons (Ashton 1996). Diseases related to obesity, cardiovascular disease and diabetes mellitus all occur more frequently amongst Australian Aborigines, Maori and Pacific Islanders than the rest of the population, and the health care system has done little to alleviate this situation (Ashton 1996; Bullen & Beaglehole 1997; Gray & Saggers 1994).

The Australian Council for Aboriginal Reconciliation has drawn public attention to the links between health and social justice (ACAR 1994). In New Zealand, the Treaty of Waitangi has attempted to achieve a similar focus. The Treaty is central to race relations and to issues affecting the social and economic position of Maori, including the health system. New Zealand's health care reforms, especially regionalisation, have allowed the Maori Health Authority to purchase health services as a joint venture with the Regional Health Authority, but this is only a recent gesture and will require evaluation to reveal whether it will result in health gains. It is a widely accepted view that the Treaty has not been honoured, and that Maori ownership, rights and privileges have been steadily undermined by the non-Maori people (Ashton 1996). The extent to which this has contributed to poor health outcomes is unknown.

In North America, race relations also dominate discussions of indigenous health. There is a view that some problems, such as drug and alcohol abuse and ill-health, have arisen from, or been exacerbated by, deprivation and the erosion of indigenous cultural integrity as a result of colonisation (Brady 1995). In Australia, disruption of cultural practices is thought to be related to loss of land. Re-connecting an Aboriginal person to his/her cultural and spiritual roots is therefore essential to recovery and ongoing wellbeing (Brady 1995). On this basis, programs that stress 'cultural' treatment models encouraging a sense of Indian-ness or Aboriginality (such as the 'sweat lodges' in North America) should be more efficacious, but there is little research evidence for this.

The other side of this treatment equation is that, even in tradition-oriented communities where social organisation remains intact and where people have retained intimate contact with their land, some still engage in unhealthy and destructive behaviours, for reasons that may have nothing to do with the health care system (Brady 1995). This leads to two important ethical dilemmas: first, without systematic evaluation of the relative merits of different types of treatment there is no assurance of appropriate allocation of resources (Gray et al. 1995). The second dilemma concerns the extent to which governments are willing to discuss issues such as land rights within the context of health care provision. Neither of these issues are readily resolvable, but both need widespread debate with community participation from all sides and at all stages of the process.

A further ethical dilemma in trying to provide culturally appropriate services occurs when some culturally prescribed practices seem to violate the principles of primary health care and, sometimes, humanity itself. For example, female circumcision is recently under debate. It appears as systematic brutality towards and abuse of women, yet it is so embedded in cultural identity that it is actively pursued and promoted by women in Northern Africa and Southern Arabia (Campbell et al. 1997). When these people migrate to other systems of care, the dilemma revolves around the extent to which cultural beliefs override those of the prevailing morality.

Indigenous understanding is therefore instrumental in guiding health services. One example concerns the way in which terminal illness is conceptualised. In many cases, death is seen in indigenous cultures as a normal progression of life, embedded with spiritual meaning. The custom in Western societies of 'diseuthanasia' or prolongation of life by all means possible, may be unethical in other cultures (Campbell et al. 1997, p. 32). Even in our own culture, the euthanasia debate needs to address the arrogance of determining the timing of another's death and of providing dehumanising and intrusive treatment solely for the purpose of prolonging life, and 'true' medical care or 'rescue' (Campbell et al. 1997, p. 160). Organ donations are a related issue. It is the conviction among Japanese people that a warm, bleeding body is alive, therefore to take organs from a brain-dead body is regarded as assault or murder (Campbell et al. 1997). To what extent, then, do we impose goals on the convictions of another's culture?

Social justice and public health

As public health advocates, we are directed by the ethics of public health beyond the biomedical map to the fundamental values of the wider society and the preservation of human rights (Leeder 1997). We need to pay close attention to the way in which public health policies place a burden on human rights (for example, in urging fitness programs and/or healthy diets on those who cannot afford it) and be aware of the damaging effects to health of human rights violations (Mann, cited in Leeder 1997). One question all health professionals must ask relates to the extent of our obligation to become involved in human rights issues. We have a responsibility to clarify what we perceive human rights to be, especially when the concerns are far removed from us geographically or socially (Driscoll 1997). This issue is currently being addressed by the WHO through the criteria set during a conference in the Netherlands, hosted by the European Consultation on the

Rights of Patients. The criteria include the following:

- Everyone has the right to respect of his or her person as a human being.
- Everyone has the right to self-determination.
- Everyone has the right to physical and mental integrity and to the security of his or her person.
- Everyone has the right to respect of his or her privacy.
- Everyone has the right to have his or her moral and cultural values and religious and philosophical convictions respected.
- Everyone has the right to such protection of health as is afforded by appropriate measures for disease prevention and health care, and to the opportunity to pursue his or her own highest attainable level of health (WHO 1995).

The ethics of resource allocation

Resource allocation has emerged as the most important ethical issue of the 1980s and 1990s. Discussion surrounding the ethics of resource allocation focuses on the major ethical principles of autonomy (individual freedom and choice), beneficence (promoting good health and preventing or curing illnesses), non-maleficence (doing no harm) and justice (proper distribution of social benefits and burdens) (Beauchamp & Walters 1989; Beauchamp 1994).

We know that there are systematic and avoidable differences among social, ethnic and geographic population groups in terms of health status, access to health services, uptake of these services, and quality of health care (Whitehead & Dahlgren 1995). However, it is the role of health planners to attempt to achieve just distribution in the allocation of resources. This creates a dilemma in deciding which principle of justice will guide our activities: distributive justice, where benefits should be given first to the disadvantaged or those who need them most; egalitarian justice, where there is equal distribution of benefits to everyone regardless of need; or restorative justice, where benefits go primarily to those who have been wronged by prior injustice (Spradley & Allender 1996).

The public health dilemma is whether to allocate according to equal distribution or need. One solution is to adopt the model of many European countries (the Netherlands, Finland, Sweden) to distribute resources, including screening services with variable uptake, consistently among the population, rather than rely on rates of health as defined by particular indices (Whitehead & Dahlgren 1995). The public health ethos tends to lean toward need as the guide for resource allocation, defined in terms of outcomes (Campbell et al. 1997). However, many competing needs require arbitration, including rural and under-served populations, and those who need life enhancement rather than life-saving interventions (Campbell et al. 1997). Another issue is related to the appropriate use of technologies. Providing accessible and expensive services may serve a number of functions, but it has a limited impact on inequalities in health (Najman 1994).

Informed and conjoint decisions must inform local debates about cost-benefit, and several fundamental questions must be addressed in relation to the ethical provision of health care. The first is related to how we define adequacy in health care. The next is linked to the evolving body of knowledge and the concomitant possibilities for improved health care provision. When supply constantly fails to meet demand, and the right to health care is impossible to implement, we must define priorities in terms of social justice and decide who gets what. Because each new innovation creates more demand, we must view health care from a population benefit perspective and in terms of efficiency, effectiveness and equity. This embodies the concept of distributive justice (Campbell et al. 1997).

Another issue in relation to equitable distribution according to need concerns the formula used to define it. Some health care planners have constructed formulas for calculating need on the basis of outcome expectation; for example, quality adjusted life years (QALYs); or the approach taken in New Zealand to define 'core health services' to prioritise urgency (Campbell et al. 1997). The problem with this approach is that all scoring and rating systems conceal value-laden judgements, such as the propensity to exclude a person with a history of alcoholism from a liver transplant (Barer, Lomas & Sanmartin 1997). Still another dilemma relates to whether aggregate improvements count for more than individual improvements.

An additional dilemma arises in relation to health insurance. Because health is not a self-limiting market we must avoid trying to save costs by cost shifting to private insurance. When this happens, private insurance becomes a major component of the health system, thereby eroding the public service. As private insurers become the major providers, costs escalate due to free market forces. This attracts professional staff into high-paid private work, increasing the cost of their services and effectively depleting services available in the public sector. As a result, consumers are pushed into the private sector. As the spiral continues, the public health system becomes less sustainable and the overall costs of health care rise exponentially (Campbell et al. 1997).

Genetic engineering

Defining need is complicated by the rapid development of new technologies and the growth in genetic engineering. Genetic engineering includes genetic screening and use of DNA probes on one hand, to pre-emptive intervention and selective abortion on the other, from genetic counselling to somatic cell gene therapy. It includes the Human Genome Project with its efforts to map the nucleotide sequence of the human genome, cloning, and human eugenics (enhancement of desirable human dispositions and characteristics by genetic means) (Campbell et al. 1997). These authors suggest that we need to determine 'the sort of interference with nature and the genome that will advance human welfare and the integrity of the planet, while respecting the dimensions of what it means to be human' (p. 75).

The 1980s saw the advent of the polymerase chain reaction (PCR) for gene reproduction. This led to ease of DNA fingerprinting and the start of gene therapy, where direct insertion of normally functioning genes were able to enter target tissue through vectors (Kerr 1996). By the 1990s, automated instrumentation and sophisticated information management had progressed the field even further. Simultaneously, and even prior to this, the entry of large corporations and laboratories engaged in widespread commercialisation of genetic research created the potential to change the political and social milieu of genetic research (Kerr 1996).

The public health issue related to genetic research is related to equity and privacy. The concern is that people possessing genes deemed harmful will be discriminated against or unfairly stigmatised (Kerr 1996). The question surrounds who will safeguard the dissemination of genetic information, particularly when 'Hyperbole, misinformation and the premature raising of expectations typically surround the press conferences of scientists and accounts in the mass media' (Kerr 1996, p. 452).

The public health ethos also tends to be suspicious of commercial imperatives, and more concerned about the morality of developing expensive high-technology strategies in a crowded world characterised by sociopolitical turbulence, environmental degradation and the resurgence of communicable diseases (Kerr 1996). A further concern relates to screening. The question is, what do we do with the results of testing children and adolescents for late-onset inherited disorders? Do we conduct pre-symptomatic screening for Alzheimer's disease? What do we do with this information? Do we limit migration and/or employment? What level of risk is acceptable before resources are deployed? Do we screen workers for drugs and alcohol, or HIV, or hepatitis B, or all those who engage in socially incorrect behaviour for mental illnesses? (Campbell et al. 1997; Downie & Calman 1994; Kerr 1996; McCallum 1994).

Health promotion ethics

An additional area of ethical concern surrounds the strategies used for health promotion. There is incontrovertible proof that smoking causes ill health, yet rather than blame the victims (the smokers), should our health budget include funding for alternative stress-alleviation strategies (Downie & Calman 1994)? Similarly, in school-based health education programs, is it an imposition for us as health professionals to get involved in character education? Governali (1995) suggests that character education is necessary to address the worst psychosocial epidemics of society—early sexual behaviour, teenage pregnancy, alcohol, drug use and drug culture, child suicide, juvenile crime, AIDS, violence, alienation, the violent and sexual excesses of the media, and societal breakdown. Every day the media communicates to young people messages that the answer to their needs lies in sexual hedonism, escape into drugs, and aggressive self-assertion by violence. He concludes that if health professionals do not become involved in guiding young people, the media will continue to do so, with more damaging results than having our views imposed on them (Governali 1995).

Labonte (1994) re-frames the problem of disseminating information as 'risk communication', suggesting that information, education and participation are entwined. He states (p. 269): 'Information forms one basis to education; education implies dialogue, reflection and critical analysis; participatory structures, with adequate resources for participation, allow the public an opportunity to act upon their knowledge at both personal and public policy levels.' His suggestion is that we try to safeguard how the media portrays health information, enacting a media advocacy approach in which the discourse on issues is challenged, rather than added to.

The importance of understanding the dynamic and complex issues surrounding health care systems should be evident from the foregoing discussion. Yet, ethical issues continue to polarise the views of many members of the health community: the 'high tech' experts against those who see themselves as humane, caring people; those who compete for resources between minimisation of disability and handicap, care of the aged and the management of chronic illness; those who advocate domiciliary and family care versus hospital care; well-informed consumers versus experts and politicians (Kalucy 1995). Each of the principles of primary health care is embodied in the way health care systems translate their strategies into maintaining the health of the community. To ensure that these strategies continue to be efficient, effective, equitable, ethical, accessible, strategic, sustainable, transparent, empowering and resourced, it is a matter of urgency that the health care system be the focus for collegial and participative community debate and decision-making.

THINKING CRITICALLY

The health care system

▶ Compare and contrast the health care systems of Australia and the US.

▶ Identify four ethical dilemmas facing all health care systems in contemporary society.

▶ Describe five cost-containment measures that have been adopted by various health care systems.

▶ Discuss the implications of creating parallel, indigenous health care systems in terms of human and resource costs.

▶ Develop a set of recommendations for the ideal health care system.

REFERENCES

Ashton, T. 1996, 'Health care systems in transition: New Zealand. Part 1, An overview of New Zealand's health care system', *Journal of Public Health Medicine*, vol. 18, no. 30, pp. 269–73.

Attenborough, R. 1997, 'The Canadian health care system: development, reform, and opportunities for nurses', *Journal of Obstetrics, Gynecology and Neonatal Nursing*, vol. 26, no. 20, pp. 229–34.

Australian Council for Aboriginal Reconciliation 1994, *Walking Together: The First Steps: Report of the Australian Council for Aboriginal Reconciliation*, AGPS, Canberra.

Barer, M., Lomas, J. & Sanmartin, C. 1997, 'Re-minding our Ps and Qs: Medical cost controls in Canada', in *Health Policy and Nursing*, 2nd edn, eds C. Harrington & C. Estes, Jones & Bartlett, Boston, pp. 380–90.

Beauchamp, T. 1994, 'The four-principles approach', in *Principles of Health Care Ethics*, ed. R. Gillon, John Wiley & Sons, Chichester, pp. 3–12.

Beauchamp, T. & Walters, L. (eds) 1989, *Contemporary Issues in Bioethics*, 3rd edn, Wadsworth, Belmont, California.

Bero, L. & Rennie, D. 1995, 'The Cochrane Collaboration: preparing, maintaining and disseminating systematic reviews of the effects of health care', *Journal of the American Medical Association*, vol. 274, no. 24, pp. 1935–8.

Blendon, R., Benson, J., Donelan, K., Leitman, R., Taylor, H. et al. 1997, 'Who has the best health care system? A second look', in *Health Policy and Nursing*, 2nd edn, eds C. Harrington & C. Estes, Jones & Bartlett, Boston, pp. 403–14.

Brady, M. 1995, 'Culture in treatment, culture as treatment. A critical appraisal of developments in addictions programs for indigenous North Americans and Australians', *Social Science and Medicine*, vol. 41, no. 11, pp. 1487–98.

Bullen, C. & Beaglehole, R. 1997, 'Ethnic differences in coronary heart disease case fatality in Auckland', *Australian and New Zealand Journal of Public Health*, vol. 21, no. 7, pp. 688–93.

Campbell, A., Charlesworth, M., Gillett, G. & Jones, G. 1997, *Medical Ethics*, 2nd edn, Oxford University Press, Aukland.

DeBois Inglis, A. & Kjervik, D. 1993, 'Empowerment of advanced practice nurses: regulation reform needed to increase access to care', *Journal of Law, Medicine and Ethics*, vol. 21, pp. 193–205.

Deyo, R. 1995, 'Promises and limitation of the patient outcome research teams: the low back-pain example', *Proceedings of the Association of American Physicians*, vol. 107, no. 3, pp. 324–8.

Downie, R. & Calman, K. 1994, *Healthy Respect. Ethics in Health Care*, Oxford University Press, New York.

Driscoll, J. 1997, 'In defence of patient/person human rights within national health care provision: implications for British nursing', *Nursing Ethics*, vol. 4, no. 1, pp. 66–77.

Engelhardt, H. 1996, *The Foundations of Bioethics*, 2nd edn, Oxford University Press, New York.

England, M. 1997, 'The evolving health care system: changing paradigms and the organized system of care', *Journal of Allied Health*, Winter, pp. 7–13.

Evans, M. 1997, 'The evolving of the United States health care delivery system', *Orthopaedic Nursing*, March/April (suppl.), pp. 7–11.

Governali, J. 1995, 'Health education and character education', *Journal of School Health*, vol. 65, no. 9, pp. 394–6.

Gray, D. & Saggers, S. 1994, 'Aboriginal ill health: the harvest of injustice', in *Just Health. Inequality in Illness, Care and Prevention*, eds C. Waddell & A. Petersen, Churchill-Livingstone, Melbourne, pp. 119–33.

Gray, D., Saggers, S., Drandich, M., Wallam, D. & Plowright, P. 1995, 'Evaluating government health and substance abuse programs for indigenous peoples: a comparative review', *Australian Journal of Public Health*, vol. 19, no. 6, pp. 567–72.

Ham, C. 1997, 'Lessons and conclusions', in *Health Care Reform: Learning from International Experience*, ed. C. Ham, Open University Press, Buckingham, pp. 119–40.

Jones, D. & Miller, M. 1992, 'Advocacy for community health', in *Community Health Policy and Practice in Australia*, eds F. Baum, D. Fry & I. Lennie, Pluto Press, Leichardt, pp. 143–53.

Kalucy, R. 1995, 'Ethics and Public Health', in *Health For All: The South Australian Experience*, Wakefield Press, ed. F. Baum, Kent Town, SA, pp. 172–90.

Kasenene, P. 1994, 'African ethical theory and the four principles', in *Principles of Health Care Ethics*, ed. R. Gillon, John Wiley & Sons, Chichester, pp. 183–92.

Kearney, P. & Engh, C. 1997, 'History of the American health care system: its cost control programs and incremental reform', *Orthopedics*, vol. 20, no. 30, pp. 236–47.

Kerr, C. 1996, 'Genetic testing and public health' (editorial), *Australian and New Zealand Journal of Public Health*, vol. 20, no. 5, pp. 451–2.

Labonte, R. 1994, '"See me, hear me, touch me, feel me": lessons on environmental health information for bureaucratic activists', in *Ecological Public Health: From Vision to Practice*, eds C. Chu & R. Simpson, Institute of Applied Environmental Research, Brisbane, pp. 269–76.

Leeder, S. 1997, 'Rights and Public Health', *In Touch*, newsletter of the Public Health Association of Australia Inc., vol. 14, no. 7, pp. 4–5.

Liaschenko, J. 1997, 'Ethics and the geography of the nurse–patient relationship: spatial vulnerabilities and gendered space', *Scholarly Inquiry for Nursing Practice*, vol. 11, no. 1, pp. 45–59.

Matseoane, S. 1997, 'South African health-care system at the crossroads', *Journal of the National Medical Association*, vol. 89, no. 50, pp. 350–6.

McCallum, R. 1994, 'Ethics in occupational health', in *Principles of Health Care Ethics*, ed. R. Gillon, John Wiley & Sons, Chichester, pp. 931–43.

Minichiello, V. 1995, 'Community care: economic policy dressed as social concern?' in *The Politics of Health: The Australian Experience*, 2nd edn, ed. H. Gardner, Churchill-Livingstone, Melbourne, pp. 453–82.

Najman, J. 1994, 'Class inequalities in health and lifestyle', in *Just Health. Inequality in Illness Care and Prevention*, eds C. Waddell & A. Petersen, Churchill-Livingstone, Melbourne, pp. 27–46.

Nishida, H. 1997, 'Perinatal health care in Japan', *Journal of Perinatology*, vol. 17, no. 1, pp. 70–4.

Pollock, A. 1997, 'The politics of destruction: rationing in the UK health care market' in *Health Policy and Nursing*, 2nd edn, eds C. Harrington & C. Estes, Jones & Bartlett, Boston, pp. 391–402.

Roos, N. & Mustard, C. 1997, 'Variation in health and health care use by socioeconomic status in Winnipeg, Canada: Does the system work well? Yes and No', *Milbank Quarterly*, vol. 75, no. 1, pp. 89–110.

Rosenbaum, S., Serrano, R., Magar, M. & Stern, G. 1997, 'Civil rights in a changing health care system', *Health Affairs*, vol. 16, no. 1, pp. 90–105.

Spradley, B. & Allender, J. 1996, *Community Health Nursing: Concepts and Practice*, 4th edn, Lippincott, Philadelphia.

Takahashi, T. 1997, 'The paradox of Japan: what about CQI in health care?' *Journal of Quality Improvement*, vol. 23, no. 1, pp. 60–4.

Thorpe, K. 1997, 'The health care system in transition: care, cost and coverage', *Journal of Health Politics, Policy and Law*, vol. 22, no. 2, pp. 339–61.

Whitehead, M. & Dahlgren, G. 1995, 'What can be done about inequalities in health?', in *Health and Disease: A Reader*, eds B. Davey, A. Gray & C. Seale, Open University Press, Buckingham, pp. 367–75.

World Health Organization 1995, *Promotion of the rights of patients in Europe. Proceedings of a WHO consultation, 1994, 28–30 March, Amsterdam, the Netherlands*, WHO Regional Office for Europe/Kluwer Law International, the Hague.

World Health Organization 1996, *The World Health Report 1996: Fighting Disease, Fostering Development*, WHO, Geneva.

17
Researching community health

In this era of rapidly changing health care trends, the need for ongoing, systematic research in community health has never been greater. There is a need for close examination of the processes and outcomes of health service restructuring, the efficacy of community-based services, measures of population health, home and community care, multidisciplinary clinical decision-making, community participation, and the mechanisms and outcomes of trying to maintain fiscal and clinical accountability in health care.

Research studies are designed by researchers from diverse fields, using a variety of approaches, to address a plethora of health-related questions. Despite differing research agendas, their common goal is to improve the health of the population either by providing small incremental contributions to knowledge, or by studies of such magnitude as to change the direction of health care. It is imperative that the growing body of evidence for clinical decision-making, quality care, efficiency and effectiveness of the health care system, preservation of the environment, and community acceptability, be given a high profile in our quest for the creation and sustainability of health. This chapter provides an overview of issues related to community health research, and suggests a number of research challenges and strategies that could be used to effect improvements in community health.

Objectives

By the end of this chapter you will be able to:

- *identify three broad areas of research interest relevant to community health*

- *provide four reasons for the use of multiple research methods in conducting community health research*

- *explain the importance of the evidence-based practice movement*

- *explain the five most important ethical issues related to conducting research studies*

- *identify three research studies that could lead to improvements in the health of your community.*

Researching communities

Research in community health has a relatively recent history. Although biomedical and clinical research have long and respected traditions, systematic examination of our communal environments and the way in which they contribute to the health of the population has only occurred throughout the past forty years (Badura & Kickbusch 1991). With increasing awareness of the inextricable links between biology, medicine and the socioecological environment, health-related research has now expanded to incorporate the social and ecological environments within which health is maintained. We know, for example, that biology both affects, and is affected by, the stress of living in an environment devoid of social support (Badura & Kickbusch 1991). This suggests a need for research related to the construction and maintenance of a socially supportive and sustainable environment within which healthy populations can thrive.

One problem in community health research has been that, despite substantial growth in the area, many researchers continue to focus on individuals and individual behaviours rather than improvements to population health and the social mechanisms that produce and support behaviours (Drevdahl 1995). In a socioecological model of health, we need to investigate the health consequences of economic policies through their effects on unemployment, inflation and income (Milio 1991). As health professionals accountable to the community, we must also address human resources and labour force issues, particularly in the organisational climate of cost containment, and an increasing trend toward international benchmarking (Ham 1997; Meleis 1989).

Features of the environment, and measures already taken to promote health, also need to be evaluated. For example, we need to examine in detail the pattern of activities certain population groups undertake to promote health. What has influenced their choices? How well has the immediate environment supported those choices? What barriers to success exist? What are the unintended consequences of certain initiatives for health promotion? How can the environment be made more supportive? (Baum 1992). Health policies must also come under scrutiny. We need to examine which policy options will make healthy choices easier for people, which in turn will make it easier for them to achieve their health goals, especially in an administrative environment that favours productivity over quality of life. The other side of this equation is to investigate the factors that make options for healthy policies easier for policy-makers and their supporters (Milio 1991).

Researching in the setting

As mentioned in previous chapters, there is currently an increased emphasis on the setting for health promotion. Because this is a relatively new development over the last decade, the need for ongoing evaluation research is acute. Some of the gaps in knowledge of settings-based health promotion are related to the relative merits of new information and educational technologies, the influence of public policy on such things as school health and workplace health promotion programs, how best to maintain linkages between settings, and the effectiveness of different approaches to promoting health among marginal and special subgroups in those settings (Mullen et al. 1995).

Research in health care settings

Although health is promoted in a number of settings, the three most attractive settings for health promotion are health (or illness) care agencies, workplaces and schools. Each of these has considerable differences in culture, physical environment and audience, suggesting a need to include many aspects of the context in our research. Health care sites are a special case. People who use health care services are usually receptive to health promotion information, and trusting of those who provide it, and this combines to produce a setting that is conducive to effective health education (Mullen et al. 1995). Research studies to date reveal positive findings of the effectiveness of health education in health care settings, especially when educational principles have been adhered to. These include individualising the messages, providing explicit feedback on learning or clinical progress, and ensuring that there are other forms of reinforcement appropriate to the situation (Mullen et al. 1995).

Despite these encouraging findings, there are still many questions to be answered in the health care setting. Some of these have less to do with the delivery of information than with the individuals who participate in the process. For example, we know little about the factors that influence health care professionals to participate in health education, and of the provider–patient role set that influences behaviour change (Mullen et al. 1995). There is also a need to investigate quality of care issues in the home and community care setting (Twinn 1997). A further area for study is the extent to which communities are receptive to community development strategies and factors influencing their participation, especially in rural areas (Glick et al. 1996; McMurray 1998).

Research in school settings

Given the importance of the school as a setting for health promotion, there is a growing need for studies in the school setting, and this is an area where research has already shown considerable gains. Since the 1980s the relative advantages of comprehensive school health programs have been the subject of several large-scale studies. Studies have revealed that curricular components dedicated to health education have been effective in improving knowledge, attitudes and behaviour related to the use of alcohol, drugs, tobacco, diet and sexual risk behaviours (Kolbe, Collins, & Cortese 1997; Mullen et al. 1995). School-based health centres are the site of studies examining critical events, primary care interventions, case management, peer partnerships and the effects of health education strategies on a range of behaviours (Hinton Walker et al. 1996; Kolbe et al. 1995).

Some researchers have found that the health centres increase students' access to care and improve their health knowledge, but the extent to which this reduces risk behaviour is less clear (Kisker & Brown 1996). Cross-cultural comparisons of these outcomes are sparse, so this is another important area for research (Baldwin et al. 1996). Studying the links between inputs (health education) and outputs (behaviour change) needs to be continued, so that young people's behaviour can be tracked over time, especially in relation to such major problems of adolescence as teenage pregnancy, substance abuse and suicide. The suggestions of those already researching the field are for extension of their work to identify and monitor critical health-related events, school interventions designed to influence those events, influences on planning strategies and the long-term effects of interventions and evaluation of interventions (Kolbe, Collins & Cortese 1997). Other studies need to examine the mechanisms for encouraging community partnerships in school health programs, and the various influences on local community participation in school-based programs (Hinton Walker et al. 1996; Kisker & Brown 1996).

Research in workplace settings

Some of the research approaches being adopted in schools are also appropriate in the workplace setting. The workplace does not have a rigorous history of research (Schulte, Goldenhar & Connally 1996). However, many health professionals involved in occupational health and safety are becoming increasingly aware of the need to evaluate workplace interventions, risks and strategies for effective organisational, as well as environmental, strategies (Khoury 1996). Of continuing interest to that setting is 'dose–response' data. This addresses the extent to which an input (the dose) will effect a desired change. This type of approach extends to field of molecular epidemiology to trace a causal pathway between an exposure and resultant disease, allowing identification of 'markers' that can be used in prevention programs (Schulte, Goldenhar & Connally 1996).

One area where there has been a dearth of workplace-based research is in examining women in various workplaces and work roles. The need for gender-oriented studies is currently being redressed on the basis of the large number of women entering, or returning to, a wide range of jobs as a result of affirmative action policies. One area of particular interest to researchers is the effect of certain types of employment on pregnancy. The research is primarily aimed at investigating the effects of certain industrial processes on the health of pregnant women and their children (Hatch 1996). This type of surveillance research investigates worker health and safety and the effects of occupational hazards. It is primarily aimed at detecting worksite conditions that need to be modified, but it is also used to follow illness and injury trends, to provide a basis for workplace policies, and to measure the outcomes of health promotion intervention (Frye 1997).

The worksite is rapidly becoming a laboratory for health promotion research, particularly with the trend toward networking studies between sites and between industries (Mullen et al. 1995; Ringen & Stafford 1996). Research studies are currently addressing such issues as smoking and the relationship between high-risk behaviours and high-risk work environments (Schulte, Goldenhar & Connally 1996). However, many gaps remain in our knowledge of health in the workplace. For example, we need to know the effects of seasonal work patterns on the health of the worker and his or her family. There is also a need for ongoing data collection to trace injury rates linked to particular industries and workplaces to inform policy makers as well as potential and current employees (Frye 1997). Risk surveillance is also a long-term endeavour and requires the commitment of workers as well as those conducting the research. For this reason, workplace-based research must also address labour relations, to ensure that the environmental or 'macro-level' factors contributing to healthy workplaces are given equal consideration (Schulte, Goldenhar & Connally 1996).

Aggregating study data to inform health practices

One problem with research into the health effects of medical intervention has been that the sample size and outcome effects of many clinical trials provided insufficient statistical power to draw definitive conclusions. The response of some medical researchers has been to conduct a meta analysis of many studies, where aggregated findings from a number of studies would lead to more reliable results. The advantages of *meta analysis* also include the ability to identify an invariant finding in a group of diverse studies, and evidence for the appropriateness of the various methodological designs used in previous research (Daly, Kellehear & Gliksman 1997).

Another advantage of meta-analytic studies is that they can be used to feed comprehensive, and thus meaningful, information back to the public. In the US, for example, patient outcome research teams (PORTs) have been organised around specific clinical conditions with a view toward synthesising the available literature, analysing data bases, conducting prospective cohort studies and disseminating the findings to practice communities. Their task is to find out what 'works' in medicine, with a subtext of eliminating unnecessary medical care and promoting cost containment (Deyo 1995).

This information is extremely useful for practitioners in rural or isolated areas who may not have access to updated information, and helps to inform practice strategies and the community.

Social scientists have also used meta-analysis to construct a more realistic view of the effects of social factors on health. For example, Daly, Kellehear and Gliksman (1997) cite the meta-analytic studies compiled by Oakley, a well-known researcher in the field of women's health. Her composite findings provided evidence for the value of social support during pregnancy. She concluded that by ignoring the social perspective, previous researchers had failed to recognise strong evidence for the positive effect of social support on reducing the incidence of low birthweight, and overcoming the effect of low social class on both mortality and morbidity (Daly, Kellehear & Gliksman 1997).

Evidence-based practice

The meta-analytic approach has gained widespread acceptance among health professionals, and has been attributed with inspiring a global movement toward evidence-based practice in the health professions (Pearson et al. 1997). The evidence-based practice movement is based on the notion that providing research evidence for all of our activities in the health professions ensures accountability to the population for clinical decision-making and subsequent interventions. The popularity of evidence-based practice surged with the establishment in the UK of the International Cochrane Collaboration, which maintains a database of systematic reviews of research on health care interventions in a wide range of clinical areas in medicine (Bero & Rennie 1995; Daly, Kellehear & Gliksman 1997). The Cochrane Database of Systematic Reviews publicises reviews of a range of health care studies from a network of centres throughout the world. It was first published in 1995, with the objective of providing widespread dissemination of the results of randomised controlled trials, and the best evidence from other sources, so that practitioners could have access to the latest research findings for clinical decision-making that is both accurate and unbiased (Bero & Rennie 1995). The nursing profession has also followed suit in several countries, combining results of clinical trials of a number of nursing interventions to provide a more accurate picture of their effectiveness (Pearson et al. 1997).

Methodological issues

One of the most fundamental tenets of research is that the question guides the method. The framing of research questions and the analysis of the research findings are linked to certain theoretical foundations, and these are often a function of the researcher's educational preparation and professional orientation. Because researchers from different backgrounds tend to gravitate to certain types of questions (clinical, social, behavioural, environmental), there is often a pattern in the methodological approaches selected for study. Psychologists, for example, seek to explain individual behaviour, and this is reflected in studies addressing explanations for health-related behaviour and the influences on behaviour change. Sociologists and others in the area of social science (social workers and many allied health professionals) tend to research aspects of the social and economic environment within which behaviour is maintained.

Medical researchers, on the other hand, have a long tradition of conducting randomised controlled trials, as the method of choice to evaluate clinical interventions. These trials are conducted according to the rigours of the scientific, positivist, method. They typically investigate the outcome of a particular intervention in two randomised cohorts of patients, one having experienced the clinical intervention, and the other (the control group) who did not. This type of approach has yielded highly effective information to inform clinical practice (Daly, Kellehear & Glicksman 1997).

Nurses and many others involved in health care research have begun to use a range of interpretive methodologies in combination with more traditional research methods that require statistical computations. Interpretive research includes a number of specific methods (phenomenological, ethnographic, participative action research) that require different skills and different ways of thinking about the data than occurs in quantitative studies. Research questions revolve around describing and interpreting information in its 'real world' context rather than in the laboratory situation (McMurray 1994). In contrast to quantitative research, interpretive studies reflect the assumption that there are multiple, socially defined realities. By adhering to the conventions for analysis, the researcher can engage with research participants while 'bracketing out' his or her assumptions and biases, to report on the views, perceptions and thus meanings that participants bring to the research situation.

The attraction of interpretive methods is that including contextualised information allows a more holistic view of the situation. Interpretive research is also conducive to explorative flexibility—that is, the opportunity to investigate the 'cultural territory' and learn from the research population. This is enhanced by using in-depth, iterative investigation, where people may be interviewed on a number of occasions, with increasing refinement and focus (Gittlesohn et al. 1996).

Because interpretive studies emphasise the uniqueness of human situations and experiences, reliability or replicability in the quantitative sense cannot be achieved. However, through sampling strategies, verification interviews, multiple data collection methods, and a systematic and auditable plan for analysis, the data can be 'triangulated' to validate findings (Gittlesohn et al. 1996). A range of other sources of data can also be incorporated into the findings to ensure adequate triangulation, including census and client data, survey reports, mortality and morbidity rates, patient satisfaction and utilisation data, environmental reports, and media content analysis (Baum 1992).

Historically, one of the problems among the health research community has been a hesitancy to look at the many dimensions of a health issue or problem using multiple methods. One reason for this is the lack exposure to multiple methods in our educational preparation. Some professions, particularly medicine, lean toward epidemiological studies because of the emphasis on exact measurements. Others from the social sciences have attempted to research lay perceptions and the *emic view*, or culturally embedded context of health behaviour (Gittelsohn et al. 1996). To make a difference to the health of the community, the use of multiple strategies is important. In some cases, this involves a collaborative approach at each stage of the research process, beginning with defining the problem or issue to be investigated. In other cases, researchers may work in isolation on aspects of a problem that can be addressed incrementally.

One such method is participatory action research (PAR). Action research is a bit like evaluation research, except that the focus in evaluation studies is usually to study outcomes of change, such as efficiency and effectiveness measures. Action research tends to focus on the big picture: what *influences* change as well as its impact; what situational variability occurs; how the change is best implemented and by whom, and the perspectives of those involved in the change as well as those affected by it. Like qualitative evaluation studies, action research may be used as a type of formative evaluation of a program—a health promotion strategy, for example. Participatory action research is typically initiated from within an organisation or a program. The researcher is therefore a co-participant in the research, which makes the notion of *conducting* the research invalid. Instead, the researcher initiates the dialogue and trains others in the use of analytic techniques (Corcega 1992).

As a form of co-operative inquiry, PAR can be empowering for its participants, and thus the research fits well with the principles of primary health care and community development. One study among Aboriginal health workers in South Australia demonstrated the empowerment that flows from melding the roles of the researcher and the researched. The study examined the training needs of the health workers from their perspective and, in the process, improved their research literacy. By allowing the participants a genuine opportunity to set the agenda for the research, the study was seen to develop initiative, strengthen decision-making, and increase self-reliance (Hecker 1997).

Community health problems are particularly amenable to the type of participative, multidimensional investigations that are gaining popularity. Chapman's work in the area of smoking cessation, for example, suggested that epidemiological studies of smoking patterns were inadequate to provide direction to smoking cessation policies. He suggested that studies using more interpretive approaches, including oral history and discourse analysis, are necessary to make the complexities of smoking cessation more transparent (Chapman, in Daly, Kellehear and Gliksman 1997). Schurman (1996) adopted a PAR approach to workplace evaluation to ensure that her research agenda did not override the needs of those working in her industry. The study was a welcome opportunity for employees to bring workplace issues to the surface and plan for further exploration of strategies to meet their needs (Schurman 1996).

Combining research methods can provide valuable and balanced information, with *informational* as well as *statistical* significance, to inform strategic planning for health. A combination of approaches is currently being used in most evaluation studies—for example, to study cost-utility and other factors that will ultimately be used to inform resource allocation strategies. Focus group interviews, where a group of people are asked to participate in an interview based on their common experiences, provide an additional dimension. The focus group often produces a larger amount of rich data than individual interviews and can provide an encouraging environment for people to voice concerns, debate differences or address potentially embarrassing topics (Daly, Kellehear & Gliksman 1997). Focus group interviews may also produce serendipitous data that inform future research studies.

The advantage of community consultation at each stage of the research process is illustrated in the research findings of a study conducted by Colomeda (1996). She set out to examine perceptions of breast cancer held by North American Indian, Inupiat and Inuit women, and learned that these women had very clear ideas about the linkages between degradation of their physical environment and the disease. Instead of informing diagnostic strategies and treatment options, as was the original intention of the study, the results of her study shifted the focus to challenging minimum standards of environmental pollutants in underdeveloped parts of the North American rural areas (Colomeda 1996).

▶ CASE STUDY

Evaluating by thinking, listening, looking, understanding

Research approaches that are both multidimensional and culturally appropriate are particularly important in evaluation research, to avoid overly simplistic explanations of health outcomes in relation to program components. The Council of Remote Area Nurses of Australia, in collaboration with the council of an indigenous community (The Nganampa Health Council) adopted a participatory approach to develop a guide for those working on indigenous health promotion projects. The guide contains a training manual for those attempting to evaluate the outcomes of their health promotion strategies. It adopts a participatory approach to evaluation that is focused on encouraging participants to consider and discuss their impressions of the program at every step of the process, rather than waiting on outcome data.

The manual is written in simple terms for those unaccustomed to the jargon of research, and illustrated with culturally appropriate symbols. The text guides the researcher through the reasons for evaluation, goals and strategic planning for evaluation, and the techniques that guide each step in the process, explained in a series of work sheets.

The guide is based on the premise that the researcher must seek understanding, not just at the end of the research process, but throughout. Watching and thinking are the key cognitive activities. Footprints through the text direct the researcher through a circular process of questioning, reflecting, maintaining continuity with thoughts and data collection, feeding information back to interested co-participants (the community, the health service, and the project funders) to gain a sense of meaning from their perspective, thinking carefully again from a personal perspective, and questioning further to gather any additional information that may have been missed. It is an excellent manual to help lay researchers, many of whom will be Aboriginal Health Workers, with the language, skills and knowledge of evaluation research. (Colin & Garrow 1996).

Research ethics

The major ethical considerations in conducting research studies are universally accepted, and these include ensuring confidentiality and anonymity of research participants, scientific validity, and protection of vulnerable people such as children and those who become powerless by institutionalisation. In the use of animals, the rules are to use as few as possible, for specified purposes only, and to ensure there are proper safeguards for their use, including avoidance of pain or discomfort (Downie & Calman 1994). Researchers are ethically accountable to both the researched and the scientific community. This holds them responsible to fully explain to research participants any risks and benefits, regardless of how small, so that participants only consent to their involvement on the basis of being fully informed (Khoury 1996). In all research, there is some opportunity cost for the researched, and this needs to be made explicit, even if it is simply the imposition on their time (Downie & Calman 1994).

Researchers must take seriously their obligation to provide feedback to those supplying information. This ensures that people and the information they hold are not exploited by researchers who simply use the data for their own purposes, whether for idealistic purposes (to improve the health of populations), career enhancement (publication), or to guide further research studies. In the workplace, there is an ethical obligation to convey research findings on minimum standards of risk, permissible exposure limits, as well as the effects of drugs and alcohol on performance (Fessendon-Raden & Gert 1989). Another workplace issue is the use of research findings as a justification for instituting screening programs. A duty of care exists for both employer and employee, but not at the expense of civil liberties (McCallum 1994).

In all research studies, the issue of cultural sensitivity must be addressed. If a research study is devised without full consultation with those being researched, there is a risk of inadequate or inappropriate information being gathered and, in some cases, misinterpretation of the subtleties that may lead to persistent health problems (Daly, Kellehear & Gliksman 1997). The use of interview or observational data poses a particular risk to accurate interpretation. Researchers must make every effort to grasp the underlying intuitions of those being questioned, as their understanding of illnesses, their causation and treatment, is embedded in personal experiences and culture-based meanings (Campbell et al. 1997; Gittlesohn et al.

1996). This is particularly important in research aimed at informing policy development. When the major players are involved in helping to frame the questions, guide the research process, and articulate the findings in language that is meaningful to them, there is a greater likelihood that their preferences will find their way into public policies. Using language specific to the culture or group also increases the likelihood of successful implementation of any policy developments that flow from the research (Garner & Barraclough 1992).

Researching the future

Many questions remain to be addressed in community health. At a 'macro' level, research questions should be directed at knowing how investment in social infrastructure affects the distribution of income and wealth. We also need to examine the influences of social trust and community co-operation on economic outcomes (Baum 1997). Another area of importance to us all concerns the environmental issues that are so important to a sustainable future. Climate change is among the most pressing problems, especially in the South Pacific region (Hales, Woodward & Guest 1995).

As health researchers we need to become involved in the type of research that will study the effects of ozone depletion on the rate of skin cancers and cataracts, and the effect of heat waves on the elderly and those who live in sub-standard housing. We also need to look at the indirect effects of climate change on health that may be demonstrated in vector-borne disease and food production, as well as social disruptions (Hales, Woodward & Guest 1995). It is predicted that climate change will increase the prevalence of such vector-borne diseases as dengue fever, and this is already being seen in Australia. Furthermore, climate change has a powerful effect on agriculture and thus nutrition-related diseases, and there is a need to study these in a cross-regional and cross-cultural context (Hales, Woodward & Guest 1995).

In addition to the wider issues, there remains little information on locally defined health issues. One important element of the local agenda is health service utilisation. We know a great deal about the provision of health services, but little of the conditions that influence people's access to, or utilisation, of health care. We need to investigate which people use which services, and whether this is based on need, perceptions or convenience. We need to know what barriers to services exist in the community—such as cost, transportation, time or location. Also, we must research the extent to which there is unmet need in a given community to inform equitable planning processes.

We also need to conduct research into the '"patterned consistency" of health status, building upon research results on the relationship between health and socioeconomic status, ethnicity, race, age and sex' so that we can create alternative classifications, constructed on a systems-environmental perspective (Kickbusch 1997, p. 432). It is also essential that any community health research portfolio includes a series of community 'snapshots' to ensure that, in the true spirit of Alma Ata, health professionals continue to 'think globally' but 'act locally' (McMurray et al. 1998). We need to study community involvement in decision-making. What are the mechanisms for collaboration? Do people see their health services as affordable, or are there competing priorities than health care professionals are not aware of? Are services culturally acceptable? Are non-professionals providing appropriate care, and at what personal cost? What are the gaps in health promotion efforts across sectors in the community (McMurray 1993)?

Another area that has been neglected in mainstream public health research is that which focuses on the family, particularly in examining variation in families' perceptions of health and how health is supported within changing family structures. It is widely accepted that a person's concept of being healthy is socially constructed within the cultural system of the family and social group (Mechanic 1992). Notions of health or healthiness may differ considerably from medical or morbidity-related definitions (Kleinman 1988). Perceptions of family health and patterns of health services utilisation should therefore be examined carefully, particularly in light of the growing body of international health services research suggesting that self-assessment of health status is one of the best predictors of use of health care services (Fylkesnes & Forde 1992; Litva & Eyles 1994).

Questions also remain in various settings. We have witnessed the beginning of evaluation strategies in comprehensive school health programs, but we know little about the perspective of students or their families. We also have few operational definitions of culturally competent care from the perspective of the recipient (Santelli et al. 1996). In the parlance of contemporary WHO initiatives, we need to know where the best investments in health lie. Some researchers contend that the two greatest investments lie in improving child health and working conditions (Whitehead & Dahlgren 1995). Our research agenda for these areas would guide us toward examining the social gradients that exist in the provision of child care and housing, poverty, unemployment, working conditions and diet. Based on a body of research evidence, we could institute programs for improving such things as antenatal care, immunisation, and programs to help mothers quit smoking, improve their education and gain social support. In addition, we could better examine dangerous working conditions, inadequate or unsafe housing, and access to a nutritious diet for both children and adults (Whitehead & Dahlgren 1995).

There are many problems related to the physical environment that have yet to be the subject of research. In some places, the problem is a dearth of information—so much minutiae, so little analysis of the cause and even less prescription of the solution (Labonte 1994). In other places, we are overwhelmed with data needing to be interpreted at the level where it can be understood as a basis for change. We also need to integrate knowledge of the social environment with what we learn about our geography. Kickbusch (1997) identifies two major challenges in relation to examining the environments supportive to health. The first is to consider the settings projects (health care, school and workplace) as standards, so that our knowledge of health technologies includes the social technology of supportive environments for health. In this way, careful evaluation studies will lead to validating the standards of best practice in health-promoting settings. Then we need to see how this technology transfers into non-traditional, non-institutional settings (Kickbusch 1997). In Kickbusch's (1997) view, health is not only created where people live, love, learn, work and play, but where they shop, get their hair done, have a drink, and go out and have fun. In all of these places, we need to think, listen, look, understand and act as we go along (Colin & Garrow 1996).

THINKING CRITICALLY

Community health research

▶ Identify three research studies that could lead to health improvements in any three population groups.

▶ Explain the links between research findings and healthy public policy.

▶ Explain why the actions of health professionals should be based on research evidence.

▶ Discuss the ethical implications of screening health care workers for HIV.

▶ Devise a strategic research plan for examining the adequacy of dietary intake among an Aboriginal population.

REFERENCES

Badura, B. & Kickbusch, I. 1991, 'Introduction' in *Health Promotion Research. Towards a New Social Epidemiology*, eds B. Badura & I. Kickbusch, WHO European Regional Publication no. 37, WHO Geneva, pp. 1–6.

Baldwin, J., Rolf, J., Johnson, J., Bowers, J., Benally, C. et al. 1996, 'Developing culturally sensitive HIV/AIDS and substance abuse prevention curricula for Native American youth', *Journal of School Health*, vol. 66, no. 9, pp. 322–7.

Baum, F. 1992, 'Researching community health—evaluation and needs assessment that makes an impact', in *Community Health Policy and Practice in Australia*, eds F. Baum, D. Fry & I. Lennie, Pluto Press, Leichardt, pp. 77–94.

Baum, F. 1997, 'Public health and civil society: understanding and valuing the connection', *Australian and New Zealand Journal of Public Health*, vol. 21, no. 7, pp. 673–5.

Bero, L. & Rennie, D. 1995, 'The Cochrane Collaboration: preparing, maintaining and disseminating systematic reviews of the effects of health care', *Journal of the American Medical Association*, vol. 274, no. 24, pp. 1935–8.

Campbell, A., Charlesworth, M., Gillett, G. & Jones, G. 1997, *Medical Ethics*, 2nd edn, Wadsworth, Belmont, CA.

Colin, T. & Garrow, A. 1996, *Thinking, listening, looking, understanding and acting as you go along. Steps to evaluating indigenous health promotion projects*, CRANA, Alice Springs.

Colomeda, L. 1996, *Through the Northern Looking Glass*, NLN Press, New York.

Corcega, T. 1992, 'Participatory research: getting the community involved in health development', *International Nursing Review*, vol. 39, no. 6, pp 185–8.

Daly, J., Kellehear, A. & Gliksman, M. 1997, *The Public Health Researcher*, Oxford University Press, Melbourne.

Deyo, R. 1995, 'Promises and limitations of the patient outcome research teams: the low back-pain example', *Proceedings of the Association of American Physicians*, vol. 107, no. 3, pp. 324–8.

Downie, R. & Calman, K. 1994, *Healthy Respect: Ethics in Health Care*, Oxford University Press, New York.

Drevdahl, D. 1995, 'Coming to voice: the posers of emancipatory community interventions', *Advances in Nursing Science*, vol. 18, no. 2, pp. 13–24.

Fessenden-Raden, J. & Gert, D. 1989, 'A philosophical approach to the management of occupational health hazards', in *Contemporary Issues in Bioethics*, 3rd edn, eds T. Beauchamp, & L. Walters, Wadsworth, Belmont, CA, pp. 618–23.

Frye, L. 1997, 'Occupational health surveillance', *American Association of Occupational Health Nurses Journal*, vol. 45, no. 4, pp. 184–7.

Fylkesnes, K. & Forde, O. 1992, 'Determinants and dimensions involved in self-evaluation of health', *Social Science and Medicine*, vol. 35, pp. 271–9.

Gardner, H. & Barraclough, S. 1992, 'The policy process', in *Health Policy: Development, Implementation and Evaluation in Australia*, ed. H. Gardner, Churchill-Livingstone, Melbourne, pp. 1–28.

Gittelsohn, J., Harris, S., Burris, K., Kakegamic, L., Landman, L. et al. 1996, 'Use of ethnographic methods for applied research on diabetes among the Ojibway-Cree in Northern Ontario', *Health Education Quarterly*, vol. 23, no. 3, pp. 365–82.

Glick, D., Hale, P., Kulbok, P. & Shettig, J. 1996, 'Community development theory. Planning a community nursing center', *Journal of Nursing Administration*, vol. 26, no. 7–8, pp. 44-50.

Hales, S., Woodward, A. & Guest, C. 1995, 'Climate change in the South Pacific region: priorities for public health research', *Australian Journal of Public Health*, vol. 19, no. 6, pp. 543–5.

Ham, C. 1997, 'Lessons and conclusions', in *Health Care Reform: Learning from International Experience*, ed. C. Ham, Open University Press, Buckingham, pp. 119–40.

Hatch, M. 1996, 'Women's work and women's health', *Epidemiological Prevention*, vol. 20, pp. 176–9.

Hecker, R. 1997, 'Participatory action research as a strategy for empowering Aboriginal health workers', *Australian and New Zealand Journal of Public Health*, vol. 21, no. 7, pp. 784–8.

Hinton Walker, P., Bowllan, N., Chevalier, N., Gullo, S. & Lawrence, L. 1996, 'School-based care: clinical challenges and research opportunities', *Journal of School and Pediatric Nursing*, vol. 1, no. 2, pp. 64–74.

Kalucy, R. 1995 'Ethics and public health', in *Health for All: The South Australian Experience*, ed. F. Baum, Wakefield Press, Kent Town, SA, pp. 172–90.

Khoury, M. 1996, 'From genes to public health: the applications of genetic technology in disease prevention', *American Journal of Public Health*, vol. 86, no. 12, pp. 1717–22.

Kickbusch, I. 1997, 'Health-promoting environments: the next steps', *Australian and New Zealand Journal of Public Health*, vol. 21, no. 4, pp. 431–4.

Kisker, E. & Brown, R. 1996, 'Do school-based health centers improve adolescents' access to health care, health status, and risk-taking behavior?', *Journal of Adolescent Health*, vol. 18, pp. 335–43.

Kleinman, A. 1988, *The Illness Narratives*, Basic Books, New York.

Kolbe, L., Collins, J. & Cortese, P. 1997, 'Building the capacity of schools to improve the health of the nation', *American Psychologist*, vol. 52, no. 3, pp. 256–65.

Kolbe, L., Kann, L., Collins, J., Leavy Small, M., Collins Pateman, B. et al. 1995, 'The school health policies and programs study (SHPPS): context, methods, general findings, and future efforts', *Journal of School Health*, vol. 65, no. 8, pp. 339–43.

Labonte, R. 1994, '"See me, hear me, touch me, feel me". Lessons on environmental health information for bureaucratic activists', in *Ecological Public Health: From Vision to Practice*, eds C. Chu & R. Simpson, Institute of Applied Environmental Research, Brisbane, pp. 269–76.

Litva, A. & Eyles, J. 1994, 'Health or healthy: why people are not sick in a southern Ontario town', *Social Science and Medicine*, vol. 38, pp. 1083–91.

McCallum, R. 1994, 'Ethics in occupational health', in *Principles of Health Care Ethics*, ed. R. Gillon, John Wiley & Sons, Chichester, pp. 931–4.

McMurray, A. 1993, *Community Health Nursing: Primary Health Care in Practice*, 2nd edn, Churchill-Livingstone, Melbourne.

McMurray, A. 1994, 'Researching rural health: the qualitative approach', *Australian Journal of Rural Health*, vol. 2, no. 4, pp. 17–24.

McMurray, A. 1998, 'Disseminating research findings for the benefit of the rural community', *Australian Journal of Rural Health*, vol 6, no. 2, pp. 89–95.

McMurray, A., Hudson-Rodd, N., Al Khudairi, S. & Roydhouse, R. 1998, 'Family health and health utilisation in Belmont, Western Australia: a community case study', *Australian and New Zealand Journal of Public Health*, vol. 22, no. 1, pp. 107–14.

Mechanic, D. 1992, 'Health and illness behavior and patient–practitioner relationships', *Social Science and Medicine*, vol. 34, no. 12, pp. 1345–50.

Meleis, A. 1989, 'International research: a need or a luxury?', *Nursing Outlook*, vol. 7, no. 3, pp. 138–42.

Milio, N. 1991, 'Making healthy public policy: developing the science by learning the art: an ecological framework for policy studies' in *Health Promotion Research. Towards a New Social Epidemiology*, eds B. Badura & I. Kickbusch, WHO European Regional Publication, no. 37, WHO, Geneva, pp. 7–28.

Mullen, P., Evans, D., Forster, J., Gottlieb, N., Kreuter, M. et al. 1995, 'Settings as an important dimension in health education/promotion policy, programs, and research', *Health Education Quarterly*, vol. 22, no. 3, pp. 329–45.

Pearson, A., Borbasi, S., Fitzgerald, M., Kowanko, I. & Walsh, K. 1997, 'Evidence-based nursing: an examination of nursing within the international evidence-based health care practice movement', Discussion Paper No. 1, Royal College of Nursing, Australia, RCNA, Canberra.

Ringen, K. & Stafford, E. 1996, 'Intervention research in occupational safety and health: examples from construction', *American Journal of Industrial Medicine*, vol. 29, pp. 314–20.

Santelli, J., Morreale, M., Wigton, A. & Grason, H. 1996, 'School health centers and primary care for adolescents: a review of the literature', *Journal of Adolescent Health*, vol. 18, pp. 357–66.

Schulte, P., Goldenhar, L. & Connally, L. 1996, 'Intervention research: science, skills, and strategies', *American Journal of Industrial Medicine*, vol. 29, pp. 285–8.

Schurman, S. 1996, 'Making the "New American Workplace" safe and healthy: a joint labor–management–researcher approach', *American Journal of Industrial Medicine*, vol. 29, pp. 373–7.

Twinn, S. 1997, 'Methodological issues in the evaluation of the quality of public health nursing: a case study of the maternal and child health centres in Hong Kong', *Journal of Advanced Nursing*, vol. 25, pp. 753–9.

Whitehead, M. & Dahlgren. G. 1995, 'What can be done about inequalities in health?', in *Health and Disease: A Reader*, eds B. Davey, A. Gray & C. Seale, Open University Press, Buckingham, pp. 367–75.

18

Healthy public policy

The role of healthy public policy is to guide the way in which governments, communities and individuals address changes that must be made to create, enhance and sustain health. At the global level, healthy public policies may be instigated by the initiatives of such agencies as the WHO and the World Bank. These are informed by comparative epidemiological data, which are then filtered down to the national, state and community level. National and state (or provincial) governments often use the international information to develop policies appropriate to the needs of their populations, but this is not always the case. Policy developments may be initiated at the local or grass-roots level, where local information may form the basis for national or international policies. Healthy policies for any one issue or population group may also be developed collaboratively across sectors and across various health issues. Policy development is therefore dependent on the population needs, the political and economic context and the capacity for intersectoral collaboration, and vertical and horizontal information sharing.

In any type of policy development, community participation is essential to identify strategic goals and culturally appropriate mechanisms for meeting health needs. This chapter examines the directions that should be taken in the development of healthy policies at all levels: community, societal and global. It provides an overview of policy developments in some geographic areas related to several of our most pressing health problems so that, in the next century, we can learn from the past and work toward the common goal of improving health in all communities.

Objectives

By the end of this chapter you will be able to:

- *identify the four most important objectives of policy development*

- *explain the difficulties faced by political decision-makers in attempting to redress societal health problems*

- *describe one successful healthy public policy*

- *identify one major health issue that requires a public policy response that is both local and global, and identify its essential elements.*

- *analyse the adequacy of at least one of your community's health policies.*

Why healthy public policy?

In providing opportunities for efficient and effective health care and health promotion, healthy policies contribute to advancing community goals for sustainable health and wellbeing. At the individual level, the industriousness of study and productivity of work contribute to personal development. Through socioeconomic opportunity, healthy workplaces and healthy schools provide enhanced opportunities in which the family can reach its full potential. Structures and processes that support healthy families contribute to community vitality. Healthy policy development is thus pivotal to the advancement of society. It is a multifaceted and multi-level undertaking where nations, states, communities and individuals become either deliberate or inadvertent participants in the creation and sustainability of health.

The model introduced in chapter 4 of this book identified community health as a product of the interactions between health status, health determinants and risk factors, health resources and health service utilisation (see figure 4.1). Each of these is either constrained or facilitated by public policies which may expedite or impede communities in overriding any disadvantages associated with biological factors, and maximising opportunities for accessing resources. Policies themselves are thus part of the social and political environment within which health is created and sustained.

The combination of factors influencing health is, to a large extent, determined by the 'mix' of public policies in a range of areas, including those governing industry, trade, other economic developments, systems of social welfare, health and education. The interdependence of health, social, industry, and economic policies is often subtle, and may be overlooked when policy planners begin to address the needs in one or another of these areas. However, at the level of implementation, resource implications of decisions in each of these areas usually override other considerations. The challenge for policy development is to recognise the financial issues and multilayered political agendas that either assist or impede community development.

The politics of policy-making

At the *macro* level, global and national economic policies create wealth which, depending on policies governing the distribution of resources, can support or constrain community development (Lee & Paxman 1997). In many cases, the implementation of these policies is left to operational decisions taken at the community level. In the process of implementation, there is an opportunity for community members to feed back information to the various health authorities, and this is usually aimed at helping improve or redirect resources or policy decisions in the future. This type of feedback often forms the basis for wider policy reviews that may reach beyond the community.

The feedback loop is illustrated by healthy workplace policies, which can be both an implementation of national health promotion policies and a mechanism for informing policy development for other settings or other industries. Similarly, policies that promote healthy organisations in any sector of the community add value to the national social and economic capacity. For example, in Queensland Health, a policy on health-promoting environments has recently been developed, to implement the 'healthy settings' initiatives of the international community as recommended by the WHO (Dwyer 1997; WHO 1995, 1996). This work can subsequently be used by the Australian Commonwealth Department of Health and Community Services or the Public Health Association, as a prototype for a national initiative.

Most countries have a public health association that is the source of policy statements. In Australia, the Public Health Association lists 64 policy statements to guide activities ranging from breastfeeding and childhood lead exposure to landmines, tobacco control, stratospheric ozone depletion and ecologically sustainable development (PHAA 1997). Most of these policies are based on a national 'report card' of how the country is doing in relation to the directives of the WHO and the benchmarks of other countries. Recommendations are based on the growing body of clinical and preventive knowledge in each of the respective areas. In each case, the Public Health Association identifies what it will undertake to change, what type of government support needs to be encouraged, and how it will work with the public, the government and non-government organisations to secure the objectives identified in the policy (PHAA 1997).

Developing policies that improve the health of any population defies a 'cook-book' approach because, with the diversity of communities, skills, values and issues, none follow a linear, ordered developmental process (Labonte 1994). In both developing and industrialised countries, healthy economic policies are needed to reduce poverty. However, the very policies that are designed to stimulate economic growth often create a wider gap between the rich and poor, leading to increased public demand for welfare services through unemployment and poverty. This depletes national resources, creating a vicious cycle of economic disadvantage. The paradox is that, when public health assistance is most necessary, it is usually least affordable (Ife 1995).

Although research in a number of countries has shown a reduction in several indicators of poverty as a result of economic growth, no definitive links can be made because of the disparate distribution of wealth (Whitehead 1995). Healthy public policies must therefore be extended to systems that would guide equitable distribution of wealth. These include employment policies that would provide people with the means to generate revenue. National economic policies must therefore be accompanied by comprehensive social welfare strategies, and local implementation processes that allow opportunities for economic development at the community level.

One of the most important lessons for policy development is to look to past experience to solve the problems of the future. It is helpful to examine what works, and what has brought about less than optimal conditions. For example, when harmful products such as tobacco and alcohol are deregulated, there is the potential for indiscriminate use of these substances by young people and the disenfranchised in society (Kalucy 1995). Yet regulation sometimes has a punitive effect, as those lobbying for the legalisation of marijuana or heroin would suggest. The most important issue is to base policy development on evaluation research, which enables us to better predict the immediate and long-term outcomes of policies, and the extent to which these make healthy choices easier for people (Milio 1991).

What will be needed for the future is a new synthesis that combines the most effective principles and strategies used in the past, with some vision of the future. This requires all of us involved in health care to become conversant with the ideology that governs decision-making, as well as the more practical issues related to health care delivery. Today's political climate in the industrialised world is somewhat conservative, and oriented more toward a capitalist than a socialist view. This has an implication for health care, particularly in sanctioning economic rationalism to create greater wealth. Navarro (1993) contends that this is not entirely healthy, as socialist regimes have experienced greater successes than capitalist forces in improving people's health (Navarro 1993). Once again, the debate must focus on issues of social justice as well as the core business of wealth creation.

Many political tensions pervade the ideological debates involved in policy-making. Tensions exist between: those who defend the welfare state with a genuine commitment to the needs of the community; the economic rationalists who would maximise efficiency, encourage competition and individual choice and accountability with minimal government interference; the corporatists who would break down barriers between public and private; and those who would dismantle capitalist structures and replace them with a socialist order (Ife 1995).

According to Ife (1995), the welfare state dehumanises, alienates and disempowers. Economic rationalism exacerbates, rather than reduces, social and economic inequalities and 'in the name of competition and individualism it negates the values of caring, social solidarity, cohesion and community' (Ife 1995, p. 7). Corporatism is only a short-term solution as it is an artificially manufactured compromise between competing interests (capital and labour) and could only succeed under relatively stable economic growth and prosperity. It also requires trade-offs to be made at the level of peak organisations, which militates against democratic or participatory forms of policy and decision-making (Ife 1995).

Ife (1995) suggests that we have a symbiotic relationship between industrial capitalism and socialism, with each necessary for the other. We need social services for capitalism to grow. In turn, social services must be supported by the finances of capitalism. Meeting human needs for stability, security, health and education is good for production and reproduction. The answer is community-based human services located within a broader program of social change based on a philosophy of sustainability, social justice and ecological community development (Ife 1995).

In developing healthy public policies, we must recognise that health-supporting or health-impeding practices range through all areas of organisation and life, from the public to the personal (Jones & Miller 1992). At the population level, we must accommodate to the plurality and secularity of our society. The growth of multiculturalism and affirmative action have increased public awareness and influenced the resource allocation debate (Kalucy 1995). We have also experienced the paradoxical effects of the success of modern clinical and public health research and practice. With reductions in perinatal and maternal mortality and increased longevity, the demand for health care has shifted to long-term care of chronically ill, disabled, aged, vulnerable and disempowered people. The full implication of this will not be known for many years.

Social justice may be an illusory goal, but we must maintain policies that strive for the greatest good, and an ecological view that sees today's participation in creating health as an investment in the future. We need to carefully examine the factors leading to lifelong wellbeing and the propensity to morbidity and mortality. Given the research findings to date, it becomes clear that these are affected by antenatal care, birthweight and perinatal care, and measures of relative advantage and disadvantage such as social class, education, employment and family background (Kalucy 1995). Genetics also has a part to play, not just biologically, but in family socialisation that affects smoking, exercise, drinking and other lifestyle behaviours. These indicate a need to continue to address health issues from within a socioecological model of health, where social and environmental policies are at least as important as policies about illness prevention and health promotion.

Components of healthy public policy

Several elements are essential for healthy public policy. At a national level, there must be structures to encourage equitable health care for all the population. The public also must have access to services and delivery mechanisms to meet the needs of special groups. Policies must also include strategies to encourage participation by all community members. Healthy policies must include some type of reward system for keeping the population healthy, rather than simply addressing illness issues. This could involve fiscal incentives that favour health promotion over technologically intense interventions (Salmon 1995).

Another element is related to quality improvement. Health policies need to include systems for performance monitoring in relation to clinical outcomes and these are dependent upon both research and information systems. Health-related research needs to be seen as the foundation of healthy policy and funded accordingly. Information systems that convey options to the periphery of decision-making must be appropriate, non-duplicative and user-friendly. A further component in healthy public policies is an adequately educated and geographically distributed workforce to provide community and hospital based services to those in need of both preventive and illness care.

To ensure equity of access, resourcing mechanisms for the health care system must have the organisational capacity to deliver co-ordinated, comprehensive health services to under-served populations, and to ensure that no new categories of under-served populations emerge. This may require privatisation of some previously public services, or alternative mechanisms to ensure access to specialist care for those in need of such services. Policies governing the delivery of health care must also be aimed at the provision of seamless services across the illness trajectory. This means that home and community care must be funded to the extent that adequate family and carer support is guaranteed.

Finally, a vital web of population-based, core public health functions must be developed to strengthen the capacity of the government and communities to identify and respond to both personal and public health problems, including the needs of informal care givers (Salmon 1995).

Types of health policies

Healthy policies fall into one or more of the following four categories: policies that strengthen individuals; those that strengthen communities; those that improve access to essential facilities and services; and those intended to effect macroeconomic and cultural change (Whitehead 1995).

■ Healthy policies in terms of individuals are person-based, and aimed at building knowledge, motivation and skills. Policies that enable workplace stress management, counselling services for people who become unemployed and smoking cessation programs fall into this category (Whitehead 1995).

■ Policies that strengthen communities guide programs to bring disadvantaged people together for mutual support and protection against health hazards. This would include, for example, healthy neighbourhood programs that promote social cohesion through strategies for social control of illegal activity and substance abuse, programs for enhancing the socialisation of young people or limiting youthful experimentation with dangerous and destructive activities, and systems that provide initial employment for young people, improve access to formal and informal health care, or that encourage the exercise of political power (Wallace, in Whitehead 1995).

- Policies that focus on improving access to essential facilities and services include ensuring that a community has clean water, sanitation, adequate housing, safe and fulfilling employment, safe and nutritious food supplies, essential health care, educational services, and welfare in times of need (Whitehead 1995).

- Policies that encourage macroeconomic or cultural changes to reduce poverty and inequalities include macroeconomic and labour market policies, and the encouragement of cultural values that promote equality of opportunities and hazard control (Whitehead 1995).

Environment policies

The environment is one area that has attracted considerable public participation, and this bodes well for the future. Policies for a healthy environment must be cognisant of the distinction between environmentalism and ecologism (Labonte 1994). *Environmentalism* tends to define the environment as external to human existence. This makes it easier to dismiss changes in local or global air, water and land, and in flora and fauna populations as directly affecting individual health or wellbeing. *Ecologism* is a contrasting paradigm emphasising the interconnectedness and interdependencies of ecosystems. Human health and wellbeing cannot be understood apart from the health of local, global or regional ecosystems (Labonte 1994).

Policies for a healthy environment must be holistic in terms of integrating and synthesising the interdependence of people and their surroundings. They must be focused on sustainability, diversity and equilibrium and responsive to changing needs and knowledge (Ife 1995; Lee & Paxman 1997). They must also respond to people's concerns for such issues as employment, housing or health care, and be based on the ecologist principle that most human activity is embedded within sets of ecosystem relations between organisms, individuals, populations and communities (Petersen & Lupton 1996). This is illustrated in policy suggestions for a carbon tax, for example, to deter those who do not use public transportation. The long-term effect of such a policy may be to attract the wealthy to cities, which would relegate the poor to suburban fringes where transportation is inadequate (Ife 1995). This type of policy often generates moral overtones but a lack of sensitivity to all that may be affected. It is essential in planning environment policy that it be sensitive to the connections between the biosphere and *all* human relations, including racism, classism, ageism, ethnocentrism, imperialism, sexism and colonialism. Healthy environmental policies must also integrate environmental analysis with community concerns, lifestyles and preferences (Labonte 1994; Petersen & Lupton 1996).

Occupational health policy

The WHO global strategy on occupational health is based on the consideration of occupational health as a basic element of sustainable development (WHO 1995). This is related to the fact that preventing occupational accidents, injuries and diseases, and protecting workers against physical and psychological overload, implies a parsimonious use of resources, minimising the unnecessary loss of human and material resources. Occupational health policy is linked to healthy environment initiatives in that the objective of healthy and safe working environments is safe, low-energy, low-emission, low-waste technology and the use of the best available production technology. In addition, policies governing the workplace are based on the capacity of workplaces to provide early detection and intervention for a range of environmental health hazards. Healthy occupational policies therefore have the capacity to foster a healthy, productive and well-motivated workforce as the means for socioeconomic, and thus community, development (WHO 1995).

Healthy occupational policies are also those that maintain ethical considerations in the workplace. Given the fact that at some time during their employment all workers encounter some type of hazard, policies and their implementation strategies must be based on accurate disclosure to workers and the duty of care by employers to eliminate or reduce harm, minimise worker exposure, and provide information and training (Fessenden-Raden & Gert 1989). Health education in the workplace should also be governed by these ethical principles, and focus on worker participation in developing strategies to implement the policy initiatives of the wider community, whether these relate to smoking cessation, health screening, stress management or nutrition (Mullen et al. 1995).

Indigenous health policy

Another policy area that is fundamental to socioeconomic development is that which guides indigenous health issues. The US policies that guide the health of American Indians have been considered among the most successful (Kunitz & Brady 1995). Although policy development in that country has been done with some degree of conflict, several policy initiatives throughout the past three decades are seen to have improved health care to indigenous people in that country. These include federal (rather than state) government administration, separation of the Indian Health Service from other Indian affairs, and the provision of an integrated health service (Kunitz & Brady 1995).

The American approach has been commended, as federal governments are seen to be better suited to guarding the interests of indigenous minorities than are state or provincial governments, who compete with them for natural resources and land. Indigenous health policy is also more effectively implemented if the agency responsible for its development is devoted to that issue alone, and not distracted by land rights, natural resources and economic development issues. A national health agency may also have better professional resources for community outreach, disease surveillance, health education and substance-abuse prevention strategies than state agencies with multiple responsibilities (Kunitz & Brady 1995). This is the basis for the development of specific, indigenous mental health policies in Australia. Separating out the local problems and culturally accepted strategies for addressing these allows the community to target specific mental health issues that may become obscured within wider policy initiatives (Queensland Health 1996).

One area that distinguishes policies for indigenous people in North America from that of other countries is related to the treaties made between indigenous and non-indigenous people (O'Neil 1995). The treaties and trust relationships established in the US and Canada provide a basis for legal standards of health care. As Kunitz and Brady (1995, p. 557) suggest, without such standards, 'indigenous people are merely supplicants, sometimes wheedling, sometimes demanding, but always unprotected by the law and dependent on the good will, guilt, and embarrassment of the majority'. Treaty provisions ensure that indigenous people's rights are fundamental to health policy, and that they have access to traditional healers as well as Western medicine (O'Neil 1995).

Canadian policy revolves around the four principles of equity, holism, indigenous control and diversity in the design of health systems and services (O'Neil 1995). People of the First Nations communities in that country contend that the fundamental ingredient in making this type of policy approach work is to ensure that when there is transfer of authority to indigenous people there must be adequate investment in the existing institutional infrastructure and human resource capacities at the community level (O'Neil 1995). These are issues currently at the heart of negotiations in Australia, New Zealand and South Africa (Ashton 1996; Gray & Saggers 1994; Gray et al. 1995; Matseoane 1997).

Mental health policy

One of the priorities for healthy public policy should be mental health. It is estimated that up to 20% of adults and 10–15% of young people may be affected by a mental disorder at any one time (Rafael, in Martin & Davis 1995). Many, especially among Aboriginal people, migrant groups and adolescents, do not find their way into treatment. One of the problems is the emphasis on management of mental illness or mental disorders, rather than on promoting good mental health (Martin & Davis 1995). Healthy public policy needs to also address the social aspects of mental health, including family relationships, interpersonal and social skills, parenting, and elements of the social environment that protect people from exposure to violence, abuse or discord (Martin & Davis 1995).

Another problem in mental health policy development is the backlash that has ensued from anti-discrimination and equal opportunity acts that have guided deinstitutionalisation of the mentally ill. These have given rise to bodies such as guardianship boards and tribunals, whose function is to ensure the civil rights of those disempowered by virtue of being diagnosed with mental illness (Kalucy 1995). The resource implications of these acts, which were overlooked at the time of their development, have resulted in excessive burdens being placed on psychiatrists and mental health nurses to 'process' rather than treat people. Resourcing policy decisions thus falls into the realm of ethics. Paradoxically, the very policies that were intended to improve conditions for the mentally ill have had the opposite effect. The need for thoughtful and thorough government planning in policy development is imperative, especially for those with mental illness, who are among the most vulnerable in society (Kalucy 1995; Minichiello 1995).

Tobacco policy

One of the most high-profile public policy issues of the 1990s has been tobacco policy and legislation (Reynolds 1995). The regulatory controls over the purchase and use of tobacco products have been a major success in making healthy choices easier for people. Policy initiatives targeting availability, pricing, labelling and promotion have acted as deterrents to smokers, and rates of those beginning to smoke are on the decline in many areas. However, more importantly, the public policies have transformed the way smoking is viewed in the community, and created a ritual of exclusion. This has had the effect of stigmatising smokers, which is either applauded or rejected by various groups in the community (Reynolds 1995). Once again, policy development must be mindful of ethical considerations and the need to preservice social justice and the rights of individuals, while targeting the greater good of the population (Reynolds 1995).

Population policies

Another policy development with ethical implications concerns the Global Burden of Disease Study. As mentioned in earlier chapters, this study is aimed at collecting global epidemiological information in an attempt to guide population-based policy development (Murray & Lopez 1997a,b,c,d). The idea is palatable to policy planners, but the methods are of concern to some. The global burden of disease is being calculated as a product of both quantity and quality of life in a composite index of Disability Adjusted Life Years (DALYs). Concern has been expressed over whether such a rational– technical approach to global policy development is warranted, particularly when the trend is toward identifying local issues from which the best return on investments in health are expected to flow. The Global Burden of Disease Study is costly, and may therefore be diverting scarce analytical resources away from more fruitful pursuits such as examining the outcomes of various clinical interventions (Mooney, Irwig & Leeder 1997). A related issue is whether the focus should be on disease or intervention. Such an approach may not be congruent with the WHO investment in health approach or reveal 'best buys' in health (Mooney, Irwig & Leeder 1997).

A similar concern has also been raised by critics of the Healthy Cities projects. Universal policy initiatives that rely on expert knowledge to solve community problems obscure the power relations, uncertainties and ambiguities of the local environment. This may convey the impression 'that national, cultural and local differences, competing interests and inequitable access to resources are irrelevant to policy outcomes' (Petersen & Lupton 1996, p. 127). Healthy cities must go beyond 'ideologically fortified declaration' (McMichael 1993, p. 295) to encompass good science and an understanding of local health status, health hazards and health services and the outcomes of previous interventions (McMichael 1993; Whitehead & Dahlgren 1995).

That unique combination of 'good science' and locally derived information is the key to healthy policies in a range of areas. One example is related to healthy eating. Nutrition is an important health issue plaguing many people, especially indigenous groups. Nutrition policies that would improve dietary patterns must be done from a deep understanding of consumption practices, structural conditions that constrain healthy eating, and economic factors that may impede improvements. Healthy nutrition policies must therefore blend ideas and strategies derived from the indigenous communities themselves with the scientific knowledge of nutrition and marketing expertise. Labonte (1994) suggests this could be done using a composite 'shopping basket' of food items based on food purchasing patterns as a basis for planning. Such a policy could be sensitive to group and community customs, cultural expectations and economic factors. The food basket approach would also allow analysis of environmental constraints such as food toxicity, and personal factors such as the patterning of actual and shifting food preferences. This provides a creative and comprehensive approach to policy development that is guided by national initiatives but dependent on local information.

Decisions for healthy public policy must also take account of collaboration and information sharing to ensure that horizontal and vertical integration is achieved wherever possible. A co-operative approach also ensures a population focus, which guides decisions for integrated or single-focus programs. For example, decisions must be made as to whether it would be more advantageous to develop child-specific policies for such things as diet, infectious disease control, immunisation and injury protection, or whether child health policies should be integrated into the settings orientation of healthy schools, healthy neighbourhoods and healthy marketplaces. Similarly, policies for women's health and men's health must be developed in the overlapping contexts of indigenous health policies, nutrition and injury protection policies, and those that address gender and race relations. Rural health policy, for example, cuts across all policy areas for reasons that are related to both the population and the setting.

> **CASE STUDY**

*Healthy public policy for rural and
remote Australia*

The residents of rural and remote areas in many countries share a number of distinctive characteristics that predispose them to poorer health status than their urban counterparts. These include geographic isolation, inaccessible and sometimes inadequate health services, maldistribution of health professionals, the special circumstances associated with what are often harsh environments, and, in many cases, specific health needs associated with particular population groups. In Australia, these groups include Aboriginal and Torres Strait Islanders, women, young people, the aged and persons experiencing mental health problems.

In 1995, the Australian Health Ministers Advisory Council reviewed the national rural health strategy (NRHS) in an attempt to ensure its continued relevance to promoting the health of people in rural and remote Australia. Their objective was to ensure that the following goals were met:

■ accessible, acceptable and affordable health care based on population needs
■ flexible approaches to address the specific needs of disadvantaged groups
■ approaches to service delivery that take account of the specific education needs of health practitioners
■ multidisciplinary approaches within a co-ordinated framework
■ an orientation to primary health care and public health
■ integration and co-ordination of activities between Commonwealth and state governments to maximise intersectoral linkages
■ consumer participation in health planning and decision-making
■ health services that are able to demonstrate improved health outcomes.

In order to achieve these formidable goals, it has been necessary for government bodies to minimise the barriers and problems that currently impede effective delivery of health services in these areas. The most important barriers to health services in rural and remote areas relate to the ubiquitous transportation and communication problems that are a characteristic of all rural and remote areas. For many areas, access in and out of remote areas is seasonal and variable. Not only does this interfere with the community accessing existing health services, but it also acts as a deterrent to health professionals for reasons that are both geographic and professional. Often acting as lone practising professionals, health practitioners are often quick to reach 'burnout' stage from overwork and the responsibility for health outcomes with insufficient infrastructure and support.

In response to the problems, the AHMAC have recommended a healthy rural health policy as follows:

■ Rural health care needs
These must be met from an understanding of the links between the special needs of rural and remote Australians and the direct causative factors. This guides health planners to improve information so that there is greater understanding of the causes of ill health, and to respond to the special needs of those population groups with special needs.
■ Resource allocation and service provision
Key issues are to identify those being unserved, underserved or inappropriately served to ensure equity and access. This guides the development of population-based funding models that ensure adequate resource allocation to rural and remote areas, with an integrated funding option, to pool resources for greater coverage of need. The recommended approach is to accelerate and expand multipurpose service arrangements, extension of mobile and

outreach services and the use of interactive technology for service delivery.

■ Rural and remote workforce issues

Given problems with recruitment and retention, the education and training of the rural and remote workforce requires ongoing support. This entails funding for education and support activities, especially for nurses and indigenous health practitioners, support for the network of Rural Health Training Units (RHTUs), instituting a system of on-site educational seminars and workshops, and maximising the potential of interactive technology.

■ Primary health care approach

The recommendations acknowledge that, while maintaining the services required to deliver acute care and emergency services, funding and educational preparation must be given to the health workforce to encourage health promotion and primary health care activities. This includes incorporating public health training with a population focus in the educational preparation of all health professionals practising in rural and remote areas and funding to develop mechanisms for community participation in planning and decision-making.

■ Evaluation and health outcomes

To ensure that resources are allocated efficiently and equitably, information systems are to be established that can create comprehensive baseline measures and monitor the health status and workforce characteristics of rural and remote communities, the level of people's accessibility to services, and the effects of different models of service delivery. This would help to ensure that funding is linked to health outcomes and that intervention measures are benchmarked to other areas and other strategies.

The policy recommendations are accompanied by a series of strategic suggestions for local and regional models for health funding and management, organisational and education issues, recruitment and retention strategies, best practice models and multiskilling of the workforce, meeting the special needs of isolated communities and those with special risks to health, and models for collaboration. It is a healthy public policy in addressing the political and economic environment within which health service provision can be improved. Another strength is its orientation toward framing health goals in terms of population health outcomes, and recognition of the need for government support and continuing education for health professionals at the vanguard of health promotion (AHMAC 1995).

The promise for the twenty-first century lies in our ability to learn from the twentieth century. The policies we have used, the process by which they have evolved, and the structural features that have enabled their implementation are all instructive. Perhaps more importantly, in the process of creating and sustaining health, we have learned much from one another. Each of us has experiences that reflect differences in gender, religion, ethnicity, socioeconomic background and the endless combinations of these. The challenge for the future is to create the kind of society in which the meanings of the past can protect and stimulate the vigour of the local community (Suzuki 1997). This includes cautious celebration of our technological capabilities. Technology has been purchased at an enormous cost: pollution, conflict, alienation, social decay, ecological breakdown and long-term nuclear risk (Beare & Slaughter 1993). Some technologies are so powerful that they need to be subjected to careful scrutiny during their development and their effects monitored over time. As the caretakers of the changing environment, our generation must adopt a form of 'cultural editing' so that we can frame alternatives and social innovations in the context of our multidimensional ways of seeing and knowing (Beare & Slaughter 1993).

The other major area for policy consideration is related to the organisation of health services. There is now unequivocal evidence to show that level of health in a population does not correlate with the level of medical consumption (Navarro 1993). Health services must be people-friendly and embodied in the principle that health is a public good, not a market commodity (Lee & Paxman 1997). For too long, communities have placed an over-reliance on outside expertise to dictate their health care needs. In the next millenium, there will be no access, equity or self-determinism unless community participation is encouraged at each stage of health care planning, from service development to outcome evaluation.

With the approach of the next millenium, the world presents some startling contrasts (Nossal 1997). We have lost faith in our governments and, in many cases, have become apathetic about unemployment, drugs, violence and the alienation of the underclass. Yet an exciting, multi-cultural, unregulated world without borders, freed from the threat of nuclear annihilation beckons (Nossal 1997). The defining achievements of the twentieth century include the end of colonialism, the emergence of independence and pride in many nations, and evolving economic development. But even as the world has been developing, poverty has left one-third of humanity bereft of a real chance to contribute to the future (Nossal 1997). To enter the next era will therefore require us to use the education and health resources that exist in our present to capitalise on the intellectual and social capital of our communities to create a better world (Beare & Slaughter 1993). Our global goal for community health in the next millenium must be to use those resources in ways that are both creative and visionary, to imbue social justice throughout the local and global landscape.

THINKING CRITICALLY

Healthy public policy

▶ Analyse the impact, in terms of health outcomes, of one public policy in your health care system.

▶ Devise a healthy public policy to counter the AIDS epidemic in your local community.

▶ Analyse a significant health issue for the next century in terms of policy requirements.

▶ Identify three barriers and three facilitating factors in successful health policy development.

▶ Identify the pros and cons of the Global Burden of Disease Study in terms of healthy public policy.

REFERENCES

Ashton, T. 1996, 'Health care systems in transition: New Zealand. Part 1. An overview of New Zealand's health care system', *Journal of Public Health Medicine*, vol. 18, no. 30, pp. 269–73.

Australian Health Ministers Advisory Council 1995, *National Rural Health Strategy Update*, AGPS, Canberra.

Beare, H. & Slaughter, R. 1993, *Education for the Twenty-First Century*, Routledge, London.

Dwyer, S. 1997, 'Improving delivery of a health promoting-environments program: experiences from Queensland Health', *Australian and New Zealand Journal of Public Health*, vol. 21, no. 4, pp. 398–402.

Fessenden-Raden, J. & Gert, B. 1989, 'A philosophical approach to the management of occupational health hazards', in *Contemporary Issues in Bioethics*, 3rd edn, eds T. Beauchamp & L. Walters, Wadsworth, Belmont, CA, pp. 618–23.

Gray, D. & Saggers, S. 1994, 'Aboriginal ill health: the harvest of injustice', in *Just Health. Inequality in Illness Care and Prevention*, eds C. Waddell & A. Petersen, Churchill-Livingstone, Melbourne, pp. 119–33.

Gray, D., Saggers, S., Drandick, M., Wallam, D. & Plowright, P. 1995, 'Evaluating government health and substance abuse programs for indigenous peoples: a comparative review', *Australian Journal of Public Health*, vol. 19, no. 60, pp. 567–72.

Ife, J. 1995, *Community Development: Creating Community Alternatives—Vision, Analysis and Practice*, Longman, Melbourne.

Jones, D. & Miller, M. 1992, 'Advocacy for community health', in *Community Health Policy and Practice in Australia*, eds F. Baum, D. Fry & E. Lennie, Pluto Press, Leichardt, pp. 143–53.

Kalucy, R. 1995, 'Ethics and public health', in *Health for All: The South Australian Experience*, ed. F. Baum, Wakefield Press, Kent Town, SA, pp. 172–90.

Kunitz, S. & Brady, M. 1995, 'Health care policy for Aboriginal Australians: the relevance of the American Indian experience', *Australian Journal of Public Health*, vol. 19, no. 6, pp. 549–58.

Labonte, R. 1994, '"See me, hear me, touch me, feel me". Lessons on environmental health information for bureaucratic activists', in *Ecological Public Health: From Vision to Practice*, eds C. Chu & R. Simpson, Institute of Applied Environmental Research, Brisbane, pp. 269–76.

Lee, P. & Paxman, D. 1997, 'Reinventing public health', *Annual Review of Public Health*, vol. 18, pp. 1–35.

Martin, G. & Davis, C. 1995, 'Mental health promotion: from rhetoric to reality?' in *Health for All: The South Australian Experience*, ed. F. Baum, Wakefield Press, Kent Town, SA, pp. 496–25.

Matseoane, S. 1997, 'South African health-care system at the crossroads', *Journal of the National Medical Association*, vol. 89, no. 5, pp. 350–6.

McMichael, T. 1993, 'Public health in Australia: a personal reflection', *Australian Journal of Public Health*, vol. 17, no. 4, pp. 295–6.

Milio, N. 1991, 'Making healthy public policy; developing the science by learning the art: an ecological framework for policy studies', in *Health Promotion Research: Towards a new Social Epidemiology*, eds B. Badura & I. Kickbusch, WHO, Copenhagen, pp. 7–28.

Minichiello, V. 1995, 'Community care: economic policy dressed as social concern?', in *The Politics of Health: The Australian Experience*, 2nd edn, ed. H. Gardner, Churchill-Livingstone, Melbourne, pp. 453–82.

Mooney, G., Irwig, L. & Leeder, S. 1997, 'Priority setting in health care: unburdening from the burden of disease', *Australian and New Zealand Journal of Public Health*, vol. 21, no. 7, pp. 680–1.

Mullen, P., Evans, D., Forster, J., Gottlieb, N., Kreuter, M. et al. 1995, 'Settings as an important dimension in health education/promotion policy, programs, and research', *Health Education Quarterly*, vol. 22, no. 30, pp. 329–45.

Murray, C. & Lopez, A. 1997a, 'Mortality by cause for eight regions of the world: global burden of disease study', *The Lancet*, vol. 349, May 3, pp. 1269–76.

Murray, C. & Lopez, A. 1997b, 'Regional patterns of disability-free life expectancy and disability-adjusted life expectancy: global burden of disease study', *The Lancet*, vol. 349, May 10, pp. 1347–52.

Murray, C. & Lopez, A. 1997c, 'Global mortality, disability, and the contribution of risk factors: global burden of disease study', *The Lancet*, vol. 349, May 17, pp. 1436–42.

Murray, C. & Lopez, A. 1997d, 'Alternative projections of mortality and disability by cause 1990–2020: global burden of disease study', *The Lancet*, vol. 349, May 24, pp. 1498–504.

Navarro, V. 1993, 'Has socialism failed? An analysis of health indicators under capitalism and socialism', *Science and Society*, vol. 57, no. 1, pp. 6–30.

Nossal, G. 1997, 'How to heal the global rift', speech given to the Centre for Australian and New Zealand Studies, Washington, Oct. 24.

O'Neil, J. 1995, 'Issues in health policy for indigenous peoples in Canada', *Australian Journal of Public Health*, vol. 19, no. 6, pp. 559–466.

Petersen, A. & Lupton, D. 1996, *The New Public Health*, Sage Publications, London.

Public Health Association of Australia, Inc. 1997, *Policy Statements 1998*, PHA, Canberra.

Queensland Health 1996, *Aboriginal and Torres Strait Islander People Mental Health Policy Statement*, Queensland Health, Brisbane.

Reynolds, C. 1995, 'Health and public policy: the tobacco laws', in *Health for All: The South Australian Experience*, ed. F. Baum, Wakefield Press, Kent Town, SA, pp. 215–29.

Salmon, M. 1995, 'Public health policy: creating a healthy future for the American public', *Family Community Health*, vol. 18, no. 1, pp. 1–11.

Suzuki, D. 1997, *The Sacred Balance. Rediscovering our Place in Nature*, Allen & Unwin, Sydney.

Whitehead, M. 1995, 'Tackling inequalities: a review of policy initiatives', in *Tackling Inequalities in Health: an Agenda for Action*, eds M. Benzeval, K. Judge & M. Whitehead, King's Fund, London.

Whitehead, M. & Dahlgren, G. 1995, 'What can be done about inequalities in health?', in *Health and Disease: A Reader*, eds B. Davey, A. Gray & C. Seale, Open University Press, Buckingham, pp. 367–75.

World Health Orgaization 1995, *Global strategy on occupational health for all*, WHO/OCH 795.1, WHO, Geneva.

World Health Orgaization 1996, *Promoting health through schools. The World Health Organization's global school health initiative*, WHO/HPR/HEP/96.4, WHO Geneva.

Index